Driving Transformational Innovation With Social Creativity

Ziska Fields
https://orcid.org/0000-0001-5353-1807
University of Johannesburg, South Africa

Lars Mackel
Chemnitz University of Technology, Germany

Stephan Sonnenburg
Department of Marketing, ICN Business School
CEREFIGE, University of Lorraine, Nancy, France

IGI Global
Scientific Publishing
Publishing Tomorrow's Research Today

Published in the United States of America by
IGI Global Scientific Publishing
701 East Chocolate Avenue
Hershey, PA, 17033, USA
Tel: 717-533-8845 | Fax: 717-533-7115
Website: https://www.igi-global.com E-mail: cust@igi-global.com

Library of Congress Cataloging-in-Publication Data

Names: Fields, Ziska, 1970- editor | Mackel, Lars, 1970- editor | Sonnenburg, Stephan editor
Title: Driving transformational innovation with social creativity / [edited by] Ziska Fields, Lars Mackel, Stephan Sonnenburg.
Description: Hershey, PA : IGI Global Scientific Publishing, [2026] | Includes bibliographical references and index. | Summary: "This book aims to explore the power of social creativity in driving transformational innovation that benefits society as a whole, ultimately leading to lasting, positive societal change"-- Provided by publisher.
Identifiers: LCCN 2025015500 (print) | LCCN 2025015501 (ebook) | ISBN 9798337327426 hardcover | ISBN 9798337327433 paperback | ISBN 9798337327440 ebook
Subjects: LCSH: Technological innovations--Social aspects http://id.loc.gov/authorities/subjects/sh2008112654 | Creative ability--Social aspects http://id.loc.gov/authorities/subjects/sh2009122251 | Social change http://id.loc.gov/authorities/subjects/sh85123918
Classification: LCC HM846 .D75 2026 (print) | LCC HM846 (ebook) | DDC 303.48/3--dc23/eng/20250526
LC record available at https://lccn.loc.gov/2025015500
LC ebook record available at https://lccn.loc.gov/2025015501

British Cataloguing in Publication Data
A Cataloguing in Publication record for this book is available from the British Library.

Table of Contents

Detailed Table of Contents

analysis reveals a lack of empirical and contextually grounded studies, concluding that leadership, creativity, and innovation are mutually reinforcing in driving systemic change.

This research examines how transformational leadership levels affect social creativity followed by their effects on OCB inside Ethiopian integrated healthcare organizations. The research uses 385 healthcare professionals' data to apply Confirmatory Factor Analysis (CFA) for model validation as well as Structural Equation Modeling (SEM) through AMOS software to test variable linkages. The research demonstrates that teams under transformational leadership display better social creativity which creates conditions for innovative healthcare practices. Social creativity shows positive associations through OCB according to the study results thus indicating creative actions produce higher employee engagement as well as proactive behaviors. Organizational culture emerges as a vital connecting factor in this model since an encouraging work environment strengthens both the social creativity outcomes from transformational leadership as well as employees' extra-role behaviors. The study verifies the validity of its analysis results through the Kaiser-Meyer-Olkin (KMO) measurement which determines

The main purpose of this chapter is to investigate the associations among leadership approaches, particularly transformational style of leadership, creativity of society, as well as innovation under corporate state of affairs. The investigation uses the approach of mixed methods, combining quantitative surveys and qualitative interviews. Quantitative data is collected using validated scales to assess leadership approaches, creativity of society, and the level of innovation among participants from various organizations. High quality interviews with leaders and team members give an additional idea of their tacit knowledge and their perception concerning the influence of leadership on creativity. The outcomes manifest a strong positive association among transformational style of leadership and creativity of society as well as innovation. Transformative leaders can greatly augment your creative team by empowering them.

Employee development is increasingly recognized as an important resource for innovation and creative processes in companies. Particularly in light of the dynamic development of technological innovations, special organizational strategies and processes are required. However, despite extensive research on organizational learning, knowledge management, and innovation, little is known about educational management in innovation processes. This multiple-case study examines the design of educational management in innovation projects by successful innovators. Educational episodes were characterized and related to the needs of the respective innovation activity. The functions of educational management for innovators were identified, and the intentions for incorporating educational measures into innovation processes were categorized. The results demonstrate that a means-end relationship exists between educational and innovation activities, and that there is a specific variation of formal and informal learning forms depending on the innovation step.

The issue of creativity is a long-debated tool of progress, innovation, and culture change, but which creates exceptional moral predicaments. The chapter reflects on how creativity may (or may not) become morally neutral, highlighting its modality as both productive and disruptive. It examines conflicts involving radical freedom moral responsibility, and unintended consequence using Nietzschean, Kantian, and utilitarian understandings. According to Nietzsche, creativity is an act of the will to power, and it has frequently gone beyond the norms of conventional morality, whereas in Kant, creativity fits within the confines of duty and the universality of principles. Utilitarianism makes judgements on creative acts, however, on their benefits towards society and so runs the risk of defining art merely in terms of consequences. The chapter posits that ethically responsible creativity should be contextual, deliberate, and considerate of implications to persons and collectives.

The research focuses on understanding how ethical leadership impacts social creativity as well as resulting organizational citizenship behavior (OCB) in integrated healthcare facilities of Ethiopia. A total of 390 healthcare employees participated in the study that used statistical approaches like Kaiser-Meyer-Olkin (KMO) as well as confirmatory factor analysis (CFA) to prove construct validity. SEM analysis through AMOS software operates as the research methodology to evaluate the proposed connections among ethical leadership, social creativity, organizational culture, as well as OCB. The study discovers that ethical leadership produces enhanced social creativity that positively affects OCB. Organizational culture serves as a mediator that intensifies the impact of ethical leadership on social creativity while boosting its influence over OCB according to this analysis. Organizations must dedicate resources to develop ethical leadership approaches as well as build powerful organizational cultures because this combination results in innovative employee behaviors.

In an era defined by complexity, traditional problem-solving approaches fall short in addressing the layered, persistent challenges known as wicked problems. This chapter explores how collaboration, when rooted in diversity and shared purpose, becomes a powerful engine for social creativity. Moving beyond the myth of the lone innovator, the chapter reframes creativity as a collective endeavor—one that thrives in spaces of dialogue, co-construction, and trust. Drawing from real-world examples, theoretical insights, and human-centered design principles, the authors

Preface

The need for transformational innovation and social creativity has never been greater. We live in a world where familiar answers no longer work. Challenges spill across boundaries, and solutions that once felt solid now dissolve in the face of uncertainty. The world is confronted with what Rittel and Webber (1973) described as *wicked problems*: climate change, inequality, health crises, and political instability. These are not puzzles to be solved once and for all. They are shifting, entangled, and difficult to name. They force us to ask: if the problems are wicked, can our responses remain conventional?

For a long time, creativity and innovation were framed in narrow ways. Schumpeter (1942) emphasized the role of disruption and the heroic entrepreneur, while much subsequent research focused on technology, efficiency, and individual achievement. These models delivered progress, yet they also revealed their limits. They encouraged disruption but often ignored connection. They celebrated novelty but sometimes deepened division. If innovation is only about new products or faster markets, how can it ever heal the fractures of society?

A different horizon is opening. Contemporary research emphasizes the centrality of collaboration, diversity, and shared imagination in addressing complex challenges (Montuori, 2012; Van Knippenberg et al., 2020). The frontier of transformational innovation is found in the interplay of social creativity, collective problem-solving, and community-driven action. Social creativity is not the flash of a single mind but the weaving of many voices. As Sawyer (2017) has argued, the most powerful ideas emerge in groups that combine dialogue, trust, curiosity, care, and imagination. It shifts the question from "What can I invent?" to "What can we create together?"

This book is grounded in that conviction. It explores how collaborative and inclusive processes can help address today's most urgent issues. But it also insists that reacting to crises is not enough. We must learn to shape the future before it arrives. What if creativity was not a privilege for the few but a practice for the many? What if innovation was measured not only by novelty but by its capacity to strengthen communities and repair the world?

The chapters that follow are written with these provocations in mind. They do not promise easy answers. Instead, they open spaces for reflection and invite us to think differently about what innovation can and should mean. The future of transformational innovation will depend less on individual breakthroughs than on our willingness to cultivate social creativity as a shared ethos. Whether that promise is fulfilled depends on all of us.

Today, innovation stands at a crossroads. Technology such as artificial intelligence, biotechnology, and digital platforms is reshaping daily life at a breathtaking pace, while societies grapple with mistrust, fragmentation, and fatigue. We have an abundance of tools, yet we remain uncertain about how to use them wisely. Innovation takes on the dual nature of both promise and problem. Does faster always mean better? And better for whom?

In this context, social creativity signals a powerful shift. It directs attention away from novelty toward the renewal of relationships. Around the world, movements show how strong this shift can be. Fridays for Future evolved from student protests into a global climate force, influencing public concern and behavior patterns (Fritz et al., 2023). During the COVID-19 crisis, communities organized to deliver food, produce protective gear, and care for vulnerable neighbors (Borkowska and Laurence, 2021). Open collaboration platforms such as Wikipedia and Linux demonstrate that collective knowledge building can challenge traditional institutions (Benkler, 2006). These examples illustrate that creativity flourishes when people connect, share, and act together.

This spirit is also visible in institutions. Companies integrate responsibility into strategy rather than treating it as symbolic reporting. Governments find that policies gain traction when shaped by citizen participation. Universities experiment with new formats of learning that connect disciplines and cultures (Fazey et al., 2020). In all these contexts, the frontier is less about new gadgets or regulations and more about new ways of organizing imagination and action.

Placing social creativity at the center of today's world means embracing interdependence. A start up, a state, or a movement can only advance so far in isolation. Progress grows when actors connect perspectives and resources. This shift is cultural as well as practical. It challenges the myth of the solitary innovator and raises a different question: how can communities, organizations, and societies imagine futures together? What if progress were measured not by speed but by the depth of participation it enables?

Social creativity therefore emerges as a necessity rather than a choice. Innovation becomes meaningful when it strengthens bonds, fosters inclusion, and opens pathways to resilience. This is where the topic fits today, at the intersection of global pressures and collective imagination, where the future will be shaped less by invention alone and more by our ability to create together.

The target audience that may find the content of the book valuable includes:

- Innovators and Entrepreneurs
- Educators and Researchers in Innovation and Social Sciences
- Nonprofit Leaders and Social Entrepreneurs
- Policymakers and Government Officials
- Corporations seeking to enhance their social responsibility and impact
- Community Organizers and Activists
- Students in social sciences, sustainability, and entrepreneurship

Below is a description of the importance of each chapter in the context of the book.

Chapter 1 explores the role of art, creativity, and innovation in advancing sustainable development in the face of ecological and social challenges. It shows how cultural practices promote sustainability through alternative imaginaries, emotional engagement, and systemic change. Drawing on interdisciplinary literature and policy frameworks, the analysis considers case studies from Denmark and Germany: the architectural installation *MY-CO SPACE*, the AI storytelling project *AGAINST ALL ODDS*, and circular design strategies by KVADRAT. These examples are assessed through the lenses of transformative innovation and aesthetic sustainability. Findings reveal that creative practices not only reflect but also shape sustainability narratives, fostering constructive hope and ecocentric values. Yet tensions remain between visionary futures and practical implementation. The chapter concludes by calling for policy and educational frameworks that position artists and designers as key agents of change, capable of linking ecological responsibility with cultural meaning and social justice.

Chapter 2 examines how leadership can drive social creativity and innovation to address global challenges such as inequality, climate change, and social exclusion. It highlights the importance of inclusive, adaptive, and emotionally intelligent leadership grounded in systems thinking and community participation. The critique challenges traditional models of innovation and argues for embedding social creativity within organizational and policy frameworks. Methodologically, the study uses a descriptive literature review supported by systematic database searches to ensure rigor and breadth. The analysis identifies a lack of empirical and context-specific studies, concluding that leadership, creativity, and innovation are mutually reinforcing in driving systemic change.

Chapter 3 investigates how transformational leadership influences social creativity and, in turn, organizational citizenship behavior (OCB) in Ethiopian integrated healthcare organizations. Using data from 385 healthcare professionals, the study applies Confirmatory Factor Analysis (CFA) for model validation and Structural Equation Modeling (SEM) with AMOS software to test relationships among variables. Findings show that transformational leadership enhances team creativity, fostering innovative healthcare practices. Social creativity is positively associated with OCB, demonstrating that creative actions increase employee engagement and proactive behaviors. Organizational culture emerges as a critical mediator, amplifying both the impact of transformational leadership on creativity and the influence of creativity on employees' extra-role behaviors. Validity is confirmed through the Kaiser-Meyer-Olkin (KMO) measure.

The aim of Chapter 4 is to examine the relationships among leadership approaches—particularly transformational leadership—social creativity, and innovation in organizational contexts. It addresses the challenge of understanding how leadership nurtures a culture of creativity and stimulates innovative outcomes. A mixed-methods approach is adopted, combining quantitative surveys with qualitative interviews. Quantitative data were gathered using validated scales to measure leadership approaches, social creativity, and levels of innovation across organizations. In-depth interviews with leaders and team members provided insights into tacit knowledge and perceptions of leadership's influence on creativity. Results reveal a strong positive association between transformational leadership, social creativity, and innovation. Transformative leaders were found to significantly enhance team creativity by empowering employees and fostering innovation.

Chapter 5 explains the positive impact of empowering employees' creative capacities through educational management, illustrated with a case study of successful innovators in Germany. Employee development is increasingly seen as a vital resource for fostering innovation and creativity in organizations. In light of rapid technological change, new organizational strategies and processes are required. Despite extensive research on organizational learning, knowledge management, and innovation, little attention has been paid to the role of educational management in innovation processes. This multiple-case study examines how successful innovators in Germany designed educational management practices within innovation projects. Educational episodes were analyzed and matched to the specific needs of innovation activities. Findings reveal that educational management fulfills key functions in supporting innovation, with formal and informal learning forms varying depending on the stage of the process. The study demonstrates a direct means-end relationship between educational and innovation activities.

Chapter 6 explores the ethics of creativity and questions whether innovation can be morally neutral. Creativity is widely recognized as a driver of progress, innovation, and cultural change, yet it raises complex ethical dilemmas. This chapter examines whether creativity can be morally neutral, highlighting its potential to be both productive and disruptive. The discussion considers conflicts between radical freedom, moral responsibility, and unintended consequences, drawing on Nietzschean, Kantian, and utilitarian perspectives. Nietzsche views creativity as an expression of the will to power, often transcending conventional morality. Kant situates creativity within the duty-bound framework of universal principles. Utilitarianism, in contrast, evaluates creative acts based on their societal benefits, risking a narrow focus on outcomes. The chapter argues that ethically responsible creativity should be contextual, intentional, and mindful of both individual and collective implications.

Chapter 7 investigates how ethical leadership shapes social creativity and organizational citizenship behavior (OCB) within Ethiopian healthcare organizations. Based on data from 390 healthcare employees, the study employs the Kaiser-Meyer-Olkin (KMO) measure, confirmatory factor analysis (CFA), and Structural Equation Modeling (SEM) using AMOS software. Results indicate that ethical leadership enhances social creativity, which in turn positively affects OCB. Organizational culture serves as a mediator, intensifying the impact of ethical leadership on social creativity and strengthening its effect on OCB. The findings highlight the importance of fostering ethical leadership and building strong organizational cultures to promote innovative and engaged employee behaviors.

Chapter 8 emphasizes that collaboration is a catalyst for social creativity and a pathway to collective solutions for wicked problems. In today's world of complexity, traditional problem-solving approaches are insufficient for addressing persistent and multidimensional "wicked problems." This chapter argues that collaboration, when grounded in diversity and shared purpose, becomes a powerful driver of social creativity. Moving beyond the myth of the lone innovator, creativity is reframed as a collective process that thrives in spaces of dialogue, trust, and co-construction. Drawing on real-world examples, theoretical insights, and human-centered design principles, the chapter demonstrates how interdisciplinary collaboration generates novel ideas and fosters inclusive, sustainable solutions. It concludes that cultivating collective imagination is essential for navigating uncertainty and building viable futures.

Chapter 9 discusses the Sharing Economy as a key example of how social creativity has reshaped resource allocation, driving transformative innovation across sectors. Using a conceptual framework, it outlines the definitions and features of the Sharing Economy and analyzes how its organizations differ. A database of roughly 1,000 cases illustrates this variety. By comparing theoretical concepts with empirical data, the chapter identifies innovations at both societal and organizational levels. The Sharing Economy is presented as a manifestation of social creativity, in which communities collectively reimagine economic participation beyond traditional market logics. The analysis shows that social creativity underpins diverse organizational models, ranging from peer-driven idealistic platforms to hybrid and commercialized ventures. The chapter concludes that social creativity remains the foundation and driver of the Sharing Economy's structural, normative, and technological evolution.

In conclusion, this book is an invitation to reimagine what creativity and innovation can achieve when they are shared. It brings together perspectives that reveal how imagination, when practiced collectively, can spark transformations reaching far beyond individual success stories. The chapters highlight pathways where social creativity becomes a living force, capable of renewing institutions, energizing communities, and opening horizons that feel both urgent and hopeful.

The contribution of this volume lies in showing that transformational innovation is never abstract. It takes shape in classrooms, workplaces, neighborhoods, and movements. It grows in the moments when people listen to each other, combine their strengths, and act with courage. Through these accounts, readers will encounter ideas and practices that move from reflection to real change.

The outlook is both challenging and inspiring. The future will test our ability to imagine together, to act across boundaries, and to sustain creativity as a common practice. Will we choose innovation that deepens divides, or innovation that creates new bonds? Will we settle for progress measured only in economic terms, or will we embrace measures of justice, resilience, and shared well-being?

This book does not provide final answers. Instead, it offers a call: to see social creativity as a resource we all carry, and to use it with intention. The pages ahead invite every reader to become an agent of transformation. The challenge is immense, but so is the potential. The question that remains is simple and open: how will you, the reader, take part in shaping the futures that lie ahead?

REFERENCES

Benkler, Y. (2006). *The wealth of networks: How social production transforms markets and freedom.* Yale University Press.

Borkowska, M., & Laurence, J. (2021). Coming together or coming apart? Changes in social cohesion during the COVID-19 pandemic in England. *European Societies, 23*(supl, suppl 1), 618–636. DOI: 10.1080/14616696.2020.1833067

Fazey, I., Schäpke, N., Caniglia, G., & Young, H. R. (2020). Transforming knowledge systems for life on Earth: Visions of future systems and how to get there. *Energy Research & Social Science, 70*, 101724. DOI: 10.1016/j.erss.2020.101724

Fritz, L., Hansmann, R., Dalimier, B., & Binder, C. R. (2023). Perceived impacts of the Fridays for Future climate movement on environmental concern and behaviour in Switzerland. *Sustainability Science, 18*(5), 2219–2244. DOI: 10.1007/s11625-023-01348-7

Montuori, A. (2012). Creative Inquiry: Confronting the challenges of scholarship in the 21st century. *Futures, 44*(1), 64–70. DOI: 10.1016/j.futures.2011.08.008

Rittel, H. W. J., & Webber, M. M. (1973). Dilemmas in a general theory of planning. *Policy Sciences, 4*(2), 155–169. DOI: 10.1007/BF01405730

Sawyer, R. K. (2017). *Group genius: The creative power of collaboration.* Basic Books.

Schumpeter, J. A. (1942). *Capitalism, socialism and democracy.* Harper & Brothers.

Van Knippenberg, D., Nishii, L. H., & Dwertmann, D. J. G. (2020). Synergy from diversity: Managing team diversity to enhance performance. *Behavioral Science & Policy, 6*(1), 75–92. DOI: 10.1177/237946152000600108

Acknowledgment

We extend our heartfelt gratitude to all the chapter contributors for their invaluable insights, expertise, and dedication. Each chapter represents a significant investment of time, effort, and intellectual energy, and this book would not have been possible without your commitment to advancing knowledge in this field.

We also wish to sincerely thank the peer reviewers, whose careful evaluations, constructive feedback, and thoughtful suggestions strengthened the quality and rigor of this work. Your contributions ensured that the book reflects both academic excellence and practical relevance.

A special note of appreciation goes to our co-editors, whose commitment, collaboration, and unwavering dedication guided this project to completion. Your vision, perseverance, and leadership turned a collective effort into a cohesive and meaningful volume.

To everyone involved in this journey—thank you.

Chapter 1
Art, Creativity, and Innovation:
A Powerful Alliance for a Sustainable Future

Anca Unertl
https://orcid.org/0009-0006-7465-720X
ArtisLogistics Cultural Management, Germany

Laura Zebisch
Goethe-Institut, Germany

ABSTRACT

*This chapter examines how art and creativity contribute to sustainable development amid global ecological and social challenges. Conceived as a statement, it draws on interdisciplinary literature and case studies from Denmark and Germany – MY-CO SPACE, the AI-based storytelling project *Against All Odds*, and Kvadrat's circular design strategies – to explore how cultural practices foster sustainability through alternative imaginaries, emotional engagement, and systemic change. Analyzing these examples through aesthetic sustainability and transformative innovation, the study finds that creative practices shape sustainability narratives, promoting hope and ecocentric values while revealing tensions between visionary futures and actionable change. It concludes by advocating for policy and education frameworks positioning artists as key agents of change, linking ecological responsibility with cultural meaning and social justice, and offers practical lessons for practitioners. Conceived as a statement, the chapter concludes by advocating for policy and educational frameworks that position artists and designers as central agents of change, capable of bridging ecological responsibility with cultural meaning and social justice. Furthermore, the conclusion provides explicit, distilled lessons for practitioners.*

DOI: 10.4018/979-8-3373-2742-6.ch001

1. INTRODUCTION

In a world increasingly defined by ecological crises, social inequality, and systemic uncertainty, the search for sustainable solutions demands more than technocratic solutions and economic adjustments. It requires imagination, cultural comprehension, and new ways of perceiving and shaping the future. With a mere five years remaining to achieve the objectives of the 2030 Agenda for Sustainable Development – the sustainable development goals (SDGs) – a critical assessment of global progress is both necessary and urgent. The Sustainable Development Report 2025 reveals that, on average, only 18% of SDG targets are currently on track to be achieved globally. The remaining 82% exhibit either moderate respectively marginal progress, stagnation or regression (United Nations Department of Economic and Social Affairs, 2025). This data underscores the limitations of current approaches and the need to reassess existing strategies for sustainable development: "With just five years to reach the Sustainable Development Goals, we need to shift into overdrive" (António Guterres, Secretary-General, United Nations). In response, this chapter explores how art, creativity, and innovation can function as powerful catalysts for sustainability by opening up alternative prospects, reconfiguring public discourse, and fostering collective resilience.

By examining theoretical concepts, cultural policy developments and global frameworks, national models – primarily in Denmark and Germany –, as well as real-world practices (case studies) the analysis demonstrates how cultural and creative industries contribute not only to economic vitality but also to ecological and social transformation. Drawing on international declarations, national strategies, and empirical indicators, it highlights practices such as circular design, sustainable architecture, and climate-oriented storytelling as meaningful responses to the United Nations Sustainable Development Goals (United Nations, 2015). The chapter closes by giving explicit, distilled guiding questions for practitioners.

2. THEORETICAL FRAMEWORKS

The relationship between culture and sustainable development has been debated in the academic literature since the 1990s. Between 2001 and 2021, numerous scholars have brought the significance of a close connection between these two domains to the fore. In this context, culture has increasingly been conceptualized and defined as a driving force for sustainability as follows: Sanz-Hernández and Covaleda emphasize that art stimulates individual and collective processes of reflection and learning or illustrates solutions through its ability to connect cognition and emotion. Art builds bridges between indifference and action, between resistance and activism based on constructive hope (Sanz-Hernández & Covaleda, 2021, p. 2).

According to Dessein et al. (2015), culture has three different roles within sustainable processes: a role *in*, *for* and *as* sustainable development. The authors understand culture *in* sustainable development as a fourth dimension in its own right, with the aim of making cultural practices and institutions more sustainable and thus promoting sustainable development. This view that the cultural and creative industries make a distinct contribution to achieving greater sustainability, for example by reducing greenhouse gas emissions, is already well established. By contrast, Dessein et al. see culture *for* sustainable development as a contextualizing and mediating force, for instance by communicating meanings, emphasizing its connecting function through its possibilities of framing and interpretation. This role is particularly important in cases of conflicting goals that arise due to different aspirations and actions in the ecological, economic and social spheres, and that are usually culturally determined. And finally, the authors identified culture *as* sustainable development as a necessary basis, structure and creating or transformative power for achieving sustainability goals because it shapes decision-making, social learning, and practices. Cultural values and norms influence actions, promote alternative cultural practices, and offer a multifaceted potential for social design. Therefore, sustainability should be internalized as a mindset (Dessein et al., 2015, pp. 28-33).

> *"Culture refers here not to particular types of knowledge, but to fundamental new processes of social learning that are nourishing, healing, and restorative. Sustainability exists thus as a process of community-based thinking that is pluralistic where culture represents both problem and possibility, form and process, and concerns those issues, values and means whereby a society or community may continue to exist." (Dessein et al., 2015, p. 32)*

Against this background, the concept of sustainability in culture respectively art, creativity, design and innovation tends to be reductive rather than expansive. It underscores the conscious renunciation of excess and aims to reduce effort, potentially even eliminating it entirely in extreme cases. At times, the most sustainable approach to design may involve non-design, the preservation of existing structures, or the transmission of knowledge. Design can also facilitate the substitution of material aspects of lifestyles with immaterial alternatives, thereby prioritizing shared use and communal access over individual ownership and accumulation (Brocchi, 2022, p. 453).

In this context, sustainability must also be understood as a practice of knowledge transmission and management. Sustainable design is not only about materials and forms, but also about preserving, sharing, and evolving knowledge that fosters ecological awareness and cultural resilience. This includes traditional ecological knowledge, artistic practices, and scientific insights that are often marginalized in dominant innovation discourses.

A compelling example of this approach is the project *Kosmoperzeptionen des Waldes (Cosmoperceptions of the Forest)* by Goethe-Institut, which explores the forest not merely as a resource, but as a space of knowledge, perception, and co-existence. Through interdisciplinary workshops, artistic interventions, and participatory formats, the project invites participants to engage with the forest as a living archive of ecological, cultural, and spiritual knowledge. Rather than extracting or transforming the forest, the project emphasizes listening, observing, and co-perceiving – practices that are inherently sustainable because they cultivate attentiveness, humility, and long-term thinking.

Such projects demonstrate that sustainability is not only a technical or ecological challenge, but also a cultural and epistemic one. They call for infrastructures of care and learning that enable the intergenerational transfer of knowledge and the co-creation of meaning. In this sense, sustainable design becomes a medium for cultivating relationships between people, places, and more-than-human worlds and for embedding knowledge in lived experience.

Accordingly, culture, or more specifically, creativity functions not merely as an artistic tool but as a societal capability that enables individuals and communities to respond to complexity and uncertainty in flexible, imaginative and innovative ways. This is particularly crucial in times of accelerating environmental and social disruption, where linear planning and rational forecasting are no longer sufficient.

The close connection between creativity, innovation, and sustainability is further emphasized by Marcus Collins, who argues:

> *"Creativity allows us to think outside the box and imagine possibilities that might not be immediately obvious... Innovation is about taking those creative ideas and turning them into practical, implementable solutions. In the context of sustainability, creativity and innovation can lead to new technologies, circular business models, and socially responsible urban or agricultural systems." (Collins, 2024)*

Collins's perspective reflects a growing consensus: sustainable solutions require the rethinking of established systems and the strategic use of human ingenuity. He also notes that sustainability itself can act as a driver of innovation, prompting businesses to explore alternatives that enhance both environmental performance and competitive advantage.

Another noteworthy position is that of Brem and Puente-Díaz (2020). They understand creativity, innovation, and sustainability as intrinsically linked. According to their model, impactful creative ideas must not only be novel and useful, but also implementable across societal, corporate, and consumer levels.

This positioning of creativity at the center of sustainability discourse is further supported by interdisciplinary research across the social sciences, which frames creativity as a dynamic process of recombination, sense-making, and value creation (Brem & Puente-Díaz, 2020). In sustainable development, this includes the ability to challenge dominant consumption patterns and envision alternatives that align with ecological limits and human well-being.

Regarding the topic of sense-making, the white paper A New Era in Climate Communications (New Zero World, 2024) provides valuable contributions and further elaborations. The white paper critiques the limitations of purely data-driven messaging and instead advocates for emotionally resonant, narrative-based approaches that foster hope, collective identity, and behavioral change. In this paradigm, the creative industries are identified as powerful agents in shaping cultural narratives that can mobilize meaningful climate action.

Similarly, *Creativity as a Driver for Green Transition* (Creative Denmark, 2023) emphasizes that creativity is essential for both individual and systemic transformation in response to climate change and environmental degradation. The paper stresses that creativity not only enables innovation, but also empowers consumers, organizations, and societies to act more sustainably by changing behaviors, redesigning systems, and imagining new futures.

> *"Creativity opens new solutions and products, generating an energy that can be channeled into the green transition of our society... It can benefit the entire planet as it moves towards a healthier, environmentally friendly, and sustainable global community." (Creative Denmark, 2023, p. 6)*

This approach aligns with the Danish model (in the fourth section introduced), which encourages cross-sectoral creativity, flat hierarchies, and collaboration rooted in high trust and open dialogue, factors referred to in the paper as the Danish "creative DNA" (Creative Denmark, 2023, p. 10).

The combination of cultural narratives, artistic production, and creative technology creates what Hjort (2023) refers to as "aesthetic sustainability" – a mode of engagement that makes sustainable living not only more accessible but more emotionally and symbolically meaningful. This emotional dimension is key to fostering long-term behavioral shifts, as people are more likely to act when sustainability resonates with identity, aesthetics, and aspiration.

In this paper, *creativity* is therefore understood as a space of possibility as well as imagination; *innovation* is conceptualized as planned and controlled change within a social system, achieved through the application of new ideas and techniques. The challenge of sustainable innovation is not to want to keep everything, but to let go, especially of the problem, in order to find new solutions. Brocchi (2025) thus speaks of exnovation (p. 26) in the context of sustainability when it comes to innovation. We follow this understanding. Finally, we turn to the understanding of *art* in this chapter in order to take account of the triadic perception of art, creativity and inspiration on which the article is based: art is created by people in a cultural context with a social function in an aesthetic dimension. It can be an artifact (the artwork in the narrower sense), a structure or a process. We therefore pursue a broad understanding of art, referring to the arts in the plural, including music, literature, film, and so on, and use the term culture synonymously as a generic term.

However, the positions presented here also have their limitations. In particular, the various dimensions of sustainability (cultural, social, ecological and economic) are not equally balanced in reality. They are always subject to conflicting goals and constant prioritisation. The theoretical concepts presented here are models that simplify reality, cannot truly do justice to its complexity and the interactions of the overall situation, are partly static and need to be adapted as they develop. It is important to bear in mind that there are many different manifestations and understandings, as well as opposing positions to the understandings of art, creativity, innovation and sustainability presented here, which we cannot all take into account. This would go beyond the scope of this chapter. Therefore, we will restrict ourselves here to pointing out a few limitations of the theories.

To conclude, it can be stated that art and creativity emerge as more than vehicles for aesthetic expression – they are critical drivers of transformative innovation. When sustainability is embraced as a mindset as already elaborated by Dessein et al. (2015), it has the potential to reshape how societies respond to environmental and social challenges. Artistic practices foster this shift by offering alternative perspectives, challenging dominant paradigms, and engaging people emotionally and intellectually in envisioning sustainable futures. Concepts such as social creativity, artistic innovation, and design thinking are central to this co-creative process.

3. CULTURAL POLICY DEVELOPMENTS AND POLITICAL FRAMEWORKS

We seek to investigate how sustainable solutions developed through governmental structures, creative practices and artistic approaches can be translated into concrete societal transformation and how the theoretical frameworks can be linked. Starting from the macro-level, the analysis focuses on identifying cultural policy frameworks that provide the foundation for sustainable change.

The value of culture as a driver of social sustainability processes is increasingly recognized in international political, scientific and creative discourses as well as in climate governance. Multilateral players such as UNESCO and individual countries are addressing the issue of culture-based climate protection measures. UNESCO has called for the explicit inclusion of culture as a standalone goal in the post-2030 sustainable development agenda. Furthermore, the Climate Heritage Network has similarly urged the United Nations Framework Convention on Climate

Change (UNFCCC) to formally integrate culture, heritage, and the creative industries into global climate policy, particularly in the lead-up to COP30 in 2025 this year in Belém, Brazil. This circumstance portrays that several initiatives – such as the International Council of Museums (ICOM), the International Alliance for the Protection of Heritage in Conflict Areas (ALIPH), and the International Institute for Conservation of Historic and Artistic Works (ICC) – support the adoption of a joint working resolution on culture and climate action. This proposed UN process intends to develop policy frameworks that recognize and enable culture's contributions to climate solutions, effectively placing culture at the heart of climate action.

The international discourse on culture-based climate action can be seen as an example for Dessein's concept of culture *as* sustainable development because the approach of culture at the heart of climate action is a kind of embodiment of changed norms and values. The discourse has evolved significantly in recent years, reflecting a growing recognition that cultural heritage, creative expression, and traditional knowledge are not only vulnerable to climate change but also essential spaces of possibilities in addressing it. This shift marks a departure from earlier climate policy frameworks, which largely focused on scientific, technological, and economic solutions.

One of the most notable developments in this discourse is the increasing acknowledgment of culture within global climate governance. Events such as the High-Level Ministerial Dialogue for Culture-Based Climate Action at COP28 in Dubai have brought together policymakers, cultural leaders, and climate experts to explore how cultural policies and institutions can contribute to climate goals. These discussions emphasize that culture is not merely a vehicle for communication but a transformative force capable of shaping values, behaviors, and collective imagination. Further, the 2023 COP28 marked a significant development in this regard with the establishment of the *Group of Friends*, a coalition comprising national governments and intergovernmental organizations, including, among others, Brazil, Germany, Egypt, the United Arab Emirates, UNESCO, the British Council, and Julie's Bicycle. The group aims to promote the integration of cultural considerations into UNFCCC processes and national climate strategies. This could lead to increased funding for artists, cultural practitioners, and traditional communities engaged in climate action (Jesus, 2024, para. 3).

A central actor in this movement is the Climate Heritage Network (CHN), which has been instrumental in advocating for the integration of culture into climate action. The CHN's Manifesto, presented at COP27, outlines a vision in which arts, culture, and heritage are mobilized to inspire climate ambition, support behavioral change, preserve cultural heritage, and empower communities – particularly Indigenous peoples and youth – to lead climate solutions. The Manifesto underscores the idea that cultural actors are not passive observers but active agents of change.

Another key theme in the international discourse is the vulnerability of intangible cultural heritage to climate change. Practices such as oral traditions, rituals, and traditional ecological knowledge are deeply rooted in specific environments and ecosystems. As these environments are altered or destroyed by the effects of climate change, the cultural practices tied to them are also at risk. Scholars and international organizations have called for a rights-based approach to protect these forms of heritage, emphasizing the need for legal recognition and support for community-led adaptation strategies (UNESCO, n.d. & IUCN, 2021).

At the same time, traditional knowledge systems are increasingly recognized as valuable resources for climate adaptation and resilience. Indigenous fire management techniques, traditional water harvesting methods, and sustainable agricultural practices offer time-tested solutions that can complement scientific approaches. These practices are often embedded in cultural and spiritual worldviews that promote harmony with nature, providing alternative paradigms to dominant models of development and consumption.

The creative industries also play a crucial role in the cultural response to climate change. Through film, literature, visual arts, and digital media, artists and storytellers can translate complex scientific data into compelling narratives that resonate emotionally with diverse audiences. Initiatives such as UNESCO's ResiliArt movement and the Climate Story Lab support cultural practitioners in addressing environmental issues through their work, fostering public engagement and climate literacy.

In addition to these grassroots and artistic efforts, there is a growing push to institutionalize culture within climate policy. International organizations like UNESCO, ICOMOS, and the CHN have advocated for the inclusion of cultural indicators in climate reporting and monitoring. They also call for the development of sustainability standards for cultural institutions and the integration of cultural knowledge into national adaptation plans and disaster risk reduction strategies.

Despite these advances, several challenges remain. Culture is still often marginalized in national climate strategies and funding mechanisms. Many cultural institutions lack the resources or technical expertise to implement sustainability measures. Furthermore, there is a need for standardized metrics to assess the impact of cultural interventions on climate outcomes.

To address these gaps, the international community is exploring new models of cross-sectoral collaboration, capacity-building, and inclusive policymaking. These efforts aim to ensure that cultural voices, especially those of marginalized and Indigenous communities, are heard and valued in climate decision-making processes.

UNESCO's report *Re|Shaping Policies for Creativity* (2022) provides evidence that national sustainable development plans (NSDPs) are beginning to incorporate cultural dimensions, although such cases are still rare and only more or less effective. Among 127 surveyed countries (92 developing countries and 35 developed countries), 88% acknowledged the strategic role of culture in national development, and 63% specifically recognized the significance of the cultural and creative industries. While there is widespread recognition of culture's contribution to social cohesion, identity, and well-being, its potential to drive climate action remains underexploited (UNESCO, 2022, p. 212). The overall integration of culture in development policy has remained relatively static since 2017. Nevertheless, several countries have already begun implementing comprehensive policies that leverage the cultural and creative sectors for climate mitigation and adaptation.

In conclusion, the international discourse on culture-based climate action is increasingly dynamic and multifaceted. It reflects a growing consensus that cultural heritage, creative expression, and traditional knowledge are not peripheral to climate action but central to its success. By embracing the cultural dimensions of the climate crisis, societies can foster more inclusive, resilient, and imaginative responses to one of the greatest challenges of our time.

4. NATIONAL MODELS: DENMARK AND GERMANY

Building upon the preceding macro-level perspective, this section shifts the analytical focus to national strategies situated at the meso-level. Denmark and the Danish model are examined within the broader framework of the Nordic countries, which are frequently cited as exemplary cases of culturally embedded and sustainability-oriented transformation. The Nordic region, particularly through the Nordic Green Roadmap for Cultural Institutions – co-authored by Danish art historian Inger Smærup Sørensen – is widely recognized as a global pioneer in the development of sustainable societal structures (Vågen Svensson & Smærup Sørensen, 2023). In contrast, the analysis also considers Germany, the authors' country of origin, whose structurally and administratively driven cultural policy in the context of sustainability is observed with analytical interest.

Denmark's national agenda aligns closely with the United Nations Sustainable Development Goals (United Nations, 2015), while grassroots initiatives such as the *Danmarks Deklarationen* emphasize ecological values in governance (Øko-net, 2000). The Ministry of Foreign Affairs of Denmark (2022) has implemented sustainability measures including carbon reduction, sustainable procurement, and inclusive hiring practices.

Denmark's National Strategy for Sustainable Development introduced in 2003 outlines eight objectives including decoupling economic growth from environmental degradation (The Danish Government, 2003). The concept of Genuine Savings integrates environmental and economic capital, supporting indicators that measure progress beyond GDP. Growth in eco-labeled products, ISO certifications, and high development aid contributions reinforce Denmark's commitment to sustainability.

As highlighted in *Denmark a Creative Toolbox* (Ministry of Foreign Affairs of Denmark, 2024), the publication demonstrates how democratic values and high trust environments promote innovation. These factors support collaborative problem-solving and creative risk-taking. Danish storytelling traditions – modernized through digital media – reinforce resilience and cultural cohesion. Within this ecosystem, industries apply aesthetic and human-centered approaches to sustainability. Examples from the white paper include SYBO's "Play 2 Plant" game, the Too Good To Go food-waste app, and zero-waste product companies like AllMatters and LastObject (Creative Denmark, 2023, pp. 16–24).

These innovations are not isolated efforts but reflect a larger ecosystem in which public funding, university partnerships, and design incubators bolster creative experimentation. For example, the Danish Creative Business Cup connects early-stage startups with sustainability mentors and investors, cultivating green entrepreneurship with global reach (Creative Denmark, 2023, p. 32).

Boer, Goduscheit, Schweisfurth, and Visser-Groeneveld (2025) accentuate the need for research that unites innovation and sustainability. They advocate for systemic changes to consumption, production, and governance structures.

Creativity as a Driver for Green Transition (Creative Denmark, 2023) documents over 20 cases where creativity catalyzes innovation – such as Circle Bank (circular construction), Nordisk Film (sustainable production), and Kvadrat (textile reuse). It emphasizes creativity as a mindset that incorporates empathy, imagination, and aesthetics in order to promote more sustainable lifestyles.

Furthermore, the Danish innovation system has been recognized for its relative success in aligning national innovation performance with sustainability goals. Gregersen and Johnson (2021) argue for a dynamic, capability-based approach to assessing innovation systems, highlighting that learning, collaboration, and institutional adaptation are key components of sustainable innovation performance. Their work shows that while Denmark scores highly on international SDG indexes, challenges remain – particularly in areas such as responsible consumption, sustainable cities, and climate action (Gregersen & Johnson, 2021).

This broader capability-oriented framework positions Denmark not merely as a producer of green technologies but as a learning society, where cross-sectoral synergies and inclusive innovation ecosystems are essential. Emphasis is placed on collaborative learning environments, vocational training for green jobs, and participatory governance that empowers communities in shaping their ecological futures (Gregersen & Johnson, 2021).

The government's 2020 strategy, *A Green and Sustainable World*, further illustrates how Denmark uses its experience in green transition to exert global influence. It outlines diplomatic efforts to raise international climate ambitions and foster climate finance flows toward low-emission pathways. Denmark's Strategic Sector Cooperation program, for instance, partners with countries like Vietnam and China to share expertise on energy efficiency and carbon reduction (Danish Government, 2020, pp. 14–16). These partnerships exemplify how Denmark combines technical knowledge with creative policymaking and public diplomacy.

Additionally, the strategy recognizes the need to shift the financial sector toward climate-resilient development. Denmark champions reforms in trade policy, green investment, and corporate responsibility, emphasizing that environmental innovation must be consistent with social justice goals (Danish Government, 2020, pp. 22–26). Non-state actors, including businesses and youth-led movements, are mobilized to scale up green solutions and foster civic engagement in climate governance.

In this context, creativity is viewed as a national strength and export commodity. Danish companies are supported not only to innovate domestically but also to act as ambassadors of green transition abroad. Through platforms such as Green Strategic Partnerships and Global Climate Diplomacy, Denmark positions itself as a "green superpower" with the soft power to influence global sustainability norms (Danish Government, 2020, pp. 6–9).

Denmark's sustainability agenda is also deeply interwoven with its cultural connection to nature, particularly as it relates to fostering creativity. Research by Plambech and Konijnendijk van den Bosch (2015) highlights how natural environments positively influence the creative capacities of Danish professionals. Through qualitative interviews with artists, designers, and innovators, the study revealed that nature enhances creativity by stimulating curiosity, fostering mental flexibility, and helping individuals generate new ideas.

Specifically, nature supports the early phases of the creative process: *preparation* and *incubation*. During these stages, individuals gather input and subconsciously reflect – functions that benefit significantly from restorative natural surroundings. The study identifies three key sensory dimensions of natural environments that are especially valued by creative professionals: *nature*, *space*, and *serene*. These characteristics enable what Kaplan (1995) described as "soft fascination", allowing attention to reset and replenish, which is crucial for complex cognitive tasks like ideation and problem-solving.

This insight reinforces the value of integrating green spaces into urban design and work environments. In Denmark, where creativity underpins much of the sustainability transition, nature is not merely aesthetic but instrumental. It is a cognitive and emotional resource that enhances innovation, demonstrating how ecological and psychological sustainability can go hand in hand.

Denmark's sustainability model flourishes through the integration of creativity, capability-building, and international collaboration, illustrating that ecological modernization is not solely a technical challenge but also a cultural and imaginative endeavor. By embedding creative practices across education, diplomacy, industry, and urban planning, Denmark presents a holistic approach to sustainable development – one that extends beyond policy into lived societal frameworks. This model shows how nations can strategically align innovation systems with storytelling traditions and participatory values to generate resilient, forward-thinking societies. The country's approach emphasizes that creative thinking should not be confined to artistic disciplines or innovation policy alone but should permeate the structures of governance, education, and community planning. Such integration nurtures the imaginative and cognitive capacities required to address complex global challenges such as climate change, biodiversity loss, and resource depletion. Rather than merely reacting to environmental pressures, Denmark's model enables societies to anticipate and shape their transitions in transformative ways. This forward-looking strategy is built on high levels of social trust, inclusive decision-making, and a shared vision for a sustainable future. By doing so, Denmark offers a replicable example of how creativity can serve as a foundational driver in the pursuit of systemic, proactive, and equitable ecological transformation on both local and global scales.

A glance at Germany shows that this nation has also committed itself to the Paris Climate Agreement to curb climate change and make its economy climate-neutral by 2045. The culture and media sector also plays a role in this, not only as a mediator, initiator and driver of innovation, but also as a source of greenhouse gas emissions. Against this backdrop, the German sustainability strategy aims to expand the introduction of environmental management systems in cultural institutions (German Sustainability Strategy, 2025, p. 166).

In addition to technical and infrastructural measures, the strategy emphasises the importance of raising awareness and promoting behavioural change through cultural engagement. Cultural institutions are encouraged to act as role models for sustainable practices and to integrate climate-related issues into their programming and public relations work. Furthermore, the strategy promotes interdisciplinary cooperation between the cultural, scientific and educational sectors in order to strengthen climate knowledge and support transformative social change. This holistic approach reflects the overarching goal of the German Sustainability Strategy to align all areas of public life – including culture – with the goals of Agenda 2030.

The Danish sustainability strategy is often chosen for further elaboration in international discussions because it exemplifies a culturally integrated and forward-thinking approach to sustainable development. Unlike Germany's strategy, which is more structurally and administratively oriented, Denmark places a strong emphasis on embedding sustainability into everyday cultural practices and creative industries.

The Danish sustainability strategy is often chosen over the German one for further elaboration because it presents a more culturally embedded and holistic approach to sustainable development. While Germany's strategy is comprehensive and institutionally robust, it tends to focus on structural coordination, environmental management systems, and sectoral monitoring. In contrast, Denmark integrates sustainability deeply into everyday life and cultural identity, using the creative and cultural sectors not only as communicators but as active drivers of innovation and behavioral change. Danish policies emphasize the role of design, architecture, and the arts in fostering climate awareness and social transformation, making culture a central pillar of their sustainability agenda. This culturally grounded model offers a compelling example of how sustainability can be both systemic and socially resonant, which is why it is frequently highlighted in international discourse. Furthermore, both nations share close ties to Agenda 2030, the SDGs and KPIs for CO_2-reduction. One difference is that in Germany, there is slightly less focus on designing a sustainable, everyday lifestyle, and the connection with nature is not as prominent.

5. REAL-WORLD PRACTICES

> *"All too often, the debate surrounding sustainability focuses on what we must give up or will be lost. The true focus, however, should be the potential rewards for everyone." (Zimmermann, 2018, p. 1)*

The following three case studies - MY-CO SPACE, Kvadrat and Against All Odds demonstrate on a micro-level how sustainability can be given a positive connotation by opening spaces of opportunity for utopian visions and culture-based calls to climate action. Engaging in an enjoyable activity that emphasizes the benefits gained, rather than the sacrifices made, motivates us to participate in building a sustainable future and the transformation leading to it (Zimmermann, 2018, p. 5). We also establish a connection to the theoretical framework and politics. It's about moving away from a problem-centric approach and towarda solution-oriented approach.

MY-CO SPACE: Fungi-Driven Design for a Sustainable Tomorrow

The sculptural architecture MY-CO SPACE is an artistic and scientific research project in which building materials and techniques, housing solutions, material cycles, and recycling issues are explored and reimagined by an interdisciplinary team of artists, designers, architects, and scientists. The research is conducted against the backdrop of ecological, social, and economic resource conservation concerns, as well as cultural aesthetics. The artwork serves as an interactive experimental space that introduces visitors to the world of fungi and allows them to experience their potential (V. meer, n.d.).

The subject of research is fungal cultures. These were chosen because fungi in nature can deconstruct, transform, and reconstruct organic material. They are metabolic artists, capable of processing residual materials – such as those from agriculture and forestry – and converting them into stable, lightweight materials. These form three-dimensional networks of, for example, interwoven sawdust or similar substances, referred to as mycelium (Pfeiffer & Meyer, 2023, p. 15).

The central research question posed by the project is: "How can biological-technological structures and essential housing functions be integrated into the smallest possible space so that people can live and work comfortably under conditions of limited resources?" (Pfeiffer & Meyer, 2023, p. 15). The project addresses the urgent need for a paradigm shift in architecture and design in light of ongoing ecological and societal transformation processes. At its core lies the development of so-called living building materials based on fungi, which grow through biological processes and exhibit properties such as self-regulation, adaptability, autonomous growth, and self-repair. These materials offer a compelling alternative to the predominantly technology-driven concepts of smart buildings. To harness the full potential of such materials, a new planning culture is required that considers the entire life cycle of materials, from the local availability of raw resources to their complete reintegration into natural material cycles. The project was conceived and collaboratively realized by the interdisciplinary and international SciArt collective MY-CO-X, which brings together expertise from the fields of science, art, architecture, and design.

The sculpture consists of a lightweight plywood arch construction mounted on a wooden base plate and clad with mycelium panels. It has the shape of a curved, ring-like half space capsule and appears worm-like. It was designed for the tinyBE • living in a sculpture open-air exhibition, which was on display from June 26 to September 26, 2021, in Frankfurt's Metzlerpark and at locations in Darmstadt and Wiesbaden.

The exterior shell comprises 330 mycelium panels, designed according to the geometric principle of hexagons, inspired by the benzene ring of fungi. The interior, covering approximately 20 square meters, is conceived as a living space that can be divided into sleep, reading, and work areas. Kitchen and sanitary facilities are not included. During the exhibition, visitors were provided with a tent and two camping mattresses, which they could integrate independently according to the co-design principle, emphasizing the systemic and self-build nature of the sculpture's architecture. Additionally, further design principles and features were included like reusability and modularity, independent assembly and disassembly, study materials, such as preserved fungal cultures in petri dishes, mycelium-based building bricks, literature, and a telescope. The goal was to offer a twofold immersive experience:

one into the fungal microcosm via the provided study materials, and the other into the surrounding natural macrocosm using the telescope (Pfeiffer & Meyer, 2023, pp. 14-27).

The interplay of art, design, and innovation as drivers of sustainable development in MY-CO SPACE becomes apparent when viewed through the analytical framework of Alexia Sanz-Hernández and Irene Covaleda – art stimulates processes of reflection. They define four key phases of sustainable creativity processes, which do not necessarily have to occur linearly (Sanz-Hernández & Covaleda, 2021, p. 4): learning experience, reflection, creative action and communication, and mobilization for change.

Phase learning experience: MY-CO SPACE enables participating artists, architects, designers, and scientists as well as visitors to acquire knowledge in the following areas: sustainable building – engaging with biodegradable materials and direct contact with mycelium fosters understanding of reusability and resource minimization; circular economy – MY-CO SPACE demonstrates how fungi process organic waste and create stable, resource-efficient building materials; symbiotic thinking – MY-CO SPACE embodies fungal networks that symbolize symbiotic communities shaping our world. The sensory and emotional experience of the sculpture invites visitors to reflect on sustainable living (Pfeiffer, Meyer 2023, p. 22); transformation – visitors learn how fungi break down, transform, and build materials, encouraging them to apply these principles themselves.

Phase reflection: as artistic reflection, the sculpture translates biological processes into aesthetic forms. It conveys the transformative power of fungi through visionary living space architecture that emphasizes total resource recycling as a future-oriented housing concept. Fungi's ability to decompose organic matter and create new life forms serves as a powerful metaphor for change, adaptability,network (trans)formation, regeneration and key aspects of sustainable architecture and society.

The aesthetic language of MY-CO SPACE is deliberately organic and non-linear, evoking the forms of nature rather than the rigid geometries of industrial modernism. This design choice reflects a deeper philosophical stance: that sustainability is not merely a technical challenge but a cultural and aesthetic one. By reimagining beauty in terms of ecological harmony and material humility, the project challenges dominant norms and invites new sensibilities.

Phase creative action and communication: For participation and co-creation as creative action, MY-CO SPACE serves as an interactive platform where visitors can actively participate in the research process. By engaging with the study materials and experiencing the living sculpture, visitors gain a deeper understanding of fungal biology and its potential applications in sustainable design. This hands-on involvement fosters a sense of ownership and responsibility toward environmental conservation. Further participation in the design process is encouraged by flexibly adapting the interior space using provided elements such as tents and mattresses. This experiential involvement facilitates the transfer of practical knowledge about compact living, analogous to life in space capsules, while also fostering sensory and emotional exploration of alternative ways of inhabiting space.

The overarching goal of such co-creative design is to cultivate resilient communities in which humans and other life forms interact and collaboratively shape shared spaces. These interactions nurture a sense of collective identity and responsibility, which serves as a vital foundation for sustainable behavior.

Moreover, the project's participatory ethos extends beyond the physical installation. Through workshops, talks, and publications, MY-CO SPACE engages diverse audiences in a broader dialogue about the future of living. It becomes a platform for interdisciplinary exchange, where artists, scientists, activists, and citizens can co-create knowledge and envision alternatives.

MY-CO SPACE sparks discussions on sustainable housing, resource consumption, and the future of nomadism. It vividly demonstrates how biological-technological structures can be integrated to enable life in resource-limited environments, inspiring new innovative architectural visions. The sculpture also communicates a sustainable design philosophy grounded in reduction, circular economy, sufficiency, and a networked future in which fungi serve as sources of biological, aesthetic, and societal inspiration. The project's communicative power lies in its ability to make abstract concepts tangible. Visitors do not merely learn about sustainability – they feel it, inhabit it, and co-create it. This embodied experience is crucial for fostering deep engagement and long-term behavioral change.

Phase mobilization for change: In a world increasingly shaped by ecological crises, MY-CO SPACE offers a hopeful vision of coexistence and creativity. It shows that sustainability is not a constraint but a catalyst for innovation, beauty, and community. By rooting design in the wisdom of fungi, the project invites us to rethink our relationship with materials, with space, and with each other.

But it is not only the theoretical framework of Sanz-Hernández and Covaleda that can be applied. With the help of Dessein's model, it can be shown that MY-CO SPACE embodies both: aspects of culture *for* sustainability due to the translation of new building materials and aspects of culture *as* sustainable development in the form of social learning, which is provided by the organism structures of the fungi and the learning stations (microscope, etc.). The artwork clearly illustrates the different levels respectively manifestations of sustainability and illustrates the limitations of theory and practice – models cannot be viewed in isolation in a complex environment.

Last but not least, it should be noted that Collins' theory can also be found in MY-CO SPACE with its outside-the-box thinking in relation to alternative building materials and vision making. In addition, the sculpture is a good visual aid for culture-based climate action. It addresses SDGs 4, 9, 11-13 and 15-17. While MY-

CO SPACE was developed in a specific European context, its core principles are globally relevant. Many regions around the world face similar challenges related to housing, waste management, and ecological degradation. The use of locally available organic waste to grow building materials can be adapted to diverse climates and cultures, making the approach both scalable and context-sensitive.

Against All Odds: Historical Women and New Algorithms – Reanimating Anne Marie Carl-Nielsen Through AI

In an age increasingly shaped by artificial intelligence (AI) and digital storytelling, the project Against All Odds – Historical Women and New Algorithms stands as a compelling example of how emerging technologies can intersect with cultural heritage. Conceived through a collaboration between the National Gallery of Denmark (Statens Museum for Kunst, SMK), the Technical University of Denmark (DTU), and the design studio Yoke, the project reimagines the legacy of Danish sculptor Anne Marie Carl-Nielsen through an innovative AI-powered chatbot. This case study explores the theoretical underpinnings, the development process, and broader implications of this project for digital humanities, feminist historiography, and cultural storytelling.

Throughout history, many women artists have been overlooked due to systemic biases in record-keeping and cultural valuation. The decision to focus on Anne Marie Carl-Nielsen is not incidental; she was one of the few women artists whose extensive personal writings (letters, diaries, and publications) are digitally archived. This abundance of data provided a foundational basis for training a machine learning model capable of emulating her persona. Yet this availability also underscores a critical issue in archival studies: the scarcity of preserved records from many of Carl-Nielsen's female contemporaries. This disparity is emblematic of what feminist theorist Joan Scott describes as the "politics of memory," wherein historical narratives are constructed based on selective preservation (Scott, 1988).

By choosing Carl-Nielsen, the project not only leverages a unique dataset but also highlights the biases embedded in data availability. As Kate Crawford argues, data is never neutral; it reflects historical, social, and political processes that determine what is remembered and what is omitted (Crawford, 2021). Thus, the chatbot is not merely a technical artifact but a commentary on historical silences and erasures.

More than a technological novelty, the Carl-Nielsen chatbot serves as a living artwork. Visitors interact with a dynamic digital interface that constructs and deconstructs pixelated portraits of the sculptor. These visual fluctuations function as metaphors for the malleability of identity and memory. The chatbot not only speaks in Carl-Nielsen's voice but does so through a constantly shifting visual field, encouraging users to reflect on the ephemeral nature of historical representation.

Yoke, the design studio responsible for the chatbot's interface, visual expression, and sound design, played a pivotal role in translating this conceptual framework into an engaging sensory experience. Their work ensures that the chatbot is not perceived as a static information source but as an interactive, interpretative medium (Manovich, 2013). This aligns with the increasing recognition that digital tools can offer new modes of storytelling that go beyond linear narratives.

Pixelated portraits that form and dissolve on screen as users interact with the system. These fragmented and reassembled images of Carl-Nielsen embody the fluctuating nature of historical memory and the instability of identity when filtered through data. The portraits visualize the process of memory-making, suggesting that identity, like history, is not a singular truth but a continuous reinterpretation. This metaphor is reinforced by the sound design – ambient tones and responsive audio cues – that further immerse the user in a layered sensory dialogue with the past.

The technical development of the chatbot was led by Professor Morten Mørup and Associate Professor Tue Herlau from DTU Compute, along with advanced students Niels Raunkjær Holm, Andreas Holmer Bigom, and Michael Alexander Harborg. Drawing on expertise in machine learning, data mining, and probabilistic modeling, the team created a system that could analyze Carl-Nielsen's writings and generate responses that closely resemble her linguistic style and thematic concerns.

Professor Mørup's background in signal processing and network analysis likely informed the chatbot's ability to detect patterns in Carl-Nielsen's language, while Herlau's specialization in statistical inference ensured that the system could make reasoned decisions about language generation (Mørup & Hansen, 2012; Herlau, 2016). The students contributed by implementing the natural language processing (NLP) frameworks, training the models, and testing user interactions to refine the chatbot's performance.

This collaborative, interdisciplinary approach exemplifies what Johanna Drucker refers to as "speculative computing", the use of digital technologies to explore humanities questions through experimental and iterative design (Drucker, 2009). In this context, the chatbot becomes a site of inquiry as well as a tool, challenging users to reconsider their assumptions about historical figures and their relevance today.

The success of the Carl-Nielsen chatbot reveals a paradox at the heart of digital heritage work. On the one hand, the artists's extensive digital archive enabled the project; on the other, most other women in the exhibition lacked sufficient digitized material to be included in a similar capacity. This discrepancy, what the project calls a "data vacuum", highlights the unequal processes of cultural preservation. The histories we choose not to preserve become ever more difficult to recover in the digital era. This reflects what Wendy Chun calls "the enduring ephemeral" of digital media, its promise of permanence often conceals deeper acts of forgetting (Chun, 2008).

In acknowledging this gap, the project foregrounds the constructed nature of data and the human decisions underlying it. The Carl-Nielsen chatbot is a version of the artist mediated through accessible texts and images, shaped by prior narratives and cultural investments. It reminds us that any digital reconstruction is partial and interpretive.

A defining feature of the project is its commitment to transparency. The exhibition clearly identifies its data sources, acknowledges the interpretive decisions involved in developing the chatbot, and emphasizes that AI is not an objective or impersonal force. Rather, it is a human product, shaped by algorithms that are themselves designed within specific epistemological frameworks.

This reflexivity is crucial in an age when AI is often perceived as autonomous or all-knowing. As Safiya Umoja Noble cautions in Algorithms of Oppression, algorithmic systems can perpetuate existing biases if not critically examined (Noble, 2018). By making its construction process visible, the Carl-Nielsen chatbot encourages users to question the authority and neutrality of technological systems, aligning with broader calls for ethical AI development.

The exhibition installation underscores this point. As users interact with the chatbot, its responses are framed not as definitive truths but as interpretations. The interface features abstract, pixel-driven portraits that assemble and dissolve in response to dialogue – a visual metaphor for how historical narratives are constructed, deconstructed, and contested.

The chatbot is a dynamic participant in cultural dialogue rather than a static repository of facts. Through user interactions, the system learns and adapts, creating new forms of engagement with Carl-Nielsen's legacy. This aligns with the concept of living history, wherein the past is continually interpreted and reinterpreted in light of present concerns.

According to cultural theorist Stuart Hall, identity is not a fixed essence but a "positioning," constantly constructed through discourse and representation (Hall, 1996). The chatbot embodies this notion by offering a platform through which Carl-Nielsen's identity can be re-explored, not as a closed chapter of history but as an evolving narrative.

This mode of storytelling repositions the museum visitor from a passive recipient to an active interlocutor. Each interaction with the chatbot becomes a co-authored moment in the unfolding of Carl-Nielsen's legacy, shaped by the user's queries, interpretations, and emotional responses. This dialogic framework aligns with Mieke Bal's assertion that narratives within cultural institutions gain meaning through interaction and reinterpretation (Bal, 1996).

Beyond its artistic and technical achievements, the project serves as a powerful educational tool. By engaging users in dialogue with a historically significant figure, the chatbot fosters curiosity about art history, feminist critique, and digital culture.

It also serves as a prototype for future cultural projects that seek to democratize access to historical knowledge through technology.

Institutions such as SMK are increasingly embracing such innovations to expand their reach and relevance. As museums grapple with how to present complex histories in the digital age, projects like Against All Odds offer a compelling model. They demonstrate that digital tools, when thoughtfully applied, can enhance rather than dilute historical understanding (Cameron & Kenderdine, 2007).

This approach also opens new avenues for participatory curatorial practice. The ability to interact with historical figures through AI challenges the traditional authority of the museum as the sole interpreter of history. Instead, it invites a multiplicity of voices and interpretations, democratizing the experience of historical knowledge and making it more accessible and emotionally resonant.

In conclusion, Against All Odds – Historical Women and New Algorithms is more than an exhibition; it is a manifesto for reimagining our relationship with the past. It also serves as a compelling example of how sustainability encompasses not only environmental concerns but also the preservation, transmission, and continual evolution of knowledge. By combining AI, design, and feminist critique, the project reveals the potential of digital humanities to not only preserve history but to revitalize it. The Carl-Nielsen chatbot stands as a testament to what can be achieved when art, technology, and critical theory converge. In doing so, the project challenges us to reconsider whose stories we tell, how we tell them, and what tools we use. It invites us to see history not as a static archive but as a living, contested space where new voices can emerge – against all odds.

Kvadrat: Reimagining Textile Waste Into Creative and Sustainable Solutions

Kvadrat, a leading Scandinavian design company, exemplifies how innovation embedded within design can drive systemic change in the circular economy by transforming textile waste into sustainable, low-carbon furniture. This section explores Kvadrat's strategic approach to sustainability, highlighting its integration of environmental, social, and economic goals within the broader framework of the United Nations Sustainable Development Goals (SDGs). A close analysis of Kvadrat's initiatives and leadership principles sheds light on the intersection of creativity, innovation, and sustainable development in the contemporary textile and furniture industry.

Kvadrat's sustainability strategy is deeply rooted in the recognition that over 80% of a product's environmental impact is determined at the design stage. This insight informs the company's holistic approach to sustainability, which begins with conscious decision-making from the earliest phases of design, including material selection and packaging considerations. Kvadrat's commitment to responsible consumption and production aligns directly with SDG 12, emphasizing the need to reduce waste and optimize resource use throughout product life cycles.

Central to this approach is the adoption of circular design principles, which prioritize durability, repairability, and recyclability. By integrating these principles, Kvadrat aims to reduce its reliance on virgin materials and significantly lower CO_2-emissions associated with manufacturing. The company's target to reduce production waste intensity by 25% by 2030 and recycle 90% of remaining waste demonstrates a concrete commitment to measurable environmental goals. These targets are not merely aspirational; they are embedded within a framework of accountability and continuous improvement.

Kvadrat's work exemplifies how creativity can function as a catalyst for sustainable innovation. By reimagining textile waste as a valuable resource rather than refuse, the company disrupts traditional linear production models. This paradigm shift is not solely technical but conceptual, challenging long-standing industry norms that prioritize speed and cost-efficiency over environmental stewardship.

The transformation of textile waste into high-quality furniture embodies an innovative closed-loop system. This system conserves resources and simultaneously redefines value creation by aligning economic incentives with ecological responsibility. Such innovation is supported by cross-disciplinary collaboration between designers, engineers, and material scientists, highlighting the importance of integrating diverse expertise to tackle complex sustainability challenges.

Moreover, Kvadrat's approach demonstrates the capacity of design to communicate sustainability narratives effectively. Through aesthetic appeal and functional excellence, their products invite consumers to engage with environmental issues on a sensory and emotional level. This engagement cultivates a deeper awareness and responsibility toward sustainable consumption practices, illustrating the power of design as both a practical and pedagogical tool.

The realization of Kvadrat's sustainability goals is underpinned by its distinctive leadership philosophy and organizational culture. The company's leadership principles – invent, execute, grow, and engage – establish a framework that encourages continuous innovation, accountability, personal development, and collaboration both within and outside the organization. The 'invent' principle challenges existing processes and fosters a mindset oriented toward improvement and experimentation. This cultural emphasis on questioning the status quo is essential in developing novel solutions that integrate sustainability without compromising quality or design integrity. 'Execute' focuses on translating vision into tangible results, ensuring that strategic sustainability objectives are met through coordinated team efforts. The 'grow' principle highlights the importance of investing in people, nurturing talents, and fostering an environment conducive to learning and adaptation, critical for long-term organizational resilience in a rapidly changing global context. Finally, 'engage' emphasizes connectivity – with teams, partners, customers, and the broader community – recognizing that sustainable transformation requires collective action and shared commitment. This leadership model illustrates how sustainability transcends technical interventions to become a cultural and relational practice embedded at every organizational level.

Kvadrat's initiatives can be situated within wider scholarly discussions on sustainability, circular economy, and the role of creative industries in addressing global challenges. Recent literature underscores the necessity of integrated approaches that combine environmental objectives with social and economic considerations to achieve transformative impact (Geissdoerfer et al., 2017; Bocken et al., 2016). In this light, Kvadrat's commitment to reducing waste, optimizing materials, and fostering innovation aligns with calls for systemic change rather than isolated interventions. The company's emphasis on design as a leverage point resonates with academic perspectives that highlight the strategic importance of early-stage decision-making in sustainability transitions (Fargnoli et al., 2019).

Moreover, the case of Kvadrat illustrates how business leadership and corporate culture influence the adoption and scalability of sustainable practices. The integration of sustainability into leadership principles and organizational values reflects best practices identified in corporate sustainability literature, which emphasize leadership as a critical enabler of innovation and change (Egri & Herman, 2000; Waldman & Siegel, 2008).

Sustainability is frequently discussed primarily in ecological terms; however, Kvadrat's holistic approach acknowledges its broader social and economic dimensions. The company's strategies contribute not only to environmental preservation but also to responsible resource management, social responsibility, and economic viability, all critical for sustainable development.

This multifaceted understanding aligns with the increasingly recognized need to address global challenges such as climate change, social inequality, and economic instability in an integrated manner (Rockström et al., 2017). The role of creativity and art in this context becomes especially salient, as they offer innovative pathways to reimagine production and consumption patterns and foster inclusive dialogue around sustainability. Kvadrat's approach exemplifies this by embedding creative processes within sustainability frameworks, thereby bridging technical innovation and cultural transformation. This intersectionality is crucial to overcoming entrenched barriers and enabling sustainable innovation to thrive at scale.

In conclusion, Kvadrat's pioneering work in transforming textile waste into sustainable furniture illustrates the powerful synergy between creativity, innovation, and sustainability. By embedding circular design principles and fostering a leadership culture grounded in innovation and engagement, the company advances a holistic vision of responsible production and consumption. Kvadrat's initiatives exemplify how creative industries can act as agents of systemic change, aligning economic success with environmental and social imperatives.

The analysis of this section naturally complements the previous discussions on the Against All Odds project, which has revitalized the legacy of Anne Marie Carl-Nielsen through AI-powered cultural storytelling, and MY-CO SPACE, visionary living and housing concepts for the future based on natural building materials such as fungi. All three projects demonstrate the transformative potential of combining technology, creativity and critical reflection to tackle historical and current challenges. While the Against All Odds initiative highlights the importance of reclaiming marginalized voices through digital humanities and artificial intelligence, the work of Kvadrat and MY-CO-X underlines how design and material innovation can contribute to environmental and social sustainability. Together, these projects affirm that sustainable futures require interdisciplinary collaboration, creative problem-solving, and an ethical commitment to inclusion and responsibility. They call for expanding our understanding of sustainability beyond traditional ecological concerns to encompass cultural, technological, and social dimensions. Through such integrative approaches, history, art, and design converge to inspire innovative solutions and foster more equitable, resilient societies.

6. CONCLUSION

This chapter has demonstrated that art, creativity, and innovation are not peripheral to sustainability but central to its cultural, social, and systemic realization. They are not mere aesthetic add-ons but powerful levers that enable societies to imagine alternative futures, question dominant paradigms, and foster emotional engagement with complex ecological and social challenges. The cases examined – from fungi-based architecture and AI-driven cultural storytelling to circular textile design – illustrate how interdisciplinary collaboration and artistic experimentation can generate new forms of knowledge, participation, and sustainability-oriented action. The actionable findings with the corresponding key questions are summarized in the following table:

Table 1. Actionable Insights for Cultural Policymakers, CEOs, and Innovation Leaders

Key Insight	Why It Matters	Guiding Questions	How to Apply
Reframe Sustainability as a Cultural Challenge	Beyond technology and economics, sustainable futures require shifts in values, narratives, and collective imagination	Does my sustainable action create a clear, mobilizing vision of the future that initiates change?	• Policymakers: invest in cultural programs • CEOs: embed sustainability in brand storytelling • Innovators: design products with symbolic as well as functional value
Harness the Arts as Catalysts for Knowledge Management and Systemic Change	Art can visualize futures, disrupt habits, and open dialogue across sectors	Do the arts preserve knowledge, pass it on, and develop it further? Who has access to it?	• Fund cross-sector residencies: artists in science labs, businesses, government • use creative works to engage communities in policy design
Build Cross-Disciplinary Alliances	Solutions emerge when creatives, scientists, and business leaders co-create	Is the approach of my sustainable action interdisciplinary and integrative?	• Establish structured collaborations: hackathons, labs, fellowships with equal voice for creative practitioners
Design for Participation, Not Just Consumption	Cultural innovation is most powerful when people co-create, not passively consume	Does my sustainable action prioritize user-centered engagement and empowerment?	• Support participatory art/science projects • design business models that invite users as co-innovator
Embrace Experimentation and Narrative Risk	Sustainability demands new myths and models, which require tolerance of creative uncertainty	Are materials used responsibly, minimally, and with reusability in mind in my sustainability measures? Is harm to people or ecosystems avoided?	• Set material-use guidelines • Measure social/ ecological impacts • Adopt circular design principles

Source: own illustration

Among this, knowledge transfer is decisive. The ways in which knowledge is created, filtered, and circulated determine who is empowered to act and which futures become possible. Who has access to knowledge, and under what conditions? Who is entitled to make decisions based on it? How is knowledge kept in circulation across disciplines, organizations, and generations? Knowledge is power, and decisions about sharing – or withholding – it directly affect opportunities for development, equity, and resilience. Embedding deliberate, participatory strategies of knowledge transfer is therefore not optional but essential for sustainable transformation and organizational development alike.

At the same time, the analysis highlights key tensions: between visionary narratives and actionable change, between symbolic engagement and structural transformation. Addressing these requires not only supportive policy frameworks but also a redefinition of sustainability as a cultural mindset – one that values imagination, empathy, and pluralism as much as efficiency and innovation.

The call to action is clear: policymakers, CEOs, and innovation leaders must recognize creativity and knowledge transfer as strategic resources, not peripheral concerns. By embedding cultural and knowledge dimensions into sustainability discourse and practice, we can cultivate inclusive, resilient, and hopeful pathways toward a just and livable future in the Anthropocene.

REFERENCES

Bal, M. (1996). *Double Exposures: The Subject of Cultural Analysis*. Routledge.

Bocken, N. M. P., Short, S. W., Rana, P., & Evans, S. (2016). A literature and practice review to develop sustainable business model archetypes. *Journal of Cleaner Production, 65*, 42–56. DOI: 10.1016/j.jclepro.2013.11.039

Boer, H., Goduscheit, R. C., Schweisfurth, T., & Visser-Groeneveld, J. (2025). The role of creativity and innovation in the quality of our lives, the planet and science. *Creativity and Innovation Management, 34*(1), 75–77. DOI: 10.1111/caim.12628

Brem, A., & Puente-Díaz, R. (2020). Creativity, innovation, sustainability: A conceptual model for future research efforts. *Sustainability (Basel), 12*(8), 3139. DOI: 10.3390/su12083139

Brocchi, D. (2022). *By Disaster or by Design? Transformative Kulturpolitik: Von der multiplen Krise zur systemischen Nachhaltigkeit*. Springer VS. DOI: 10.1007/978-3-658-38965-9

Cameron, F., & Kenderdine, S. (Eds.). (2007). *Theorizing Digital Cultural Heritage: A Critical Discourse*. MIT Press. DOI: 10.7551/mitpress/9780262033534.001.0001

Chun, W. H. K. (2008). The Enduring Ephemeral, or the Future Is a Memory. *Critical Inquiry, 35*(1), 148–171. DOI: 10.1086/595632

Collins, M. (2024). Chat: Creativity, innovation & sustainability. https://chatmtc.com/c/cb7jq1fx177hmxzzqvwfo7nl

Crawford, K. (2021). *Atlas of AI: Power, Politics, and the Planetary Costs of Artificial Intelligence*. Yale University Press.

Creative Denmark. (2023). Creativity as a driver for green transition. https://www.creativedenmark.com

Creative Denmark. (2025). Creativity as a driver for sustainability. https://www.creativedenmark.com/in-focus/creativity-as-a-driver-for-sustainability

Danish Government. (2020). A green and sustainable world: The Danish Government's long-term strategy for global climate action. https://um.dk/en/foreign-policy/green-diplomacy

Dessein, J., Soini, K., Fairclough, G., & Horlings, L. (2015). *Culture in, for and as sustainable development*. European Union/University of Jyväskylä.

Drucker, J. (2009). *SpecLab: Digital Aesthetics and Projects in Speculative Computing*. University of Chicago Press. DOI: 10.7208/chicago/9780226165097.001.0001

Egri, C. P., & Herman, S. (2000). Leadership in the North American environmental sector: Values, leadership styles, and contexts of environmental leaders and their organizations. *Academy of Management Journal, 43*(4), 571–604. DOI: 10.2307/1556356

Europa Regina. (2024). Denmark creative industries. https://europaregina.eu

Fargnoli, M., Testa, F., Boiral, O., & Iraldo, F. (2019). The role of design in sustainability transitions: Contributions and research agenda. *Journal of Cleaner Production, 231*, 1145–1158. DOI: 10.1016/j.jclepro.2019.05.286

Geissdoerfer, M., Savaget, P., Bocken, N. M., & Hultink, E. J. (2017). The Circular Economy – A new sustainability paradigm? *Journal of Cleaner Production, 143*, 757–768. DOI: 10.1016/j.jclepro.2016.12.048

German Federal Government. (2025). Further development of the German Sustainability Strategy: Shaping transformation together and fairly. 2030 Agenda. https://www.2030agenda.de/de/article/weiterentwicklung-der-deutschen-nachhaltigkeitsstrategie-veroeffentlicht

Gregersen, B., & Johnson, B. (2021). The measurement and performance of the Danish innovation system in relation to sustainable development. In Christensen, J. L., Gregersen, B., Holm, J. R., & Lorenz, E. (Eds.), *Globalisation, new and emerging technologies, and sustainable development: The Danish innovation system in transition* (pp. 252–266). Routledge. DOI: 10.4324/9781003037750-18

Hall, S. (1996). Cultural Identity and Diaspora. In Mongia, P. (Ed.), *Contemporary Postcolonial Theory: A Reader* (pp. 110–121). Arnold.

Hjort, M. (2023). Aesthetic sustainability and creative practices. In Denmark, C. (Ed.), *Creativity as a driver for green transition* (pp. 38–41). https://www.creativedenmark.com

IUCN. (2021). Rights-based approaches must be placed at the heart of conservation efforts. https://iucn.org/news/governance-and-rights/202112/rights-based-approaches-must-be-placed-heart-conservation-efforts

Jesus, T. (2024). COP 30: For climate action rooted in culture. https://peoplespalaceprojects.org.uk/en/cop-30-for-climate-action-rooted-in-culture/

Kvadrat. (n.d.-a). About us – People and culture. Retrieved June 5, 2025, from https://www.kvadrat.dk/en/about/people-and-culture

Kvadrat. (n.d.-b). Sustainability. Retrieved June 5, 2025, from https://www.kvadrat.dk/en/sustainability

Manovich, L. (2013). *Software Takes Command*. Bloomsbury. DOI: 10.5040/9781472544988

Ministry of Foreign Affairs of Denmark. (2022). Sustainability strategy and implementation. https://um.dk

Ministry of Foreign Affairs of Denmark. (2024). Denmark: A creative toolbox. https://denmark.dk

Mørup, M., & Hansen, L. K. (2012). Archetypal analysis for machine learning and data mining. *Neurocomputing*, *80*, 54–63. DOI: 10.1016/j.neucom.2011.06.033

New Zero World. (2024). A new era in climate communications – White paper. https://newzeroworld.org

Noble, S. U. (2018). *Algorithms of Oppression: How Search Engines Reinforce Racism*. NYU Press. DOI: 10.18574/nyu/9781479833641.001.0001

Øko-net. (2000). DanmarksDeklarationen – Erklärung über eine dänische Agenda für nachhaltige Entwicklung im 21. Jahrhundert. https://www.oeko-net.dk

Pfeiffer, S., & Meyer, V. (2023). Engage with Fungi. Berlin Universities Publishing. DOI: https://berlinup.books.tu-berlin.de/produkt/978-3-98781-008-4/

Plambech, T., & Konijnendijk van den Bosch, C. C. (2015). The impact of nature on creativity – A study among Danish creative professionals. *Urban Forestry & Urban Greening*, *14*(2), 255–263. DOI: 10.1016/j.ufug.2015.02.006

Rockström, J., Steffen, W., Noone, K., Persson, Å., Chapin, F. S., Lambin, E., & Foley, J. (2017). A safe operating space for humanity. *Nature*, *461*(7263), 472–475. DOI: 10.1038/461472a PMID: 19779433

Sanz-Hernández, A., & Covaleda, I. (2021). Sustainability and creativity through mail art: A case study with young artists in universities. *Journal of Cleaner Production*, *318*, 128525. DOI: 10.1016/j.jclepro.2021.128525

Scott, J. W. (1988). *Gender and the Politics of History*. Columbia University Press. DOI: 10.7312/scot91266

Statens Museum for Kunst (SMK). (2024). Anne Marie Carl-Nielsen Chatbot: Against All Odds – Historical Women and New Algorithms. https://www.smk.dk/en/article/anne-marie-carl-nielsen-chatbot/

The Danish Government. (2002). A shared future: Balanced development. Denmark's national strategy for sustainable development. https://mst.dk

UNESCO. (2022). UNESCO global report 2022: Reshaping policies for creativity – Addressing culture as a global public good. .DOI: 10.18356/9789210015240

UNESCO. (n.d.). Cultural heritage and climate change. Intangible Cultural Heritage. https://ich.unesco.org/en/climate-change

United Nations. (2015). Transforming our world: The 2030 agenda for sustainable development. https://sdgs.un.org/2030agenda

United Nations Department of Economic and Social Affairs. (2025). The Sustainable Development Goals Report 2025. New York. (revision August 2025). https://unstats.un.org/sdgs/report/2025/

V. meer. (n.d.). MY-CO SPACE. https://www.v-meer.de/my-co-space

Vågen Svensson, L. E., & Smærup Sørensen, I. (2023). *Nordic Green Roadmap for Cultural Institutions (Nord 2023:041).* Nordic Council of Ministers. DOI: 10.6027/nord2023-041

Waldman, D. A., & Siegel, D. (2008). Defining the socially responsible leader. *The Leadership Quarterly, 19*(1), 117–131. DOI: 10.1016/j.leaqua.2007.12.008

Zimmermann, O. (2018). Sustainability culture: Fresh thinking is what the country needs! On the cultural dimension of the sustainability debate. In: German Almanac of Sustainability 2018: Ideas and actions. *Transformation (Durban)*, 50–57. https://www.nachhaltigkeitsrat.de/wp-content/uploads/2019/02/Almanac_2018_Zimmermann_190213EN.pdf

Chapter 2
The Role of Leadership in Social Creativity and Innovation

Yohannes Mekonnen Yesuf
https://orcid.org/0000-0003-2448-8656
University of Johannesburg, South Africa

Ziska Fields
https://orcid.org/0000-0001-5353-1807
University of Johannesburg, South Africa

ABSTRACT

This chapter explores how leadership advances social creativity and innovation to address global challenges, including inequality, climate change, and social exclusion. It advocates for inclusive, adaptive, and emotionally intelligent leadership grounded in systems thinking and community participation. The chapter critiques traditional innovation models and calls for embedding social creativity in organizational and policy frameworks. Methodologically, the study employs a descriptive review, complemented by systematic database searches, to ensure rigor and breadth. The analysis reveals a lack of empirical and contextually grounded studies, concluding that leadership, creativity, and innovation are mutually reinforcing in driving systemic change.

INTRODUCTION

In the modern era, societies face various complex and interrelated ecological, societal, and governmental concerns, such as global warming, economic hardship, and

DOI: 10.4018/979-8-3373-2742-6.ch002

the exploitation of individuals that no single societal sector can effectively manage. Social, financial, and political inequality persists worldwide, with income, rights, privileges, educational attainment, and social position gaps. These disparities are closely linked to different adverse outcomes, including lower health, more violence, diminished social trust, and other negative consequences for both marginalized and privileged societies (van Bezouw et al., 2021; Wilkinson & Pickett, 2009). Addressing these complex societal challenges requires coordinated efforts among public-sector stakeholders, non-profit, and industry players to enhance innovative and sustainable solutions. Instead of relying solely on traditional notions of innovation commonly emphasized in business literature, which are primarily concerned with increasing a firm's ability to outperform rivals (Farida & Setiawan, 2022), these complex issues demand a shift toward social creativity and innovation (CI) (Pless et al., 2021).

Social CI is motivated by a drive to address social gaps or, more broadly, pursue social possibilities, with the benefits primarily aimed toward society (Qureshi et al., 2021). The relevance of this research has been amplified by the global focus on the UN's Sustainable Development Goals. As stakeholder expectations for the role of business organizations and their management in responding to critical social issues rise, so does the need to better understand leaders' motives and methods for stakeholder engagement. Such understanding is necessary to evaluate the consequences of leadership engagement with social CI processes and their potential outcomes. This study looks primarily at the organizational aspects of this leadership role.

Organizational research aims to uncover the primary drivers that drive social CI to develop conceptual frameworks and practical solutions for improvement (Zhou & Hoever, 2014). Leaders play a crucial role by shaping tasks, allocating resources, and influencing the work environment (e.g., Javed et al., 2021). Leaders can also significantly affect their employees' behavior by using their existing skills, such as motivation, or learning new skills (Fischer et al., 2017). This illustrates how important leadership is in developing a creative and innovative workplace. There has never been a greater need for innovative, significant, and long-lasting solutions in a time of progressively complex social issues, from inequality and systemic poverty to public health emergencies and climate change (Mulgan, 2019). Social innovation, which is the practice of creating and implementing novel ideas, services, or models that better suit societal requirements than current options, is at the core of overcoming these obstacles. Solis-Navarrete et al. (2021) stated that social innovation seeks to develop enduring value to society through enhancing the welfare of people, communities, and society as a whole, in contrast to conventional innovation, which is primarily concerned with economic results.

Leadership is widely acknowledged as essential to fostering social CI (van Bezouw et al., 2021). Despite a few recent academic publications (e.g., Herrera, 2016; Parés et al., 2017; Qureshi et al., 2021; Shier & Handy, 2020), a systematic study on the relationship between leadership and social CI persists. While a large body of literature has investigated the role of leadership in promoting tech-driven and managerial innovations in enterprise contexts (Banmairuroy et al., 2022; Nani & Safitri, 2021), these findings are limited in their applicability to understanding how leadership influences social CI, which is the primary focus of this study. This distinction results from the fact that, while social CI share some fundamental characteristics with technological and administrative innovation, such as creativity and idea implementation, they are ultimately motivated by different objectives: social impact in the latter case, and business success in the former. Consequently, the incubation, design, and development stages will probably differ. Pless et al. (2021) underline the ethical and psychological factors that might transform empathy into socially conscious business practices, including systems-based thinking, community-oriented value analysis, and a sincere desire to lessen human suffering. There is an urgent need to deepen our understanding of the function of leadership in advancing social CI, especially in light of the increasing demand for these capabilities and the expanding involvement of organizations across corporate and nonprofit domains in tackling societal challenges.

Although historically associated with nonprofits and social enterprises (Farinha et al., 2020), social CI has gained traction within the corporate sphere, often as an extension of corporate social responsibility (Agostini et al., 2017) or through emerging models of corporate social innovation (Souto, 2022). This area of research remains emergent and is still establishing its theoretical and empirical foundations (Tabares, 2020). However, skepticism persists: critics note that corporate leaders may be constrained by profit motives or ethical lapses, contributing to economic crises and ongoing social inequities (Carberry et al., 2019). Evidence suggests that business leaders' engagement in social CI is growing and influential, underscoring the importance of understanding how leadership can effectively guide, inspire, and sustain social CI in diverse organizational settings.

Framing social innovation within the broader concepts of creativity and leadership emphasizes that leaders are not simply facilitators but active architects of inclusive, culturally attuned solutions (Qureshi et al., 2021). They shape collaborative networks, mobilize resources, frame shared visions, and empower communities to take ownership of change (Mariani et al., 2022). By exploring the role of leadership in social CI, this study addresses a notable gap in the literature: while there is extensive research on leadership and employee creativity in general (see Asbari, 2021), the specific leadership roles, behaviors, and strategies that enable social CI remain underexamined and theoretically fragmented (Hughes et al., 2018; van Bezouw et al., 2021).

To advance both scholarship and practice, this study identifies four interrelated research imperatives that directly reflect the chapter's central focus. First, examining how leadership fosters social creativity within organizational contexts and across sectors is essential. Second, there is a need to clarify the specific leadership roles, visionary, collaborative, ethical, and facilitative, that enable the effective development and implementation of social innovation. Third, further investigation should explore how leadership drives transformational innovation to address complex societal challenges. Finally, it is essential to identify and evaluate organizational strategies leaders can employ to cultivate, sustain, and scale social CI.

This chapter advances the field's theoretical foundations and generates actionable insights by positioning leadership as the primary analytical lens through which social creativity and innovation are examined. Leaders can use these insights to design and implement socially meaningful and innovative interventions, bridging the gap between conceptual understanding and practical application.

METHODOLOGY

This chapter was developed using a descriptive literature review approach, complemented by systematic search procedures to provide a comprehensive and reliable synthesis of contemporary knowledge on leadership in social creativity and innovation. Given the interdisciplinary nature of the topic, which spans management, social entrepreneurship, and organizational studies, this approach ensures both breadth and depth of understanding. The narrative approach helps bring together different theories and research findings (Sukhera, 2022), while the systematic approach improves transparency, rigor, and the ability to replicate the review when selecting and evaluating relevant studies.

We searched multiple scholarly databases, including Web of Science, Scopus, Google Scholar, JSTOR, ProQuest, and SSRN, as they provide comprehensive and reliable coverage of management and social science research. The search used key terms such as “leadership,” “creativity,” “innovation,” “social creativity,” “social innovation,” “transformational leadership,” “collaborative leadership,” and “social entrepreneurship.” These terms were combined with Boolean operators (e.g., AND, OR, NOT) to improve accuracy and breadth. For example, one representative search string was:

(“leadership” AND (“creativity” OR “innovation”) AND (“social creativity” OR “social innovation”) AND (“transformational leadership” OR “collaborative leadership” OR “social entrepreneurship”)).

The review included only English-language, peer-reviewed journal articles published between 2000 and 2024. This structured approach helped ensure that the literature captured was comprehensive and directly relevant to the study's variables, encompassing both theoretical and practical perspectives.

A clearly defined set of inclusion and exclusion criteria was employed to guide the selection of studies. Eligible publications addressed leadership about creativity, innovation, and social impact, particularly on social enterprises, nonprofit organizations, hybrid firms, and community-based initiatives. Studies were excluded if they focused exclusively on technological or purely commercial innovation without a social dimension, were published in languages other than English, or lacked sufficient methodological rigor. The screening process aligned with these predefined criteria (see Table 1). As a result, 59 rigorously selected studies were identified for detailed analysis (see Table 2).

Table 1. Inclusion Parameters and Rationale

Criteria	Justification
Peer-reviewed journal articles (2000–2024)	Guarantees up-to-date, reliable, and high-quality research.
Focuses on the role of leadership in social creativity and innovation.	Ensures relevance to the study's core topic.
Empirical or theoretical works	Captures both practical insights and conceptual developments.
Covers all sectors related to leadership, social creativity, and innovation	Enables a comprehensive understanding of social creativity and innovation across various sectoral applications.
Includes studies from all countries	Enables a global perspective and cross-contextual view
English-language publications	Ensures accessibility and consistency in analysis.

Table 2. Summary of Reviewed Articles

Thematic cluster	Key focus	Selected studies
Leadership roles in promoting social creativity	Leader behaviors, motivation, and organizational culture that support creative thinking.	(Ahlin et al., 2014; Asbari et al., 2021; Clydesdale, 2006; Çokpekin & Knudsen, 2012; Cropley, 2006; Csikszentmihalyi, 2014; Dolejšová et al., 2021; Fields, 2016; Fischer, 2004; Gilson, 2024; Glăveanu, 2020; Jefferson & Anderson, 2017; Jeong & Shin, 2019; Karwowski et al., 2020; Khedhaouria et al., 2017; Koppl et al., 2015; Liv et al., 2020; Nisula et al., 2022; Politis, 2005)
Leadership roles in promoting social innovation	Transformational, transactional, empowering, and entrepreneurial behaviors and their impact on social creativity and innovation processes.	(Acar et al., 2019; Agostini et al., 2017; Audretsch et al., 2022; Blanco & León, 2017; Carberry et al., 2019; Caulier-Grice, 2012; Eichler & Schwarz, 2019; Herrera, 2016; Iqbal & Piwowar-Sulej, 2022; Manzini, 2015; Mongelli & Rullani, 2017; Mulgan, 2006, 2019; Murray, 2010; Phills et al., 2008).
Leadership drives transformational innovation to tackle complex societal problems.	Strategic decisions, vision setting, and ethical practices that turn creativity into real social impact.	(Acar, Tarakci, & van Knippenberg, 2019; Amit & Zott, 2020; Asbari, 2021; Avelino et al., 2019; Begum et al., 2022; Hansen & Pihl-Thingvad, 2019; Lévesque, 2013; Ma & Jiang, 2018; Purwati et al., 2021; Ruben & Gigliotti, 2016; Shier & Handy, 2020; Suriyankietkaew et al., 2022).
Effective organizational strategies	Developing, maintaining, and expanding social creativity and innovation.	(Amabile & Pratt, 2016; Anderson & Dees, 2006; Banmairuroy et al., 2022; Buonocore et al., 2024; Farinha et al., 2020; Heeks et al., 2014; Kolasani, 2023; Kolk & Lenfant, 2015; Parés et al., 2017; Pless et al., 2021; Politis, 2005; Tabares, 2020; Van Tulder & Van Mil, 2022).

A literature matrix was employed to systematically extract and analyze data, documenting key study characteristics such as year, context, methodology, theoretical framework, primary findings, and authors. A thematic analysis was conducted, structured explicitly around the chapter's four research objectives:

1. Explore how leadership encourages social creativity, focusing on leader behaviors, motivation, and organizational culture that support creative thinking.
2. Explain specific leadership roles in promoting social innovation, including transformational, transactional, empowering, and entrepreneurial behaviors and their impact on social creativity and innovation processes.
3. Examine how leadership drives transformational innovation to tackle complex societal problems, looking at strategic decisions, vision setting, and ethical practices that turn creativity into real social impact.
4. Identify effective organizational strategies for developing, maintaining, and expanding social creativity and innovation, including governance, stakeholder engagement, resource management, and ethical practices like data stewardship.

The review provides a structured narrative synthesis that reflects theoretical diversity and contextual variation across sectors and regions by clustering codes under these objective-aligned themes. A critical appraisal of each study was also performed to ensure methodological robustness and relevance; studies lacking clarity, rigor, or contribution to the field were excluded from the final synthesis. While this review offers an integrative understanding of leadership's role in social creativity and innovation, certain limitations should be noted. Limiting the search to English-language publications may have excluded relevant studies from non-English-speaking contexts, and the rapidly evolving nature of the field means some emerging studies may not have been captured.

In conclusion, this methodology integrates narrative synthesis with systematic rigor and aligns thematic analysis directly with the chapter's four research objectives. This approach provides a solid foundation for identifying patterns, knowledge gaps, and practical insights, ensuring the chapter's findings are academically robust and directly relevant to understanding the role of leadership in social creativity and innovation.

CREATIVITY AND INNOVATION (CI)

Understanding the link between the processes of CI has grown more critical due to business globalization, which has boosted managers' worldwide mobility and the propensity to spread innovative activity across national borders (Amabile & Pratt, 2016; Raisch & Birkinshaw, 2008). CI significantly enhances individual and organizational achievements, drives broader economic growth, and fosters social progress worldwide. By encouraging novel ideas and solutions, they stimulate competitive advantage, improve productivity, and open new markets. (Acar et al., 2019; Westwood and Low, 2003).

Both creativity and innovation are complex ideas that involve various distinct and frequently related consequences (Gilson, 2024). Even with the multifaceted and constantly changing aspects of CI (Mumford, Steele, et al., 2017), both emphasize the creation and execution of innovative knowledge (Weisberg, 2016). Liu et al. (2020) added that information specialists of today desire elements of CI to be relevant. The trans disciplinary nature of both constructs is supported by research findings (Frederico & Amorim, 2008; Heye, 2006; Nakano & Wechsler, 2018). Additionally, most research on the relationship between CI is still considerably more investigative than properly supported by theoretical frameworks. As a result, three different kinds of relationships between CI have been covered.

First, consider CI as being synonymous. According to this perspective, both structures are similar because the result is the same (Nakano & Wechsler, 2018).

For example, Mostafa (2012) employed both terms synonymously and explained that "innovation or creativity refers to the systemic development and practical application of a new idea." Nevertheless, previous studies have questioned this assumption, arguing that being creative does not always lead to innovation but can contribute to its advancement or serve as one of its sources (Campos et al., 2014). This understanding has been criticized since, if we treat these concepts as synonyms, we would miss some critical differences between them (Koppl et al., 2015). While innovations require that an idea is executed, about moving forward, creativity first demands something appropriate, such as a concept, understanding, or remedy aimed at solving a problem. Innovation, as opposed to creativity, requires moving beyond idea generation to overcome practical challenges and execute steps, such as problem study, appraisal, and implementation (Zeng et al., 2011).

Second, according to some academics, individual creativity has been cited as the most significant factor influencing innovation (e.g., Asbari et al., 2021; Hughes et al., 2018; Liu et al., 2020; Politis, 2005; Rosso, 2014). In this regard, creativity is significant and is often viewed as a prerequisite to innovation (West & Richter, 2024), yet this relies on both creativity and outside factors like the market and its regulating forces; the relationship between the two ideas cannot be seen as straightforward and linear (Acar et al., 2019). Moreover, Weisberg (2016) emphasized that because creativity serves as the groundwork for innovation, gaining insight into the creative process and the elements that foster it is crucial. It is common to think that bottom-up causation operates: creative individual behavior, under the right conditions, can result in innovative organizations (Ahlin et al., 2014; Karwowski et al., 2020). Sarooghi et al. (2015) extensively reviewed the link between CI. Their meta-analysis revealed a positive association between the two, particularly at the individual level. Later research examining different circumstances further supported the link between creative processes and innovation outcomes (Hwang, 2017; Valaei et al., 2017).

Third, on the other extreme, creativity and innovation are seen as separate and independent ideas (Černe et al., 2013; Reiter-Palmon, 2018). According to this perspective, researchers point out that the terms are used imprecisely because both CI can be understood from the viewpoint of the outcome, evaluated by its originality and adequacy for creativity, or by its practicality for innovation (Nakano & Wechsler, 2018). Clydesdale (2006) distinguished creativity from innovation by proposing that innovation results from external incentives or the desire to challenge established methods, while creativity is fueled by internal motivation. Another distinction is that although innovation must be examined from a team or organizational level, creativity must be researched on a personal scale (Černe et al., 2013). Therefore, numerous processes exist between developing and implementing a concept, increasing the possibility of a communication breakdown between these two points (Nakano & Wechsler, 2018).

In summary, CI is a closely associated but fundamentally unique notion in academic discourse. While these terms are frequently used interchangeably in daily conversation, especially by non-experts, it is vital to note that they differ in several key ways. Specifically, creativity involves the creation of novel and valuable ideas, which is frequently fueled by individual cognitive processes, intrinsic motivation, and a supportive sociocultural environment. On the other hand, innovation takes a step further by emphasizing the execution and application of creative ideas in practical, organizational, or market situations. Individual, social, motivational, and evaluative characteristics express these differences in various ways (see Table 3). For example, creativity is evaluated by how original and unique the ideas are. At the same time, innovation is measured by how well those ideas are implemented and how useful they are. Because of these subtle differences, it is crucial to approach creativity and innovation as distinct but interrelated phenomena, particularly in empirical studies. Ignoring this could result in measurement errors, conceptual ambiguity, and difficulties developing and implementing theories. The ongoing interplay between idea creation and concept implementation necessitates that scholars use precise terminology and frameworks when examining individual, team, or organizational outcomes.

Table 3. Comparative Overview of the Conceptual Definitions of CI

Bases for comparison	Creativity	Innovation	Reference
Meaning	Involves producing original ideas or practical solutions, drawing on imagination, originality, and the potential to generate value.	Involves effectively putting creative ideas into action, leading to new or enhanced products, services, processes, or practices that add value.	(Amabile, 1988)
Process	Ideation	Implementation	(Anderson et al., 2014)
Risk	Free	High	(Tidd & Bessant, 2014)
Motivation	Intrinsic	Extrinsic	(Amabile, 1996)
Criteria for evaluation	Prioritizes originality	Prioritizes effectiveness	(Farr & Ford, 1990; Runco & Jaeger, 2012)

SOCIAL CREATIVITY (SC) AND ATTRIBUTES

Definition of Social Creativity

"Social creativity" describes how an individual's creative process arises from interactions with their social and cultural surroundings rather than being an isolated mental process. A person's relationship with their work and relationships with others are their sources. Cooperation, dialogue, and idea sharing stimulate creativity in a social setting. Because they offer resources that aid in developing and shaping creative ideas, artifacts, such as tools, knowledge, and shared experiences, also play a vital role in this process (Sawyer, 2014).

In essence, SC acknowledges that creativity is a dynamic, collective process. Social creativity is not just about an individual's thoughts; it also involves how those thoughts engage with and get influenced by the surrounding socio-cultural environment. People can create something new by interacting with others and drawing on shared knowledge, demonstrating that creativity is inherently social. This concept challenges the idea that creativity is a solitary activity, highlighting the importance of social contexts in supporting and improving creative outcomes (Csikszentmihalyi & Csikszentmihalyi, 2014; Moran, 2010).

SC emerges from the active engagement between individuals and their socio-cultural contexts. While individual creativity is often viewed as a solitary activity, much of human creativity results from collaboration and shared experiences with others (Glăveanu, 2020; van Bezouw et al., 2021). It is not confined to the individual mind. However, it is enhanced through connections with others and with the artifacts that represent collective knowledge. Creativity, in this sense, is deeply rooted in social contexts where exchanges of ideas, emotions, and experiences play crucial roles in generating innovative outcomes (Amabile & Pratt, 2016; Fischer, 2013). To foster SC, environments must be open-ended and multifaceted, offering conditions that challenge users to come across new and uncertain situations, leading to moments of reflection and learning (Fischer et al., 2005; Jefferson & Anderson, 2017). These breakdowns, though difficult, create growth opportunities, enabling individuals and groups to develop new insights and approaches (Fischer, 2004). Co-creation is another critical component of SC: the cooperative creation of new concepts and interpretations in a socio-technical setting (Giaccardi, 2004). Participants must synchronize and improvise during the situated experience of co-creation, which is not linear (Kimmel et al., 2018). People can share feelings, experiences, and representations through this approach, frequently in a setting motivated by group intent rather than clear objectives, such as informal social structures or art.

Co-creation can manifest in various forms, including:

1. **Serial co-creation**: an individual creates something, which is then brought into a shared social space where others can build upon it.
2. **Parallel co-creation**: individuals create separate elements later combined into a new, collective creation.
3. **Simultaneous co-creation**: participants collaboratively create something in real-time, with everyone contributing simultaneously.

Beyond these forms, SC also involves the exchange of diverse perspectives, the leveraging of collective intelligence, and the ability to adapt to shifting environments. It is driven by shared goals, mutual support, and a willingness to embrace ambiguity, which enhances the creative potential of groups and organizations (Jeong & Shin, 2019; Kolasani, 2023). In summary, social creativity is a complex, collaborative process where the boundaries between individual and collective contributions blur, fostering innovation through shared learning and joint problem-solving.

Attributes of Social Creativity (SC)

A complex concept, SC describes how individuals or groups develop original and worthwhile ideas in social settings, especially in response to societal issues and group demands. Collaboration stands as a crucial part of social creativity. Unlike independent creativity, SC frequently comes via partnership, dialogue, and co-creation. The various actors' diverse viewpoints, experiences, and cultural backgrounds enrich the creative process (Fischer et al., 2005). Collaborative engagement encourages trust, shared ownership, and the integration of diverse knowledge systems, improving the quality and feasibility of socially creative results. Individuals can build on each other's contributions when collaborating creatively in teams or organizations (Sawyer, 2010). In this way, social creativity is fundamentally relational, reliant on interaction, collaboration, and collective learning dynamics.

Another core attribute of SC is empathetic understanding. This refers to the capacity to recognize and empathize with the emotions, needs, and views of another. Empathy allows people to frame challenges not just from a technical or abstract perspective, but also from the actual experiences of those affected. As a result, empathy drives socially creative ideas that are aligned with the particular social context and centered on human needs, an essential quality for advancing social innovation, sustainable development, and grassroots problem-solving (Manzini, 2015).

A further significant attribute is value orientation, notably a dedication to social good. SC is more than just novelty or innovation for its justification; it also develops ideas and solutions that promote equity, justice, sustainability, and wellbeing (Souto, 2022). This ethical and moral dimension sets social creativity apart from other types of creativity that may focus on profit or efficiency. Socially creative individuals or groups are frequently motivated by a well-defined goal or direction, societal accountability, and a desire to confront systemic social problems (Cropley, 2006). As a result, social creativity is fundamentally normative; it measures success not just by novelty but also by the ability to enhance social contexts.

Cultural context greatly influences SC, which shapes how individuals see issues, develop solutions, and collaborate. Human-centered solutions are supported by cultures that prioritize empathy and harmony, whereas collectivist cultures encourage collaboration through principles like community and shared responsibility. Traditional knowledge and cultural narratives inspire locally relevant and meaningful socially creative thoughts (Larraz-Rábanos, 2021). Therefore, culture is an active force that propels socially creative activities rather than just a background aspect. Understanding cultural effects makes creative remedies more effective in tackling complex societal issues by ensuring they are context-specific, broadly accepted, and long-lasting.

Finally, an attribute that defines SC is adaptive problem-solving. Social problems are often dynamic, complex, and challenging to solve straightforwardly (Loseke, 2017). Cognitive and emotional flexibility allows socially creative actors to rethink issues, try different strategies, and stay receptive to stakeholder input and shifting circumstances. This flexibility is crucial to navigating ambiguity and effectively coping with social setbacks. Social creativity promotes ongoing social system transformation and improvement through open-ended inquiry and iterative learning (Dolejšová et al., 2021). In conclusion, the defining attributes of SC, empathetic understanding, collaborative engagement, value orientation, and adaptive problem-solving, collectively empower individuals and groups to imagine and implement meaningful solutions to social challenges. These attributes highlight the importance of SC in areas such as social entrepreneurship, education, community development, and policymaking. Through interaction and mutual support, they foster a collaborative, socially engaged, and resource-sharing environment that nurtures creativity. Moreover, the social setting, cultural context, and opportunities for reflection are essential in generating and sustaining creativity within groups and organizations.

SOCIAL INNOVATION (SI) AND ATTRIBUTES

Definition of Social Innovation

Although social innovations (SIs) are crucial for societal and technological advancement, they are insufficient to address the primary issues of the twenty-first century. Instead, SIs aim to address, or at least mitigate, some of these pressing problems. SIs' roles in information technology (e.g., the creation of free open-source software; Qureshi et al., 2021), the health sector (e.g., improvements in dementia research; Igarashi & Okada, 2015), and housing and community development (Blanco & León, 2017) have all been the subject of various disciplines' research.

Social innovation is innovative practices, procedures, and services that meet social demands and improve community well-being (Mulgan, 2006, p. 146). It covers a broad spectrum of organizational forms, from hybrid organizations that achieve a balance between social and financial objectives in for-profit firms that adopt corporate social responsibility programs to incorporate social value into their commercial plans. Benefit Corporations (B-Corps) and Low-Profit Limited Liability Companies (L3Cs) are examples of these hybrid models. They operate within organizational frameworks that prioritize both social impact and economic sustainability (Anderson & Dees, 2006; Reiser & Dean, 2017).

The initiatives of social entrepreneurs primarily fuel SI; they use corporate concepts to provide novel answers to societal problems. Unlike regular business owners, social entrepreneurs prioritize social transformation over monetary gain (Morris et al., 2021). Across multiple sectors, such as healthcare, education, technology, and environmental sustainability, they introduce scalable and sustainable solutions essential in filling established systems' gaps. Their goals are to empower underprivileged groups, enhance the quality of life, and bring about sustainable social change.

Academics and researchers have offered different definitions to encapsulate the essence of social innovation. According to Phills et al. (2008), it represents an innovative solution to a social issue that is more sustainable, impactful, and efficient than existing practices. It delivers value to society collectively, rather than benefiting only specific individuals. Similarly, social innovation is defined by Murray (2010) as novel concepts, models, and methods that tackle urgent societal issues and support systemic change. Moreover, social innovation involves changing systems and structures and developing new ideas, as stressed by Westley and Antadze (2010). According to them, it entails new social practices that profoundly change societal norms, habits, and governance structures, considerably influencing how social and economic activities are carried out.

Social innovation's novelty and interdisciplinary nature have contributed to the lack of consensus on a single definition (Pellicer-Sifres et al., 2017). Due to its broad scope, SI has been studied across multiple academic disciplines, each offering unique perspectives on its meaning and significance. A comprehensive analysis of existing definitions identified five core elements that best describe social innovation (Eichler & Schwarz, 2019):

1. Addressing a social need: SI responds to pressing social issues like economic disparity, impoverishment, and environmental degradation. It aims to create solutions that improve social well-being.
2. Innovative approach: It involves new methods, strategies, or models that differ from conventional solutions, introducing fresh perspectives and creativity to problem-solving.
3. Implementation of a product or service: SI goes beyond merely coming up with ideas; it requires practical application through products, services, or new processes that bring about real change.
4. Improvement of existing conditions: The overarching aim of social innovation is to enhance current situations, ensuring a measurable positive impact on individuals, communities, or systems.
5. Building new relationships and collaborations: SI fosters cooperation across sectors (public, private, and nonprofit) to maximize impact and sustainability. Strong networks, knowledge sharing, and partnerships are essential for scaling and sustaining social innovation.

Beyond these five elements, social innovation is deeply interconnected with systemic change. It introduces new ideas and transforms existing institutions, policies, and social structures to create long-term improvements (Westley & Antadze, 2010). This systemic nature ensures that SI is a temporary fix and a sustainable mechanism for continuous development. Moreover, SI's digital transformation and technological advancements are growing, enabling broader participation, enhanced data-driven decision-making, and global connectivity. Platforms for open innovation, social entrepreneurship, and co-creation have amplified the impact of social innovation across different sectors. SI is emerging as a powerful force in shaping more inclusive, equitable, and resilient societies by integrating community-driven solutions, policy support, and cross-sectoral collaboration.

Co-creation and Inclusive Innovation

Aiming primarily to improve individual and communal well-being, SI refers to innovative approaches, concepts, ideas, and organizational structures that address urgent social needs more successfully than current solutions. SI is intrinsically mission-driven, addressing systemic problems like poverty, injustice, environmental degradation, and social exclusion, in contrast to traditional innovation, which frequently prioritizes technological advancement or market competitiveness (Audretsch et al., 2022).

The modern view of SI centers on co-creation and inclusive innovation, emphasizing working together and ensuring fairness for everyone involved. According to

Voorberg et al. (2015), co-creation involves the engaged collaboration of multiple stakeholders. In the ideation, design, implementation, and assessment of solutions, particularly those directly impacted by the issue. Participatory development theory, which promotes community empowerment via engagement in decision-making and knowledge-sharing, is the foundation of this participatory strategy (Castro-Arce & Vanclay, 2020)—recognizing local knowledge, experience, and context as crucial elements of creativity challenges top-down intervention methods.

Simultaneously, inclusive innovation aims to provide chances for people who are frequently left out of innovation processes, including low-income groups, women, youth, people with disabilities, and rural populations, to both contribute to and profit from innovation (Heeks et al., 2014). The capability theory, Sen (1999), which emphasizes expanding people's freedoms and capacities to live the kinds of lives they value, is consistent with this approach. Thus, inclusive innovation democratizes access to resources, technologies, and solutions by moving the innovation center from prestigious institutions to the local level. Co-creation and inclusive innovation work together to broaden the meaning of social innovation beyond just new products to include the methods used to get there. Integrating innovation into community structures fosters sustainability, trust, and ownership (Ciasullo et al., 2020). These approaches are critical in emerging countries where forced solutions have historically failed to consider cultural, economic, and political difficulties.

Theoretically, this shift aligns with social constructivist perspectives on innovation, which maintain that solutions and knowledge are not transmitted from experts but co-produced through social interaction (Polk, 2015). Additionally, it embodies the principles of complex adaptive systems theory and systems thinking, which highlight the interdependence of societal issues and the necessity of cooperative, situation-specific methods for systemic change (Nisula et al., 2022).

In summary, how SI is framed through co-creation and inclusive innovation highlights the structure and ethics of the innovation process and the significance of the results. These strategies guarantee that social change is significant, long-lasting, and able to address the underlying causes of societal issues by placing communities at the core of innovation. This approach has enormous potential for achieving inclusive and transformative development, strengthening communities, and fostering resilience.

Attributes of Social Innovation (SI)

According to Caulier-Grice (2012), SI is distinct from other types of innovation in eight critical ways. Even though these qualities are deemed desirable, not all social innovations meet all requirements because time and circumstance can affect how they are implemented. An organized description of these elements can be found below:

Intersectoral nature: any sector- public, commercial, or nonprofit- can give rise to SI, which frequently moves between them as it matures. This adaptability promotes cross-sector cooperation by enabling solutions to change to meet different institutional and societal needs (Kolk & Lenfant, 2015).

Open and collaborative approach: a transparent and cooperative method, SI needs to be inclusive and promote widespread involvement from various stakeholders. Technology is essential to promoting this inclusivity because it makes sharing concepts, codes, and solutions easier across settings. This openness makes social innovations more scalable and flexible (Qureshi et al., 2021).

Bottom-Up development: development from the bottom up, in contrast to top-down strategies, SI is frequently spearheaded by beneficiaries and the community. In addition to ensuring that solutions are more pertinent, efficient, and long-lasting, this grassroots development promotes empowerment. SI fosters long-term involvement and boosts efficiency by actively incorporating stakeholders (Castro-Arce & Vanclay, 2020).

Prosumption and Co-Production: The lines between producers and consumers are being distorted by social innovation. Users frequently assume the position of co-creators, changing from being passive consumers of services to being actively involved in the creation and upkeep of the solution. This shared accountability guarantees that inventions are long-lasting and fulfill their intended function (Caulier-Grice, 2012).

Utilitarianism: The foundation of SI is the notion that the welfare of the individual and the group are intertwined. Mutual reliance builds social links and resilience as communities collaborate to achieve shared objectives. Numerous community-led and cooperative projects are based on this idea (Avelino et al., 2019).

Establishment of new roles and relationships: Social innovation revolutionizes traditional service delivery by encouraging new connections between service providers and users. Beneficiaries actively contribute to developing and improving solutions rather than acting as passive recipients. According to Lévesque (2013), this participative strategy improves ownership and involvement in social programs.

Improved use of resources and assets: successful SI identifies, uses, and organizes already-existing social resources, such as networks, expertise, and knowledge. By making the most of available resources, social projects can have a bigger impact with fewer inputs, resulting in more effective and long-lasting solutions (Ziegler, 2017).

Building assets and capabilities: SI aims to develop communities' long-term capabilities and fix urgent problems. Cultivating resilience, knowledge, and abilities equips people and organizations to handle obstacles on their own in the future. This focus on developing capacity guarantees social innovation will have a transformative and long-lasting effect (Stroh, 2015).

The process of SI is dynamic and complex, and it depends on community involvement, cooperation, and inclusivity. While not every innovation addresses every facet simultaneously, these ideas provide a framework to enhance sustainability and social impact. As society continues to confront intricate issues, embracing these traits can contribute to significant and enduring transformation.

THE DIFFERENCE BETWEEN SC AND SI

While they have conceptual similarities, SC and SI serve different purposes in creating and enacting significant social change. The ability of people, groups, or organizations to envision new possibilities, question accepted wisdom, and generate unique concepts in response to social needs or injustices is known as SC (Glăveanu, 2020). This cognitive and cultural process includes divergent thinking, introspection, storytelling, and reinterpreting commonplace experiences. As a bottom-up force that reflects local reality and different worldviews, SI frequently arises from marginalized groups or those closest to social problems. SC involves creating new ideas and working together to co-create meaning, which can impact how communities define issues and envision change (Gilson, 2024).

SI, on the other hand, focuses more on the valuable aspects of social transformation. It entails transforming innovative concepts into concrete interventions that enhance people's and communities' well-being in scalable and sustainable ways, such as new services, goods, organizational structures, or regulations (Avelino et al., 2019). Innovation entails systematic design, testing, adaptation, and institutionalization procedures, whereas creativity drives the ideation stage. Thus, SI is a more result-driven and action-oriented phenomenon frequently involving cross-sector cooperation between civil society actors, governments, non-profits, and enterprises (Fields, 2016). It is becoming increasingly important to address complicated and systemic societal issues that traditional methods have not been able to handle, such as inequality, environmental degradation, or health crises.

The two have a symbiotic, iterative, and sequential interaction. Applying those concepts to real-world situations allows SI to impact, whereas social creativity supplies the creative spark for innovation by presenting new viewpoints (Howaldt et al., 2016). Without originality, innovation risks becoming incremental and replicating current standards without having the capacity to change them. Creative ideas, on the other hand, could stay theoretical or unrelated to execution in the absence of innovation. According to Manzini (2015), creativity gains social significance when it manifests as new social norms, organizations, or behaviors. So, fostering social creativity is crucial to opening up new possibilities for social change, and funding social innovation guarantees that those ideas become action that improves people's lives.

In this way, the two ideas are not just distinct in their emphasis- ideation versus implementation- but also complementary components of a larger ecosystem for bringing about change. A society that encourages and fosters imaginative creativity, particularly from its most marginalized or vulnerable sections, develops the ability to challenge the status quo. This creativity leads to significant, inclusive advancement combined with innovation's strategic and structural instruments. In the end, creating solutions that are not just innovative and successful but also fair and sensitive to the various demands of society requires acknowledging and enhancing the connection between SC and SI.

LEADERSHIP IN SC AND SI

Over the decades, leadership has been thoroughly studied, revealing a plethora of evidence and varied conceptualizations (Bass & Stogdill, 1990). Previously considered a simple concept, leadership has become a complex and diverse phenomenon formed by several disciplinary perspectives and contextual goals (Van Fleet & Yukl, 1986; Yukl, 2009). Despite these differences, a common thread runs across many definitions: leadership is fundamentally a process of influence to direct collective activity toward shared objectives. Organizations are social platforms where human creativity and collective action come together, acting as more than just economic systems in today's socially complex and more interconnected world (Daft & Armstrong, 2021). Because of this, leadership is increasingly commonly viewed as a dynamic, reciprocal process of social impact rather than only a directive position (Ruben & Gigliotti, 2016; Uhl-Bien, 2006). This viewpoint is relevant in settings where social creativity and innovation are crucial to solving intricate societal issues and producing long-term value (Daft & Armstrong, 2021; West & Farr, 1990).

The ability of both individuals and groups to come up with original and significant ideas that address societal problems is known as social creativity. In this field, leadership encourages inclusive discourse, facilitates cross-border cooperation, and stimulates creative potential among varied actors (Khan et al., 2018). Similarly, social innovation, which is the generation and use of innovative solutions that enhance the welfare of people and communities, needs leaders who can advance beyond established hierarchies and unite diverse stakeholders around a common goal (Mulgan, 2019). For this research, leadership is therefore defined as a socially rooted process that enables individuals to persuade others to co-create, test, and apply creative solutions for the good of all (Daft & Armstrong, 2021; Mendenhall, 2017). In line with the changing needs of a society where innovation is not limited to the business but rather permeates the wider societal domain, this definition places leadership at the nexus of influence, creativity, and purpose. In light of this, the chapter delves into four contemporary leadership styles: transactional, transformational, empowering, and entrepreneurial leadership, and how each fosters SC and SI in a volatile and fast-changing global economy.

Transactional leadership is built on relationships between leaders and their subordinates, emphasizing structure, performance standards, and reward-based responsibility. Despite being perceived as more managerial than visionary, transactional leadership is highly beneficial when SI necessitates consistency, discipline, and coordination. Transactional leaders assist in transforming innovative concepts into workable plans in socially conscious contexts, like government agencies, nonprofit organizations, or social businesses, by defining precise objectives, deadlines, and accountability systems (J. A. Hansen & Pihl-Thingvad, 2019). While transactional leadership may not be the primary source of creative enthusiasm, it fosters innovation by establishing circumstances for stability and dependability, particularly in contexts with limited resources or high levels of regulatory supervision. When combined with participative and inclusive approaches, it can promote incremental innovation and provide a stable foundation for more visionary types of leadership to thrive. Transactional leadership is a practical facilitator, ensuring that innovative social ideas are effectively implemented and sustained (Ma & Jiang, 2018).

In contrast, transformational leadership is critical in leading SC and nurturing breakthrough innovation. Transformational leaders inspire people with a compelling vision, emotional devotion, and ethical behavior. They encourage innovative mindsets, challenge assumptions, and enhance an inclusive environment in which various perspectives and unusual ideas are welcome (Begum et al., 2022). This leadership style is especially effective in addressing complex social challenges because it inspires individuals and teams to look beyond their interests and commit to communal well-being. Transformational leaders promote an innovative culture, inspire trust, and help people see the larger purpose of their job. They catalyze significant systemic change by combining creative energy with socially desirable goals, transforming bold ideas into robust, long-term solutions (Suriyankietkaew et al., 2022).

Transactional and transformational leadership approaches work well simultaneously to promote social innovation. The creative energy and ethical values required to initiate and drive significant change come from transformational leadership, while transactional leadership ensures operational consistency and efficient execution. In dynamic social settings, both are necessary: one provides discipline and structure, while the other offers inspiration and vision. These elements create an effective balance that fosters and sustains social creativity and innovation.

Empowering leadership helps drive innovation by promoting autonomy, shared ownership, and participation in decision-making. Unlike transactional leadership, which focuses on control, or transformational leadership, which emphasizes vision, empowering leadership builds trust and confidence in people. Empowering leaders give authority to others, involve them in decisions, and create safe spaces where different ideas and creativity are welcome (Faulks et al., 2021). This style works exceptionally well in inclusive innovation environments, where people are motivated to take initiative, try new things, and work together to solve problems that benefit society. In this way, empowering leadership supports grassroots innovation and teamwork, helping organizations grow and improve from within (Jung et al., 2020).

Finally, pursuing social change is aided by entrepreneurial leadership's proactive, opportunity-driven approach. In contrast to empowering leadership, which emphasizes autonomy, and transformational leadership, which emphasizes moral vision, entrepreneurial leadership focuses on seeing and seizing opportunities, especially in environments with limited resources or uncertainty (Renko et al., 2015). Innovative solutions and systemic change require leaders willing to take risks, challenge established standards, and creatively deploy resources (Amit & Zott, 2020). Entrepreneurial leaders are visionaries and implementers who turn concepts into workable, scalable solutions with tangible social effects in start-ups, social enterprises, and grassroots movements (Purwati et al., 2021).

Addressing global problems such as climate change, systemic poverty, global health crises, and forced migration requires leadership approaches that generate innovative ideas and ensure effective implementation. Focusing on social creativity and innovation provides a unifying framework for tackling these challenges because it integrates problem-solving with a commitment to social impact, inclusivity, and sustainability. Global problems are inherently complex, cross-sectoral, and deeply embedded in socio-political contexts, which means that no single leadership style can meet the diverse demands of problem-solving at this scale. Instead, a portfolio of leadership approaches, transactional, transformational, empowering, and entrepreneurial, offers a complementary set of capabilities for initiating, developing, and sustaining solutions that are both creative and socially relevant.

Transformational leadership addresses global problems by presenting a clear vision, building moral commitment, and bringing together diverse stakeholders around shared values (Suriyankietkaew et al., 2022). It effectively drives systemic change, forms coalitions, and keeps long-term issues, such as climate action and reducing global inequalities, at the center of attention. Transactional leadership, often seen as more managerial, ensures that visionary ideas are implemented through strong operational discipline, accountability, and performance standards (Hansen et al., 2019). This is especially useful in regulated or resource-limited contexts, such as humanitarian relief work, where precision, coordination, and compliance are essential. Empowering leadership adds to these approaches by encouraging autonomy, shared responsibility, and collaborative problem-solving, which are vital for inclusive innovations that depend on local knowledge and grassroots participation (Faulks et al., 2021). Finally, entrepreneurial leadership brings a proactive, opportunity-focused mindset that helps leaders deal with uncertainty, find new solutions, and use limited resources creatively, an approach well-suited to emerging crises or rapidly changing situations (Amit & Zott, 2020; Persson-Fischer & Liu, 2021).

The uniqueness of each global problem demands a flexible and context-sensitive application of leadership styles, where effectiveness lies in shifting emphasis according to situational demands rather than adhering to a single model (Kaul et al., 2020). Climate change mitigation, for instance, requires transformational leadership to inspire collective behavioral change, co-creative and transactional leadership to coordinate international agreements and enforce compliance, and entrepreneurial leadership to accelerate the adoption of new technologies and sustainable practices (Hofstad et al., 2022). In contrast, global health crises such as pandemics benefit from transactional leadership for rapid logistical mobilization, empowering leadership to engage communities in preventive measures, and transformational leadership to sustain trust and solidarity across borders (Balasubramanian & Fernandes, 2022). Social justice movements to reduce systemic inequalities rely more heavily on empowering and transformational leadership to elevate marginalized voices and reshape institutional norms. In contrast, entrepreneurial leadership identifies innovative platforms and models for economic inclusion (Udin, 2024). This adaptability reflects an "ambidextrous leadership" approach, blending exploration-oriented transformational behaviors with exploitation-oriented transactional practices to meet each challenge's scale, urgency, and socio-cultural complexity (Mascareño et al., 2021).

In sum, a leadership focus on social creativity and innovation addresses global problems by combining vision with operational discipline, empowering communities while seizing opportunities, and adapting to the unique demands of each challenge. By integrating transformational, transactional, empowering, and entrepreneurial leadership strengths, leaders can foster inclusive, resilient, and innovative responses that are effective in the short term and sustainable over time. This multifaceted leadership approach ensures that solutions are globally informed, drawing on broad networks, resources, and expertise, and locally grounded, reflecting the cultural, political, and economic realities of the contexts in which they are implemented. In doing so, leadership bridges global problem awareness and the practical realization of transformative, socially impactful solutions.

ROLE AND IMPORTANCE OF LEADERSHIP IN DRIVING TRANSFORMATIONAL INNOVATION TO ADDRESS SOCIETAL ISSUES

Transformational innovation means moving away from familiar ways of doing things and exploring new, often unknown areas (Denning, 2005). Unlike incremental innovation, which improves existing systems by making them faster, cheaper, or more efficient, transformational innovation brings entirely new products, services, or processes that change how value is created and can disrupt existing markets. Because it challenges the current way of doing things and affects long-standing interests, it often requires significant organizational changes, something many companies are naturally hesitant to accept (Kotter et al., 2025).

The transformative aspect of transformational innovation is evident in its external market ramifications and the internal upheaval it generates within organizations. Jones Christensen et al. (2014) stated that driving such innovation requires leaders to fundamentally convince managers and employees to rethink their roles, habits, and assumptions. This may involve changing long-held strategies, challenging established processes, and reshaping organizational culture, customer relationships, and brand identities. Importantly, such a change must not occur gradually or reluctantly, but with urgency and enthusiastic dedication, a requirement that heightens the leadership challenge.

There is increasing agreement that little steps are no longer enough at a time of complicated and interconnected problems, from political unrest and institutional fragility to social inequality, climate change, and global health emergencies. Because these issues are dynamic and systemic, traditional government, healthcare, education, and economic development systems frequently find it challenging to address them. A crucial reaction mechanism in this situation is transformative innovation. It symbolizes significant shifts in principles, procedures, frameworks, and results that seek to enhance systems and rethink and rebuild them (Schot & Steinmueller, 2018).

Schot & Steinmueller (2018) discussed that transformational innovation challenges the status quo and seeks daring alternatives that address the underlying causes of societal dysfunction, in contrast to incremental innovation, which concentrates on efficiency or optimization within preexisting frameworks. Transformational approaches include, for instance, moving away from traditional aid models and toward community-led development, reconsidering urban planning to give justice and sustainability priority, or switching from fossil fuel-based energy systems to decentralized renewable solutions. The UN's Sustainable Development Goals (SDGs), which call for systemic changes rather than discrete initiatives, can only be achieved with these technologies (Assembly, 2015).

However, achieving transformational innovation is not a simple process. It entails negotiating social conflicts, political risk, resource limitations, and institutional resistance. At this point, leadership becomes essential. Leadership is a key factor in starting, establishing, and maintaining transformative change, broadly defined as persuading and inspiring people toward a common goal (Deng et al., 2023). Effective leadership facilitates systemic change rather than merely managing it in this situation. It creates an atmosphere that allows for the emergence of fresh concepts, stakeholder collaboration, and cross-border learning. According to Westley et al. (2013), leaders construct "innovation niches," safe havens where experimentation and adaptation can occur without the pressure to fit in with preexisting norms.

Furthermore, presenting societal issues in novel ways requires strong leadership. Narrow perspectives frequently result in fragmented or temporary solutions to poverty, environmental degradation, or violence. Visionary leaders can reframe these problems as interrelated, systemic issues that require collaborative, cross-sectoral solutions (Van Tulder & Van Mil, 2022). For example, tackling young unemployment is a challenge in governance, education, and innovation, in addition to being an economic one. Crucially, leadership quality is inextricably linked to the impact of transformational innovation. Leaders must be inclusive, morally upright, resilient, flexible, and have a clear vision (Newstead et al., 2020).

Furthermore, another common component of transformational innovation is changing power dynamics, such as empowering underrepresented groups, decentralizing decision-making, or upending elite control over resources. Those with vested interests may oppose such changes. Thus, Leadership is instrumental in managing the politics of change and entrepreneurship. Leaders must reconcile ambition, diplomacy, disruption, and inclusiveness to steer sustainable and impactful innovations (Dreier et al., 2019).

Transformational innovation offers an essential opportunity to address today's complex societal issues, ranging from inequality to environmental degradation. However, this type of innovation does not happen by luck; it takes deliberate and imaginative leadership. Leadership serves as a link between ideas and action, assisting in aligning short-term pressures with long-term objectives. Leaders inspire change and lay the groundwork for innovation to develop, take root, and thrive by encouraging inclusive involvement, handling uncertainty, and remaining focused on common goals. To realize the full potential of transformational innovation, we must invest as much in leadership development as we do in the innovation itself. This means cultivating leaders who are adaptive, empathetic, and capable of mobilizing diverse stakeholders. Such leadership ensures that innovation efforts are technically successful, socially meaningful, and sustainable. Through strong, value-driven leadership, innovation can be scaled to produce systemic impact and create a more equitable and resilient future.

SIGNIFICANCE AND IMPACT OF LEADERSHIP, SOCIAL CREATIVITY, AND TRANSFORMATIONAL INNOVATION TO ADDRESS SOCIETAL ISSUES

As the complexity of societal challenges increases, from global inequality and climate change to public health emergencies and political instability, leadership becomes a critical factor in driving deliberate and coordinated action (Head, 2022). Effective leadership turns ideas into action by bringing people together, using different resources, and encouraging teamwork across various sectors. Liu et al. (2022) assert that it is essential for addressing key issues, serving as a compass that aligns institutional efforts with societal needs. With inclusive, ethical, and adaptive leadership, communities and organizations are better equipped to handle unpredictability and build long-term resilience.

SC is complementary and revolutionary in this process since it allows individuals and societies to rethink current circumstances and develop innovative solutions to complex problems (Paulus & Nijstad, 2019). In contrast to conventional approaches to problem-solving, social creativity entails questioning prevailing beliefs, involving underrepresented viewpoints, and collaboratively developing socially and contextually appropriate solutions. By utilizing local expertise, interdisciplinary views, and cultural understanding, it goes beyond technical solutions to encourage holistic thinking. According to a study by Khedhaouria et al. (2017), SC, when backed by visionary leadership, creates trusting, experimental, and transparent environments, all essential for creating long-lasting solutions that tackle the underlying causes of societal problems.

Building on SC and leadership, transformational innovation reshapes markets, institutions, and practices through disruptive, systems-level change (Dreier et al., 2019). This form of innovation goes beyond incremental improvements by fundamentally altering the structure and functioning of societal endeavors. It challenges governments and organizations to question the status quo, reform outdated systems, and embrace new perspectives that drive social progress. Transformational innovation requires leaders who effectively communicate change narratives, build strategic alliances, manage conflict, and align innovative efforts with ethical and inclusive outcomes. Without such leadership, transformational initiatives risk being co-opted, fragmented, or rendered ineffective (Buonocore et al., 2024).

The synergy between leadership, social creativity, and transformational innovation is a powerful catalyst for systemic change. Together, they empower individuals, transform institutions, and foster cultures of continuous learning and adaptation, shifting the transition from short-lived solutions to approaches that ensure long-term sustainability. Through proactive engagement, in which communities are not merely recipients of change but active participants in its design and implementation, this triad enables societies to move from reactive responses to proactive strategies. Given today's interconnected and complex challenges and the growing demand for dynamic, inclusive, and forward-thinking solutions, such an integrated approach is more critical than ever.

In conclusion, integrating strong, responsible leadership, creative social innovation, and bold transformational innovation offers a strategic pathway for addressing today's most pressing societal challenges. When intentionally cultivated and aligned, these elements can reshape how problems are perceived and addressed, paving the way for more equitable, inclusive, and sustainable futures. Societal progress depends not only on what we innovate, but also on how and why we lead, and on whom we empower to shape that innovation.

DATA TRUST AND THE SUSTAINABILITY OF SOCIAL CREATIVITY AND INNOVATION

Social creativity and innovation are inherently collective processes that depend on active participation, open dialogue, and knowledge sharing among diverse stakeholders. These interactions often involve sensitive information, personal experiences, and community-specific data, making trust a critical prerequisite for engagement (Bryson, 2018). Leadership plays a decisive role in cultivating this trust by setting explicit norms for data governance, ensuring transparency in information use, and modeling respect for all contributions (Van Ooijen et al., 2019). Leaders who embed ethical considerations into collaborative structures create the conditions for stakeholders to share diverse perspectives and engage in the creative risk-taking essential to social CI. Without this foundation of trust, the generative potential of social creativity and innovation is significantly diminished (Pasricha et al., 2018).

The ethical handling of data is a moral obligation and a strategic lever that directly supports the chapter's fourth research imperative: identifying effective organizational strategies leaders can use to cultivate, sustain, and scale social CI. Through clear policies, participatory decision-making, and consistent enforcement, leaders who institutionalize robust data ethics strengthen long-term stakeholder confidence and engagement (Zheng et al., 2022). This ongoing trust sustains social innovation initiatives beyond their inception, enabling them to adapt to evolving challenges while retaining legitimacy. Ethical leaders thus bridge the gap between the immediate creative energy of co-creation and the enduring resilience required for scaling innovative solutions across contexts.

By positioning data ethics as an integral component of leadership strategy, this chapter highlights a critical yet underexplored dimension of advancing social creativity and innovation. Ethical leaders safeguard the integrity of collaborative processes, protect the intellectual and social capital that stakeholders contribute, and reinforce the credibility of innovation outcomes (Ciulla, 2020). As organizations increasingly address complex societal challenges, the ability of leaders to integrate ethical data stewardship into their leadership practice becomes a determining factor in the continuity and sustainability of social CI (Fry & Egel, 2021). In this way, data ethics is not peripheral to the leadership agenda but central to fulfilling the chapter's overarching aim: to understand and strengthen the role of leadership in shaping socially meaningful, innovative change.

SOLUTIONS AND RECOMMENDATIONS

To effectively address today's complex socioeconomic challenges, it is essential to deliberately focus on developing inclusive and flexible leadership. Effective leaders must possess systems thinking and emotional intelligence and be able to navigate diverse professional and cultural contexts. Leadership skills emphasizing partnership, empathy, and strategic vision are crucial for guiding collective efforts toward sustainable solutions. Furthermore, leadership development must intentionally promote the empowerment and inclusion of marginalized groups to ensure credibility and fairness in decision-making. By investing in these leadership pathways, societies can foster their ability to adapt and build resilience in complex social issues.

It is essential to institutionalize social creativity alongside strong leadership to generate creative and contextually relevant solutions. Societal challenges often stem from deep-rooted cultural, economic, and political systems, requiring innovative responses grounded in meaningful engagement and co-creation with affected communities. Creating spaces for participation within organizations, civil society, and government allows diverse perspectives to be shared and dominant assumptions to be challenged. Educational reforms emphasizing experimentation, critical thinking, and interdisciplinary collaboration also cultivate the creative capacities needed for social innovation. In this way, social creativity enables communities to reframe problems and co-develop practical, sustainable, and socially just solutions.

Establishing and scaling transformational innovation ecosystems that facilitate disruptive, systems-level change is essential to go beyond incremental change. Cross-sector cooperation between public organizations, academic institutions, business enterprises, and civil society is necessary for these ecosystems to promote an atmosphere that encourages experimentation and taking risks. Policy frameworks must change to encourage social entrepreneurs and innovators who question the status quo and offer regulatory freedom. Evaluation standards should simultaneously move from immediate efficiency to long-term social benefit, ensuring that innovation initiatives align with general societal objectives. Supporting transformational innovation can radically alter social, economic, and environmental structures, resulting in more resilient and just futures.

Finally, incorporating leadership, social creativity, and transformational innovation into organizational and policy strategies is essential for addressing societal problems sustainably. When these elements are integrated into development agendas and governance frameworks, they become foundational to how societies operate and evolve, rather than being treated as separate or secondary efforts. This integration enables flexible, forward-looking systems that can adapt to emerging challenges. It also promotes a culture of continuous learning, inclusive participation, and ethical accountability across all levels of society. By embedding innovative approaches, creative problem-solving, and leadership development within strategic frameworks, societies can effectively catalyze systemic change and tackle the root causes of pressing social issues.

FUTURE RESEARCH DIRECTIONS

There is considerable scope for further investigation to expand and deepen understanding through empirical investigation, particularly given that the current study is based on a descriptive literature review complemented by a systematic overview of related research. While previous studies offer valuable conceptual insights into the relationship between leadership and SI, a lack of robust, context-specific evidence remains regarding how different leadership styles function across various cultural contexts. Future studies should prioritize qualitative and mixed-method approaches, such as ethnographies, participatory action research, and case studies, to build a broader perspective of how leaders enhance creativity and innovation at the grassroots level.

Future research must actively investigate which leadership behaviors and skills most effectively encourage creativity and innovation for social impact. How, for instance, do leaders balance stability and experimentation, or control and autonomy, to improve community problem-solving? Examining these relationships can help reveal the specific ways in which leadership unlocks creativity. Future research should also discuss how leaders foster community ownership, psychological safety, and inclusion, which are critical prerequisites for promoting innovative contributions from all facets of society, particularly underrepresented or marginalized groups.

Furthermore, longitudinal research could offer valuable insights into how social creativity and leadership develop in time, particularly in response to crises such as pandemics, climate change, or political instability. These disruptive events may present unique opportunities for leaders to reframe challenges, renew collective purpose, and drive transformative change. Exploring the temporal dimension of leadership, particularly how vision, values, and creative strategies evolve as societies navigate different stages of change, can lead to a more dynamic and nuanced view of leadership's role in advancing social innovation.

Finally, multidisciplinary approaches that incorporate knowledge from leadership studies, community development, psychology, innovation management, and social entrepreneurship might benefit future research. Cross-cutting viewpoints help build a comprehensive framework for understanding how leadership can best promote inclusive, innovative, and meaningful change in communities.

CONCLUSION

By expanding our knowledge of leadership's significant impact on advancing SC and driving transformative innovation within organizational contexts, this chapter significantly advances our understanding at the management, social, and theoretical levels. In terms of management, the chapter highlights the value of developing leadership philosophies that encourage innovative processes and creative capacities, such as transformational, empowering, and entrepreneurial leadership. These leadership philosophies offer valuable guidance for managers who foster inclusive workplaces where various views are respected and social innovation may thrive. The chapter provides practical insights for leaders seeking to overcome challenging organizational and societal environments by highlighting particular leadership roles and behaviors that support transforming innovative ideas into significant social initiatives.

From a social perspective, the chapter highlights the significance of leadership in uniting individuals to address pressing societal issues. It emphasizes how leaders can encourage engagement, trust, and a shared goal among stakeholders, enabling groups and communities to develop creative solutions collaboratively. This emphasis aligns with the increasing calls for moral, inclusive, and social value-creating leadership. The chapter advances a better understanding of how flexible, contextually grounded innovation emerges and scales to address several social demands by clarifying the link between leadership and SI.

This chapter advances theoretical understanding in leadership and innovation studies by integrating the concepts of SC and transformational innovation into a coherent framework. It clarifies leadership's diverse roles across various phases of innovation, from fostering intellectual curiosity and articulating vision to enabling risk-taking and managing transformative change. The chapter also identifies key areas for future research, notably how leadership can more effectively support transformational innovation to address complex, systemic social challenges. This theoretical advancement deepens our understanding of leadership as a dynamic process that actively shapes and is simultaneously shaped by organizational and societal innovation contexts.

To achieve the objectives of this chapter, the study first examined how leadership supports the development of social creativity within organizations, highlighting cooperation, empowerment, and trust as key enablers. Second, it explored the leadership roles essential for initiating and implementing social innovation, particularly competence in sharing information, inspiring ideas, and managing different stakeholders' engagement. Third, it emphasized the necessity for additional empirical studies on the influence of leadership in driving transformational innovation that addresses complex societal challenges. Finally, the chapter underscored the critical importance of organizational strategies that intentionally foster and enhance social creativity and innovation.

This chapter's key insight is that leadership, social creativity, and transformative innovation are inextricably linked and mutually reinforcing concepts. Leadership is more than a catalyst for innovation; it is also a key architect of the social environments where creative ideas can be nurtured and scaled to drive systemic change. This finding encourages scholars and practitioners to adopt more integrated approaches integrating leadership development, creative support, and managing innovation to address today's complex social concerns effectively.

REFERENCES

Acar, O., Tarakci, M., & van Knippenberg, D. (2019). Why Constraints Are Good for Innovation. *Harvard Business Review*.

Acar, O. A., Tarakci, M., & van Knippenberg, D. (2019). Creativity and Innovation Under Constraints: A Cross-Disciplinary Integrative Review. *Journal of Management*, *45*(1), 96–121. DOI: 10.1177/0149206318805832

Acar, O. A., Tarakci, M., & Van Knippenberg, D. (2019). Creativity and innovation under constraints: A cross-disciplinary integrative review. *Journal of Management*, *45*(1), 96–121. DOI: 10.1177/0149206318805832

Agostini, M. R., Vieira, L. M., Tondolo, R., & Tondolo, V. (2017). An overview of social innovation research: Guiding future studies. *BBR. Brazilian Business Review*, *14*(4), 385–402. DOI: 10.15728/bbr.2017.14.4.2

Ahlin, B., Drnovšek, M., & Hisrich, R. D. (2014). Entrepreneurs' creativity and firm innovation: The moderating role of entrepreneurial self-efficacy. *Small Business Economics*, *43*(1), 101–117. DOI: 10.1007/s11187-013-9531-7

Amabile, T. M. (1988). A model of creativity and innovation in organizations. *Research in Organizational Behavior*, *10*(1), 123–167.

Amabile, T. M. (1996). Creativity and Innovation in Organizations. Harvard Business School Industry and Background Note 396-239.

Amabile, T. M., Conti, R., Coon, H., Lazenby, J., & Herron, M. (1996). Assessing the work environment for creativity. *Academy of Management Journal*, *39*(5), 1154–1184. DOI: 10.2307/256995

Amabile, T. M., & Pratt, M. G. (2016). The dynamic componential model of creativity and innovation in organizations: Making progress, making meaning. *Research in Organizational Behavior*, *36*, 157–183. DOI: 10.1016/j.riob.2016.10.001

Amit, R., & Zott, C. (2020). *Business model innovation strategy: Transformational concepts and tools for entrepreneurial leaders*. John Wiley & Sons.

Anderson, B. B., & Dees, J. G. (2006). Rhetoric, reality, and research: Building a solid foundation for the practice of social entrepreneurship. *Social Entrepreneurship: New Models of Sustainable Social Change*, 144–168.

Anderson, N., Potočnik, K., & Zhou, J. (2014). Innovation and creativity in organizations: A state-of-the-science review, prospective commentary, and guiding framework. *Journal of Management*, *40*(5), 1297–1333. DOI: 10.1177/0149206314527128

Asbari, M. (2021). From leadership to innovation: managing employee creativity. *Available at SSRN* 4708682.

Asbari, M., Prasetya, A. B., Santoso, P. B., & Purwanto, A. (2021). From Creativity to Innovation: The Role of Female Employees' Psychological Capital. *International Journal of Social and Management Studies, 02*(02), 66–77. https://ijosmas.org/index.php/ijosmas/article/view/18

Assembly, U. N. G. (2015). *Transforming our world: the 2030 agenda for sustainable development, 21 October 2015.* A/RES/70/1.

Audretsch, D. B., Eichler, G. M., & Schwarz, E. J. (2022). Emerging needs of social innovators and social innovation ecosystems. *The International Entrepreneurship and Management Journal, 18*(1), 1–38. DOI: 10.1007/s11365-021-00789-9

Avelino, F., Wittmayer, J. M., Pel, B., Weaver, P., Dumitru, A., Haxeltine, A., Kemp, R., Jørgensen, M. S., Bauler, T., Ruijsink, S., & O'Riordan, T. (2019). Transformative social innovation and (dis) empowerment. *Technological Forecasting and Social Change, 145*, 195–206. DOI: 10.1016/j.techfore.2017.05.002

Balasubramanian, S., & Fernandes, C. (2022). Confirmation of a crisis leadership model and its effectiveness: Lessons from the COVID-19 pandemic. *Cogent Business & Management, 9*(1), 2022824. DOI: 10.1080/23311975.2021.2022824

Banmairuroy, W., Kritjaroen, T., & Homsombat, W. (2022). The effect of knowledge-oriented leadership and human resource development on sustainable competitive advantage through organizational innovation's component factors: Evidence from Thailand's new S-curve industries. *Asia Pacific Management Review, 27*(3), 200–209. DOI: 10.1016/j.apmrv.2021.09.001

Bass, B. M., & Stogdill, R. M. (1990). *Bass & Stogdill's handbook of leadership: Theory, research, and managerial applications.* Simon and Schuster.

Begum, S., Ashfaq, M., Xia, E., & Awan, U. (2022). Does green transformational leadership lead to green innovation? The role of green thinking and creative process engagement. *Business Strategy and the Environment, 31*(1), 580–597. DOI: 10.1002/bse.2911

Blanco, I., & León, M. (2017). Social innovation, reciprocity and contentious politics: Facing the socio-urban crisis in Ciutat Meridiana, Barcelona. *Urban Studies (Edinburgh, Scotland), 54*(9), 2172–2188. DOI: 10.1177/0042098016659044

Bryson, J. J. (2018). Patiency is not a virtue: The design of intelligent systems and systems of ethics. *Ethics and Information Technology, 20*(1), 15–26. DOI: 10.1007/s10676-018-9448-6

Buonocore, F., Annosi, M. C., de Gennaro, D., & Riemma, F. (2024). Digital transformation and social change: Leadership strategies for responsible innovation. *Journal of Engineering and Technology Management, 74*, 101843. DOI: 10.1016/j.jengtecman.2024.101843

Campos, C. R., Nakano, T. D. C., & Ribeiro, W. D. J. (2014). Criatividade e Inovação : uma revisão da produção científica no Brasil. *Revista Faculdades Do Saber,* 168–179.

Carberry, E. J., Bharati, P., Levy, D. L., & Chaudhury, A. (2019). Social movements as catalysts for corporate social innovation: Environmental activism and the adoption of green information systems. *Business & Society, 58*(5), 1083–1127. DOI: 10.1177/0007650317701674

Castro-Arce, K., & Vanclay, F. (2020). Transformative social innovation for sustainable rural development: An analytical framework to assist community-based initiatives. *Journal of Rural Studies, 74*, 45–54. DOI: 10.1016/j.jrurstud.2019.11.010

Caulier-Grice, J. (2012). Defining social innovation. *A Deliverable of the Project: The Theoretical, Empirical and Policy Foundations for Building Social Innovation in Europe (TEPSIE), European Commission 7th Framework Programme/European Commission, DG Research, 18.*

Černe, M., Jaklič, M., & Škerlavaj, M. (2013). Authentic leadership, creativity, and innovation: A multilevel perspective. *Leadership, 9*(1), 63–85. DOI: 10.1177/1742715012455130

Ciasullo, M. V., Troisi, O., Grimaldi, M., & Leone, D. (2020). Multi-level governance for sustainable innovation in smart communities: An ecosystems approach. *The International Entrepreneurship and Management Journal, 16*(4), 1167–1195. DOI: 10.1007/s11365-020-00641-6

Ciulla, J. B. (2020). Ethics and effectiveness: The nature of good leadership. In *The search for ethics in leadership, business, and beyond* (pp. 3–32). Springer. DOI: 10.1007/978-3-030-38463-0_1

Clydesdale, G. (2006). Creativity and competition: The beatles. *Creativity Research Journal, 18*(2), 129–139. DOI: 10.1207/s15326934crj1802_1

Çokpekin, Ö., & Knudsen, M. P. (2012). Does Organizing for Creativity Really Lead to Innovation? *Creativity and Innovation Management, 21*(3), 304–314. DOI: 10.1111/j.1467-8691.2012.00649.x

Cropley, A. (2006). Creativity: A social approach. *Roeper Review, 28*(3), 125–130. DOI: 10.1080/02783190609554351

Csikszentmihalyi, M. (2014). The systems model of creativity and its applications. *The Wiley Handbook of Genius*, 533–545. DOI: 10.1002/9781118367377.ch25

Csikszentmihalyi, M., & Csikszentmihalyi, M. (2014). Creativity and genius: A systems perspective. *The Systems Model of Creativity: The Collected Works of Mihaly Csikszentmihalyi*, 99–125.

Daft, R. L., & Armstrong, A. (2021). *Organization theory and design*. Cengage Canada.

Deng, C., Gulseren, D., Isola, C., Grocutt, K., & Turner, N. (2023). Transformational leadership effectiveness: An evidence-based primer. *Human Resource Development International, 26*(5), 627–641. DOI: 10.1080/13678868.2022.2135938

Denning, S. (2005). Transformational innovation: A journey by narrative. *Strategy and Leadership, 33*(3), 11–16. DOI: 10.1108/10878570510700119

Dolejšová, M., Ampatzidou, C., Houston, L., Light, A., Botero, A., Choi, J., Wilde, D., Altarriba Altarriba Bertran, F., Davis, H., & Gonzales Gonzales Gil, F. (2021). Designing for transformative futures: creative practice, social change and climate emergency. *Proceedings of the 13th Conference on Creativity and Cognition*, 1–9.

Dreier, L., Nabarro, D., & Nelson, J. (2019). *Systems leadership for sustainable development: strategies for achieving systemic change*. Harvard Kennedy School.

Eichler, G. M., & Schwarz, E. J. (2019). What sustainable development goals do social innovations address? A systematic review and content analysis of social innovation literature. *Sustainability (Basel), 11*(2), 522. DOI: 10.3390/su11020522

Farida, I., & Setiawan, D. (2022). Business strategies and competitive advantage: The role of performance and innovation. *Journal of Open Innovation, 8*(3), 163. DOI: 10.3390/joitmc8030163

Farinha, L., Sebastião, J. R., Sampaio, C., & Lopes, J. (2020). Social innovation and social entrepreneurship: Discovering origins, exploring current and future trends. *International Review on Public and Nonprofit Marketing, 17*(1), 77–96. DOI: 10.1007/s12208-020-00243-6

Farr, J. L., & Ford, C. M. (1990). *Individual innovation*. Academic Press.

Faulks, B., Song, Y., Waiganjo, M., Obrenovic, B., & Godinic, D. (2021). Impact of empowering leadership, innovative work, and organizational learning readiness on sustainable economic performance: An empirical study of companies in Russia during the COVID-19 pandemic. *Sustainability (Basel), 13*(22), 12465. DOI: 10.3390/su132212465

Fields, Z. (2016). Using creativity and social innovation to create social value and change. In *Incorporating business models and strategies into social entrepreneurship* (pp. 97–112). IGI Global Scientific Publishing. DOI: 10.4018/978-1-4666-8748-6.ch006

Fischer, G. (2004). Social creativity: turning barriers into opportunities for collaborative design. *Proceedings of the Eighth Conference on Participatory Design: Artful Integration: Interweaving Media, Materials and Practices-Volume 1*, 152–161. DOI: 10.1145/1011870.1011889

Fischer, G. (2013). Learning, social creativity, and cultures of participation. In *Learning and Collective Creativity* (pp. 198–215). Routledge.

Fischer, G., Giaccardi, E., Eden, H., Sugimoto, M., & Ye, Y. (2005). Beyond binary choices: Integrating individual and social creativity. *International Journal of Human-Computer Studies*, *63*(4–5), 482–512. DOI: 10.1016/j.ijhcs.2005.04.014

Fischer, T., Dietz, J., & Antonakis, J. (2017). Leadership process models: A review and synthesis. *Journal of Management*, *43*(6), 1726–1753. DOI: 10.1177/0149206316682830

Frederico, R., & Amorim, M. C. S. (2008). Criatividade, inovação e controle nas organizações. *Revista de Ciências Humanas, 42*(1-2), 75–89.

Fry, L. W., & Egel, E. (2021). Global leadership for sustainability. *Sustainability (Basel)*, *13*(11), 6360. DOI: 10.3390/su13116360

Giaccardi, E. (2004). Principles of Metadesign: Processes and Levels of Co-Creation in the New Design Space. *Leonardo Electronic Almanac, 12*(10).

Gilson, L. L. (2024). Why be creative: A review of the practical outcomes associated with creativity at the individual, group, and organizational levels. *Handbook of Organizational Creativity*, 303–322.

Glăveanu, V. P. (2020). A sociocultural theory of creativity: Bridging the social, the material, and the psychological. *Review of General Psychology*, *24*(4), 335–354. DOI: 10.1177/1089268020961763

Grojean, M. W., Resick, C. J., Dickson, M. W., & Smith, D. B. (2004). Leaders, values, and organizational climate: Examining leadership strategies for establishing an organizational climate regarding ethics. *Journal of Business Ethics*, *55*(3), 223–241. DOI: 10.1007/s10551-004-1275-5

Hansen, J., Hellin, J., Rosenstock, T., Fisher, E., Cairns, J., Stirling, C., Lamanna, C., van Etten, J., Rose, A., & Campbell, B. (2019). Climate risk management and rural poverty reduction. *Agricultural Systems, 172*, 28–46. DOI: 10.1016/j.agsy.2018.01.019

Hansen, J. A., & Pihl-Thingvad, S. (2019). Managing employee innovative behaviour through transformational and transactional leadership styles. *Public Management Review*, *21*(6), 918–944. DOI: 10.1080/14719037.2018.1544272

Head, B. W. (2022). *Wicked problems in public policy: Understanding and responding to complex challenges*. Springer Nature. DOI: 10.1007/978-3-030-94580-0

Heeks, R., Foster, C., & Nugroho, Y. (2014). New models of inclusive innovation for development. *Innovation and Development*, *4*(2), 175–185. DOI: 10.1080/2157930X.2014.928982

Herrera, M. E. B. (2016). Social innovation for bridging societal divides: Process or leader? A qualitative comparative analysis. *Journal of Business Research*, *69*(11), 5241–5247. DOI: 10.1016/j.jbusres.2016.04.119

Heye, D. (2006). Creativity and innovation: Two key characteristics of the successful 21st century information professional. *Business Information Review*, *23*(4), 252–257. DOI: 10.1177/0266382106072255

Hofstad, H., Sørensen, E., Torfing, J., & Vedeld, T. (2022). Designing and leading collaborative urban climate governance: Comparative experiences of co-creation from Copenhagen and Oslo. *Environmental Policy and Governance*, *32*(3), 203–216. DOI: 10.1002/eet.1984

Howaldt, J., Domanski, D., & Kaletka, C. (2016). Social innovation: Towards a new innovation paradigm. *RAM. Revista de Administração Mackenzie*, *17*(6), 20–44. DOI: 10.1590/1678-69712016/administracao.v17n6p20-44

Hughes, D. J., Lee, A., Tian, A. W., Newman, A., & Legood, A. (2018). Leadership, creativity, and innovation: A critical review and practical recommendations. *The Leadership Quarterly*, *29*(5), 549–569. DOI: 10.1016/j.leaqua.2018.03.001

Hwang, S. Y. (2017). Rethinking creativity: Present in expression in creative learning communities*. *Educational Philosophy and Theory*, *49*(3), 220–230. DOI: 10.1080/00131857.2016.1225559

Iqbal, Q., & Piwowar-Sulej, K. (2022). Sustainable leadership in higher education institutions: Social innovation as a mechanism. *International Journal of Sustainability in Higher Education*, *23*(8), 1–20. DOI: 10.1108/IJSHE-04-2021-0162

Javed, B., Fatima, T., Khan, A. K., & Bashir, S. (2021). Impact of Inclusive Leadership on Innovative Work Behavior: The Role of Creative Self-Efficacy. *The Journal of Creative Behavior, 55*(3), 769–782. DOI: 10.1002/jocb.487

Jefferson, M., & Anderson, M. (2017). *Transforming schools: Creativity, critical reflection, communication, collaboration*. Bloomsbury Publishing.

Jeong, I., & Shin, S. J. (2019). High-performance work practices and organizational creativity during organizational change: A collective learning perspective. *Journal of Management, 45*(3), 909–925. DOI: 10.1177/0149206316685156

Jones Christensen, L., Mackey, A., & Whetten, D. (2014). Taking responsibility for corporate social responsibility: The role of leaders in creating, implementing, sustaining, or avoiding socially responsible firm behaviors. *The Academy of Management Perspectives, 28*(2), 164–178. DOI: 10.5465/amp.2012.0047

Jung, K. B., Kang, S.-W., & Choi, S. B. (2020). Empowering leadership, risk-taking behavior, and employees' commitment to organizational change: The mediated moderating role of task complexity. *Sustainability (Basel), 12*(6), 2340. DOI: 10.3390/su12062340

Karwowski, M., Jankowska, D. M., Brzeski, A., Czerwonka, M., Gajda, A., Lebuda, I., & Beghetto, R. A. (2020). Delving into Creativity and Learning. *Creativity Research Journal, 32*(1), 4–16. DOI: 10.1080/10400419.2020.1712165

Kaul, V., Shah, V. H., & El-Serag, H. (2020). Leadership during crisis: Lessons and applications from the COVID-19 pandemic. *Gastroenterology, 159*(3), 809–812. DOI: 10.1053/j.gastro.2020.04.076 PMID: 32425233

Khan, M. K., Sandano, I. A., Pratt, C. B., & Farid, T. (2018). China's Belt and Road Initiative: A global model for an evolving approach to sustainable regional development. *Sustainability (Basel), 10*(11), 4234. DOI: 10.3390/su10114234

Khedhaouria, A., Montani, F., & Thurik, R. (2017). Time pressure and team member creativity within R&D projects: The role of learning orientation and knowledge sourcing. *International Journal of Project Management, 35*(6), 942–954. DOI: 10.1016/j.ijproman.2017.04.002

Kimmel, M., Hristova, D., & Kussmaul, K. (2018). Sources of embodied creativity: Interactivity and ideation in contact improvisation. *Behavioral Sciences (Basel, Switzerland), 8*(6), 52. DOI: 10.3390/bs8060052 PMID: 29882858

Kolasani, S. (2023). Leadership in business innovation and transformation, navigating complex digital landscapes and enterprise technology ecosystems and achieving sustainable growth in today's rapidly evolving market. *International Journal of Holistic Management Perspectives*, *4*(4), 1–23.

Kolk, A., & Lenfant, F. (2015). Cross-sector collaboration, institutional gaps, and fragility: The role of social innovation partnerships in a conflict-affected region. *Journal of Public Policy & Marketing*, *34*(2), 287–303. DOI: 10.1509/jppm.14.157

Koppl, R., Kauffman, S., Felin, T., & Longo, G. (2015). Economics for a creative world. In *Journal of Institutional Economics* (Vol. 11, Issue 1). DOI: 10.1017/S1744137414000150

Kotter, J. P., Akhtar, V., & Gupta, G. (2025). *Change: How organizations achieve hard-to-imagine results in uncertain and volatile times*. John Wiley & Sons.

Larraz-Rábanos, N. (2021). Development of creative thinking skills in the teaching-learning process. *Teacher Education-New Perspectives*, 307–322.

Lévesque, B. (2013). Social innovation in governance and public management systems: toward a new paradigm. *The International Handbook on Social Innovation*, 25–39.

Liu, B. F., Shi, D., Lim, J. R., Islam, K., Edwards, A. L., & Seeger, M. (2022). When crises hit home: How US higher education leaders navigate values during uncertain times. *Journal of Business Ethics*, *179*(2), 353–368. DOI: 10.1007/s10551-021-04820-5 PMID: 34002104

Liu, H. Y., Chang, C. C., Wang, I. T., & Chao, S. Y. (2020). The association between creativity, creative components of personality, and innovation among Taiwanese nursing students. *Thinking Skills and Creativity*, *35*(January), 100629. DOI: 10.1016/j.tsc.2020.100629

Liv, H., Xing, Z., Min, Y., & Liu, G. (2020). Everyone is Creative? Research on the Relationship Between the Work Orientation and Employee Creativity. *DEStech Transactions on Social Science, Education and Human Science,* 514–524. DOI: 10.12783/dtssehs/ssme2019/34817

Loseke, D. (2017). *Thinking about social problems: An introduction to constructionist perspectives*. Routledge. DOI: 10.4324/9781315135601

Ma, X., & Jiang, W. (2018). Transformational leadership, transactional leadership, and employee creativity in entrepreneurial firms. *The Journal of Applied Behavioral Science*, *54*(3), 302–324. DOI: 10.1177/0021886318764346

Manzini, E. (2015). *Design, when everybody designs: An introduction to design for social innovation*. MIT Press. DOI: 10.7551/mitpress/9873.001.0001

Mariani, L., Trivellato, B., Martini, M., & Marafioti, E. (2022). Achieving sustainable development goals through collaborative innovation: Evidence from four European initiatives. *Journal of Business Ethics*, *180*(4), 1075–1095. DOI: 10.1007/s10551-022-05193-z PMID: 35855697

Mascareño, J., Rietzschel, E. F., & Wisse, B. (2021). Ambidextrous leadership: Opening and closing leader behaviours to facilitate idea generation, idea promotion and idea realization. *European Journal of Work and Organizational Psychology*, *30*(4), 530–540. DOI: 10.1080/1359432X.2021.1872544

Mendenhall, M. E. (2017). Leadership and the birth of global leadership. In *Global leadership* (pp. 3–27). Routledge. DOI: 10.4324/9781315232904-1

Mongelli, L., & Rullani, F. (2017). Inequality and marginalisation: social innovation, social entrepreneurship and business model innovation: The common thread of the DRUID Summer Conference 2015. *Industry and Innovation*, *24*(5), 446–467. DOI: 10.1080/13662716.2017.1295365

Moran, S. (2010). The roles of creativity in society. *The Cambridge Handbook of Creativity*, 74–90.

Morris, M. H., Santos, S. C., & Kuratko, D. F. (2021). The great divides in social entrepreneurship and where they lead us. *Small Business Economics*, *57*(3), 1089–1106. DOI: 10.1007/s11187-020-00318-y

Mostafa, M. (2012). Factors affecting organisational creativity and innovativeness in Egyptian business organisations: An empirical investigation. *Journal of Management Development*, *24*(1), 7–33. DOI: 10.1108/02621710510572326

Mulgan, G. (2006). The process of social innovation. *Innovations: Technology, Governance, Globalization*, *1*(2), 145–162. DOI: 10.1162/itgg.2006.1.2.145

Mulgan, G. (2019). *Social innovation: How societies find the power to change*. Policy Press.

Mumford, M. D., Mulhearn, T. J., Watts, L. L., Steele, L. M., & McIntosh, T. (2017). Leader Impacts on Creative Teams. *Team Creativity and Innovation*, 131.

Mumford, M. D., Steele, L. M., Mulhearn, T. J., McIntosh, T., & Watts, L. L. (2017). Leader planning skills and creative performance: Integration of past, present, and future. In *Handbook of research on leadership and creativity*. Edward Elgar Publishing. DOI: 10.4337/9781784715465.00009

Murray, R. (2010). *The open book of social innovation*. National Endowment for Science, Technology and the Art.

Nakano, T. de C., & Wechsler, S. M. (2018). Creativity and innovation: Skills for the 21st Century. *Estudos de Psicologia (Campinas)*, *35*(3), 237–246. DOI: 10.1590/1982-02752018000300002

Nani, D. A., & Safitri, V. A. D. (2021). Exploring the relationship between formal management control systems, organisational performance and innovation: The role of leadership characteristics. *Asian Journal of Business and Accounting*, *14*(1), 207–224. DOI: 10.22452/ajba.vol14no1.8

Newstead, T., Dawkins, S., Macklin, R., & Martin, A. (2020). The virtues project: An approach to developing good leaders. *Journal of Business Ethics*, *167*(4), 605–622. DOI: 10.1007/s10551-019-04163-2

Nisula, A.-M., Blomqvist, K., Bergman, J.-P., & Yrjölä, S. (2022). Organizing for knowledge creation in a strategic interorganizational innovation project. *International Journal of Project Management*, *40*(4), 398–410. DOI: 10.1016/j.ijproman.2022.03.011

Parés, M., Ospina, S. M., & Subirats, J. (2017). *Social innovation and democratic leadership: Communities and social change from below*. Edward Elgar Publishing. DOI: 10.4337/9781785367885

Pasricha, P., Singh, B., & Verma, P. (2018). Ethical leadership, organic organizational cultures and corporate social responsibility: An empirical study in social enterprises. *Journal of Business Ethics*, *151*(4), 941–958. DOI: 10.1007/s10551-017-3568-5

Paulus, P. B., & Nijstad, B. A. (2019). *The Oxford handbook of group creativity and innovation*. Oxford Library of Psychology. DOI: 10.1093/oxfordhb/9780190648077.001.0001

Pellicer-Sifres, V., Belda-Miquel, S., López-Fogués, A., & Boni Aristizábal, A. (2017). Grassroots social innovation for human development: An analysis of alternative food networks in the city of Valencia (Spain). *Journal of Human Development and Capabilities*, *18*(2), 258–274. DOI: 10.1080/19452829.2016.1270916

Persson-Fischer, U., & Liu, S. (2021). The impact of a global crisis on areas and topics of tourism research. *Sustainability (Basel)*, *13*(2), 906. DOI: 10.3390/su13020906

Phills, J. A., Deiglmeier, K., & Miller, D. T. (2008). Rediscovering social innovation. *Stanford Social Innovation Review*, *6*(4), 34–43.

Pless, N. M., Murphy, M., Maak, T., & Sengupta, A. (2021). Societal challenges and business leadership for social innovation. *Society and Business Review*, *16*(4), 535–561. DOI: 10.1108/SBR-10-2020-0129

Politis, J. D. (2005). Dispersed leadership predictor of the work environment for creativity and productivity. *European Journal of Innovation Management*, *8*(2), 182–204. DOI: 10.1108/14601060510594693

Polk, M. (2015). Transdisciplinary co-production: Designing and testing a transdisciplinary research framework for societal problem solving. *Futures*, *65*, 110–122. DOI: 10.1016/j.futures.2014.11.001

Purwati, A., Budiyanto, B., Suhermin, S., & Hamzah, M. (2021). The effect of innovation capability on business performance: The role of social capital and entrepreneurial leadership on SMEs in Indonesia. *Accounting*, *7*(2), 323–330. DOI: 10.5267/j.ac.2020.11.021

Qureshi, I., Pan, S. L., & Zheng, Y. (2021). Digital social innovation: An overview and research framework. *Information Systems Journal*, *31*(5), 647–671. DOI: 10.1111/isj.12362

Raisch, S., & Birkinshaw, J. (2008). Organizational ambidexterity: Antecedents, outcomes, and moderators. *Journal of Management*, *34*(3), 375–409. DOI: 10.1177/0149206308316058

Reiser, D. B., & Dean, S. A. (2017). *Social enterprise law: Trust, public benefit, and capital markets*. Oxford University Press. DOI: 10.1093/oso/9780190249786.001.0001

Reiter-Palmon, R. (2018). Are the outcomes of creativity always positive? *Creativity*, *5*(2), 177–181. DOI: 10.1515/ctra-2018-0016

Renko, M., El Tarabishy, A., Carsrud, A. L., & Brännback, M. (2015). Understanding and measuring entrepreneurial leadership style. *Journal of Small Business Management*, *53*(1), 54–74. DOI: 10.1111/jsbm.12086

Rosso, B. D. (2014). Creativity and constraints: Exploring the role of constraints in the creative processes of research and development teams. *Organization Studies*, *35*(4), 551–585. DOI: 10.1177/0170840613517600

Ruben, B. D., & Gigliotti, R. A. (2016). Leadership as social influence: An expanded view of leadership communication theory and practice. *Journal of Leadership & Organizational Studies*, *23*(4), 467–479. DOI: 10.1177/1548051816641876

Runco, M. A., & Jaeger, G. J. (2012). The Standard Definition of Creativity. *Creativity Research Journal*, *24*(1), 92–96. DOI: 10.1080/10400419.2012.650092

Sarooghi, H., Libaers, D., & Burkemper, A. (2015). Examining the relationship between creativity and innovation: A meta-analysis of organizational, cultural, and environmental factors. *Journal of Business Venturing*, *30*(5), 714–731. DOI: 10.1016/j.jbusvent.2014.12.003

Sawyer, R. K. (2010). Individual and group creativity. *The Cambridge Handbook of Creativity*, 366–380.

Sawyer, R. K. (2014). *Group creativity: Music, theater, collaboration*. Psychology Press. DOI: 10.4324/9781410609090

Schot, J., & Steinmueller, W. E. (2018). Three frames for innovation policy: R&D, systems of innovation and transformative change. *Research Policy*, *47*(9), 1554–1567. DOI: 10.1016/j.respol.2018.08.011

Sen, A. (1999). *On ethics and economics*. OUP Catalogue.

Shier, M. L., & Handy, F. (2020). Leadership in nonprofits: Social innovations and blurring boundaries. *Voluntas*, *31*(2), 333–344. DOI: 10.1007/s11266-018-00078-0

Solis-Navarrete, J. A., Bucio-Mendoza, S., & Paneque-Gálvez, J. (2021). What is not social innovation. *Technological Forecasting and Social Change*, *173*, 121190. DOI: 10.1016/j.techfore.2021.121190 PMID: 36536954

Souto, J. E. (2022). Organizational creativity and sustainability-oriented innovation as drivers of sustainable development: Overcoming firms' economic, environmental and social sustainability challenges. *Journal of Manufacturing Technology Management*, *33*(4), 805–826. DOI: 10.1108/JMTM-01-2021-0018

Stein, S. M., & Harper, T. L. (2012). Creativity and innovation: Divergence and convergence in pragmatic dialogical planning. *Journal of Planning Education and Research*, *32*(1), 5–17. DOI: 10.1177/0739456X11417829

Stroh, D. P. (2015). *Systems thinking for social change: A practical guide to solving complex problems, avoiding unintended consequences, and achieving lasting results*. Chelsea Green Publishing.

Sukhera, J. (2022). Narrative reviews: Flexible, rigorous, and practical. *Journal of Graduate Medical Education*, *14*(4), 414–417. DOI: 10.4300/JGME-D-22-00480.1 PMID: 35991099

Suriyankietkaew, S., Krittayaruangroj, K., & Iamsawan, N. (2022). Sustainable Leadership practices and competencies of SMEs for sustainability and resilience: A community-based social enterprise study. *Sustainability (Basel)*, *14*(10), 5762. DOI: 10.3390/su14105762

Tabares, S. (2020). Insights from corporate social innovation: A research agenda. *Social Enterprise Journal, 16*(3), 317–338. DOI: 10.1108/SEJ-08-2019-0057

Tidd, J., & Bessant, J. R. (2014). *Strategic innovation management*. John Wiley & Sons.

Udin, U. (2024). Leadership styles and sustainable performance. *Multidisciplinary Reviews, 7*(8), 2024171. DOI: 10.31893/multirev.2024171

Uhl-Bien, M. (2006). Relational leadership theory: Exploring the social processes of leadership and organizing. *The Leadership Quarterly, 17*(6), 654–676. DOI: 10.1016/j.leaqua.2006.10.007

Valaei, N., Rezaei, S., & Ismail, W. K. W. (2017). Examining learning strategies, creativity, and innovation at SMEs using fuzzy set Qualitative Comparative Analysis and PLS path modeling. *Journal of Business Research, 70*, 224–233. DOI: 10.1016/j.jbusres.2016.08.016

van Bezouw, M. J., van Der Toorn, J., & Becker, J. C. (2021). Social creativity: Reviving a social identity approach to social stability. *European Journal of Social Psychology, 51*(2), 409–422. DOI: 10.1002/ejsp.2732

Van Fleet, D. D., & Yukl, G. A. (1986). *Military leadership: An organizational behavior perspective*. No Title.

Van Ooijen, C., Ubaldi, B., & Welby, B. (2019). *A data-driven public sector: Enabling the strategic use of data for productive, inclusive and trustworthy governance*. Academic Press.

Van Tulder, R., & Van Mil, E. (2022). *Principles of sustainable business: Frameworks for corporate action on the SDGs*. Routledge. DOI: 10.4324/9781003098355

Voorberg, W. H., Bekkers, V. J. J. M., & Tummers, L. G. (2015). A systematic review of co-creation and co-production: Embarking on the social innovation journey. *Public Management Review, 17*(9), 1333–1357. DOI: 10.1080/14719037.2014.930505

Weisberg, R. W. (2016). *Creativity: Understanding innovation in problem solving, science, invention, and the arts*. John Wiley & Sons.

West, M. A., & Farr, J. L. (1990). *Innovation at work*. John Wiley & Sons.

West, M. A., & Richter, A. W. (2024). Climates and cultures for innovation and creativity at work. In *Handbook of organizational creativity* (pp. 211–236). Psychology Press. DOI: 10.4324/9781003573326-11

Westley, F., & Antadze, N. (2010). Making a difference: Strategies for scaling social innovation for greater impact. *The Innovation Journal, 15*(2).

Westley, F. R., Tjornbo, O., Schultz, L., Olsson, P., Folke, C., Crona, B., & Bodin, Ö. (2013). A theory of transformative agency in linked social-ecological systems. *Ecology and Society, 18*(3), art27. DOI: 10.5751/ES-05072-180327

Westwood, R., & Low, D. R. (2003). The multicultural muse: Culture, creativity and innovation. *International Journal of Cross Cultural Management, 3*(2), 235–259. DOI: 10.1177/14705958030032006

Wilkinson, R. G., & Pickett, K. E. (2009). Income inequality and social dysfunction. *Annual Review of Sociology, 35*(1), 493–511. DOI: 10.1146/annurev-soc-070308-115926

Yukl, G. (2009). Leading organizational learning: Reflections on theory and research. *The Leadership Quarterly, 20*(1), 49–53. DOI: 10.1016/j.leaqua.2008.11.006

Zeng, L., Proctor, R. W., & Salvendy, G. (2011). Can traditional divergent thinking tests be trusted in measuring and predicting real-world creativity? *Creativity Research Journal, 23*(1), 24–37. DOI: 10.1080/10400419.2011.545713

Zheng, Y., Epitropaki, O., Graham, L., & Caveney, N. (2022). Ethical leadership and ethical voice: The mediating mechanisms of value internalization and integrity identity. *Journal of Management, 48*(4), 973–1002. DOI: 10.1177/01492063211002611

Zhou, J., & Hoever, I. J. (2014). Research on Workplace Creativity: A Review and Redirection. *Annual Review of Organizational Psychology and Organizational Behavior, 1*(1), 333–359. DOI: 10.1146/annurev-orgpsych-031413-091226

Ziegler, R. (2017). Social innovation as a collaborative concept. *Innovation (Abingdon), 30*(4), 388–405. DOI: 10.1080/13511610.2017.1348935

Chapter 3
Influence of Transformational Leadership in Social Creativity on OCB:
Mediating Role of Organization Culture Integrated Healthcare in Ethiopia

Hirut Assegid
https://orcid.org/0009-0003-6192-459X
Bule Hora University, Ethiopia

Wako Jio
Bule Hora University, Ethiopia

Shashi Kant
https://orcid.org/0000-0003-4722-5736
Lovely Professional University, India

Zerihun Kinde Alemu
https://orcid.org/0000-0002-8546-2882
Ethiopian Civil Service University, Ethiopia

ABSTRACT

This research examines how transformational leadership levels affect social creativity followed by their effects on OCB inside Ethiopian integrated healthcare organizations. The research uses 385 healthcare professionals' data to apply

DOI: 10.4018/979-8-3373-2742-6.ch003

Confirmatory Factor Analysis (CFA) for model validation as well as Structural Equation Modeling (SEM) through AMOS software to test variable linkages. The research demonstrates that teams under transformational leadership display better social creativity which creates conditions for innovative healthcare practices. Social creativity shows positive associations through OCB according to the study results thus indicating creative actions produce higher employee engagement as well as proactive behaviors. Organizational culture emerges as a vital connecting factor in this model since an encouraging work environment strengthens both the social creativity outcomes from transformational leadership as well as employees' extra-role behaviors. The study verifies the validity of its analysis results through the Kaiser-Meyer-Olkin (KMO) measurement which determines

INTRODUCTION

Transformational leadership proves essential to develop social creativity while boosting organizational citizenship behavior (OCB) in healthcare facilities along through other complex environments (Qalati et al., 2022). The analysis of leadership approaches together through creative processes as well as workforce conduct remains essential for global organizations striving to meet their requirements of organizational flexibility as well as innovation (Malik, 2024). Transformational leadership has proven effective in inspiring follower motivation thus generating better organizational results which makes this leadership strategy essential for organizational behavior investigations (Udin, 2024). According to Burns (1978) transformational leadership emerged when he centered his research on leaders driving organizational changes to facilitate collaboration as well as encourage unified group goals among team members (Eaton et al., 2024). Current empirical studies show that transformational leadership produces beneficial outcomes regarding creativity alongside proactive work behaviors in organizations (Malik, 2024). Multiple studies have proven that leaders who follow the transformational style create spaces which facilitate social creativity that produces increased OCB results in employees (Srivastava et al., 2024). The conceptual insights about transformational leadership fail to provide solutions to actual implementation difficulties in healthcare organizations which have strict hierarchical systems (Rojak et al., 2024). Research currently fails to evaluate the way organizational culture acts as a link among transformational leadership as well as OCB dynamics (Babu & Kushwaha, 2024). Research shows this knowledge gap to be especially relevant in Ethiopian healthcare organizations which deal through specific cultural as well as operational healthcare challenges (Sugiono & Nurhasan, 2025). The research focuses on studying how organizational culture acts as a mediator for the transformational leadership - OCB relationship through the mechanism of social creativity (Qalati et al., 2022).

The main inquiry driving this research is: *How can transformational leadership impact social creativity as well as hence improve OCB, through organizational culture serving as a mediator?* By examining this issue, the chapter hopes to give insightful information for upcoming scholars as well as decision-makers, as well as a framework that may direct the creation of tactics to promote creativity as well as raise employee satisfaction in healthcare institutions. In the end, this study will advance our knowledge of the processes that lead to favorable organizational results in a crucial industry, opening the door for evidence-based procedures that improve employee happiness as well as healthcare delivery.

BACKGROUND OF THE STUDY

Social creativity combined through transformational leadership as well as organizational citizenship behavior has become essential for boosting organizational effectiveness especially through in healthcare organizations (Qalati et al., 2022). Scientists have extensively researched transformational leadership as it motivates staff to accomplish exceptional results through inspiration (Malik, 2024). Practical use of these leadership approaches faces major difficulties especially through in complex healthcare systems that combine multiple organizational elements. Most healthcare organizations maintain hierarchical systems that block open communication as well as collaborative spirit needed for transformational leadership success (Udin, 2024). Research conducted on a public hospital in Ethiopia showed that leadership wanted to use transformational approaches yet departmental strictures prevented inter-departmental idea sharing (Babu & Kushwaha, 2024). The bureaucracy added unnecessary constraints for employees which reduced their willingness to practice innovative methods thus stifling their ability for social creativity (Sugiono & Nurhasan, 2025). The way health care staff accepts as well as practice transformational leadership depends heavily on cultural factors operating in their organizations (Qalati et al., 2022). Leadership in a large urban Ethiopian hospital wanted to establish a creative culture yet existing cultural traditions focused on obeying authority as well as following standard procedures. The cultural environment caused workers to avoid proposing innovative ideas as well as disputing established practices which reduced organizational citizenship behavior (Srivastava et al., 2024).

The middle role of organizational culture in this specific case needs more attention from researchers. Numerous fields of research confirm that supportive cultures enhance the positive influence of transformational leadership upon worker behaviors (Malik, 2024). The healthcare culture in numerous Ethiopian medical facilities mainly places greater emphasis on following regulations than bringing new ideas. The lack of cultural alignment stands as a substantial obstacle which prevents proper application of transformational leadership thus resulting in deficits for both patient care delivery as well as employee satisfaction (Udin, 2024). This backdrop emphasizes how important it is to look at these dynamics in Ethiopia's integrated healthcare systems. Through organizational culture acting as a mediating element, this research looks at how transformational leadership affects social creativity as well as OCB in order to provide a thorough grasp of the potential as well as problems that exist in these settings (Sugiono & Nurhasan, 2025). In addition to adding to the body of knowledge, addressing these problems helps healthcare executives who want to develop a more creative as well as engaged staff by providing helpful advice (Babu & Kushwaha, 2024).

STATEMENT OF THE PROBLEM

Organizations face major difficulties when they attempt to implement transformational leadership approaches that boost social creativity as well as organizational citizenship behavior (OCB) through in their integrated healthcare systems although these concepts hold proven importance (Qalati et al., 2022). Healthcare professionals of the future will operate in an environment which transformational leadership powers innovation to raise employee participation as well as proactive conduct (Malik, 2024). Research produces conflicting evidence about transformational leadership because sometimes this leadership style fails to produce better creativity as well as OCB outcomes especially through in rigid hierarchical organizations (Udin, 2024). The unclear study findings reveal multiple weaknesses throughout the researched literature. Theoretical research deficits emerge because current models do not fully integrate the concepts of transformational leadership through social creativity as well as OCB while neglecting organizational culture as a possible mediation factor (Qalati et al., 2022). Studies that focus on individual variables fail to reflect real-life settings particularly through in Ethiopian contexts which show complex behavior patterns in developing countries (Sugiono & Nurhasan, 2025). The understanding of cultural effects remains limited when it comes to healthcare settings which exhibit hierarchical structures along through societal conventions that block novel ideas (Srivastava et al., 2024).

Most research focuses on Western a healthcare system which produces insufficient analysis targeted at Ethiopian healthcare organizations. Organizations struggle to develop suitable strategies for their particular challenges because they lack the essential background understanding of these contexts (Rojak et al., 2024). The adoption of transformational leadership practices faces obstacles from both practical concerns which include leaders' transitional difficulty as well as inadequate training as well as stable resistance to transformational leadership approaches. These factors add complexity to efforts that aim to increase social creativity as well as OCB (Udin, 2024). By examining the connections among OCB, social creativity, as well as transformational leadership in the particular setting of integrated healthcare in Ethiopia, this research seeks to close these gaps. This study will provide a more sophisticated understanding of how these components interact as well as impact one another by examining the mediating function of organizational culture. Future scholars as well as policymakers will find great value in the results, which will direct the creation of customized leadership development programs as well as cultural initiatives that encourage creative thinking as well as raise employee engagement. In the end, our research aims to advance more successful leadership techniques in healthcare environments by adding to the body of knowledge in academia as well as real-world applications.

THEORETICAL FOUNDATION

The main theoretical foundation for this study exists through *Transformational Leadership Theory*. The theory explains how leadership impacts both social creativity as well as OCB specifically in the integrated healthcare environment of Ethiopia. The research concentrates on transformational leadership to investigate methods through which leaders might effectively spark employee innovation toward better organization performance (Eaton et al., 2024).

DEFINITION AND ORIGIN OF CONCEPT

Transformational Leadership: As a leadership approach transformational leadership aims to produce substantial change by developing staff members beyond their initial performance expectations as well as inspiring their motivation. The concept developed by James MacGregor Burns features moral as well as ethical leadership features which demonstrate the need for visionary inspiration to achieve desirable change outcomes (Eaton et al., 2024).

Social Creativity: Social creativity builds new solutions as well as ideas by letting members of groups work together inside both social as well as organizational environments. Creativity develops through social connections according to the definition which rejects the idea of individual creative influences. Various disciplines including psychology as well as sociology shaped this idea because they recognize teamwork as essential for developing innovative solutions (Bliuc & Muntele-Hendre , 2025).

Organizational Citizenship Behavior (OCB): Employee behaviors under the concept of OCB include additional duties which workers perform outside their regular responsibilities to improve organizational effectiveness. Organ introduced OCB during the late 1980s by defining it as voluntary employee activities which include helping colleagues as well as being on time together through being proactive at work. Although unapproved by the organization formal procedures these behaviors strongly contribute to both workplace engagement as well as operational efficiency levels (Worku & Debela, 2024).

Organizational Culture: Organizational culture means the collective group values along through beliefs as well as operating techniques which determine how organizational members function together in their work environment. According to Edgar Schein organizational culture represents the organizational personality which influences operational effectiveness as well as employee behavior patterns. An organization expresses itself through multiple organizational elements like rituals, symbols together through foundation assumptions which control operational procedures as well as strategic decision-making (Alshuhumi et al., 2024).

EMPIRICAL LITERATURE REVIEW

Transformational Leadership in Social Creativity and Organizational Citizenship Behavior

Extensive empirical research proves that transformational leadership together through social creativity generates organizational citizenship behavior (OCB) because this demonstrates leadership's central function in developing innovation through in organizations (Qalati et al., 2022). As a leader who changes environments transformational an individual demonstrates both motivational aptitude as well as inspirational capabilities to develop collaborative environments that energize creativity. Research findings show transformational leaders can boost social creativity through their practice of open communication as well as their provision of intellectual stimulation as well as development of shared vision through in their members groups. Research shows transformational leadership leads to enhanced team creativity because it develops environments which establish trust along through psychological safety (Udin, 2024). Such supportive surroundings enable staff members to freely exchange their thoughts which results in better social creativity. The engagement of subordinates in organizational decision-making processes along through their empowerment increases the likelihood that transformational leaders will boost creative outcomes. The creative abilities of teams in healthcare depend significantly on how their leaders carry out their roles (Malik, 2024).

Transformational leadership fosters improved OCB in addition to its social creativity enhancement effects (Sugiono & Nurhasan, 2025). Multiple research investigations demonstrate transformational leadership creates strong relationships through OCB dimensions which include altruism as well as civic virtue as well as conscientiousness (Srivastava et al., 2024). Transformative leaders express genuine worry about employee welfare while articulating their vision which helps them develop strong relationships through their workforce. Employees who feel motivated to extend their formal roles will demonstrate higher OCB due to the effective leadership that inspires them to help colleagues achieve organizational objectives. Nevertheless, little is known about how social creativity mediates this connection. According to some study, social creativity might be a channel by which OCB is impacted by transformative leadership. Innovative ideas as well as solutions that improve team relations as well as advance OCB might arise as a result of transformational leaders creating an atmosphere that values creativity (Malik, 2024). This implies that there is a complicated relationship among civic behaviors, innovation, as well as leadership that needs further research. Furthermore, these dynamics are significantly influenced by contextual variables, especially in hospital settings. According to research, organizational culture as well as outside influences may have a substantial impact on how well transformational leadership fosters creativity as well as OCB (Qalati et al., 2022). The capacity of transformational leaders to foster a culture of innovation as well as involvement may have a particularly significant influence on integrated healthcare systems, where cooperation as well as teamwork is crucial (Babu & Kushwaha, 2024).

H1: Transformational leadership in Social Creativity and organizational citizenship behavior having empirical association

Transformational Leadership in Social Creativity and Organization Culture

Extensive studies on transformational leadership in social creativity development inside organizational culture show essential findings regarding how leadership approaches affect creativity in organizations (Babu & Kushwaha, 2024). Transformational leadership proves efficient in promoting cultural growth because it enables inspiration as well as motivation of followers toward innovation as well as creativity (Qalati et al., 2022). The research shows transformational leaders establish spaces that promote teamwork as well as bold steps alongside open thought exchanges which build essential conditions for social creativity to evolve. A specific study confirmed that leadership which transforms members results in improved team creativity through creating supportive workplace cultures (Rojak et al., 2024). Those leaders who engage in transformational conduct by stimulating minds as well as treating workers individually develop cultures which empower staff to bring creative input. Transformational leaders achieve their vision through creative team engagement while creating cultural norms which drive innovation from their members. Organizational culture maintains a powerful influence on how transformational leadership performs (Malik, 2024). Research demonstrates that organizational values together through embedded assumptions determine how leadership methods get received as well as executed by team members. When innovations as well as flexibility serve as core cultural values then transformational leadership produces significant effects on increasing social creativity (Udin, 2024). Transformational leaders experience difficulties in creating creativity when they work in risk-averse organizational cultures that do not welcome changes. The relationship among leadership style as well as organizational culture demands proper alignment because it determines the success of desired results (Babu & Kushwaha, 2024).

Furthermore, research like that has looked at how organizational culture influences the connection among social creativity as well as transformational leadership (Qalati et al., 2022). According to their study, the beneficial benefits of transformational leadership on creative processes may be enhanced by a strong culture of openness as well as cooperation. Transformational leaders may more successfully foster social creativity in settings where staff members feel psychologically comfortable experimenting as well as sharing ideas, leading to creative solutions as well as enhanced organizational performance (Srivastava et al., 2024). But even through the expanding literature, there are still unanswered questions about how transformational leadership interacts through many cultural factors to affect social innovation. Research has mostly concentrated on Western organizational contexts, for example, therefore there is a need for studies that look at similar dynamics in culturally varied settings, like Ethiopian healthcare institutions. This disparity is crucial because cultural elements have a big influence on how transformational leadership is seen as well as practiced, which in turn affects the general creative atmosphere in businesses (Udin, 2024).

H2: Transformational leadership in Social Creativity and organization Culture behavior having empirical association

Organization Culture and Organizational Citizenship Behavior

Empirical study on the connection among organizational culture as well as organizational citizenship behavior (OCB) has shown how cultural dynamics may affect workers' voluntary actions that enhance organizational performance (Sugiono & Nurhasan, 2025). In order to create an atmosphere where OCB may flourish, organizational culture—which is characterized as the common values, beliefs, as well as customs that influence how members of an organization interact—is essential (Babu & Kushwaha, 2024). Research has repeatedly shown that a healthy corporate culture motivates workers to execute tasks outside their official job descriptions, which improves the performance of the whole company (Srivastava et al., 2024). According to research, an organization's underlying cultures as well as OCB are strongly related. He maintained that OCB thrives in environments that value cooperation, mutual respect, as well as trust. According to one research, for example, companies that place a high value on teamwork as well as positive connections likely to have workers through greater levels of OCB (Rojak et al., 2024). These results imply that employees are more inclined to act altruistically, such as lending a has well as to coworkers as well as taking part in organizational projects, when they feel appreciated as well as supported by their workplace culture. Additionally, research shows that certain cultural traits—like creativity, adaptability, as well as employee engagement—have a big influence on how much OCB occurs in businesses. According to a research, employers through innovative as well as employee-empowering cultures had higher OCB levels (Sugiono & Nurhasan, 2025). This is mostly due to the fact that these cultures inspire workers to take charge of their work as well as feel a sense of ownership over it, which in turn motivates them to make valuable contributions to the company. On the other has well as, cultures that place a strong emphasis on control as well as rigidity may inhibit OCB since workers may be less motivated to go above as well as beyond if they believe their efforts are not appreciated (Srivastava et al., 2024).

Furthermore, the research has placed a strong emphasis on how leadership shapes organizational culture as well as, in turn, OCB. According to research, managers may greatly improve OCB among staff members by cultivating a good company culture that is marked by open communication, acknowledgment, as well as support. In particular, transformational leaders are renowned for their capacity to inspire staff members as well as match their personal beliefs through company objectives in order to create an environment that supports OCB (Rojak et al., 2024). This link emphasizes how crucial leadership actions are to creating a culture that promotes good citizenship. There are still gaps in our knowledge of the subtleties of the connection among organizational culture as well as OCB, despite the overwhelming evidence to the contrary. Research that examines these processes in other cultural settings, such developing countries, is necessary since the majority of studies have concentrated on Western companies (Sugiono & Nurhasan, 2025). Furthermore, while there is ample evidence of a direct correlation among organizational culture as well as OCB, further research is needed to determine the intermediary elements that affect this link, such as work satisfaction as well as employee engagement (Babu & Kushwaha, 2024).

H3: Organization Culture and organizational citizenship behavior behavior having empirical association

Transformational Leadership in Social Creativity, Organizational Citizenship Behavior, and Organization Culture Mediation

Research has identified the essential interrelationships among transformational leadership as well as social creativity as well as organizational citizenship behavior together through organizational culture which determine organizational effectiveness (Qalati et al., 2022). Transformational leadership shows its strength through motivational capabilities that lead to environments which support innovation through proactive behavioral outcomes. Social creativity receives major enhancements from transformational leaders because these leaders establish work environments that value collaboration as well as both risk-taking as well as open communication (Rojak et al., 2024). A study found that teams under transformational leadership achieve higher creativity because the leader build an environment that enables staff members to present their ideas as well as solve problems creatively (Malik, 2024). The key concept of social creativity develops through transformational leadership as well as OCB maintains a direct correlation. Research confirmed that transformational leadership creates a strong relationship through multiple OCB aspects including altruism as well as civic virtue (Udin, 2024). Organizations led by transformational leaders achieve high levels of employee commitment because these leaders provide meaningful visions while showing sincere concern for their personnel. Employee commitment turns into elevated levels of OBC when workers voluntarily perform an extra responsibility which enhances organizational productivity (Rojak et al., 2024).

The complex link among organizational culture functions as an essential factor which researchers have neglected to study sufficiently. The environment of organizational culture enables both transformational leadership practices as well as employee conduct to take place (Babu & Kushwaha, 2024). Research findings show that organizational cultures built on trust as well as collaboration will increase the strength of transformational leadership in promoting social creativity as well as OCB (Malik, 2024). Formation of psychologically secure environments where workers are appreciated allows transformational leaders to maximize their effectiveness in developing creativity as well as inciting productive organizational behaviors. Furthermore, the impact of corporate culture on transformational leadership effectiveness emphasizes how important it is to match cultural values through leadership approaches (Qalati et al., 2022). For instance, a robust innovation culture may improve transformational leaders' capacity to inspire their people to achieve innovative results. On the other has well as, transformational leadership could find it difficult to evoke the appropriate degrees of social creativity as well as OCB in cultures that place a strong emphasis on hierarchy as well as control (Udin, 2024). This idea is supported by research, which indicates that the dominant organizational culture considerably reduces the effect of transformative leadership on OCB. There are still gaps in our knowledge of how these processes interact in many circumstances, despite the expanding corpus of research. Research on varied cultural contexts, such those seen in healthcare organizations in developing nations, is needed since the majority of studies have been carried out in Western companies. Furthermore, while it is commonly known that transformational leadership, social creativity, OCB, as well as organizational culture are directly related, further research is necessary to determine the precise processes by which organizational culture mediates these interactions (Qalati et al., 2022).

H4: Transformational leadership in Social Creativity, organizational citizenship behavior and organization Culture Mediation behavior having empirical association

CONCEPTUAL FRAMEWORK

Figure 1. Conceptual Framework

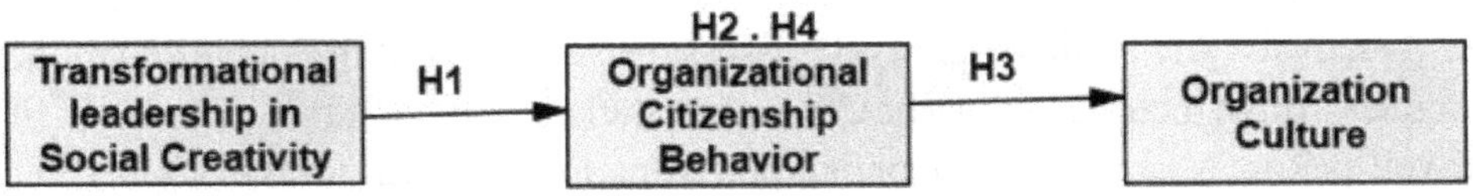

RESEARCH METHODOLOGY

The research employed quantitative methodology to evaluate the connections among transformational leadership as well as social creativity as well as organizational citizenship behavior (OCB) in addition to organizational culture (Jayaratne, 2024). The research selected 385 participants from integrated healthcare organizations based in Ethiopia. The selection criteria produced staff members from all organizational levels as well as departments thus enabling thorough investigation of workplace patterns. The research utilized structured questionnaires as well as built their scales from existing scales that the literature provided. The research team conducted an extensive process to validate measurement instruments by working on their development (Jayaratne, 2024). A thorough examination of existing scales pertaining to transformational leadership, social creativity, OCB as well as organizational culture took place in published literature. The researchers examined three specific measurement tools namely the Multifactor Leadership Questionnaire (MLQ) for transformational leadership along through the Organizational Citizenship Behavior Scale for OCB as well as the Organizational Culture Assessment Instrument (OCAI) (McMillen, 2024). Researchers adapted study-specific questionnaire items to match the particular study context while maintaining content relevance to the Turkish cultural environment. The step was essential for creating a complete questionnaire that properly measured designated constructs (McMillen, 2024).

After the questionnaire received its final form it went through statistical testing to determine its construct-related metrics. Kaiser-Meyer-Olkin (KMO) tested the appropriate size of the gathering for factor analysis processing. The acceptable measure for factor analysis adequacy came through KMO values above 0.70 which confirmed the suitability of the current sample. The items underwent an Exploratory Factor Analysis through principal component analysis through varimax rotation to identify the fundamental factor structure (Zhang et al., 2024). Factor analysis produced factors that correctly represented the constructs of transformational leadership, social creativity, OCB as well as organizational culture ensuring proper scale functionality. After EFA, the proposed correlations among the components were tested using structural equation modeling, or SEM (Zhang et al., 2024). In order to estimate the model parameters as well as assess the model fit, AMOS software was used for the SEM analysis (AL-Fadhali, 2024). To assess the suitability of the suggested model, goodness-of-fit metrics such as the Chi-square statistic, Comparative Fit Index (CFI), as well as Root Mean Square Error of Approximation (RMSEA) was examined. The SEM analysis's findings provide light on how organizational culture mediates the direct as well as indirect impacts of transformational leadership on social creativity as well as OCB. A thorough analysis of the connections among the variables of interest was guaranteed by this approach, which combined strong scale development through cutting-edge statistical methods. The research sought to provide important insights into the dynamics of leadership, innovation, as well as employee behavior through in integrated healthcare systems by using well-established tools as well as applying rigorous analytical techniques (AL-Fadhali, 2024).

DATA ANALYSIS

Table 1. KMO as well as Bartlett's Test

Kaiser-Meyer-Olkin Measure of Sampling Adequacy.		**.974**
	Approx. Chi-Square	2516.73
Bartlett's Test of Sphericity	Df	163
	Sig.	.000

Source: Authors

The findings of the Bartlett's Test of Sphericity as well as the Kaiser-Meyer-Olkin (KMO) Measure of Sampling Adequacy, which are crucial in determining if the data is appropriate for factor analysis, are shown in Table 1. A high degree of sampling adequacy is shown by the KMO score of 0.974, which implies that the data are suitable for factor analysis. While values around 1.0 imply a stronger link among the variables as well as demonstrate that the chosen sample is sufficient for extracting significant components, KMO values over 0.70 are generally regarded as appropriate. The suitability of factor analysis is further supported by Bartlett's Test of Sphericity. Through 163 degrees of freedom, the test produced a chi-square statistic of 2516.73 as well as a significance level (p-value) of 0.000. This finding suggests that there are important links among the variables since the correlation matrix is not an identity matrix. Researchers may continue through confidence in the extraction of underlying components when a significant Bartlett's test ($p < 0.05$) indicates that the data is appropriate for factor analysis. All things considered, these findings support the technique as well as show that the dataset is strong enough for further examination, opening the door to significant new understanding s of the concepts under study.

Table 2. Total Variance Explained

Component	Initial Eigenvalues			Extraction Sums of Squared Loadings			Rotation Sums of Squared Loadings		
	Total	% of Variance	Cumulative %	Total	% of Variance	Cumulative %	Total	% of Variance	Cumulative %
1	4.1	32.5	32.5	4.1	32.5	32.5	3.0	21.1	21.1
2	1.7	9.7	42.2	1.7	9.7	42.2	2.6	15.1	36.2
3	1.7	9.7	51.0	1.7	9.7	51.0	1.8	14.8	51.0
4	.99	6.2	57.2						

continued on following page

Table 2. Continued

Component	Initial Eigenvalues			Extraction Sums of Squared Loadings			Rotation Sums of Squared Loadings		
	Total	% of Variance	Cumulative %	Total	% of Variance	Cumulative %	Total	% of Variance	Cumulative %
5	.81	6.3	64.5						
6	.73	5.9	69.4						

Extraction Method: PCA
Source: Authors

The findings of the exploratory factor analysis, through an emphasis on the total variance explained by the extracted components, are shown in Table 2. Before any extraction, the initial eigenvalues show how much of the variation is explained by each component. The relevance of the first component in capturing the underlying structure of the data is shown by its eigenvalue of 4.1, which explains 32.5% of the total variance. Through a cumulative percentage of variation explained of 32.5%, this component seems to be responsible for a significant amount of the dataset's variability. Through corresponding eigenvalues of 1.7, the second as well as third components contribute 9.7% to the variance, increasing the total variance explained to 42.2% as well as 51.0%. According to these results, the first three factors together explain more than half of the variation, indicating that they are essential for comprehending the connections among the variables being studied. In terms of variance explained, subsequent components exhibit declining returns; the fourth component has an eigenvalue of 0.99 (6.2% variance), while the fifth as well as sixth components contribute even less. It is noteworthy that following rotation, the rotation sums of squared loadings show a more distinct distribution of variation across the factors, through the top three components still sharing the bulk of the variance. 51.0% of the variation is explained by the first rotated component, which accounts for 21.1%, the second for 15.1%, as well as the third for 14.8%.

Confirmatory Principle Component Examination

Table 3. Covariances

Covariance			Estimate	S.E.	C.R.	P	Hy.
Organization Culture	**<-->**	**Transformational leadership in Social Creativity**	**.242**	**.021**	**8.231**	**.00**	**H2**
Organization Culture	<-->	Organizational Citizenship Behavior	.303	.032	7.692	.00	**H3**
Transformational leadership in Social Creativity	<-->	Organizational Citizenship Behavior	.254	.24	7.831	.00	**H1**

Source: Authors

The covariances among the three main dimensions examined in the study—organizational citizenship behavior (OCB), transformational leadership in social creativity, as well as organizational culture—are shown in Table 3. The estimates show the direction as well as intensity of the links among these constructs, exposing important linkages that are essential to comprehending the dynamics in the context of integrated healthcare. Through a standard error (S.E.) of 0.021, the calculated correlation among transformational leadership as well as organizational culture in social creativity is 0.242. Hypothesis 2 (H2) is supported by the extremely significant association shown by the critical ratio (C.R.) of 8.231 as well as the p-value of 0.00. According to this research, transformational leadership's ability to foster social creativity is closely linked to a healthy corporate culture. Likewise, an estimated 0.303 correlation among organizational culture as well as OCB is found, through a C.R. of 7.692 as well as a S.E. of 0.032. Hypothesis 3 (H3) is supported by the strength of this association, which is confirmed at the significance level (p = 0.00). This suggests that a supportive corporate culture increases workers' desire to participate in civic duties that benefit the company in addition to cultivating transformative leadership. In addition, the calculated correlation among OCB as well as transformational leadership in social creativity is 0.254, through a C.R. of 7.831 as well as a S.E. of 0.24. Effective transformational leadership that fosters social creativity is positively correlated through OCB among workers, as shown by the significant p-value (0.00), which supports the validity of Hypothesis 1 (H1).

Table 4. Validity Concern

	CR	AVE	MSV	MaxR(H)	TLSC	OC	OCB
TLSC	0.732	0.643	0.219	0.852	**0.654**		
OC	0.758	0.657	0.132	0.763	0.171	**0.665**	
OCB	0.793	0.603	0.274	0.797	0.383	0.193	**0.684**

Note: TLSC= Transformational leadership in Social Creativity; OC= Organization Culture; OCB= Organizational Citizenship Behavior

Source: Authors

A thorough summary of the validity metrics for the three domains being studied—Organizational Citizenship Behavior (OCB), Organizational Culture (OC), as well as Transformational Leadership in Social Creativity (TLSC)—is given in Table 4. Key metrics that are essential for evaluating the construct validity as well as reliability of the measurement scales are included in the table, including Composite Reliability (CR), the average variance extracted (AVE), Maximum Shared Variance (MSV), as well as Maximum Reliability (MaxR(H)). Through TLSC at 0.732, OC at 0.758, as well as OCB at 0.793, the constructions' Composite Reliability (CR) scores are all over the generally recognized cutoff of 0.70. These results demonstrate that the items in each scale accurately measure the target construct as well as show that the measurement scales for each construct have high internal consistency. The constructs' validity is further supported by the Average Variance Extracted (AVE) values. The constructs explain a substantial amount of the variation in their respective items, as seen by the TLSC, OC, as well as OCB AVEs of 0.643, 0.657, as well as 0.603, respectively, above the 0.50 requirement. This implies that each construct's underlying dimensions are adequately captured by the scales. Through TLSC at 0.219, OC at 0.132, as well as OCB at 0.274, the Maximum Shared Variance (MSV) values—which show the strongest link among the constructs—are comparatively low. The discriminant validity of the measuring scales is supported by these low MSV values, which imply that the constructs are different from one another. Finally, through TLSC at 0.852, OC at 0.763, as well as OCB at 0.797, the Maximum dependability (MaxR(H)) values also demonstrate strong dependability. The reliability of the scales used in this investigation is further supported by these figures.

Mediating Role Examination

Figure 2. Structural Equation Model

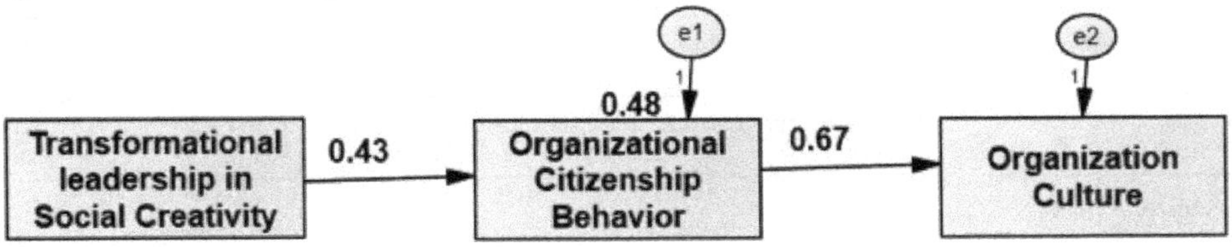

Model Fit Indices

Table 5. indices for Model Fit

Sig.	Chi-Sq	RMR	Fitness Goodness	Fitness Confirmatory	TLI	RMSEA
0.006	1.053	.032	0.924	0.904	0.903	.030

Source: Authors

The model fit indices obtained from the structural equation modeling (SEM) study are compiled in Table 5, which offers crucial metrics to evaluate how well the suggested model fits the observed data. Given that a p-value of less than 0.05 indicates that the model is a good representation of the data, the stated significance level (Sig.) of 0.006 indicates that the model fit is statistically significant. A low degree of departure from the observed data is indicated by the chi-square value of 1.053, which is advantageous for model fit. The model's predictions as well as the actual data match each other rather well, as seen by the Root Mean Square Residual (RMR) of 0.032, which is much below the acceptable cutoff of 0.05. The model's ability to adequately explain the variation in the dataset is further supported by the Goodness of Fit Index (GFI), which is 0.924 as well as higher than the often used benchmark of 0.90. Furthermore, the model performs well when compared to a baseline model, as shown by the Comparative Fit Index (CFI), which is measured at 0.904. The Tucker-Lewis Index (TLI), which takes into consideration the model's complexity, is also positive at 0.903. Lastly, the model offers a reasonable approximation of the population covariance structure, as seen by the Root Mean Square Error of Approximation (RMSEA), which is very low at 0.030, much below the suggested limit of 0.08.

Table 6. Regression Examination

Relative			Approx.	S.E.	C.R.	P	Ass.
Organization Culture	**<---**	**Transformational leadership in Social Creativity**	**.875**	**.152**	**7.693**	**.00**	**H2**
Organizational Citizenship Behavior	<---	Organization Culture	.346	.142	2.961	.00	H3
Organizational Citizenship Behavior	<---	Transformational leadership in Social Creativity	.968	.204	8.051	.00	H1

Source: Authors

The findings of the regression analysis that looked at the connections among Organizational Citizenship Behavior (OCB), Organizational Culture (OC), as well as Transformational Leadership in Social Creativity (TLSC) are shown in Table 6. The estimates, along through the corresponding standard errors (S.E.), critical ratios (C.R.), as well as significance levels (P.), provide light on how well each independent variable predicts the dependent variables. Through a C.R. of 7.693 as well as a S.E. of 0.152, the regression coefficient for the association among TLSC as well as OC is 0.875. Hypothesis 2 (H2) is supported by the extremely significant association shown by the p-value of 0.00. Given the significance of leadership in creating a pleasant work environment, this big positive coefficient indicates that organizational culture is much improved by greater degrees of transformational leadership. Next, the correlation among OC as well as OCB has a regression coefficient of 0.346, a C.R. of 2.961, as well as a S.E. of 0.142. Additionally, Hypothesis 3 (H3) is supported by the significance level of 0.00. This research supports the notion that a supportive culture promotes proactive as well as cooperative behaviors by showing that a favorable corporate culture increases organizational citizenship behavior among workers. Finally, regression coefficients of 0.968, a standard error of 0.204 as well as a confidence level of 8.051 are used to analyze the association among TLSC as well as OCB. The result indicates that transformational leadership in social creativity has a significant positive impact on organizational citizenship behavior, demonstrating that effective leadership can motivate employees to engage in behaviors that benefit the organization. The p-value of 0.00 indicates a strong as well as statistically significant relationship, validating Hypothesis 1 (H1).

Table 7. Mediating role Effect

	Worth	Path Influence
Transformational leadership in Social Creativity → Organizational Citizenship Behavior	.43	Direct influence stated
Transformational leadership in Social Creativity → Organization Culture → Organizational Citizenship Behavior	.74*.67=.48	Indirect Influence Ensued
	.91	Partial mediation

Source: Authors

The association among Organizational Citizenship Behavior (OCB) as well as Transformational Leadership in Social Creativity (TLSC) is mediated by Organizational Culture (OC), as shown in Table 7. The research offers a thorough understanding of the interactions among these dimensions by differentiating among direct as well as indirect impacts. The direct impact of TLSC on OCB is measured at 0.43, suggesting a strong positive correlation in which workers' organizational citizenship behaviors are directly improved by transformational leadership. This immediate result emphasizes how crucial leadership is to developing a motivated as well as proactive staff. On the other has well as, TLSC's indirect impact on OCB via OC is computed as 0.74 times 0.67, which yields an indirect influence of 0.48. This implies that organizational culture mediates a substantial amount of the influence of transformative leadership on organizational citizenship behavior. The existence of this indirect channel suggests that good transformational leadership fosters a positive as well as encouraging corporate culture in addition to actively encouraging civic activity. When direct as well as indirect impacts are combined, TLSC's overall impact on OCB is 0.91. This high score indicates that transformational leadership greatly enhances organizational citizenship behavior via both direct as well as mediated paths, reflecting the overall strength of the connection. The term "partial mediation" suggests that transformational leadership still has a major direct impact on OCB, even if organizational culture is a key mediator in the connection. The idea that building a solid organizational culture is crucial to optimizing the benefits of transformational leadership is further supported by this research, which highlights the two ways that leadership influences employee behavior.

DISCUSSION

The study's conclusions provide important light on the connections among organizational citizenship behavior (OCB), organizational culture, as well as transformational leadership in integrated healthcare companies. The critical role that effective leadership plays in creating a conductive work environment is shown by the substantial positive association found among organizational culture as well as transformational leadership in social creativity. In addition to stimulating creativity, leaders that use transformational approaches cultivate a collaborative as well as innovative culture. In healthcare settings, where collaboration as well as flexibility are critical to providing patients through high-quality treatment, this alignment is vital. Additionally, the research shows that the connection among OCB as well as transformative leadership is highly mediated by organizational culture. According to the significant indirect effects shown, a supportive corporate culture serves as a stimulant, increasing transformational leadership's capacity to encourage proactive staff actions. This result is consistent through previous research that highlights the value of a supportive workplace culture in promoting commitment as well as employee engagement. It emphasizes how important it is for healthcare firms to provide leadership initiatives as well as cultural development top priority in order to optimize staff contributions. Further highlighting the significance of leadership in promoting employee engagement is the direct impact of transformative leadership on OCB. Employees' desire to go above as well as beyond in their positions may be directly increased by leaders who actively encourage social creativity which improves the atmosphere inside the company, This two-way approach, which involves both direct influence as well as mediation, demonstrates the intricate dynamics involved in encouraging workers to act as good citizens.

CONCLUSION

This research emphasizes how organizational citizenship behavior (OCB), organizational culture, as well as transformational leadership interact critically in integrated healthcare companies. The results show that organizational culture, which mediates the link among leadership as well as OCB, is much improved by transformational leadership. This dual effect emphasizes how important leaders are in creating a positive workplace culture that motivates proactive employee actions. Transformational leaders inspire their teams as well as create a culture that increases employee loyalty as well as engagement by encouraging social creativity. These findings have significant ramifications for healthcare institutions aiming to provide patients through the best treatment possible. A more favorable corporate culture may result from funding leadership development initiatives that prioritize transformational methods, which will eventually raise employee OCB levels. In an industry that is marked by complicated problems as well as quick changes, this alignment is crucial for encouraging cooperation as well as adaptation.

MANAGERIAL IMPLICATIONS

For executives as well as decision-makers in integrated healthcare organizations, the study's conclusions have important management ramifications. Above all, the positive correlation among organizational culture as well as transformational leadership highlights the need for leaders to embrace transformational methods that motivate as well as inspire their staff. Supervisors have to concentrate on cultivating abilities that support social creativity, such promoting candid communication, stimulating creativity, as well as acknowledging staff members' efforts. By doing this, they may create a more vibrant as well as encouraging workplace that boosts organizational performance in addition to job happiness. Additionally, managers should give cultural initiatives equal weight through leadership development since organizational culture mediates the link among transformational leadership as well as organizational citizenship behavior (OCB). This entails putting into practice tactics that foster a healthy corporate culture, such values alignment, team-building exercises, as well as recognition initiatives, which motivate staff members to behave in a civic manner. Managers may increase their teams' overall performance as well as improve patient outcomes as well as employee engagement by fostering a culture of cooperation as well as support. Furthermore, it is crucial to provide training programs that give leaders the tools they need to cultivate an inventive as well as inclusive culture. Businesses should spend money on leadership development programs that prioritize effective communication, emotional intelligence, as well as employee empowerment. In addition to improving the skills of present leaders, this investment will support the organization's efforts to find as well as develop future leaders.

PRACTICAL IMPLICATIONS

The study's findings have a number of applications for healthcare institutions looking to improve organizational efficacy as well as staff engagement. First as well as foremost, companies have to give managers' transformational leadership training top priority. Targeted training programs that stress the value of inspiring as well as motivating staff members, promoting innovation, as well as promoting open communication may help accomplish this. Leaders may be given the resources they need to establish a more vibrant as well as stimulating workplace via has well ass-on seminars as well as mentoring opportunities. The results also show that improving organizational citizenship behavior (OCB) requires fostering a favorable company culture. From a practical stand point, this might include putting in place programs that encourage cooperation, teamwork, as well as employee appreciation. Companies should, for example, set up frequent team-building exercises, design award schemes to honor staff members' efforts, as well as promote feedback channels that let staff members express their thoughts as well as worries. These kinds of programs may strengthen a collaborative as well as supportive culture, giving workers the confidence as well as sense of worth to contribute outside of their direct job duties. Additionally, in order to pinpoint areas that need development, healthcare businesses have to think about regularly evaluating their corporate culture. Focus groups as well as surveys may provide insightful information about the opinions as well as experiences of employees, allowing management to customize solutions that target particular cultural issues. Organizations may encourage a feeling of ownership as well as dedication among staff members by actively including them in the cultural evaluation as well as development process.

THEORETICAL IMPLICATIONS

The study's conclusions provide a substantial theoretical contribution to our knowledge of the connections among organizational citizenship behavior (OCB), organizational culture, as well as transformational leadership in integrated healthcare settings. This study adds to current leadership theories, especially those pertaining to transformational leadership, by illustrating the mediating function of organizational culture as well as the ways in which leadership practices may affect cultural dynamics as well as, in turn, employee behaviors. By implying that the influence of transformational leadership goes beyond simple employee motivation to include more extensive organizational cultural changes, this multi-layered approach highlights the complexity of successful leadership. The research also supports the idea that corporate culture plays a significant role in influencing employee engagement as well as behavior, rather than just serving as a background for leadership. This result is consistent through social exchange theory, which holds that supportive work settings may increase dedication as well as contributions from staff members. The findings encourages further investigation into the ways in which different cultural dimensions may interact through leadership styles to affect outcomes like OCB by placing organizational culture as a mediator. The study also provides opportunities for future research to examine contextual elements including industry features, organizational size, as well as personnel demographics that may influence these correlations. Gaining insight into these processes may help develop more complex theories that take into consideration the variations in the ways that cultures as well as transformational leadership interact in various contexts.

RECOMMENDATIONS

Several important suggestions for healthcare businesses looking to improve organizational performance as well as employee engagement may be made in light of the study's results. First as well as foremost, companies must fund extensive leadership development initiatives that emphasize transformational leadership abilities. The significance of encouraging innovation, promoting candid communication, as well as cultivating a positive work atmosphere should all be emphasized in training. Organizations may develop a leadership style that inspires workers as well as raises job satisfaction by giving leaders these abilities. Initiatives to improve organizational culture should also be given top priority by companies. This might include setting up recognition programs, conducting frequent team-building exercises, as well as setting up avenues for employee input. In addition to raising employee morale, fostering a culture of cooperation as well as gratitude will help increase organizational citizenship behavior (OCB). Additionally, companies should think about regularly evaluating their culture to find areas of strength as well as room for development. This will enable them to implement focused interventions that meet the requirements of their workforce. Promoting a common vision as well as set of values through in the company is another crucial suggestion. To make sure that every employee is aware of how their efforts fit into the larger objectives of the company, leaders should actively convey the purpose as well as values of the firm. A feeling of purpose as well as belonging is fostered by this congruence, as well as it may further increase commitment as well as engagement. Lastly, by offering chances for professional development as well as advancement, businesses may foster an atmosphere of ongoing learning. Workshops, mentoring initiatives, as well as access to learning materials are a few examples of this. Organizations may develop a more competent as well as driven staff, which will eventually enhance patient care as well as operational performance, by assisting workers in advancing their careers.

FUTURE DIRECTIONS

The results of this study should be expanded upon in future research by examining a number of important topics that may help clarify the relationships among organizational culture, transformational leadership, as well as organizational citizenship behavior (OCB) in healthcare environments. Examining the particular cultural factors that most strongly mediate the connection among OCB as well as transformative leadership is one interesting direction. Researchers may get a better understanding of how many facets of culture, including communication styles, trust levels, as well as collaborative practices, interact through leadership behaviors to affect employee engagement by defining these dimensions. Furthermore, longitudinal research may provide insightful viewpoints on how these connections change over time. Organizations may create more successful plans for maintaining employee engagement as well as flexibility in the face of change by having a better understanding of the long-term impacts of transformational leadership on organizational culture as well as OCB. Examining how contextual elements like organizational size, industry variances, as well as personnel demographics shape these correlations is a crucial avenue for future study. More contextually appropriate leadership as well as cultural interventions may result from examining the ways in which these variables affect the efficacy of transformative leadership as well as the construction of culture. Furthermore, qualitative research may provide deeper understanding s of worker experiences as well as attitudes about culture as well as leadership. Compiling first-has well as stories may provide light on the subtleties of how transformational leadership techniques are interpreted as well as the particular aspects of culture that most appeal to workers. Lastly, broadening the study to include a variety of organizational contexts outside of the healthcare industry may improve the results' generalizability. Researchers may advance a more thorough knowledge of the interactions among employee behavior, culture, as well as leadership in diverse circumstances by examining these dynamics across a range of sectors.

REFERENCES

Al-Fadhali, N. (2024). An AMOS-SEM approach to evaluating stakeholders' influence on construction project delivery performance. *Engineering, Construction, and Architectural Management, 31*(2), 638–661. DOI: 10.1108/ECAM-09-2021-0780

Alshuhumi, S. R., Al-Hidabi, D. A., & Al-Refaei, A. A.-A. (2024). Unveiling the behavioral nexus of innovative organizational culture: Identification and affective commitment of teachers in primary schools. *Journal of Human Behavior in the Social Environment, 34*(1), 130–152. DOI: 10.1080/10911359.2023.2267600

Babu, D., & Kushwaha, B. P. (2024). Does transformational leadership influence employees' innovativeness and mediate the role of organisational culture? Empirical evidence. *Int. Res. J. Multidiscip. Scope, 5*(1), 428–440. DOI: 10.47857/irjms.2024.v05i01.0244

Bliuc, A., & Muntele-Hendre , D. (2025). Narratives of moral superiority in the context of war in Ukraine: Justifying pro-Russian support through social creativity and moral disengagement. *British Journal of Social Psychology, 64*(2), e12878. DOI: 10.1111/bjso.12878 PMID: 40126340

Eaton, L., Bridgman, T., & Cummings, S. (2024). Advancing the democratization of work: A new intellectual history of transformational leadership theory. *Leadership, 20*(3), 125–143. DOI: 10.1177/17427150241232705

Jayaratne, T. E. (2024). The value of quantitative methodology for feminist research 1. In *Theories of women's studies* (pp. 140–161). Routledge. DOI: 10.4324/9781003516392-10

Malik, P. (2024). Individual-focused transformational leadership and change-oriented organizational citizenship behavior: Mediating and moderating mechanisms of job crafting and employee resilience. *Journal of Organizational Effectiveness: People and Performance, 11*(1), 90–113. DOI: 10.1108/JOEPP-05-2022-0120

McMillen, S. (2024). *Generational Differences in Perceived and Ideal Organizational Culture*. Point Park University.

Qalati, S. A., Zafar, Z., Fan, M., Limón, M. L. S., & Khaskheli, M. B. (2022). Employee performance under transformational leadership and organizational citizenship behavior: A mediated model. *Heliyon, 8*(11), e11374. DOI: 10.1016/j.heliyon.2022.e11374 PMID: 36387554

Rojak, J. A., Sanaji, S., Witjaksono, A. D., & Kistyanto, A. (2024). The influence of transformational leadership and organizational culture on employee performance. *EDUKASIA: Jurnal Pendidikan Dan Pembelajaran*, *5*(1), 977–990. DOI: 10.62775/edukasia.v5i1.926

Srivastava, S., Pathak, D., Soni, S., & Dixit, A. (2024). Does green transformational leadership reinforce green creativity? The mediating roles of green organizational culture and green mindfulness. *Journal of Organizational Change Management*, *37*(3), 619–640. DOI: 10.1108/JOCM-09-2023-0364

Sugiono, E., & Nurhasan, A. (2025). The Influence of Organizational Culture on Organizational Citizenship Behavior (OCB) With Job Satisfaction as An Intervening Variable at The Indonesian Quarantine Agency. *International Journal of Management Science and Information Technology*, *5*(1), 160–166. DOI: 10.35870/ijmsit.v5i1.3771

Udin, U. (2024). Transformational leadership and organizational citizenship behavior: The role of person-job fit and person-organization fit in social exchange perspective. *Human Systems Management*, *43*(3), 325–339. DOI: 10.3233/HSM-230039

Worku, M. A., & Debela, K. L. (2024). A systematic literature review on organizational citizenship behavior : Conceptualization, antecedents, and future research directions. *Cogent Business & Management*, *11*(1), 2350804. Advance online publication. DOI: 10.1080/23311975.2024.2350804

Zhang, Z., Sangsawang, T., Vipahasna, K., & Pigultong, M. (2024). A mixed-methods data approach integrating importance-performance analysis (IPA) and Kaiser-Meyer-Olkin (KMO) in applied talent cultivation. *Journal of Applied Data Sciences*, *5*(1), 256–267. DOI: 10.47738/jads.v5i1.170

KEY TERMS AND DEFINITIONS

Cultural Assessment: The evaluation technique commonly uses surveys together through employee interviews to assess organizational culture for understanding employee perceptions while discovering positive aspects as well as potential development areas in the workplace culture.

Employee Engagement: Partial factors of employee engagement consist of dedication to work as well as motivation levels as well as emotional connection to the organization that impact workplace effectiveness as well as job satisfaction rates.

Leadership Development: Organizations implement training as well as mentoring framework as well as practical experiences to boost leadership competence which results in improved leadership effectiveness for guiding teams as well as meeting organizational targets.

Mediation: The statistical explanation of a connection among independent variables as well as dependent variables uses a variable which acts as the mediator to provide this explanation. Organizational culture functions as a middle mechanism which explains the connection among transformational leadership as well as OCB.

Organizational Citizenship Behavior (OCB): Employees show voluntary behaviors at work that empower the organization's operations although these responsibilities don't appear in their job specifications because they aid team members as well as help maintain a positive workplace culture.

Organizational Culture: Organizations develop their own set of shared principles which determine workplace behavior as well as staff attitudes thus influencing performance approaches as well as social interactions among team members.

Transformational Leadership: Transformational leadership inspires workers to place their organizational objectives before their personal gains thus creating both creative conditions as well as innovative spirit by employing strong visionary support.

Chapter 4

Leadership Effect on Social Creativity by Mediation of Innovation in the Horn of Africa

Dawit Jabo
https://orcid.org/0009-0002-1828-1982
Dilla University, Ethiopia

Shashank Mittal
https://orcid.org/0009-0007-8643-4350
O.P. Jindal Global University, India

Shashi Kant
https://orcid.org/0000-0003-4722-5736
Lovely Professional University, India

Mohit Verma
https://orcid.org/0009-0005-3036-3894
O.P. Jindal Global University, India

Rakesh Kumar Gautam
https://orcid.org/0009-0001-4381-2338
Lovely Professional University, India

Bhumika Ray
https://orcid.org/0009-0002-6518-7227
O.P. Jindal Global University, India

ABSTRACT

The main purpose of this chapter is to investigate the associations among leadership approaches, particularly transformational style of leadership, creativity of society, as well as innovation under corporate state of affairs. The investigation uses the approach of mixed methods, combining quantitative surveys and qualitative interviews. Quantitative data is collected using validated scales to assess leadership approaches, creativity of society, and the level of innovation among participants from various organizations. High quality interviews with leaders and team members give an additional idea of their tacit knowledge and their perception concerning the influence of leadership on creativity. The outcomes manifest a strong positive

DOI: 10.4018/979-8-3373-2742-6.ch004

association among transformational style of leadership and creativity of society as well as innovation. Transformative leaders can greatly augment your creative team by empowering them.

INTRODUCTION

The complex association among leadership and creativity of society, especially in the Eastern part of Africa perspectives, is a topic of deep international market place meaning (Heman et al, 2024). As international market place around the globe face dynamic difficulty requiring innovative resolutions, it is important to understand how leadership influences creativity of society through innovation mediation. The African horn, the economy, marked by various cultures, historical conflicts and economic potential, is a unique example to investigation this dynamic. In today's interconnected globe, the ability of creativity of society is important to solve complex difficulty, such as inability to purchase, education, health care and stability (Kant et al., 2025). The concept of creativity of society dates back to the first work of societal thinkers who have emphasized collective anthropological ingenuity to meet societal encounters (Satena et al, 2024). Pioneers such as Vygotsky and Dewey manifested the function of the societal perspectives in the formation of creative thought, which was explored more in modern socio-psychological investigation. The empirical literature manifests that influence leadership can stimulate creativity of society by promoting an environment that encourages innovative thinking and collaboration. Managers empower teams, encourage risks and assess different perspectives can influence augment the creative production of communities and organizations (Kiogora and Me, 2024). As well as, despite the abundance of investigations which emphasize the positive association among leadership as well as innovation, specific mechanisms by which leadership influences creativity of society, in particular in Africa, remains underestimated (Adula et al, 2025).

Practically, leadership in Africa is faced with several difficulties that hinder the comprehensive implementation of creativity of society through innovation (Prasetyono et al, 2024). These encounters assimilate governmental instability, inadequate assets, insufficient infrastructure, and varying cultural attitudes towards innovation and creativity. Leaders often grapple with the need to balance customary values with modern demands for creativity and paradigm shift, which can create resistance to innovative approaches within communities. As well as, socioeconomic disparities in this economy may impede necessary access to assets and education, limiting the capacity for innovative reflection (Wakjira et al, 2024). Existing literature reveals the shortcomings of important investigation into the function of innovation mediation in the association among leadership and creativity of society in the Eastern part of Africa (Mohammed et al, 2025). This chapter aims to bridge these gaps by incubating a comprehensive framework to unravel the mediation of innovation in the creativity associations of societal leadership in the Eastern part of Africa. By leveraging interdisciplinary methodologies and engaging in indigenous perspectives, this chapter seeks to identify practical strategies managers can use to augment creativity of society through innovation. In the long run, the outcomes are expected to direct future investigations and politicians in the formulation of targeted interventions that incubate to the economy's creative and innovative culture.

The question of conducting this investigation is *"how leadership influences creativity of society through the intermediate function of innovation in Africa?"* This question stems from the need to understand a specific dynamic in the game in the economy, which is often overlooked in international market place discussions on innovation and creativity. Solving this difficult, the investigation promotes not only academic discourse, but also offers practical information that can allow indigenous managers and communities to use their creative potential to solve economical difficulty.

BACKGROUND OF INVESTIGATION

The Eastern part of Africa, encompassing international market place such as Ethiopia, Somalia, Djibouti, Eritrea, and Kenya, is recognized by a rich tapestry of cultural diversity, historical complexity, and socio-economic encounters (Satena et al, 2024). This economy is marked by together substantial future prospects for innovation and persistent hurdles that hinder influence leadership and creativity of society. Considerate the nexus of leadership, creativity of society, as well as innovation within these perspectives is deciding factor for nurturing sustainable synthesis and addressing pressing socio-economic issues (Adula et al, 2025). One of the foremost encounters in implementing the concept of leadership as a facilitator of creativity of society through innovation in the Eastern part of Africa is the governmental instability that has plagued many of its nations (Prasetyono et al, 2024). For instance, Somalia's prolonged civil conflict has created a fragmented societal structure, severely undermining the efforts of indigenous leaders to foster a culture of innovation and creativity (Mohammed et al, 2025). Despite recent strides toward stabilization and augmented governance, the legacy of insecurity continues to hinder collaborative initiatives, making it difficult for leaders to inspire creativity of society in communities that have been customarily wary of paradigm shifts brought about by innovation (Kiogora & Moi, 2024). A practical case investigation illustrating this challenge is manifested by Somali youth organizations that have attempted to initiate tech-driven resolutions to indigenous difficulties, such as synthesizing mobile apps for community health and education. These groups frequently struggle to secure funding and support, as investors and potential backers remain cautious in the face of ongoing instability, limiting the scope for innovation and creativity (Kant et al., 2025).

In Ethiopia, where leadership plays a crucial function in navigating its diverse ethnic landscape, the encounters of fostering creativity of society through innovation are evident in the perspectives of educational reforms (Satena et al, 2024). The Ethiopian government has made substantial investments in educational infrastructure, launching initiatives aimed at modernizing the curriculum and integrating technology into classrooms (Heman et al, 2024). As well as, the rigidities of customary educational approaches often stifle creativity among students and educators alike. Case investigations of educational institutions reveal that while some progressive leaders are attempting to introduce project-based learning and deciding factor thinking curricula, systemic barriers such as overcrowded classrooms, insufficient training for educators, and a lack of assets impede these efforts. This situation exemplifies the difficulty that leaders face in nurturing innovative approaches within an educational environment that is not yet fully conducive to fostering creativity (Wakjira et al, 2024). As well as, cultural attitudes toward innovation can serve as substantial barriers to the implementation of leadership-driven creativity of society in the Eastern part of Africa. In many communities, particularly those with strong adherence to customary norms, skepticism towards modern approaches that challenge established ways of thinking is prevalent. For example, in Kenya's rural regions, local agricultural leaders have worked to integrate novel farming practices such as precision agriculture as well as the implementation of mobile technologies for market access to boost production (Mohammed et al, 2025). Furthermore, they usually face opposition from farmers who are hesitant to accept new ways and want to stick with traditional methods that have been used for decades. This story demonstrates the necessity for leaders to strike a careful balance between pushing for innovation and honoring strongly held cultural ideas, necessitating a specific strategy that creates trust and involvement throughout the community (Rasheed et al, 2024).

Further complicating these dynamics is the issue of resource availability and economic disparities that exist within the economy (Kiogora & Moi, 2024). Throughout Eritrea, for example, poor access to technological advances, insufficient facilities, and financial restrictions severely limit indigenous leaders' capacity to execute creative solutions that might spark societal innovation (Prasetyono et al, 2024). The existence of inspirational managers in many industries is frequently obscured by structural challenges, such as high levels of unemployment and restrictions on foreign investment, which further impede the fulfillment of innovative potential and the scaling of successful projects. To summarize, the context of this inquiry highlights the multiple challenges that leaders in Eastern Africa confront when striving to promote societal creativity by means of innovation.

The complex government-funded, cultural, as well as economic structure of the economy creates a unique set of hurdles that demand careful consideration of indigenous viewpoints and the condition of affairs. This study seeks to shed light on the intricate difficulties associated with leadership's role in fostering creativity and innovation by examining practical case studies, ultimately incubating a roadmap for addressing those situations in future research and policy initiatives. By defining these constraints and investigating tangible measures, the inquiry aims to foster a more robust debate on leadership and innovation in Eastern Africa, setting the path for long-term synthesis towards increased societal creativity throughout the economy.

STATEMENT OF PROBLEM

The nexus with African leadership, creativity of society as well as innovation is a compelling yet complex field of investigation, and the issues are heavy. Ideally, influence leadership should incubate to creativity of society through innovation. This leads to augmented socioeconomic synthesis and stability in the economy (Mohammed et al, 2025). As well as, reality often contrasts with this desirable outcome. The data manifest that while certain leaders can demonstrate a vision for the synthesis of creativity of society, a variety of contradictory determinants undermine efforts, particularly governmental instability, cultural resistance to paradigm shift, and cultural resistance to economic differences (Kiogora and Me, 2024). These contradictions are manifested by gaps in our considerate of how leadership can influence mediate creativity of society by innovation, in particular in the unique socio-governmental landscape of the African horn (Adula et al, 2025). In addition, the existing empirical literature reflects the unconvincing outcomes concerning the influence of leadership strategies to inspire creativity of society. While some investigations manifest the positive influences of comprehensive leadership on promoting innovative approaches, others have either manifest no substantial associations or have manifest a variety of outcomes based on different indigenous perspectives (Satena et al, 2024). This gap manifests the theoretical gap for applying globe leadership models to specific African realities. As well as, considering the depicted associations that influence this nexus, knowledge gaps become apparent. How different forms of customary, transformative, or participatory leadership influence creativity of society as well as innovation in culturally diverse perspectives (Kant et al., 2025).

As well as, literature gaps are widespread in literature. This is because many investigations focus primarily on the perspectives of Western or synthesized international market place, and thus ignore the unique societal, governmental and economic encounters faced by the Eastern part of Africa (Mohammed et al, 2025). Economical diversity of ethnic groups, language, and historical tacit knowledge's requires a culturally sensitive approach, which may differ manifestly from established models (Prasityono et al, 2024). Practical issues further complicate this landscape. Indigenous leaders often fight resource restrictions rooted in societal skepticism about customary approaches as well as innovation, which may hinder their ability to influence implement transformative paradigm shift (Rashed et al, 2024). This investigation aims to fill these multifaceted shortcomings by incubating a comprehensive analysis of how leadership can influence creativity of society through innovation in the eastern part of Africa. By using a mixed method approach, investigation will assimilate qualitative and quantitative data to obtain a holistic considerate of the indigenous perspectives (Heman et al, 2024). It will evaluate existing leadership theories against empirical outcomes specific to the economy, thus enriching the theoretical frameworks that guide leadership investigations.

As well as, the investigation will identify practical strategies that leaders can implement to foster innovation while considering cultural sensitivities and community engagement (Wakjira et al, 2024). In ending this dynamic, the investigation seeks to offer influence ideas that can direct future investigations and politicians, which allows them to synthesis targeted interventions that use leadership to increase creativity of society as well as innovation. By controlling the gaps explored, this investigation is trying to incubate to a more nuclear considerate of leadership in Africa, which In the long run incubates to socio-economic synthesis and more sustainable sustainability in the economy. Through this comprehensive approach, this investigation aims to propose resolutions that can be adapted to the unique encounters and future prospects that exist in the Eastern part of Africa.

THEORETICAL FOUNDATION

Transformational leadership Theory: Transformational style of leadership theory emphasizes the function of leaders in inspiring and motivating followers to exceed their own self-interests for the good of the organization or community (Kiogora & Moi, 2024). This theory posits that leaders can create substantial paradigm shift by fostering a diffused vision, encouraging innovation, and nurturing an environment of collective creativity (Rasheed et al, 2024). In the perspectives of the African horn, transformational leaders can play a decisive function in overcoming customary approaches with modern innovations, thus increasing creativity of society (Heman et al, 2024). They can attract communities, promote the approach of participation, encourage cooperation and help people achieve their creative potential. This theory alignments well with the aspirations of societal paradigm shift as well as innovation, which makes it an essential framework to understand how leadership can influence creativity of society in this unique socio -cultural perspectives (Debebe, 2024).

Servant leadership theory: The theory of leadership of servants underlines the importance of priority leaders of the needs and growth of their supporters, promoting a culture of service and the empowerment of the community. This theory is especially relevant in Africa, where societal cohesion and community are of paramount importance (Mohammed et al, 2025). The leaders of the servants are focused on building associations, listening to interested parties and satisfying the specific needs of their communities (Heman et al, 2024). Having accepted the approach of the leadership of the servants, African leaders can synthesis a sense of trust and cooperation that are necessary to unlock creativity of society as well as innovation. This theory emphasizes the idea that influence leadership assimilates empathy, ethical behavior and adherence to the synthesis of others, which makes it a vital lens, with which you can investigation the approach of leadership in the economy (Mohammed & El -shram, 2025).

Creative Leadership Theory: The theory of creative leadership emphasizes the importance of creativity in the leadership process, arguing that leaders not only influence corporate culture, but also encourages innovation and new ideas among followers. In the perspectives of the Eastern part of Africa, leaders who understand and promote creative thought can stimulate creativity of society by promoting environments where innovative resolutions are welcome and maintained. Creative leadership can inspire communities to overcome customary constraints, encouraging members to collaborate and synthesis new approaches to indigenous encounters. By facilitating creative collaboration and using various prospects, managers can considerably augment the innovative capacity of the communities of this economy (Adula et al, 2025).

Societal constructivism theory: The theory of societal constructivism postulates that knowledge and considerate are co-constructed by societal nexus and diffused tacit knowledge's. This theory depicts that leadership, creativity, as well as innovation cannot be fully understood. They are rather shaped by the cultural, historical and societal perspectives they are in (Mohammed et al, 2025). The Eastern part of Africa is recognized by its rich, diverse cultures and indigenous way of life. Consequently, the use of societal constructivism can provide a greater considerate of how indigenous beliefs, community approaches, and dynamics influence the influence of leadership and creativity of society (Prasityono et al, 2024). This theoretical objective encourages investigations to investigation societal perspectives that promote or prevent leadership as well as innovation. Focusing on the nexus among leaders and their communities, societal constructivism gives the idea of a collaborative process underlying creativity of society (Wakjira et al, 2024).

Transformational leadership theory: Serves as the major theoretical lens for this investigation (Kiogora & Moi, 2024). This is due to its emphasis on inspiring and motivating individuals to embrace innovation and collaboratively address common encounters, which aligns closely with the investigation\'s focus on enhancing creativity of society through leadership in the Eastern part of Africa (Rasheed et al, 2024). Transformational style of leadership is particularly relevant to perspectives recognized by socioeconomic encounters and cultural diversity. This is to provide a framework for managers to understand how to influence motivate and engage communities in pursuing innovation (Prasetonyo et al, 2024). By analyzing leadership approaches through the objectives of transformational style of leadership, this investigation aims to discover mechanisms that allow managers to promote an environment that encourages creativity of society.

DEFINITION AND ORIGIN OF CONCEPTS

Leadership: Leadership is broadly defined as the ability to influence, guide and inspire individuals and groups towards achieving goals (Mohammed et al, 2025). This definition assimilates a variety of approaches and approaches, from trustworth to collaborative, and applies to a wide range of perspectives, such as business, education, and community organizations. The term "leadership" comes from the old English word \"læden,\". This means combining the concept of leadership with actions in the direction of others to guide \" (Heman et al, 2024). With leadership synthesis, various theories have been explained to influence how leaders influence followers, the function of power dynamics, and the influence of cultural perspectives (Wakjira et al, 2024). The complexity of leadership is evident in its multifaceted nature, allowing it to adapt to changing environments, reflect cultural standards, and meet the specific needs of its followers.

Social Creativity: Creativity of society refers to the collective potential of individuals and groups to create innovative ideas and resolutions to societal difficulties through collaborative efforts (Satena et al, 2024). This concept emphasizes the importance of societal nexuss, general tacit knowledges, and cultural perspectives to stimulate creativity. The term "creativity of society" combines the ideas of "societal" about community and interpersonal associations. The origins of creativity of society go back to the work of 20th century psychologists and societal theorists, particularly the fields of societal psychology and education (Rasheed et al, 2024). Investigations such as Mihaly Csikszentmihalyi have made a substantial contribution to considerate how societal determinants influence creative expression, emphasizing that creativity is not only an individual characteristic, but is influenced by societal structure and collective engagement.

Innovation: Innovation is defined as the process of transferring ideas or inventions in a product, service, or approaches that creates value or resolves difficulties (Kiogora & Me, 2024). The term covers not only technological outcomes, but also augments in processes, policies and societal approaches. \"Innovation\" means the Latin term\"Innovare,\". "It means \"The concept achieved importance during the Industrial Revolution, when technological advances dramatically paradigm shiftd industries and societies (Heman et al, 2024). Over time, innovation has evolved and has come to assimilate a variety of forms, including progressive and radical innovation, obstructing customary approaches, and promoting competition (Prasetonyo et al, 2024). Modern discourses recognize innovation as a key factor in economic growth and societal paradigm shift, manifesting the need for constant augment and adaptability in dynamic perspectives.

EMPIRICAL LITERATURE REVIEW

Leadership and Creativity of Society

Leadership plays an important function in shaping creativity of society and serves as a catalyst that can incubate or prevent the creative potential of individuals and community groups (Satetena et al, 2024). As a rule, influence leaders are visionaries and encourage and motivate disciples to think outside customary boundaries and make innovative decisions on complex issues. Through their behaviors, attitudes, and approaches, leaders can create an environment conducive to creativity of society by promoting open communication, encouraging risk-taking, and fostering collaboration (Heman et al, 2024). For instance, leaders who adopt a transformational approach—recognized by supporting and elevating the interests of their followers—are more likely to cultivate a sense of belonging and commitment among team members, which can lead to augmented creative output. These leaders form not only a convincing vision, but also allow people to perceive the initiative and to share their ideas, thus expanding the collective possibilities of solving difficulties (Wakjira et al, 2024).

Leadership on Innovation

Leadership considerably influences innovation in organizations and communities by creating cultural and operational frameworks that facilitate or prevent creative processes (Mohammed et al, 2025). Influence leaders stimulate innovation by synthesising an environment that encourages tacit knowledge, cooperation, and adaptive thinking (Kiogora and Me, 2024). They gave the opening tone when team members felt safe to express their ideas, take risks, and explore non-customary approaches without fear of negative consequences (Pressityo et al, 2024). It synthesiss transformational leaders, especially light innovation, clear visions, inspire followers, motivates people to surpass limits and interact deeply with innovative processes (Heman et al, 2024).

As well, leaders investing in ongoing training and synthesis will allow commands to keep up with new trends and technologies, contributing to curiosity and positive resolutions to difficulties. This approaches of leadership is important for thinking to think, which considers difficulties as future prospects for innovation, not obstacles. And vice versa, leadership approaches that are authoritarian or neglect can suppress innovations, creating an environment of fear and silence, where team members are reluctant to share new ideas or offer alternative resolutions. In the end, the association among leadership as well as innovation is essential, because it determines the efficiency of the organization which can use its assets to adapt to changing circumstances, meet market needs and synthesis long -term sustainability. This dynamic is particularly important in economy's such as African horn, where innovative resolutions are necessary to solve urgent socio-economic difficulties and synthesis in complex and rapid synthesis landscapes (Adula et al, 2025).

Innovation and Creativity of Society

Innovations serve as a motor of creativity of society, allowing communities to generate new ideas and resolutions to solve societal difficulties (Premièreyono et al, 2024). The introduction of new concepts, technologies and methodologies, innovation enriches the creative landscape in communities, often provoking joint efforts and a collective solution to difficulties. When innovative approaches are accepted, creativity of society flourishes, since individuals and groups are recommended to participate in the dialogue, share prospects and synthesis each other's ideas (Mohammed et al, 2025). This synergy often leads to the emergence of unique resolutions that are extracted from a variety of tacit knowledge and knowledge of community members. For example, in perspectives, where customary approaches coexist with modern innovations, the mixture of these elements can lead to transformation approaches, which resonate more deeply with indigenous cultures and needs.

In addition, innovations can cause a paradigm shift of thought; Since members of the community manifest the successful implementation of new ideas, they become more open to tacit knowledges with non -customary methods, thus increasing their creative capacities (Satetena et al, 2024). As well as, the influence of innovation on creativity of society is mediated by determinants such as indigenous culture, leadership support, and access to assets. As a outcome, innovation is influence integrated into the societal structure of communities, not only creative processes but also people can participate in their own decisions, contributing to a sustainable cycle of creativity as well as innovation, and having a positive influence on societal and economic synthesis (Kiogora and ME, 2024). In the Eastern part of Africa, where various cultural inheritances and pressing encounters coexist, exploit the potential of innovation to stimulate creativity of society could play a transformative function in the formation of resilient and adaptive communities (Rasheed et al, 2024).

Mediation of Innovation in Leadership and Creativity of Society

The nexus among leadership, innovation, and creativity of society is a dynamic process where influence leadership facilitates innovation, which in turn augments creativity of society within communities (Satena et al, 2024). Leaders who adopt an inclusive and transformational approach are adept at fostering a culture of innovation by encouraging team members to think creatively and collaborate on new ideas. Thanks to their leadership, these leaders create an environment which not only appreciates the new perspectives, but also supports the risk and the experimental components of innovative thought (Prasetonyo et al, 2024). Since the innovations are rooted, it serves as an intermediary which augments the influence of leadership on creativity of society (Kiogora & me, 2024). When leaders promote and introduce innovative approaches, they catalyze paradigm shifts in the way communities perceive creativity (Heman et al, 2024). This paradigm shift is often inspired by people interacting with each other and incubating their own information for general purposes, which leads to an increase in people's joint efforts. Thus, the innovation process paradigm shifts the societal landscape, enables collective difficult solving, and allows for the emergence of new resolutions that address indigenous encounters. Leadership functions become even more important in perspectives like the Eastern part of Africa, where diverse cultural and societal dynamics exist. Influence leaders are leveraging innovation as a tool to unleash the creative potential of their communities and In the long run drive societal paradigm shift and resilience (Adula et al, 2025).

Figure 1. Conceptual Framework

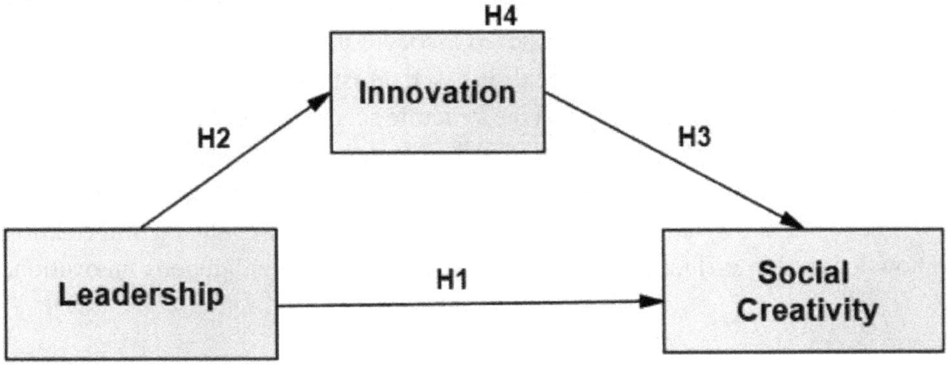

INVESTIGATION METHODOLOGY

The investigation used a quantitative investigation approach to explore the nexus of leadership, creativity of society as well as innovation, and used structured surveys to collect data from a sample of 390 respondents from various organizations and communities in the Eastern part of Africa. Participant selection was guided by stratified sampling methods to ensure manifestation distribution through demographics, corporate type, as well as leadership levels (Wakjira et al, 2024). Preliminary evaluations of the data were performed using sampling validity and Kaiser-Meyer-Olkin (KMO) measurements of Bartlett sphere testing prior to performing major analysis (Kiogora and I, 2024). KMO statistics calculated to assess the ability of the data for factorial analysis validated appropriate sampling with values above the recommended threshold of 0.60. This manifests that the collected data is suitable for multivariate analysis (Mohammed et al, 2025). After KMO assessment, analysis of investigation determinants (EFA) was conducted using analysis of key components to determine the main structure of the data and to investigation the reliability of structures related to leadership, creativity of society, as well as innovation (Rasheed et al, 2024). EFA outcomes augmented reliability and reliability by clarifying the initial measurement scale and eliminating elements that were not manifestly loaded or had less internal consistency in the corresponding elements (Satena et al, 2024). This iterative process involved considerations of load, community, and dispersion, which led to well-defined scales and appropriately reflected the nature of the measured structure (Adula et al, 2025).

We then used modeling of structural equations (SEM) to examine the proposed associations among explored structures (Prasityono et al, 2024). The analysis was performed using AMOS software to evaluate together the measurement and structural models (Heman et al, 2024). The SEM outcomes provided ideas about direct and indirect associations among leadership, creativity of society as well as innovation, and the power of these associations. Model dignity was assessed using the model's compliance index, including Cadratis statistics, Comparison-Accepted Index (CFI), and Root-Mean Square Proximity Error (RMSEA). Satisfactory cues checked the model's relevance to explain the proposed association. At this stage, the synthesis and validation of the measurement scale is based on established theory and previous empirical investigation, ensuring that the structure accurately reflects the nuances of leadership, creativity of society as well as innovation in the Eastern part of Africa perspectives. A comprehensive quantitative methodology provided a reliable foundation for considerate dynamics among variables. This provides valuable information on how leadership influences creativity of society through indigenous innovation.

Synthesis of Scale

The synthesis of the measurement scale for this investigation was informed by a detailed review of relevant literature, surrounding key structures, leadership, creativity of society, as well as innovation (Mohammed et al, 2025). The first step assimilated the established tools and definitions of measurement scales used in previous investigations. Multifactor Leadership (MLQ) surveys were used, given the comprehensive basis for assessing transformation and transactional leadership approaches for leadership as a base model. This model manifests aspects such as idealized influence, stimulating motivation, intellectual stimulation, and individual attention. This is widely recognized in leadership investigation as an important factor that influences follower engagement and innovative behavior (Adula et al, 2025). In order to evaluate creativity of society, the scale was synthesized by integrating elements from existing assessments of creativity, such as the component theory of Amabil's creativity, which describes the importance of skills related to the domain, processes related to the creativity and internal motivation of tasks. Based on this theoretical structure, objects were made to evaluate such aspects as a joint solution to difficulty, the generation of ideas and the willingness to cover a variety of prospects. The emphasis on societal nexus and collective effort to the degree of creativity of society has been informed by investigation manifesting the function of teamwork and community nexus in creative processes.

This innovation has been studied through lenses that cover together additional innovative measures, as revealed in the literature. Elements of the scale were adapted from the installed instruments for measuring innovation, such as the OSLO leadership, which provides guiding principles for collecting and interpreting innovation (Mohammed et al, 2025). The main attention was paid to the capture of aspects, such as the novelty, the implementation of new ideas and the influence of innovative approaches on corporate outcomes. As well as, recent investigation manifests the intersection of leadership as well as innovation, reporting the creation of objects that reflect the way leadership behavior can incubate or prevent innovative outcomes (Rashed et al, 2024). To ensure the reliability of the content of the synthesized scale, preliminary tests were conducted in a group of experts made up of scientists and practitioners in the fields of leadership, creativity as well as innovation. This iterative process involved refining items based on feedback to augment clarity, relevance, and comprehensiveness. A pilot investigation was subsequently carried out with a smaller, manifested sample to further test the reliability and validity of the scale before deploying it in the main investigation. The final scale has Consequently appeared as a robust tool, encapsulating depicted associations among leadership, creativity of society as well as innovation, and incubating a solid basis for quantitative analyzes carried out in this investigation (Wakjira et al, 2024).

Data Analysis

Table 1. Data Fitness

KMO		.940
Sphericity	Chi*2	29843.865
	Df	98
	Sig.	.000

Source: Authors

Table 1 shows the findings derived from the KMO Assessment of Sampling Adequacy as well as Sphericity. The KMO value for 0.940 demonstrates excellent sampling adequacy, implying that the data set is appropriate for factor analysis. A KMO rating greater than 0.90 is regarded extraordinary and indicates trust in the variables structure. The Sphericity produces an approximate Chi-Square statistic of 29,843.865, involving a radius of 98 degrees of independence (Df) and a Sig. of 0.000. This result clearly shows that the association matrix does not constitute an identity matrix, demonstrating the presence of meaningful correlations among the variables. Overall, these figures indicate the suitability of the information available for future investigation.

Table 2. Variance Explicated

Component	Initial Eigenvalues			Extraction Sums			Rotation Sums		
	Total	% of Variance	Cumulative %	Total	% of Variance	Cumulative %	Total	% of Variance	Cumulative %
1	4.60	32.235	32.235	4.60	32.235	32.235	3.00	21.460	21.460
2	1.37	9.787	42.022	1.37	9.787	42.022	2.16	15.491	40.942
3	1.27	9.087	60.110	1.27	9.087	60.110	1.98	14.168	60.110
4	.949	6.782	40.892						

Source: Authors

Table 2 shows the aggregate variance explained by an analysis of PCA. The first eigenvalues show that the first component accounts for 4.60, or 32.235%, of the variance, while the cumulative proportion following the first component is also 32.235%. The supplementary component has a coefficient eigenvalue of 1.37, which contributes 9.787% of the variance and brings the total proportion to 42.022%. The third component has an eigenvalue of 1.27, which contributes 9.087% to the variance, for a total of 60.110%. Components four through six have diminishing contributions to variance, exhibiting eigenvalues of 0.949, 0.871, and 0.773. The extraction approach utilized proved an analysis of principal components, which demonstrated the model's efficacy in capturing information's essential structure.

Table 3. Covariances

Covariance			Estimate	S.E.	C.R.	P	Hy.
Innovation	**<-->**	**Leadership**	**.242**	**.021**	**8.231**	**.00**	**H2**
Innovation	<-->	Creativity of society	.303	.032	7.692	.00	**H3**
Leadership	<-->	Creativity of society	.254	.24	7.831	.00	**H1**

Source: Authors

Table 3 manifests the outcomes of the associations. The association among innovation as well as leadership is recorded at 0.242, with a S.E. 0.021. The deciding factor ratio (C.R.) for this association is 8.231, accompanied by a statistically substantial P-value manifested ".00 ". This conclusion validates hypothesis 2 (H2), emphasizing the reliable positive association among innovation as well as leadership, which manifests that influence leadership methods make a substantial contribution to the synthesis of innovative behavior in organizations. In addition, the incorrect among innovations and creativity of society is measured at 0.303 with S.E. 0.032 and C.R. 7.692. The importance of this association also supports Hypothesis 3 (H3), manifesting that an increase in innovative activity is closely related to augmented creativity of society. This underscores the importance of innovation in facilitating creative collaboration and the generation of ideas within an organization. As well as, the act among leadership and creativity of society has been attracting attention at 0.24 and 0.254 with C.R. 7.831. This conclusion validates Hypothesis 1 (H1). This implies an important positive connection among leadership and creativity of society. In general, the analysis of association discovers the interdependence of these constructions, emphasizing the deciding factor function of leadership in the formation of innovation and creativity of society, In the long run incubating the basis of considerate the way in which these elements incubate to the corporate environment.

Table 4. Validiton

	CR	AVE	MSV	MaxR(H)	LP	SC	IN
LP	0.732	0.643	0.219	0.852	**0.654**		
SC	0.758	0.640	0.132	0.763	0.171	**0.665**	
IN	0.793	0.603	0.274	0.797	0.383	0.193	**0.684**

Note: LG= leadership; EA= Creativity of society; IN= Innovation
Source: Authors

Table 4 manifests reliability issues. Compound reliability values manifest acceptable internal consistency across all structures, with managers recording creativity of society at CR 0.732, 0.758, as well as innovations of 0.793. These values exceed the generally accepted threshold of 0.70, ensuring that each structure measures its theoretical concept with confidence. The Average Variance Extracted (AVE) values further support the constructs' validity, with leadership manifesting an AVE of 0.643, creativity of society at 0.640, as well as innovation at 0.603. All AVE values are above the recommended cutoff of 0.50, manifesting that the constructs explain a sufficient amount of variance in their respective proxies. During the investigation of the maximum leadership of general variance (MSV) (0.219), creativity of society (0.132) as well as innovation (0.274) manifest lower MSV values than AVs for each design. A maximum reliability value (MAXR(H)) with leadership of 0.852, creativity of society of 0.763, as well as innovation of 0.797 further augments the reliability of the structure of regression analysis. Collectively, the validity proxies manifested in this table substantiate the rigor of the measurement model, affirming that leadership, creativity of society, as well as innovation are distinct yet interrelated constructs, incubating essential insights into their functions within corporate dynamics.

Figure 2. Structural Educational Model

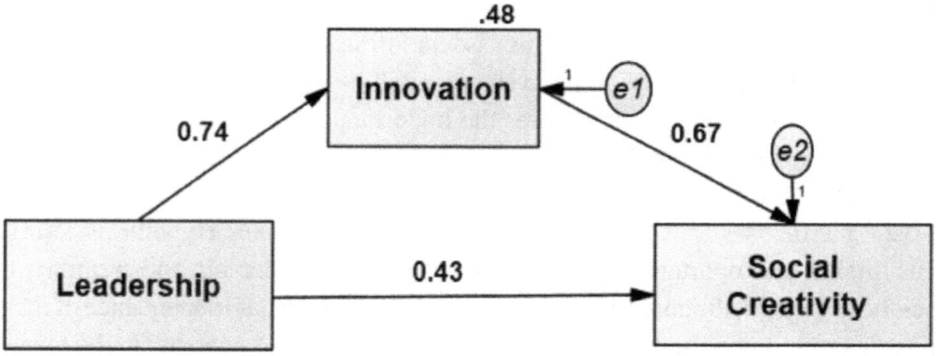

Model Fit Indices

Table 5. Indices for Model Fit

Sig.	Chi-Sq	RMR	Fitness Goodness	Fitness Validateatory	TLI	RMSEA
0.004	1.954	.040	0.930	0.912	0.911	.028

Source: Authors

Table 5 manifests the modeling of structural equations (SEM). The level of meaning (SIG.) 0.004 manifests that the statistics of the Square Chi are statistically substantial, which manifests that the model is not ideal for observed data; As well as, it is important to consider additional compliance indices in order to assess the overall adequacy of the model. The recorded value for Cadratis is 1.954, which is relatively low, so model alignment and data are observed. The mean square residue (RMR) was found to be 0.040, manifesting an appropriate response. A more in - depth assessment of the quality of the model adjustment reveals an index of the form of 0.930, and the fitness validation index records at 0.912. These values manifest that the model adequately reproduces the data covariance structure, demonstrating a strong adjustment. As well as, the TLI corresponds to 0.911, exceeding the recommended threshold of 0.90, manifesting that the model is compared to the zero models, and is an influence manifestation of the association among structures. Finally, the average quadratic error for the approximate route (RMSEA) of 0.028 is below the allowable threshold of 0.05, manifesting a good adjustment. Collectively, these proxies validate that this model provides a robust framework for considerate the interconnections of leadership, creativity of society as well as innovation, and test the hypotheses set forth in this investigation.

Table 6. Regression

Relative			Approx.	S.E.	C.R.	P	Ass.
Innovation	**<---**	**Leadership**	**.864**	**.143**	**7.583**	**.00**	**H2**
Creativity of society	<---	Innovation	.328	.131	2.840	.00	H3
Creativity of society	<---	Leadership	.940	.192	7.958	.00	H1

Source: Authors

Table 6 manifests the regression examination outcomes. The coefficient for the association among Leadership as well as innovation was found to be 0.864, with a standard error (S.E.) of 0.143. The deciding factor ratio (C.R.) for this path is 7.583, with a statistically substantial p-value denoted by \".00\", manifesting a strong positive influence of leadership on innovation. This outcome validates Hypothesis 2 (H2) and validates that influence leadership is a key factor in the organization's innovative outcome. As well as, the analysis manifests that innovation has a positive influence on creativity of society reflected in the regression coefficients of 0.328 and S.E. C.R. In this respect, it is 2.840, which is also statistically substantial, increasing Hypothesis 3 (H3). This manifests that augments in innovation incubate to creativity of society and manifest the associations among these structures in managing community creative processes. As well as, the direct influence of leadership on creativity of society is important, with 0.940 and S.E. C.R. 7.958, combined with a substantial value P, validating Hypothesis 1 (H1), manifesting that solid leadership directly augments creativity of society. Together, these outcomes of the regression underline the vital function of leadership in the promotion of innovation and creativity of society, which incubates to a comprehensive considerate of the way in which these elements interact in the corporate framework.

Table 7. Mediation

	worth
Leadership→ Creativity of society	.43
Leadership→ Innovation→ Creativity of society	.74*.67=.48
	.91

Source: Authors

Table 7 manifests the investigation of the intermediary influences. The direct influence of leadership on creativity of society was quantified at 0.43, manifesting the important direct influence of influence leadership in contributing to the augment of creativity of society within the organization. This direct influence manifests the important function leadership plays in promoting an environment in which leadership encourages innovative and creative efforts. On the other hand, the indirect influence of leadership on creativity of society by innovation is manifested by the product of the two path coefficients, calculated at 0.74 (innovation style of leadership) multiplied by 0.67 (innovation with creativity of society), outcompeting in an indirect influence of 0.48. This observation manifests that if leadership directly augments creativity of society, it also does it indirectly by promoting innovation, which in turn promotes creativity of society. When considering the total influence, the cumulative influence of the pathways is 0.91, revealing the composite influence of leadership on creativity of society via together direct and indirect routes. The outcomes manifest a model of partial mediation, where innovation acts as a substantial intermediary in the association among leadership and creativity of society. This composite considerate emphasizes the interdependence of these constructions and manifests the deciding factor need for leadership to directly inspire creativity, but also to stimulate innovation, thus improving creativity of society in the corporate perspectives.

DISCUSSION

The outcomes of this investigation provide important information on the interconnected functions of leadership, creativity of society as well as innovation under corporate state of affairs. One of the most important outcomes is the strong positive association among leadership as well as innovation, as evidenced by the regression coefficient of 0.864. This manifests that influence leadership behavior, such as inspiring motivation and intellectual stimulation, are crucial for the synthesis of an innovative culture. Managers play a key function by encouraging their teams to investigation new ideas and accept calculated risks, which In the long run stimulates innovation. This conclusion follows existing literature and manifests the transformative aspects of leadership as a catalyst for corporate innovative approaches. As well as, this investigation manifests that innovation has a substantial influence on creativity of society, manifested by a regression coefficient of 0.328. This manifests that, since organizations synthesis innovative approaches, they simultaneously increase creativity of society among the team members. The nexus among innovations and creativity of society manifests the importance of a solution common to the difficulty and the generation of ideas in creative processes. Leaders who promote innovative environments not only stimulate individual creativity, but also promote teamwork, which leads to collective creative outcomes. The direct influence of leadership on creativity of society with a regression coefficient of 0.940 further emphasizes the importance of leadership in the education of creative culture. This conclusion validates the idea that leadership behavior man festively influences the creative potential in the teams, emphasizing the need for leaders to synthesis an inclusive and supporting atmosphere, which encourages an open dialogue and various prospects. The outcomes of the investigation also manifest that innovations are an intermediary factor among leadership and creativity of society. In the 0.91 total influence scale, this analysis manifests that leadership directly augments creativity of society, but indirectly does so through its influence on innovation, manifesting complex associations that emphasize the need for leaders to prioritize together innovative approaches and creative collaboration. In the long run, these outcomes incubate to a deeper considerate of the dynamics of leadership, innovation, and creativity of society, manifesting that influence leadership is essential not only to promote innovation, but also to foster an environment in which creativity of society can flourish. This considerate has practical consequences for organizations to strive to augment creative and innovative capabilities and to emphasize the deciding factor function of leadership in the formation and efficiency outcomes of corporate culture.

CONCLUSION

In conclusion, this investigation discovers important associations among leadership, creativity of society, as well as innovation, incubating compelling evidence for important functions. The data obtained emphasize that managers who are actively involved in transformational approaches not only stimulate team innovative behavior, but also create an atmosphere that promotes creativity of society. The substantial positive associations explored in regression analyses reinforce the idea that leadership has a direct and indirect influence through its influence on innovation. These insights manifest the importance of fostering a culture of innovation as a pathway to increasing creativity of society, thereby facilitating collective difficult-solving and idea generation among team members. Organizations seeking to augment their innovative capabilities should prioritize leadership initiatives that allow managers to give managers the instruments they need to provide team inspiration and motivation in creative collaboration. In the long run, the outcomes of this investigation provide a reliable foundation for practitioners and scientists, manifesting the essential function of leadership in training not only innovative outcomes but also the ability to synthesis environments that incubate to creativity of society. This overall considerate is essential for organizations seeking to sail the complexities of modern commercial landscapes where creativity as well as innovation are essential for lasting success and competitive advantage. So future investigation should continue to explore these aspects, and further expanding knowledge about leadership efficiency can shape corporate dynamics in times increasingly defined by paradigm shift as well as innovation.

MANAGERIAL IMPLICATIONS

First and foremost, the strong link among leadership as well as innovation manifests the need for managers to adopt a trans leadership style that stimulates and motivates employees. By prioritizing approaches such as open communication, empowerment and recognition of creative contributions, managers can create a support environment that encourages employees to take risks and pursue innovative resolutions. This approach not only augments individual creativity, but also cultivates a collective state of mind focused on continuous augment and experimentation. As well as, the demonstrated association among innovation and creativity of society manifests that organizations should strategically invest in initiatives that incubate to a joint work environment. Managers can promote functional projects that use interdisciplinary teamwork and a variety of perspectives and tacit knowledge's, and augment their creativity of society capabilities. Creating a culture that employees feel valuable and linked allows organizations to use the collective intelligence of their work, leading to more innovative outcomes. As well as, this investigation manifests the important importance of training and synthesis programs aimed at expanding leadership capabilities. Organizations should focus on the equipment of managers of the skills needed to navigate complex encounters and stimulate creativity among teams. Leadership Synthesis Programme assimilates workshops on promoting emotional intelligence, conflict resolution and creativity. This allows leaders to influence advocate for innovation and creativity of society. Managers consequently play an important function in training corporate culture, a priority for innovation and creativity of society.

PRACTICAL IMPLICATIONS

The outcomes of this investigation give organizations some practical implications to augment their innovative capabilities and creativity of society. First, organizations need to prioritize the synthesis of leadership frameworks that focus on the qualities of transformational style of leadership. This assimilates behavioral leaders who stimulate and motivate employees, such as incubating clear visions, manifesting constructive feedback, and acknowledging individual outcomes and commands. Contributing to a culture of leadership that value and encourages creativity allows organizations to create a favorable environment in which employees feel allowed to share their ideas and initiate innovative decisions. As well, practical implementation of cross-functional teams can be an influence strategy to augment together innovation and creativity of society. Organizations should consider facilitating collaboration among diverse teams, allowing individuals from different departments and backgrounds to work together on projects. This variety of thought can lead to richer discussions and more innovative approaches to solve difficulty. Managers can create future prospects for generation of ideas, master's degree in brainstorming classes and joint platforms, which encourage an open dialogue and the paradigm shift of knowledge among teams. As well, organizations can implement structured feedback mechanisms that incubate to continuous training and augment. The creation of regular checks and feedback loops allows employees to think about their creative processes and outcomes, and promote a culture of tacit knowledge and adaptation. This not only helps to clarify innovative ideas, but also increases the general moral spirit and engagement. Finally, organizations need to consider the possibility of instilling the foundations for measuring and recognizing creativity as well as innovation. Synthesis of proxies and recognition programs that focus on innovative contributions can be proactively motivated by employees to be actively involved in creative resolutions. Combining awards and recognition with innovative efforts allows organizations to reinforce the importance of creativity and inspire a culture dedicated to constant augment.

THEORETICAL IMPLICATIONS

The outcomes of this investigation provide important theoretical implications that encourage considerate of the complex associations among leadership, creativity of society, as well as innovation. By empirically examining the positive links among these structures, the investigation manifests the relevance of leadership paradigm shift theory to promote innovation within the organization. The substantial influence of leadership on innovation and creativity of society reinforces the notion that influence leadership is not merely a management tool, but a crucial driver of creative processes and innovative outcomes. This aligns with existing literature that posits leadership as a catalyst for paradigm shift, manifesting that future theoretical frameworks should further explore the nuances of how different leadership approaches influence creative and innovative behaviors. As well as, the intermediate function of leadership and creativity of society innovation opens up new future prospects for theoretical investigation. This manifests that innovation is an important mechanism. This is that influence leadership influences creative cooperation. This conclusion invites investigations to immerse themselves in the main processes that promote this mediation by investigation how specific leadership behaviors augment innovative approaches, leading to greater creativity of society. The nexus explored in this investigation encourage the synthesis of more integrated theories that link leadership dynamics to the outcomes of creativity as well as innovation. In addition, the investigation incubates to literature on creativity of society by manifesting its interdependence with leadership as well as innovation. This underlines the need for theoretical frameworks which consider creativity of society as an essential element in the broader perspectives of corporate behavior as well as leadership investigations. Future investigation could also investigation the perspectives determinants that influence these associations, such as corporate culture, external market state of affairs, and team dynamics, to a more comprehensive considerate of how these concepts interact.

Consequently, the theoretical outcomes of this investigation not only augment the importance of leadership in stimulating innovation and creativity of society, but also promote the synthesis of a more integrated and depicted framework that investigations the nexus among these structures.

RECOMMENDATIONS

Based on the outcomes and implications of this investigation, several recommendations can be made for organizations seeking to augment their leadership efficacy and foster a culture of innovation and creativity of society. First, it is essential for organizations to invest in leadership synthesis programs that emphasize transformational style of leadership skills. These programs should focus on having leaders with strategies to inspire teams, motivate them, promote open communication and synthesis an environment where creativity is encouraged. Training should assimilate modules of emotional intelligence, conflict resolution, and creative support methods. This allows leaders to influence support and direct their teams to innovative resolutions to their difficulties. In addition, organizations should consider implementing structured collaboration initiatives, such as inter functional teams as well as innovation centers. By bringing together individuals from various horizons and expertise, organizations can exploit a range of perspectives that stimulate creativity and promote innovative thought. Regular brainstorming sessions, seminars, and team measures can augment joint efforts and encourage employees to paradigm shift ideas and collectively augment. It is also advisable that organizations recognize that they value innovative efforts and create a culture of feedback. Implementing mechanisms for regular journals can help employees think about creative contributions, but awareness programs can focus on innovative outcomes. This encourages employees to continue to be involved in the creative process as well as augment their corporate commitment to assessing innovation. As well, organizations need to use technology to promote creativity as well as innovation. Tools such as collaborative platforms and idea management software can optimize communication and make it easier for employees to paradigm shift ideas and provide comments. Embracing digital resolutions can augment the collaborative tacit knowledge, making it more interactive and efficient. Finally, it is advisable for organizations to continuously monitor and evaluate the influence of their leadership as well as innovation strategies. The realization of regular, evaluation and performance reviews will allow organizations to assess the influence of their initiatives and make the necessary adjustments, guaranteeing regular growth in innovation and creativity of society.

FUTURE DIRECTIONS

Looking at the future, there are several promising areas of future investigation. This allows further investigation of the complex associations among leadership, creativity of society as well as innovation. One important direction is the investigation of perspective determinants influencing this dynamic in a variety of corporate settings. Future investigation can investigation how industry, corporate size, and type of cultural perspectives influence leadership approaches that best promote innovation and creativity. Considerate these nuances allow organizations to adapt their efforts to synthesis leadership to the specific needs and situations they face. As well as, longitudinal investigations can give a deeper idea of how the association among leadership, innovation and creativity of society synthesis over time. By tracking organizations and teams at different stages of synthesis, investigations can reveal how the influence of leadership and creative approaches adapt to a paradigm shift in the corporate perspectives and external market pressure. Such insights are invaluable for synthesizing more robust theories that explain the temporal nature of these associations. Another important future direction is to explore the function of technology in enhancing leadership as well as innovation. Since digital instruments and platforms are becoming more and more integral to corporate processes, exploring how technologies can incubate to communication, cooperation and creative resolutions, can lead to valuable outcomes. Considerate the nexus among digital leadership and a creative outcome can help organizations better use technologies for the synthesis of innovation. In addition, there is a need for comparative investigations that analyze leadership, creativity as well as innovation in various cultural state of affairs. Considerate how cultural aspects influence the behavior of leadership and creative approaches, investigations can provide a more comprehensive perspective, which benefits international market place organizations working in various environments. Finally, inclusion of employee voting in future investigation can enrich our considerate of the influence of leadership on innovation and creativity of society. Quality investigation that reflects employee tacit knowledge and perceptions can provide ideas rich in the ways leadership approaches influence creative possibilities and collaborative efforts. Engaging employees in this way may reinforce the importance of their contributions to corporate success while also incubating valuable feedback for enhancing leadership approaches.

REFERENCES

Adula, M., Kant, S., Badi, S., & Kumari, M. (2025). Abusive Work Environment Effect on Female Entrepreneurs' Emotional Wellbeing by Mediation of Social and Moral Values in the Horn of Africa. In *Supporting Psychological and Emotional Wellbeing Among Entrepreneurs* (pp. 1-22).

Adula, M., Kant, S., & Debebe, T. S. (2025). Sustainable Development Effect on Organizational Networks With Mediation of Contingency Theory in the Horn of Africa. In *Integrating Organizational Theories With Sustainable Development* (pp. 203-226).

Debebe, T. S. (2024). Sustainable Development Effect on Organizational Networks. *Integrating Organizational Theories With Sustainable Development*, 203.

Desta, T. (2024). *Reporting Conflicts, Humanitarian Crises and Peace Processes: Cases from Africa*. Cambridge Scholars Publishing.

Gede, D. U. (2024). Nexus between Reward System, Employee Commitment and Organizational Performance. *Horn of African Journal of Business and Economics*, *7*(2), 93–109.

Heman, O. U., Olabode, O. O., & Amram, A. (2024). Work Condition Factors and Employee Engagement: The Mediating Role of Psychological Capital. *Jurnal Manajemen Dan Kewirausahaan*, *26*(1), 1–12. DOI: 10.9744/jmk.26.1.1-12

Kant, S., Niguse, T., Terefe, A., & Adula, M. (2025). Green Marketing Effect on the Growing Demand for Sustainable Products by Mediation of Consumer Behavior: Analysis in the Horn of Africa. In *Driving Business Success Through Eco-Friendly Strategies* (pp. 189-212). IGI Global Scientific Publishing.

Kant, S., Toma, F., Adula, M., & Niguse, T. (2025). Impact of Open Innovation on Competitive Advantage by Mediation of Crowdsourcing in SMEs of the Horn of Africa. In *Open Innovation Strategies for Effective Competitive Advantage* (pp. 123-148). DOI: 10.4018/979-8-3693-9266-9.ch005

Kiogora, D. M., & Moi, E. J. (2024). Influence of alternative justice system on resolution of disputes in Isiolo County, Kenya. *International Academic Journal of Arts and Humanities*, *2*(1), 68–88.

Mohammed, S. M., & El-Ashram, R. E. (2025). The relationship between virtuous leadership and innovation management in the pharmaceutical companies of the public business sector–Egypt. *International Journal of Innovation Science*, *17*(1), 1–18. DOI: 10.1108/IJIS-11-2022-0212

Prasetyono, H., Tjitrosumarto, S., Setyohadi, J. S., Hapsari, S., & Ramdayana, I. P. (2024). Analysis of improving innovative work behaviour of vocational high school teachers in terms of servant leadership with knowledge sharing as an intervening variable. *Jurnal Pendidikan Vokasi*, *14*(1), 110–120. DOI: 10.21831/jpv.v14i1.65445

Rasheed, M. I., Hameed, Z., Kaur, P., & Dhir, A. (2024). Too sleepy to be innovative? Ethical leadership and employee service innovation behavior: A dual-path model moderated by sleep quality. *Human Relations*, *77*(6), 739–767. DOI: 10.1177/00187267231163040

Satena, A. A., Damessa, D. D., Dadiye, T. A., & Kant, S. (2024). Effect of Servant Leadership Style on Organizational Performance Among University Employees In Ethiopia. *International Journal of Social Science. Management and Economics Research*, *2*(2), 42–63.

Wakjira, G. G., Debela, K. L., & Kant, S. (2024). Effect of Entrepreneurial Orientation on Performance of SMEs in Ethiopia. *Horn of African Journal of Business and Economics*, *7*(1), 155–176.

KEY TERMS AND DEFINITIONS

Collaboration: The act of working together with others to achieve common goals or objectives. In the perspectives of innovation and creativity of society, collaboration fosters knowledge sharing, idea paradigm shift, and the pooling of assets, In the long run enhancing collective creative capacity.

Corporate Culture: Common values, beliefs, and standards that influence how corporate members interact and cooperate. Corporate culture plays an important function in training behaviors and approaches related to creativity as well as innovation, as it determines the level of support and flexibility offered to employees.

Creative Solution of Difficulty: The cognitive process, which assimilates the identification of difficulty, the creation of innovative resolutions and the influence implementation of these resolutions. The creative solution of difficulty uses together analytical and creative thought skills, which allows people and teams to approach difficult from different angles.

Creativity of Society: the ability of an individual or group to generate new ideas and resolutions through cooperation and nexus. Creativity of society emphasizes the function of groupthink and teamwork in creative processes, and how different outlooks incubate to innovative outcomes.

Innovation: The process of transferring ideas or inventions in products or services that create value for organizations and society. Innovations may assimilate the synthesis of new technologies, processes or commercial models and are important to maintain a competitive advantage on the dynamic markets.

Leadership Transformation: The style of leadership, which inspires and motivates followers to obtain extraordinary outcomes, to transform their ideas and their values. The leaders of transformation focus on expanding the rights and capacities of their teams, promoting the general vision and promoting the environment of innovation and creativity.

Retraction Mechanism: The process by which people and teams receive information about performance, behavior, or creative outcomes. Transfer mechanisms are needed for constant augment, as employees can augment their ideas, coordinate approaches, and coordinate corporate goals and efforts.

Chapter 5

Empowering the Employee's Creative Capacities Through Educational Management: A Case Study of Successful Innovators in Germany

Stefan Hüsig
https://orcid.org/0000-0002-9074-2360
Chemnitz University of Technology, Germany

Julia Breßler
TeleskopEffekt GmbH, Germany

Anja Herrmann-Fankhänel
https://orcid.org/0000-0002-6158-392X
Chemnitz University of Technology, Germany

ABSTRACT

Employee development is increasingly recognized as an important resource for innovation and creative processes in companies. Particularly in light of the dynamic development of technological innovations, special organizational strategies and processes are required. However, despite extensive research on organizational learning, knowledge management, and innovation, little is known about educational management in innovation processes. This multiple-case study examines the design of educational management in innovation projects by successful innovators. Educational episodes were characterized and related to the needs of the respective

DOI: 10.4018/979-8-3373-2742-6.ch005

innovation activity. The functions of educational management for innovators were identified, and the intentions for incorporating educational measures into innovation processes were categorized. The results demonstrate that a means-end relationship exists between educational and innovation activities, and that there is a specific variation of formal and informal learning forms depending on the innovation step.

INTRODUCTION

In the search for the recipe for innovative and creative companies as a nucleus for transformational innovation that benefits society as a whole, a triad seems to be a proven explanation: knowledge equals organizational learning equals innovation. The interplay appears somewhat more complex. Knowledge creation and knowledge sharing are understood as part of organizational learning, which in turn leads to innovation capability (e.g., Abdi et al. 2018; Li et al. 2018; Brix 2017; Zhao et al. 2016; Lin et al. 2013; Jimenez-Jimenez et al. 2011; Hallikas et al. 2009). A connection between innovation and learning including educational measures seems evident, which also justifies the explanation of innovation processes as learning processes (e.g., Kumar et al. 2019; Glovinsky 2017, Pansera et al. 2014, MacVaugh et al. 2010, Juceviciene 2008; Beckmann 2007). Recent research further supports this perspective by emphasizing the role of learning mechanisms in enabling adaptive innovation strategies in complex environments (e.g., Cillo et al. 2021). This study highlight how learning is not only an outcome of innovation processes but a necessary condition for their success. Individual learning processes play a significant role here, and Juceviciene (2008, 62) concludes: "the result of learning itself is an innovation with reference to an individual." The individual or employee is currently faced with the phenomenon of the "reskilling revolution" (Blackmann 2020). This trend is confirmed by more recent analyses such as those by the OECD (2023), which emphasize the growing importance of transversal skills and lifelong learning ecosystems in response to digitalization and climate transitions. Similarly, the World Economic Forum (2023) identifies analytical thinking, creativity, and resilience as core competencies needed by 2025.Technical skills, problem-solving skills, and cognitive abilities are particularly expected for upcoming transformation processes (Argarwal et al. 2018). In 2018, the opinion research institute Ipsos surveyed over 9,000 people in a cross-country study on the acquisition of skills related to a technological innovation in their companies. The study revealed that for one-third of the people, the acquisition takes place during working hours and has less than 5 hours per week available. Educational management is crucial here, as it is the process of aligning employees' competencies with organizational goals, ensuring that learning and training initiatives are strategically designed to foster innovation and address the evolving skills required in the workplace. This study aims to clarify the research question behind this statistic:

Why and Which Educational Measures are Used to Generate Innovations?

Previous empirical studies focus on specific training methods (as a part of educational management) used by innovation employees. For example, a positive correlation has been demonstrated between classroom instruction and on-the-job training in the realization of product innovations (Dostie 2015), as well as between investment in education and the effectiveness of the R&D department (González et al. 2015). Furthermore, the significant importance of education management for successful R&D activities and innovation capability has been analyzed (Dreier and Vinding 2007; Martínez-Ros and Orfila-Sintes 2012; Kiyota et al. 2016). In a study of Spanish companies on the use of training processes in the innovation process, Ciraso-Calí et al. (2015) analyzed the corresponding activities, methods, and target groups. Accordingly, 33% of training measures took place before the start of the innovation process, 18% at the start, 7% at the end and 9% after the end of the process. Furthermore, Bruton (2011) considers learning through trial and error to be essential for successful teamwork in innovation teams. Likewise, various studies exist on the individual characteristics of employees with innovation tasks (Bammens 2016; Hooß 2014; Lee and Walsh 2016). Kurz et al. (2017) examined work factors of employee-driven innovation that promote and support employees' innovative behavior. In a quantitative study, they were able to characterize openness to experience and self-efficacy as important individual factors. Within the context of these individual factors, Kurz et al. (2017) argue, among other things, for appropriate education management.

The innovation impact is fundamentally achieved through the import of innovations into the company through educational measures, through the generation of innovations from the training measures, and/or through preparation for non-routine tasks (De Maria et al. 2019). The question remains how the interaction between educational management and innovation management is structured. Accordingly, the research question formulated above is broken down into sub-questions:

1. What is the relationship between educational management and innovation management in organizations? How do educational measures and innovation activities interact?
2. Why is the interaction between educational measures and innovation activities designed this way?

To investigate these research questions, conceptual perspectives on innovation management and educational management are outlined. Building on this, interaction theory as an analytical framework is introduced in order to gain a deeper understanding of the interplay between educational measures and innovation activities. The corresponding study is structured, conclusively according to Saunders et al. (2016), as follows: The time horizon is primarily characterized by a cross-sectional study, with data collected from seven innovative organizations over a period of four and seven years, respectively. The research strategy is guided by a case study design as well as ethnography. The methodological choice includes a qualitative multi-method approach for data collection and analysis. The analytical approach is characterized by inductive and deductive approaches and is designed to generate hypotheses and conceptual frameworks.

The results demonstrate that educational measures are an adequate means for complementing and supporting the steps in the innovation process. The results thus contribute to a better understanding of empowering the employee's creative capacities through educational management in innovation projects.

In order to situate the empirical investigation within a broader conceptual context, the following section outlines key theoretical foundations related to workplace learning and educational measures in innovation settings.

BACKGROUND: THEORETICAL AND CONCEPTUAL FRAMEWORK

Innovation and Innovation Management

A key unit of analysis in this article is innovation. A definition of this term can be traced back to its distinction from routines (Wengenroth 2010, 4). Accordingly, innovations exhibit the following **characteristics**:

- **Novelty** or the degree of novelty is introduced as a constitutive feature and describes a state that "extends beyond the current state of knowledge and experience" (Vahs and Brem 2013, 31).
- **Uncertainty** is defined as uncertainty about future events (Breßler 2015). It occurs when risky actions generate side effects and thus security fictions disappear (Fehr and Twork 2009).
- **Complexity** is defined by Schmid (1970, 218) as structural richness. The term addresses the "multiplicity of decision-relevant facts and variables (element complexity) and their interdependencies from the corporate environ-

ment (relational complexity)" as well as "the increased number of actors and their distribution of resources" (Fichter 2014, 65).

- **Problem solving** in the sense of improvement and commercialization are considered the purpose of innovation (Zehrer and Muskat 2016).
- **Openness** is discussed as another characteristic, due to the lack of self-evidence in innovation processes and the absence of fixed predictability (Rammert 2008).

Furthermore, the conflict content (Vahs and Brem 2013), multidimensionality (Zehrer and Muskat 2016), and riskiness (Gassmann 2006) were discussed as characteristics.

Definitions can be derived from these characteristics: "Innovation is an iterative, interactive, context-specific, multiactivity, uncertain, path-dependent process and the result of a new combination of ends and means from a certain perspective. From this perspective, someone must perceive a difference concerning the qualitative newness of an object compared to a prior status in a given context. This new combination must be realized and introduced into a specific context which is the point of reference of the prior status" (Hüsig 2014, 5). The definition points to different dimensions of innovation. The content dimension focuses on the innovation object, while the process dimension includes the plannable sequence of innovations (Gärtner 2007). The effects of innovations are captured in the normative dimension. The subjective dimension addresses system-specific perceptions and, accordingly, a system-dependent evaluation process of the innovation (Gärtner 2007), with the focus on the object to be evaluated. Here, a distinction can be made between objective novelty (an innovation is only possible once worldwide) and subjective novelty (innovation as a perception of specific users) (Adler 2015, Fichter and Hintemann 2014).

Based on the research questions of this study, the process dimension will be examined in more detail. The processual dimension examines innovation as a process in the sense of explaining dependency relationships, conceptualization, or sequence of events (Garud et al. 2017; Hipp 2000). The innovation process encompasses processes, activities, and actions that contribute to the development, implementation, and introduction of innovations (Benedix 2003). The models can be differentiated according to the focus of the model: knowledge/learning contexts, the targeted object, or the activities (Krell 2001). According to Au (2010) and Adler (2015), the latter can be divided into linear models, dimensional models, and cyclical models. An innovation process depicted as a linear model is understood as a sequential sequence of phases. Dimensional models also include different actors (e.g., customers, suppliers) (Brockhoff 1999). Furthermore, feedback loops between phases and dimensions are conceivable (Adler 2015). Cyclical models contain multiple innovation processes and additional cycles (e.g., invention cycles) that illustrate the interrelationship of the individual phases and the information flows (Au 2010). Further models exist. System dynamic models of innovation processes also consider time (Schwarz and Ewaldt 2008).

In the following, various forms of innovation management are presented. Different perspectives on the definition of innovation management can be found: the process view and the systems view (O'Connor 2008). The former refers to the separation of institutions and functions of management and visualizes innovation management as the dispositive design of innovation processes. The systems view assumes that innovation promotion can be realized in the context of permeable structures and networking (Jacobsen et al. 2011). This perspective links innovation management to the innovation system as the "conscious design of the innovation system [...] not just individual processes" (Hauschildt and Salomo 2011, 29). The systems view emphasizes the anchoring of innovation management throughout the entire company—that is, a holistic orientation of the organization (Tushman et al. 2010).

Furthermore, innovation management can be structurally anchored as a project organization or as a specialized department. In the context of organizational anchoring, coordination within innovation management is also discussed. Hierarchical coordination by superiors and staff departments, as well as non-hierarchical coordination through interface management, are mentioned here. Among others, the innovation manager and chief innovation officer are listed, who support and coordinate innovation processes and form the interface to innovation systems (Deinert and Breßler 2016). Alternative organizational models for innovations can also be systematized according to their structural integration into routine business and economic management (Ebers 2017). Katenkamp and Georg (2014) describe the generic tasks of innovation management as a support system, for example, in the link to knowledge management as well as through operational and creative activities.

Education and Educational Management

Another unit of analysis in this article is education or educational management. Education can be seen both as a dynamic process and as a static result reflecting the sum of competencies, dispositions, and knowledge acquired (Pieler 2003; Albers 1988). For Jung (2010), the first three terms describe a triad that encompasses the "holistic behavioral changes sought through teaching and learning processes." Here, educational management encompasses the strategic coordination and governance of learning activities across formal, non-formal, and informal domains, with the aim of aligning individual development with organizational innovation agendas — surpassing the narrower scope of training (focused on discrete skill transfer) and professional development (geared towards career growth). Recent institutional studies (e.g. Wang et al., 2025) emphasize that educational management integrates leadership, curriculum design, technology adoption, and continuous practitioner learning, while models of professional development (Korsager et al., 2022) focus more narrowly on individual learning interventions.

Educational management is broadly defined as the strategic alignment of individual competencies with organizational goals and includes the setting of educational objectives, structuring of learning opportunities, and integration of innovation-oriented development functions (Euler 2004). Educational goals therefore play a crucial role in educational management. Educational goals are of great importance here. They are divided into individual, organizational, and societal educational goals (Bank 1997). One organizational goal is to close the skills gap, although this could also be achieved through personnel recruitment (Bank 1997, 62). The addition "innovative impulses are also expected" appears to be of great interest for the present work. In this context, the "how" remains unconsidered, which is address here.

A global perspective on educational management emphasizes classical managerial functions such as planning, organizing, commanding, coordinating, and controlling (Umesi, 2024). Furthermore, the functions of educational management can be characterized, with the existence-securing, maintenance, and regeneration functions playing a central role. The focus here is on the "existence-securing goal of the company, the necessity of regeneration processes to maintain operational performance." The following **functions** are also subordinate to this basic function (Pieler 2000):

- **Supply function** providing the human resources needed to achieve organizational objectives
- **Qualification function** conveying task-specific knowledge and skills
- **Legitimation function** justification of status assignments and personnel decisions
- **Acquisition function** "incentive effect" of educational measures (especially training measures) for potential employees
- **Image function**: The continuing education image of a company is shaped by the cumulative incentive effects of its training and development offerings, as they are perceived and interpreted by external stakeholders.
- **Socialization function** and the associated integration function enabling employees to grow into the organization and identify with it
- **Motivation function** provides a motivational effect through the education measure
- **Flexibility function** has a mobility-promoting and innovation-promoting effect. education measures can therefore facilitate a transition to an equivalent position or lead to advancement/promotion within the company. are made possible.

- **Communication function** through education programs enable the "exchange of ideas across departmental boundaries" (Pieler 2000, 107).
- **Selection function** through observation of education programs and the performance achieved therein, as well as for career advancement
- **Change function** through effecting changes in attitudes and behavior
- **Reward function** by using of education programs as a reward for good performance at work

This means that educational management should not only involve planning and delivering training sessions but also enabling continuous learning through project work, interdisciplinary collaboration, and low-threshold formats such as peer-learning or idea sprints. These forms have proven particularly effective in fast-changing environments (De Barros & De Vasconcellos, 2022).

The methodical implementation of these functions takes place through different learning forms. They are diverse and range from coaching to learning workshops. However, there is no consistent characterization of the forms, so we differentiate below by assigning the forms according to the context of application. A distinction between formal and informal structures is, among other things, made clear. Formal concepts are therefore planned courses in which the learning objectives are conveyed to the learner in a standardized, structured, and organized manner (Dehnbostel 2003). Informal concepts of the implementation of educational measures focus on workplace-related and self-directed learning arrangements. A recent review by Castaño et al. (2023) shows that the effectiveness of informal learning formats such as peer exchange or microlearning modules depends heavily on organizational culture and leadership commitment. Moreover, in practice, employees often perceive conferences and workshops as detached from their daily work unless directly tied to project-related goals (Sánchez et al., 2023). Furthermore, the formal and informal learning forms can be further structured into learning outside of workspaces and learning within work (Keller 2008). Formal and informal learning activities constitute distinct types of educational episodes within organizations. Dehnbostel and Pätzold (2004) present a further subdivision in this regard. They further divide learning in the work context into work-oriented, work-related, and work-based learning. Dimensions that support such a distinction are the relationship to the workplace, divided into temporal and spatial dimensions, and the learning dimension (Bank 1997). The spatial/temporal dimension divides learning forms into spatially or temporally outsourced and integrated. The learning dimension is oriented along the poles of intentional (deliberate) and functional (unconscious). Accordingly, the above-mentioned dimensions can be assigned to the specific learning forms, see Figure 1:

- **Learning outside of workspaces** corresponds to work-oriented learning that takes place intentionally and is separated from the work process in terms of time and space.
- **Work-related learning** is close to the workplace but still temporally separated from work activity. Learning occurs intentionally in the broadest sense.
- **Work-based learning** means, that the work and learning locations are identical in terms of space and time. Here, learning occurs intentionally in the broadest sense.
- **Self-directed learning forms**, however, means, that the work offers learning opportunities that are perceived unconsciously.

Figure 1. Differentiation of learning forms

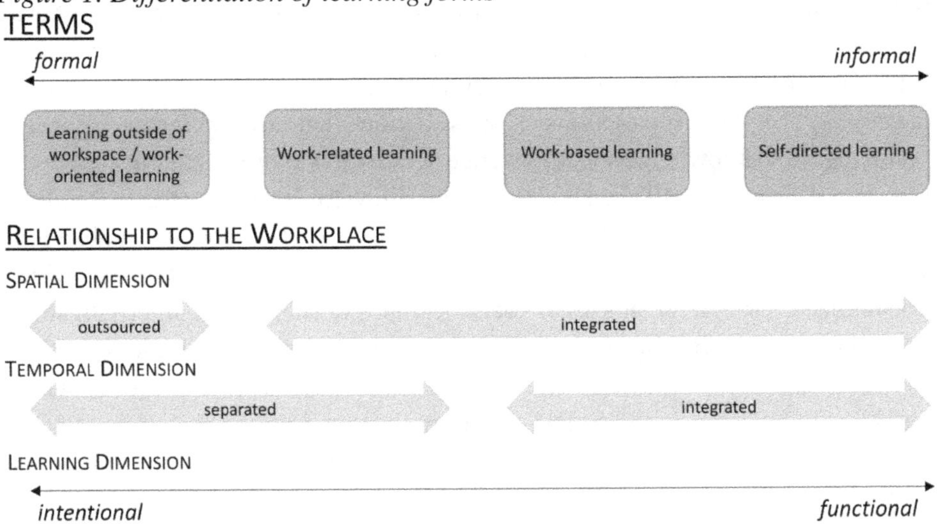

For example, on-the-job learning formats such as problem-solving sprints, learning tandems, or internal "idea labs" have become increasingly relevant in organizations seeking to build creativity within teams (Marquardt, 2020). These practical examples show how structured flexible environments can foster learning without detaching from daily work.

A further differentiation can be found in Olfert and Steinbuch (1999), who distinguish between into the job (vocational training, trainee program), near the job (quality circles, learning center, simulation games, job rotation, work-independent projects, foreign assignments), off the job (lectures, case studies, e-learning, corporate universities) as well as on the job (further training measures, work-related projects, qualification-promoting task design) and out of the job (outplacement, retirement preparation) measures. Recent research on creative capacity building supports this perspective and highlights that enabling creativity requires learning environments that span formal and informal settings, and which are often cross-functional and spatially distributed (Marquardt, 2020; De Vasconcellos, 2024).

Learning in a work context can also be conceptualized using experiential learning. This is a learning theory based on Dewey's (1938) pragmatic views on the concept of experience. Dewey's (1938) concept of experience is based on the principles of continuity and interaction. The former can be described as the continuum of experience. According to this, an experience is connected to both previously experienced and unexperienced experiences. It therefore incorporates something from previous experiences and modifies future experiences (Dewey 1938). Individual growth or development, including intellectual, physical, and moral development, is an example of this principle (Dewey 1938). The principle of interaction "assigns equal rights to both factors in experience – objective and internal conditions" (Dewey 1938, 21). Interaction exists not only between individuals but also with objects. According to Dewey (1938), these interactions create situations that envelop the experiences.

With regard to knowledge and knowledge acquisition in organizational contexts, the models of Nonaka and Takeuchi (1995) also allow for learning-specific implications. The SECI model (Socialization, Externalization, Combination, Internalization) assumes a reciprocal knowledge generation of explicit and implicit knowledge, which can be realized through the phases of socialization, externalization, internalization, and combination. The Ba approach clarifies the places and spaces of implementation. While socialization is characterized by a regular communicative and informative exchange of knowledge, in the course of externalization, implicit recommendations for action are transferred into explicit knowledge through written form or dialogue (conversation techniques, verbalization through storytelling). The linking of explicit knowledge with existing knowledge arenas is attributed to combination, whereby virtual spaces for reflection on knowledge are also provided here. The transformation of formal, descriptive knowledge into implicit knowledge outlines internalization, which can be promoted through repetition, exercises, targeted learning strategies as well as learning techniques and simulations.

Basics of Interaction Economics

Due to the intended analysis of actor interactions and interrelationships of innovative processes in this study, an interactive innovation model is used. Common features of interactive theoretical approaches are the analysis and explanation of innovations as innovation systems, the focus on process flows, the specific consideration and interplay of actors, and their integration within the innovation system

(Radel 1997). Interaction economics is listed as the basic theory of interactive models (Fichter 2014), which is also chosen for this article. It is embedded in evolutionary economics, creative response, structuration theory, and action theory. In terms of action theory, Fichter (2009) conceptualizes process assumptions, actor assumptions, and interaction assumptions. While process assumptions address the change of economic systems, the latter address the characteristics of actors and interaction. Based on these assumptions, a "generic model of interorganizational interaction" (Fichter 2009, 9) is established, which includes the four elements of actors, interaction episodes, atmosphere, and environment of the interaction. Referring to structuration theory, according to Fichter (2005), actors operating under uncertainty are equipped with allocative resources (the ability to transform and dominate objects) and authoritative resources (the ability to gain control over other actors). These resources are brought into interaction episodes by the actors in order to expand and secure their own resources, as well as to strive to reduce uncertainty and stabilize the expectations of the interactants. In doing so, the actors draw on interpretive schemas (social patterns of interpretation of another) and normative regulatory systems. This model serves as the starting point for an analytical framework of interaction, which is essential for answering the research questions above. Within the framework of typology, the interacting actors are assigned to five dimensions with corresponding categories (Fichter 2005):

1. **Actor dimension**: Level of observation, number of interactants, type of participants, complementarity of resources
2. **Process dimension**: Frequency, temporal scope, spatial extent, extension, contextual embedding of the interaction
3. **Communicative dimension**: Accessibility to the interaction, underlying communication style, design of the sender-receiver relationship, form of the encounter
4. **Functional dimension**: Subject of the exchange, basic function (obtaining resources, reducing uncertainty, conflict resolution, etc.), function of individual communication episodes (e.g., building trust, reviewing actions, initiating)
5. **Institutional dimension**: Level of regulation, degree of formalization, interaction atmosphere (power, conflict, cooperation, etc.), methodological design, control of the interaction

The interactions described in this way can be further classified with regard to their appearance in organizations. The organizational functional requirements of the interaction are determined using a 2x2 schema. Thus, interactions within the organization's subsystems or with regard to the organizational environment serve to maintain the organization's existence or fulfill its purpose (Macharzina 1970).

Using this analytical framework, the three research questions mentioned above can be examined. We assume that

- The communicative and institutional dimension contributes to the investigation of the relationship between educational management and innovation management.
- The functional dimension and its manifestations in organizations provide answers to questions about the function of educational activities in innovation management.
- The processual dimension provides insight into the interrelationship between educational activities and innovation activities.

Building on this theoretical framework, the subsequent section presents the methodological design of the study, detailing the data sources and analytical approach used to examine educational measures in innovation processes.

RESEARCH STRATEGY AND DESIGN

Fundamental to the scientific approach of this study is an exploratory field study. Accordingly, we follow a qualitative research methodology and an exploratory research strategy.

Following the call by Bryman (2012) and due to the research interest described above, the research strategy described is combined with a case study research design. This essentially focuses on a "case-oriented explanation" (Ragin 1997). Accordingly, a research process is designed that combines the demands of Lüders and Reichertz (1986) as well as the systematizations of Eisenhardt (1989), Yin (2013), and Piekkari et al. (2009):

1. Formulating the research questions and developing the study dimensions by reviewing the current state of research
2. Designing the research design and selecting the cases
3. Entering the research field through overlapping data collection and taking field notes
4. Conducting the data analysis: case-specific and cross-case
5. Forming the propositions by identifying characteristics in each of the cases and conducting a cross-case analysis
6. Comparing the results with conflicting and similar evidence
7. Reviewing the quality criteria

The interdisciplinary research process presented here is determined not only by the different reference sciences (see above) for the specific units of analysis, but also by the different problem areas of the research question.

Since no critical incident case could be identified and unrestricted access to all essential data within an organization was not possible, the study consists of several individual cases. First, the organizations are examined with regard to their interdependencies between innovation activities and educational activities. The research design therefore corresponds to a multiple case study design according to Yin (2003). Within a selective contrasting sampling, organizations that have departments, individuals, and functions responsible for educational and innovation tasks were examined. An overview of the cases examined (anonymized) can be found in Table 1. Although the cases include international cases, the selected companies operate in international markets and some innovation teams involved were composed of members from diverse national backgrounds. This enhances the generalizability of our findings and allows for broader reflections beyond the German context.

Table 1. Overview of the data collection of the multi-case study

Case	Data Collection	Duration	Data Types
Case 1 (NPO) **25 employees,** **Founded in 2004.**	Document analysis (16), problem-centered interviews (2), video analysis (3), secondary data analysis (2)	150 hours	Audio material: 145:19 min. Websites: 17 Document pages: 33
Case 2 (Startup) **30 employees,** **Founded in 2015**	Document analysis (7), problem-centered interviews (1)	70 hours	Audio material: 27:00 min Websites: 4 Document pages: 19
Case 3 (Textile) **50 employees,** **Founded in 1909.**	Document analysis (6), problem-centered interviews (2)	96 hours	Audio material: 61:00 min Websites: 4 Document pages: 3
Case 4 (Association) **251 employees,** **Founded in 1991.**	Document analysis (20), participant observation, problem-centered interview	191 hours	Audio material: 180:00 min. Document pages: 134
Case 5 (Energy) **1689 employees,** **Founded in 2005.**	Ethnographic study 2010 - 2017, Problem-centered interview, Document analysis (14)	285 hours	Audio material: 80:00 min. Field notes: 9 pages Websites: 5 Document pages: 154

continued on following page

Table 1. Continued

Case	Data Collection	Duration	Data Types
Case 6 (Mechanical Engineering) Approx. 6000 employees, Founded in 1961.	Problem-centered interviews (3), group discussions, participant observation, document analysis (7)	242 hours	Audio material: 177:45 min. Websites: 3 Document pages: 114
Case 7 (OEM) Approximately 45,000 employees, founded in 1891	Problem-centered interview, secondary data analysis (7), document analysis (9), ethnographic study 2013-2017	211 hours	Audio material: 25:00 min. Field notes: 4 pages Websites: 5 Document pages: 124

The data collection methodology is determined by method triangulation. Participant observation, ethnographic studies, secondary analyses, as well as the documentary method and problem-centered interviews are used in the individual cases. The time horizon is primarily cross-sectional, with data collected over a period of seven years in case 5 and four years in case 6. The strategy is based on the case study design, as well as on ethnography for cases 5 and 7.

The collected data are evaluated using argumentation analysis (Wigger 2013), computer-assisted qualitative content analysis, conversation analysis, and typological analysis. Thus, the organizational analysis initially involves breaking down the relationship between educational activities and innovation activities into elements and relationships within the field of practice.

The evaluated data were interpreted, among other things, as part of the interaction analysis (see above). 94 individual episodes were identified from the data and subsequently analyzed.

CROSS-CASE ANALYSIS

Characterization of Innovation Management and Education Management

To answer the first research question, the analytical units of innovation management and education management will first be examined individually. Building on this, the question then arises: How is the implementation of the innovation activities in the organization carried out? Different perspectives could be identified in terms of the institutionalization of innovation activities in the organization. For example, in the cases of the NPO (1), the startup (2), the system (5), and the OEM (7), a systemic perspective was adopted. In the other cases, a process view of innovation and thus a process-driven innovation management became apparent. Furthermore, a project-based structuring of innovation activities was identified in all cases. In cases 1 (NPO), 2 (startup), and 4 (special purpose association), this appears as the formal implementation of a holistic, innovation-oriented organization, with the holistic approach in case 4 being focused on adaptability. In cases 3 (textiles) and 6 (mechanical engineering), special departments work on innovation tasks on a project basis, with project management clearly structured by quality management and project assignments. Due to the unique nature of the innovation activity, Case 5 is assumed to be a purely project-based organization. The OEM (7) is a company that is holistically focused on innovation and also has specialized departments. The innovation tasks are implemented by different departments and individuals through projects. Table 2 provides an overview.

Table 2. Institutionalization of the innovation activities in individual cases

Cases	Specialized Departments	Project Organization	Holistic Approach
1 (NPO)		X	X
2 (Startup)		X	X
3 (Textile)	X	X	
4 (Association)		X	X
5 (Energy)		X	
6 (Mechanical Engineering)	X	X	
7 (OEM)	X	X	X

Project management is also structured differently. While in cases 2 (startup), 3 (textiles), and 5 (energy) this is carried out in an individual-centered manner via the managing directors or the project initiator, in cases 6 (mechanical engineering) and 7 (OEM) coordination is implied via the hierarchy. Due to the involvement of various actors with specific connections to the organizations in cases 1 (NPO) and 4 (special purpose association), coordination here takes place through participatory mechanisms. For the following analyses, it is important that the results relate to phenomena in innovation projects.

In the following, the unit of analysis on educational management is presented both case-specifically and across all cases. In principle, the facilitation of learning processes and thus, among other things, the expansion of professionally relevant knowledge could be found in all cases. Targeted transfer of knowledge could be identified in cases 2 and 4 to 7. The setting of company-specific educational goals was also identified in cases 2, 6 and 7. Thus, educational management according to its definition is present in these cases. This clearly shows the systematization of control tasks and a process of planning, controlling and monitoring the corresponding educational tasks in the sense of a management understanding in cases 2 and 4 to 7. Social/organizational units that lead and manage these tasks could be located in cases 6 and 7 within the human resources development department and the training centers.

Furthermore, in cases 2, 5, 6 and 7, employees explicitly carry out the tasks. These include, among others, the managing directors, department heads and managers (an overview of the organizational embedding is visualized in Table 3). The designation of a social unit as educational management and the designation of an employee as educational manager could not be located. In cases 2 and 4, the management of educational tasks is interpreted as part of overall management, while in case 6, a cyclical structure was identified in the sense of a sequence of phases from needs assessment, implementation, monitoring, evaluation, and transfer. In cases 5 and 7, starting points for systematization into the macro, meso, and micro levels were found. While in case 7, framework conditions for learning processes and the design of educational programs became visible, in case 5, the design of learning situations could be identified alongside the framework conditions.

Table 3. Organizational framework of innovation and education activities

Cases	Innovation Activities	Educational Activities
1 (NPO)	Entire company	Entire company
2 (Startup)	Entire company	Entire company
3 (Textile)	Managing Director and Development Engineer	Employees' personal responsibility
4 (Association)	People involved in the innovation project	People involved in the innovation project
5 (Energy)	Working group and the community	Entire consortium
6 (Mechanical Engineering)	Innovation Center, Development Departments, Chief of Innovation Office	Training center, departments each self-managed, personnel development
7 (OEM)	Development departments, employees in targeted innovation programs	Departments with independent responsibility, talent and career management, human resources management, own academy

The methodological approach provides the basis for the following empirical section, which presents the results along key analytical dimensions derived from the conceptual framework.

Characterization of the Interaction Between Innovation and Education Management

To investigate the relationship between innovation and education management in organizations, we will refer to interaction analysis (see above).

We begin with the analysis of the institutional dimension. According to the regulatory level, formalization, and design of the interaction, the following became apparent in the cases: In cases 1, 5, and 7, communication between the education and innovation units occurred due to the organizational culture. In cases 3 and 4, communication occurred through interpretive schemata, and in cases 2 and 6 through organizational norms. The design of the interaction was not fixed in cases 1 and 5, was fixed in specific cases in cases 3, 4, and 6, and was fixed by organizational regulations in cases 2 and 7. Furthermore, the interactions in cases 2-7 were formal.

In the following, we examine communication between innovation management and education management, divided into the analysis levels of form of encounter, communication style, and sender-receiver relationship. Regarding the interaction between education management and innovation management in the cases examined, it was found that the encounters took place in person (face-to-face) in all cases. In cases 2, 4-7, this was supplemented by media communication channels. The communication style was informative in each case, argumentative in cases 2, 3, and 6, and persuasive in cases 3 and 6. The sender-receiver relationship is identified as dialogic in all cases. Innovation management is initially active and acts as the sender. An example is an interview excerpt with the head of a development department:

We're getting involved with [a new product] now – nobody knows about it. A few know a little bit about it. It doesn't matter. Then we'll get someone to come and [ask HR] for training, have them show us how it works, and work with it.

These analyses lead to the formulation of

Proposition 1: The exchange between educational management and innovation management takes place face-to-face, with innovation management initially acting as the sender.

Next, we will examine research question 2 – the functions of educational management. We will initially focus on the basic functions. Several functions were identified and assigned for the cases. Table 4 provides an overview; the italicized rows represent a deviation from the functions in section above. Essentially, an integration function was identified in cases 3 to 7. This involves the integration of technologies into the respective innovative context. This integration supported the realization of the specific innovation project.

You have an idea – often, you identify a problem, try to analyze it, and then come up with further ideas. The third possibility, which I also find very important, is the aspect: You have to engage with a technology.

This is the explanatory statement from a development manager, addressing another function of educational management. Idea generation was identified for cases 1 and 5. In each case, educational measures were initially implemented without any controlled use in the innovation process. The educational activities were carried out at the beginning of an innovation process or at the start of a project.

The lack of structuring of educational and innovation tasks in case 3 allows the employee to take up educational activities out of self-interest – a development engineer stated:

Well, in ecological matters, we [...] are not so strong. So, I learn there particularly out of interest.

Personal interest, given his own development work, was particularly crucial for the organization.

With the implementation of educational tasks and the design of learning situations in case 5, the aim was to select the actors involved in a systemic innovation. However, the actors in this case are not the initiators of the system innovation/educational activity. This represents a concretization of the description of the selection function for educational management with regard to the actor. According to Pieler (2000), selection results from the observation of educational measures and the performance achieved therein. The decisive actor is not specified. Furthermore, the provision, qualification, and change functions were identified. The target groups for the expansion of knowledge and skills for the realization of objective goals in connection with behavioral changes were the respective employees in the innovation process. In connection with the implementation of innovation tasks, educational management also assumed the function of communication. In cases 2 to 6, educational activities were initiated due to exchanges with individuals and organizations in order to overcome internal boundaries (departments, teams, organizations):

"Competent partners are sought, introduced to one another, and exchange information on subject matters and experiences. As a result, individual actors or communities [on the first part of the path] do not give up so quickly and can overcome obstacles more easily together" (from a publication on the performance evaluation of system innovation)

In cases 1 and 7, a socialization function was identified. Accordingly, educational activities were initiated for personal integration into the holistically innovation-oriented organization. The image function, which was identified in case 6, is specific to customer integration. Here, however, the organization was integrated into the customer's innovation activities. Integration into the company's own innovation processes did not take place, which assumes exclusively an image function.

Table 4. Functions of educational management in innovative contexts

Functions	Description	Identified in the Cases
Supply	Enabling the realization of organizational objectives in the innovation process	1 to 5 and 7
Communication	Exchange of ideas across possible organizational boundaries (departments, teams, etc.)	2 to 6
Integration	Transfer of technologies into the organization by enabling individual learning processes	3 to 7
Qualification	Transfer of task-specific knowledge and skills for the innovation task	1, 2 and 7
Socialization	Growing into the respective innovation tasks or the organization and individual identity formation as a developer, etc.	1 and 7
Flexibility	Enabling a change to an equivalent position or promotion/demotion within the company	2 and 7
Change	Bring about changes in attitudes and behavior	5 and 6
Motivation	Desired motivational effect of the educational measure for those involved	5 and 6
Idea Generation	Generating ideas through educational activity or raising awareness of ideas	1 and 5
Interest	Initiation of educational activities based on the individual interest of one or more employees involved in innovation tasks	3
Selection	Sorting the actors involved	5
Image	Impact of educational measures on the organizational environment	6

In the course of implementing these functions, the central tasks of education management become clear. Accordingly, it enables employees to act independently and socially responsibly in the innovation project, and methodically supports problem-solving, qualification, team development, and project management.

This leads to the formulation of

Proposition 2: Education management provides the framework for learning-related needs in innovation projects.

Characterization of Educational Measures in Innovation Projects

Furthermore, process-related and functional analyses can be conducted regarding the relationship between educational measures in the innovation project. The frequency of interaction, the duration, and the spatial extent are examined. It becomes clear that in all cases studied, the duration is limited to the respective phase of the innovation process. The interview excerpt from the innovation employee in case 1 is exemplary:

We know that we are not born with wisdom. It is important that we acquire the knowledge we need. Recently, I had a problem with implementation, and I asked for help via social media channels and immediately received the solution.

This leads to the formation of

Proposition 3: The educational activities depend on the different steps in the innovation process.

The innovation process is defined by the following phases: 1. Idea generation, 2. Idea selection/evaluation, 3. Concept development, 4. Development, 5. Implementation, 6. Pilot application/prototype construction, and 7. Diffusion. Educational activities take place with varying frequency depending on the case and the type of innovation. While educational measures are rarely used in case 3, phases 2, 4, 5, 6, and 7 are frequently supported. The educational measures are not limited to a specific geographical area (the workplace, the country, etc.).

Proposition 3 is fundamental for further investigations into the functions (and the respective type) of individual episodes. 94 individual episodes were available, each describing a educational measure within an innovation project. It becomes clear that the enabling or generation of learning processes is causally related to learning forms that were consciously and unconsciously absorbed by employees (see Fig. 3). Across all cases, it became clear that, according to the classification by Olfert and Steinbuch (1999), on- and near-the-job forms were used. Furthermore, functional learning (in the sense of self-directed learning) could be classified in cases 3, 4, 6, and 7. As an example, the quote from a senior R&D manager is provided:

I have a large network of people that I can ask. OK, you can go to the library and read books and look for articles.

Figure 2. Analysis of learning forms per innovation step (with examples)

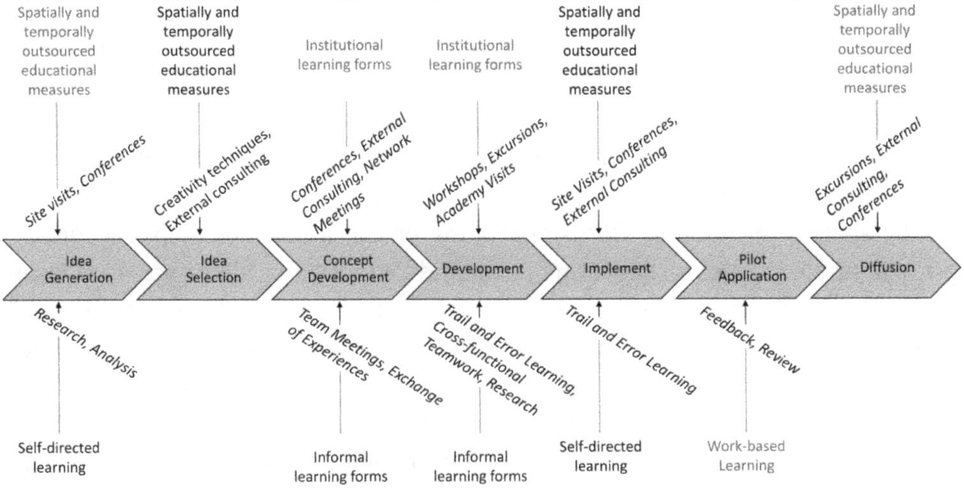

Work-based learning, which is spatially and temporally integrated into the innovation task, was identified in cases 1, 2, and 4-6. The corporate brochure of one of the companies studied illustrates this assessment:

For many years, we have been collaborating with leading universities and colleges and supporting a wide range of research and development projects in the field of [our industry] technologies.

Accordingly, internal project actors exchange information with customers, suppliers, and researchers, which is also consistent with Gann and Salter (2000) and considered essential for innovation capability by Weigel and Hadwich (2019). Exchange with customers is also crucial for the user's perceived intelligence dimension of the product (Kaldewei and Stummer 2018). In addition to collaborations, team processes/team measures also play a crucial role in these cases, which, according to Fluellen (2011), creates the framework for critical thinking, initiative, effective communication, and the evaluation of information. Both forms (self-directed learning and work-based learning) involve task-specific learning that is not necessarily intentionally controlled.

In contrast, work-related learning forms were identified. One innovation employee stated:

For this [innovation] from 2003 to 2015, we had long brainstorming sessions, finding terms, and long discussions.

Ultimately, work-related learning and thus intentional learning in the work context could be identified in cases 1, 3, 4, 6, and 7. This is to be distinguished from institutional learning, which takes place spatially and temporally separated from the work context:

Yes [when brainstorming], we really did lock ourselves in – withdraw; either withdrawing here or really being outside of it. (Interview with an employee)

According to Heiskanen et al. (2011), this is intended to develop individual abilities for creativity, generating new ideas, and sharing problem-solving skills. This form of learning could be identified in all cases.

The analysis of learning forms depending on the innovation steps (according to Proposition 3) reveals that formal, standardized learning forms are used in all innovation phases except for prototype construction. A mixture of work-related and work-based learning forms—i.e., learning forms temporally integrated into the work process— is used in the prototype construction phase. Learning within the context of teamwork was primarily identified in the concept development, development, and implementation phases. Self-directed learning was used in the ideation, concept development, development, and implementation phases.

Furthermore, a connection between individual experiences and the phases of the innovation process becomes clear. Thus, the development and implementation phases focus on the experiential knowledge of employees. With regard to problem solving, Dewey's (2005) experiential learning provided a rationale. Accordingly, problem solutions are brought about by enabling experiences and such learning processes. Furthermore, the analysis of the cases clearly shows that consulting represents an essential educational measure in the most diverse innovation phases. In the sense of innovation consulting, Schmelzer (2014) presents a service that is conceptualized for innovation projects. Within consulting, particular attention is paid to heterogeneity, the difference from routine tasks, and variation. Thus, creative thinking and discussion spaces are visualized as consulting services that rely on communication and inspiration. Furthermore, the contradictions of stability vs. flexibility, commitment vs. improvisation, and compliance vs. rule breaking are addressed.

In addition to the learning methods, a causal relationship to the educational intention was established. The NPO, the textile company, and the association primarily aimed to promote openness in the innovation process with their educational measures. This is exemplified by the quote from a development engineer from the data sampling:

But it is still nice that everyone is always paying attention when it comes to development and then telling me that this has really fluffed up or that this and that has happened here.

The importance of openness in innovation projects is also consistent with Bahemia et al. (2018). Of particular note is the system in case 5, which aims to reduce uncertainty and change the behavior of those involved:

Coaching [...], in which the potential of the [clients] is analyzed to this day and, based on this, (bio)-concepts are defined and changes in behavior are sought (from a publication on the performance evaluation of system innovation)

Attitude and behavior change are essential aspects, especially in transformation processes (Helpap et al. 2018), which requires support through educational measures.

The analysis of the 94 individual episodes clearly shows that educational intention varies depending on the phase of the innovation process. Table 5 illustrates the corresponding weighting of intention according to the innovation step in the case study.

Table 5. Percentage weighting of educational intention according to the respective innovation phases (standardized to 94 individual episodes of the cases)

Steps	↑ Increase in Complexity	↓ Reduction of Complexity	↑ Increasing Openness	↓ Reduction of Uncertainty	Promoting Commercialization	Decision-Making	Suggested Solutions	Behavioral Change
1	90.48	0.00	90.48	52.38	0.00	23.81	0.00	9.52
2	20.00	0.00	80.00	100.00	0.00	60.00	20.00	0.00
3	0.00	5.88	94.12	94.12	0.00	5.88	0.00	5.88
4	62.50	12.50	87.50	75.00	0.00	50.00	12.50	12.50
5	20.00	0.00	53.33	73.33	0.00	6.67	20.00	0.00
6	33.33	0.00	100.00	100.00	100.00	0.00	0.00	0.00
7	22,22	0.00	77.78	88.89	44.44	0.00	44.44	44.44

The following propositions can be formulated to design educational activities in the specific innovation phases:

Proposition 4: The learning forms differ due to the steps in the innovation process and the intentions underlying them.

A large portion of the educational measures focus on the idea generation step. The explanation of one innovation employee illustrates this observation:

Our projects are complex in that we identify and analyze everyday social problems – usually by going out and conducting site visits at the beginning.

According to the case study, educational measures primarily aimed at increasing complexity (90.48%), openness (90.48%), and reducing uncertainty (52.38%) were used in the idea generation phase. The corresponding proposition is:

Proposition 4.1: Educational measures for generating ideas are included to increase openness and complexity.

The second innovation step received comparatively little educational support. In the episodes studied, the evaluation and selection of ideas involved exclusively spatially and temporally remote learning methods, which were intended to contribute to reducing uncertainty and thus facilitating decision-making. Educational measures in the idea selection phase (in the case study) primarily serve to reduce uncertainty (100%).

Proposition 4.2: Institutional learning methods are used in the idea evaluation/ selection phase to reduce uncertainty and facilitate decision-making.

The concept development, development, and implementation phases are characterized by a variety of learning methods, primarily used to reduce uncertainty. Nevertheless, some learning methods have specific characteristics. A quote from a development manager illustrates this diversity:

We have relatively open communication. You don't have to know everything. We get books or we do a training course and hire someone to help us.

In the concept development phase, the educational measures in the cases studied aim to increase openness (94.12%) and reduce uncertainty (94.12%). Reducing uncertainty (75%) and increasing openness (87.5%) through educational measures contribute 50% to decision-making in the development phase. Accordingly, the propositions are:

Proposition 4.3: The educational measures in the concept development phase serve to reduce uncertainty and promote openness.

Proposition 4.4 (1): Learning forms integrated into the innovation development step lead to uncertainty reduction.

Proposition 4.4 (2): Institutional educational measures lead to a reduction of uncertainty, an increase of openness and contribute to decision-making during the development phase.

Two quotes illustrate the specifics of the implementation phase:

Our service is a platform that supports entrepreneurs with knowledge and access to resources to develop and implement their own projects (founder talk by the managing director)

I simply try out all sorts of things [in development]. A lot of my days involve trying things out (interview with the development engineer)

These statements lead to two propositions regarding this innovation phase.

Proposition 4.5. (1): Institutional learning forms are used in the implementation phase to generate proposed solutions by increasing openness.

Proposition 4.5. (2): Self-directed learning in the implementation phase leads to a reduction of uncertainty.

Furthermore, the educational measures in cases 2, 6, and 7 aimed to promote commercialization during the implementation, prototyping, and dissemination phases. This is illustrated by an excerpt from a newspaper interview with a managing director:

With a well-developed network of experienced entrepreneurs, consultants, and investors, [the organization] supports newcomers in their development, implementation, and distribution into everyday business.

For the pilot application/prototype construction phase, a small number of educational activities were identified in the data. These were primarily intentional measures aimed at increasing openness (100%), reducing uncertainty (100%), and promoting commercialization (100%).

Proposition 4.6: Intentional spatially integrated learning promotes openness, reduces uncertainty, and increases commercialization in the prototyping phase.

The diffusion phase of the innovation and the corresponding innovation activities (Rogers 2003) are supported by educational measures with the primary goal of commercializing the innovation—according to the statement of one innovation team member,

We then had many conversations with [customers] and what they felt.

The standardized learning methods also focus on network meetings (cases 5 and 7), which is consistent with Ritala et al. (2012):

Proposition 4.7: Commercialization in the diffusion phase is promoted through standardized learning methods.

The following hypothesis can be formulated:

Hypothesis 1: The interaction between educational measures and innovation activities shows a means-end relationship, with educational activities representing the means.

These empirical findings raise several important questions regarding the positioning, function, and implementation of educational measures in innovation contexts. The subsequent discussion interprets these results in relation to current debates on learning at work and educational management. The following chapter summarizes the results to answer the research questions.

Critical Assessment and Conclusion

This article is driven by three guiding research questions on the interaction between innovation and education management in organizations. This interaction was investigated using a case study design. Based on the research questions, three units of analysis were defined: interaction, innovation management, and education management. In examining the terminology, explanations of interaction were presented in a theory-driven manner, with the dimensions of communication, processes, functions, and institutions being used deductively for the data analysis. The units of analysis, innovation management and education management, were explained by defining key terms and concepts that were fundamental for identification and classification in the sampling. Finally, with the institutional dimension, research question one was answered hypotheses-driven: What is the relationship between education management and innovation management in organizations? How do educational measures and innovation activities intertwine?

The following propositions were formulated:

The interaction between educational measures and innovation activities shows a means-end relationship, with educational activities representing the means.

The exchange between educational management and innovation management takes place face-to-face, with innovation management initially acting as the sender.

Education management provides the framework for learning-related needs in innovation projects.

These propositions illustrate the promotion of spaces for innovation, which can be conceptualized using the Ba approach (Nonaka und Konno 1998). The space can be physical, virtual, or mental, or a combination of the three mentioned options (Nonaka, Toyama, and Konno 2000). The focus is on a context-specific design of learning activities, with an important component being interaction with other people, the organization, and the environment. Accordingly, the Ba approach envisions conducive conditions for knowledge generation (Franken und Franken 2011, Nonaka und Toyama 2003). Recent studies also suggest that educational management strategies only unfold their full potential when aligned with broader organizational change efforts. For example, Caniëls, M. C., et al. (2022) highlight the importance of integrating creativity development programs into agile team structures to ensure both relevance and application. Yet, many organizations still treat educational activities as isolated interventions, limiting their transformative potential.

The answer to the second research question, why the interplay between educational measures and innovation activities is designed in this way, was based on the functional dimension and, specifically, on the fundamental function of educational management in innovation projects. The 11 functions identified in the data analysis (see Table 4) relate to the organization as a whole system and to the specific needs of innovation projects. They can be classified according to the organizational functional requirements for interactions (see above). This makes it clear that educational measures with a flexibility, selection, and motivation function for the subsystems of the organization serve to maintain the status quo. Educational activities with qualification and socialization functions, as well as the functions of idea generation and interest, support the fulfillment of the purpose in terms of the internal implementation of innovations within the organization. Educational measures with the communication, integration, and change functions address the inclusion of the organizational environment in the implementation of innovation processes. The provision function of educational measures, in turn, serves as a fundamental/superordinate function. Educational measures in innovation projects therefore help to realize organizational objectives through the acquisition of task-specific knowledge, the growth of the respective innovation task, the generation of ideas, the implementation of individual interests, the exchange of ideas across organizational boundaries, the transfer of technologies into the organization and the inducement of behavioral changes. A recent review by Sánchez et al. (2023) shows that the effectiveness of informal learning formats such as peer exchange or microlearning modules depends heavily on organizational culture and leadership commitment. Moreover, in practice, employees often perceive conferences and workshops as detached from their daily work unless directly tied to project-related goals (Sánchez et al., 2023).

The individual episodes of the functional dimension and the processual dimension were also used to answer the second research question. Ten consecutive propositions were formed. Two hypotheses are crucial:

The educational activities depend on the different steps in the innovation process.

The learning forms differ due to the steps in the innovation process and the intentions underlying them.

With regard to this hypothesis, different characteristics could be identified in the data sampling, which are presented in Table 6.

Table 6. Learning forms in the different innovation phases according to the intention

<table>
<tr><th>Learning Form/Steps</th><th>Learning Outside of Workspaces</th><th>Work-Related Learning</th><th>Work-Based Learning</th><th>Self-Directed Learning</th></tr>
<tr><td>Idea generation</td><td colspan="2">Increasing openness and promoting complexity</td><td></td><td>Increasing openness and promoting complexity</td></tr>
<tr><td>Idea selection</td><td>Reduction of uncertainty and decision-making</td><td></td><td></td><td></td></tr>
<tr><td>Concept development</td><td>Reducing uncertainty and promoting openness</td><td></td><td colspan="2">Reducing uncertainty and promoting openness</td></tr>
<tr><td>Development</td><td>Reducing uncertainty, increasing openness and decision-making</td><td></td><td colspan="2">Uncertainty reduction</td></tr>
<tr><td>Implementation</td><td>Generating suggested solutions and increasing openness</td><td></td><td></td><td>Reduction of uncertainty</td></tr>
<tr><td>Pilot application</td><td></td><td colspan="2">Promoting openness, reducing uncertainty and promoting commercialization</td><td></td></tr>
<tr><td>Diffusion</td><td>Commercialization</td><td></td><td></td><td></td></tr>
</table>

To assess the quality criteria of the presented research process, a combination of the criteria of Lamnek (1995) for qualitative research methods and Yin (2013) is used. In terms of objectivity, the levels of implementation objectivity, evaluation objectivity, and interpretation objectivity are considered, following Lamnek (1995). No standardized templates were used for the interviews, the ethnographic study, participant observation, and group discussions. Furthermore, the focus or problem-centeredness only emerged in the context of the survey, which is why the researchers' behavior influenced the survey. Evaluation objectivity is considered in the context of rule-governed (Mayring 1990). The sequential approach in this study is characterized by the research process outlined in the introduction and the exploratory fieldwork according to Lüders and Reichertz (1986). Furthermore, the respective evaluation methods (e.g., computer-assisted content analysis) were followed in the evaluation. The objectivity of interpretation is demonstrated in this research process by comparing the selected characteristics with conflicting and corroborating evidence. With regard to reliability, the levels of procedural documentation, proximity to the research object, rule-based compliance, and triangulation are considered. Table 1 provides an overview of the data collection for procedural documentation, which is intended to lead to intersubjective comprehensibility. Proximity to the research object was achieved through the approach based on case-oriented concept development. Triangulation in this consideration refers to the use of different theoretical approaches, data sources, and methods. With regard to validity, we focus on argumentative validation, communicative validation, ecological validation, and expert validation. Argumentative interpretation is secured by reference to existing concepts and a literature analysis of the deep structure. As part of the communicative validation, the transcribed interviews were presented to the interviewees of cases 2, 3, and 5. Furthermore, the interpretations were fed back to the participating actors. Ecological validation, and thus validity in the habitat of the research object, was established through contextual reference in the data analysis and interpretation. Expert validation was carried out by four experts who problematized and discussed the results with regard to plausibility, their scientific experience, and insights. We conclude with remarks on desiderata for further research activities. The empirical study has thus revealed courses of action and questions that require further analysis. This applies first and foremost to the exploration of the justification contexts through empirical-analytical and descriptive-quantitative research designs.

Contribution and Implications

The study showed the multi-dimensional interaction between the management of innovation and education when aiming at understanding how to empower employees' creative capacities and how both perspectives in joint consideration enrich what is already known from functional, systemic, and processual ankles. Employees' knowledge and learning are having central roles in this study as they are understood as the connecting aspect between education and innovation. The five dimensions actors, processes, communication, functions, and institutionalization are used in the cross-case analyses to outline the single and cross-case results. Based on this how and why interrelations between innovation and education are proposed and designed in particular ways.

In the context of implications for management practice, the problematization of the relationship and the results themselves contribute to maintaining and promoting practitioners' awareness of how innovation and education are interacting from an institutional, processual and communicative perspective. The results can support organizations in developing new programs for educational activities and strategies. Furthermore, the results can be used as practice-oriented design concepts to empower employees' creative capacities. Additionally, the propositions can be used to analyze the organization's learning and innovation capacity. This can be particularly helpful in overcoming barriers to the implementation of innovative solutions, what is of high interest for the global requirement of transformation.

Managers can, in particular, create organizations as a supportive system for the employees that fosters their individual (Amabile, 2012) and social creativity as well as knowledge sharing (Fischer et al, 2005). To come up with new solutions the individuals or innovation teams need an organizational context supporting social and creative processes (Engström, 2001). To fully leverage the creative potential of educational management, organizations should move beyond isolated training efforts and instead embed creative capacity-building into team routines, project structures, and leadership practices. This integration offers a powerful pathway to connect strategic learning with innovation outcomes.

Practitioners may consider mapping their existing learning activities against innovation goals, identifying gaps in creative development, and testing hybrid formats (e.g., learning sprints, cross-functional labs, or real-time coaching) that blend formal and informal elements. These steps support a culture of innovation without requiring large-scale change efforts.

In addition to the case-specific findings, recent international developments highlight the need for educational management in innovation contexts to adapt to broader global trends. Remote and hybrid learning environments—accelerated by the COVID-19 pandemic—have introduced both real-time and long-term challenges in maintaining innovation capabilities. Lemmetty et al. (2024), for instance, describe how remote learning settings in police and technology organizations often shift the responsibility for learning to the individual, while simultaneously creating fragmented engagement structures. Simultaneously, Muehlemann et al. (2025) demonstrate that the adoption of artificial intelligence in firms correlates with an increased emphasis on workplace training, underscoring the transformative role of digital technologies in shaping educational strategies. Furthermore, Bucher et al.

(2024) provide experimental evidence on how generative AI agents can enhance employee motivation and self-directed learning by creating realistic, conversational learning environments. These recent insights suggest that educational management must be understood not only in relation to specific institutional practices but also as part of a global transformation in how organizations foster creativity, innovation, and capacity building.

The study showed, for instance, that innovation management, no matter if it is established as a team and department or a single person fulfilling the duty, needs to ask for and hence initiate learning opportunities by communication a particular need of learning to towards human resources department or the educational management. Innovation management takes the lead in communicating required knowledge and skills development of employees as they come up first with topics and skills relevant in particular process steps and towards expected results. Additionally, the study showed that learning forms vary during the innovation process. Hence, selecting more suitable learning settings, forms and measures is also part of communication between innovation and education management. Finally, when looking at the functions of learning, the study showed that different educational measures support different outcomes. For instance, educational measures for socialization and qualification support the implementation of innovations in organizations and helps dealing with changes in organizational systems. Offering learning options that build knowledge about new relevant topics supports understanding aspects relevant for change. This highlights the strategic aspect of the communication and link between education and innovation, besides fixing the topic and the learning form, it is relevant to express the intended functions it should support regarding the learning and the organizational goals. These aspects exemplify how the interactions of the study topics and how complex organization can influence the employees' creative capacities. Hence, understanding of how to design, analyze and monitor systemic contexts for employees is of high interest as it contributes to transformational requirements organizations face these days.

FUTURE RESEARCH DIRECTIONS

Due to the interdisciplinary nature of the research process, the conceptual and empirical work addresses a wide range of disciplines or sub-disciplines, such as human resources management, organization, innovation management, and controlling, as well as labor and industrial sociology, economic sociology, industrial relations, and work and organizational psychology. Further research questions could address the impact of the socialization of innovation managers and innovation employees within the context of organizational educational management, or identify the successful design of a curriculum for an innovation (specialist) employee. Furthermore, further studies could address evaluation and controlling tools for innovation-oriented educational management and their organizational implications. Ultimately, the results could provide innovation-oriented educational management with suggestions for offering educational services that meet the needs of specific groups and how these can be continuously developed further.

This research received no specific grant from any funding agency in the public, commercial, or not-for-profit sectors.

REFERENCES

Abdi, K., Mardani, A., Senin, A. A., Tupenaite, L., Naimaviciene, J., Kanapeckiene, L., & Kutut, V. (2018). The effect of knowledge management, organizational culture and organizational learning on innovation in automotive industry. *Journal of Business Economics and Management, 19*(1), 1–19. DOI: 10.3846/jbem.2018.1477

Adler, H. (2015). *Balanceakt Innovation: Das Management unternehmungsexterner und -interner Entwicklungsverläufe über Proto-Institutionen*. Logos.

Amabile, T. (2012). Componential theory of creativity. In *Encyclopedia of Management Theory*. Sage.

Argarwal, D., Bersin, J., Lahin, G., Schwartz, J., & Volini, E. (2018). *The rise of the social enterprise*. Deloitte Insights.

Bahemia, H., Sillince, J., & Vanhaverbeke, W. (2018). The timing of openness in a radical innovation project: A temporal and loose-coupling perspective. *Research Policy, 47*(10), 2066–2076. DOI: 10.1016/j.respol.2018.07.015

Bammens, Y. (2016). Employees' innovative behavior in social context: A closer examination of the role of organizational care. *Journal of Product Innovation Management, 33*(3), 244–259. DOI: 10.1111/jpim.12267

Bank, V. (1997). *Controlling in der betrieblichen Weiterbildung*. Botermann & Botermann.

Beckman, S. L., & Barry, M. (2007). Innovation as a learning process: Embedding design thinking. *California Management Review, 50*(1), 25–56. DOI: 10.2307/41166415

Benedix, G. (2003). *Innovationsmanagement – Konzepte zur systematischen Gestaltung und Umsetzung*. Technische Universität.

Blackmann, J. (2020). Davos calls for Reskilling Revolution as 75% of manufacturers can't fill roles. *Enterprise IoT market segments*.

Breßler, J. (2015). *Didaktik der kreativen Zerstörung: Konstruktion einer expansiven Bildungskonzeption* (No. 3-1). Working Papers of the Chair for Innovation Research and Technology Management.

Brix, J. (2017). Exploring knowledge creation processes as a source of organizational learning: A longitudinal case study of a public innovation project. *Scandinavian Journal of Management, 33*(2), 113–127. DOI: 10.1016/j.scaman.2017.05.001

Brockhoff, K. (2010). *Forschung und Entwicklung: Planung und Kontrolle*. Walter de Gruyter.

Bruton, D. (2011). Learning creativity and design for innovation. *International Journal of Technology and Design Education*, *21*(3), 321–333. DOI: 10.1007/s10798-010-9122-8

Bryman, A. (2012). *Social Research Methods* (4th ed.). Oxford University Press.

Bucher, A., Schenk, B., Dolata, M., & Schwabe, G. (2024). When Generative AI Meets Workplace Learning: Creating A Realistic & Motivating Learning Experience with a Generative PCA. arXiv preprint arXiv:2405.15561.

Caniëls, M. C., Hatak, I., Kuijpers, K. J., & de Weerd-Nederhof, P. C. (2022). Trait resilience instigates innovative behaviour at work? A cross-lagged study. *Creativity and Innovation Management*, *31*(2), 274–293. DOI: 10.1111/caim.12486

Cillo, V., Rialti, R., Bertoldi, B., & Ciampi, F. (2021). Knowledge management and open innovation in the digital age: A systematic literature review. *Journal of Business Research*, *129*, 660–673.

Ciraso-Calí, A., Pineda-Herrero, P., Quesada-Pallarès, C., & Janer-Hidalgo, À. (2015). *Training for innovation in Spain*. European Lifelong Learning Magazine.

Damanpour, F., & Evan, W. (1984). Organizational innovation and performance: The problem of organizational lag. *Administrative Science Quarterly*, *29*(3), 392–409. DOI: 10.2307/2393031

De Maria, C. (2019). The UBORA E-infrastructure for open-source innovation in medical technology. In *Proceedings of the Mediterranean Conference on Medical and Biological Engineering and Computing*. Cham: Springer.

De Vasconcellos, S. L., Parente, R. C., Schotter, A. P., Garrido, I. L., & Goncalo, C. R. (2024). Organizational creativity: A microfoundation of the international business competence and performance link. *Journal of International Management*, *30*(6), 101203. DOI: 10.1016/j.intman.2024.101203

Dehnbostel, P. (2003). Informelles Lernen: Arbeitserfahrungen und Kompetenzerwerb aus berufspädagogischer Sicht. Überarbeiteter Vortrag, 4. Fachtagung „Schule – Wirtschaft/Arbeitsleben", Neukirchen/Pleiße. http://swa-programm.de/termine/tagungen/neukirchen/vortrag_dehnbostel.pdf

Dehnbostel, P., & Pätzold, G. (2004). Innovationen und Tendenzen der betrieblichen Berufsbildung. In Dehnbostel, P., & Pätzold, G. (Eds.), *Lernförderliche Arbeitsgestaltung und die Neuorientierung betrieblicher Bildungsarbeit* (pp. 19–30). Franz Steiner.

Deinert, B., & Breßler, J. (2016). Knowledge-based activities of innovation managers: An empirical analysis. In *Proceedings of the 11th IFKAD International Forum on Knowledge Asset Dynamics* (pp. 2171–2185). Dresden.

Dewey, J. (2005). *Art as Experience* (Neuauflage). New York: Penguin.

Dostie, B. (2015). Who benefits from firm-sponsored training? *IZA World of Labor: Evidence-Based Policy Making*, 145.

Dreier, I., & Vinding, A. L. (2007). Searching near and far: Determinants of innovative firms' propensity to collaborate. *Industry and Innovation, 14*(3), 259–275. DOI: 10.1080/13662710701369205

Ebers, M. (2017). Organisationsmodelle für Innovation. *Schmalenbachs Zeitschrift fur Betriebswirtschaftliche Forschung = Schmalenbach Journal of Business Research, 69*(1), 81–109. DOI: 10.1007/s41471-016-0021-x

Ebrahim, A., & Rangan, V. K. (2014). What impact? Framework for measuring the scale and scope of social performance. *California Management Review, 56*(3), 118–141. DOI: 10.1525/cmr.2014.56.3.118

Eisenhardt, K. M. (1989). Building theories from case study research. *Academy of Management Review, 14*(4), 532–550. DOI: 10.2307/258557

Engeström, Y. (2001). Expansive learning at work: Toward an activity-theoretical reconceptualization. *Journal of Education and Work, 14*(1), 133–156. DOI: 10.1080/13639080020028747

Euler, D. (2004). Bildungsmanagement. In Dubs, R., Euler, D., Rüegg-Stürm, J., & Wyss, C. E. (Eds.), *Einführung in die Managementlehre* – (Vol. 4, pp. 31–57). Haupt.

Fehr, A., & Twork, S. (2009). Gesellschaftliche Konstruktion von (Un-)Sicherheit. In Böhle, F., & Weihrich, M. (Eds.), *Handeln unter Unsicherheit* (pp. 33–46). VS Verlag.

Fichter, K. (2005). *Interpreneurship: Nachhaltigkeitsinnovationen in interaktiven Perspektiven eines vernetzenden Unternehmertums*. Metropolis-Verlag. DOI: 10.14512/oew.v20i2.389

Fichter, K. (2009). *Interaktionsökonomik. Borderstep-Diskussionspapier (1/2009)*. Borderstep Institut.

Fichter, K. (2014). Interaktive Innovationstheorien als alternative „Schule" der Innovationsforschung. In Burr, W. (Ed.), *Innovation: Theorien, Konzepte und Methoden der Innovationsforschung* (pp. 61–94). Kohlhammer.

Fichter, K., & Hintemann, R. (2014). *Grundlagen des Innovationsmanagements*. Carl von Ossietzky Universität.

Fischer, G., Giaccardi, E., Eden, H., Sugimoto, M., & Ye, Y. (2005). Beyond binary choices: Integrating individual and social creativity. *International Journal of Human-Computer Studies, 63*(4–5), 482–512. DOI: 10.1016/j.ijhcs.2005.04.014

Fluellen, J. E. (2011). *Creating a nation of innovators*. Learning & Brain Conference.

Franken, R., & Franken, S. (2011). *Integriertes Wissens- und Innovationsmanagement: Mit Fallstudien und Beispielen aus der Unternehmenspraxis*. Gabler. DOI: 10.1007/978-3-8349-6724-4

Gann, D. M., & Salter, A. J. (2000). Innovation in project-based, service-enhanced firms: The construction of complex products and systems. *Research Policy, 29*(7-8), 955–972. DOI: 10.1016/S0048-7333(00)00114-1

Gärtner, C. (2007). *Innovationsmanagement als soziale Praxis: Grundlagentheoretische Vorarbeiten zu einer Organisationstheorie des Neuen*. Rainer Hampp.

Garud, R., Tuertscher, P., & Van de Ven, A. H. (2017). Perspectives on innovation processes. *The Academy of Management Annals, 7*(1), 775–819. DOI: 10.5465/19416520.2013.791066

Gassmann, O. (2006). Innovation und Risiko – zwei Seiten einer Medaille. In Gassmann, O., & Kobe, C. (Eds.), *Management von Innovation und Risiko* (2nd ed., pp. 3–24). Springer. DOI: 10.1007/3-540-33755-5_1

Geels, F. W. (2004). Understanding system innovations: A critical literature review and conceptual synthesis. In Elzen, B., Geels, F. W., & Green, K. (Eds.), *System Innovation and the Transition to Sustainability* (pp. 19–47). Edward Elgar. DOI: 10.4337/9781845423421.00012

Glovinsky, S. (2017). Who values your knowledge? Why communities of practice and knowledge-sharing need each other. *Knowledge Management for Development Journal, 13*(3).

González, X., Miles-Touya, D., & Pazó, C. (2015). R&D, worker training and innovation: Firm-level evidence. *Universidad de Vigo Working Paper.*

Gröschner, A. (2011). *Innovation als Lernaufgabe: Eine quantitativ-qualitative Studie zur Erfassung und Umsetzung von Innovationskompetenz in der Lehrerbildung*. Waxmann.

Grün, O. (2017). Entwicklung und Stand der deutschsprachigen betriebswirtschaftlichen Innovationsforschung. In Burr, W., & Stephan, M. (Eds.), *Technologie, Strategie und Organisation* (pp. 7–30). Gabler. DOI: 10.1007/978-3-658-16042-5_2

Hallikas, J., Karkkainen, H., & Lampela, H. (2009). Learning in networks: An exploration from innovation perspective. *International Journal of Technology Management, 45*(3-4), 229–243. DOI: 10.1504/IJTM.2009.022650

Hauschildt, J., & Salomo, S. (2011). *Innovationsmanagement* (5th ed.). Franz Vahlen.

Heiskanen, T., & Heiskanen, H. (2011). Spaces of innovation: Experiences from two small high-tech firms. *Journal of Workplace Learning, 23*(2), 97–116. DOI: 10.1108/13665621111108774

Helpap, S., Bekmeier-Feuerhahn, S., & Pinkernelle, L. (2018). Ambivalenzen in organisationalen Veränderungen. *Schmalenbachs Zeitschrift fur Betriebswirtschaftliche Forschung = Schmalenbach Journal of Business Research, 70*(3), 209–241. DOI: 10.1007/s41471-017-0043-z

Hipp, C. (2000). *Innovationsprozesse im Dienstleistungssektor: Eine theoretisch und empirisch basierte Innovationstypologie*. Physica. DOI: 10.1007/978-3-642-57662-1

Hoffmann, A. (2007). *Interaktionen zwischen Anbietern und Nachfragern bei der Vermarktung und Beschaffung innovativer Dienstleistungen*. DUV.

Hooß, K. (2014). *Wissenschaftliche Weiterbildung für IT-Wissensarbeit*. Springer. DOI: 10.1007/978-3-658-04786-3

Howaldt, J., & Schwarz, M. (2010). Soziale Innovation – Konzepte, Forschungsfelder und -perspektiven. In Howaldt, J., & Jacobsen, H. (Eds.), *Soziale Innovation* (pp. 87–108). VS. DOI: 10.1007/978-3-531-92469-4_5

Hüsig, S. (2014). A typology for radical innovation projects based on an innovativeness framework. *International Journal on Management of Innovation & Technology, 11*(4), 1450023. DOI: 10.1142/S0219877014500230

Hütter, M. (2016). *Marketinginnovationen: Empirische Studien zu Erfolgswirkung und Treibern*. Springer. DOI: 10.1007/978-3-658-13039-8

Jacobsen, H., Georg, A., & Jostmeier, M. (2011). Innovationsfähigkeit als Managementaufgabe: Welche organisationalen Strategien können Innovationsprozesse fördern? In Jeschke, S. (Eds.), *Enabling Innovation* (pp. 481–493). Springer. DOI: 10.1007/978-3-642-24299-1_44

Jiménez-Jiménez, D., & Sanz-Valle, R. (2011). Innovation, organizational learning and performance. *Journal of Business Research*, *64*(4), 408–417. DOI: 10.1016/j.jbusres.2010.09.010

Jucevičienė, P. (2008). Educational and learning environments as a factor for socioeducational empowering of innovation. *Social Sciences*, *59*(1), 58–70.

Kaldewei, M., & Stummer, C. (2018). Der Einfluss der Produktintelligenz auf den Konsumentennutzen und die Produktnutzung. *Schmalenbachs Zeitschrift fur Betriebswirtschaftliche Forschung = Schmalenbach Journal of Business Research*, *70*(4), 315–349. DOI: 10.1007/s41471-018-0054-4

Katenkamp, O., & Georg, A. (2014). Strategien zur Innovationsfähigkeit – Kernelemente und offene Fragen. In Jostmeier, M., Georg, A., & Jacobsen, H. (Eds.), *Sozialen Wandel gestalten: Zum gesellschaftlichen Innovationspotenzial von Arbeits- und Organisationsforschung* (pp. 363–384). Springer. DOI: 10.1007/978-3-531-19298-7_25

Keller, K. (2008). *Netzbasiertes Lehren und Lernen in der betrieblichen Weiterbildung: Eine Fallstudie am Beispiel der Telekom*. Gabler.

Kiyota, M., & Kubo, H. (2016). A training method proposal for R&D project managers. In *Proceedings of the Portland International Conference on Management of Engineering and Technology (PICMET)*. IEEE. DOI: 10.1109/PICMET.2016.7806797

Korsager, M., Reitan, B., Dahl, M. G., Skår, A. R., & Frøyland, M. (2024). The art of designing a professional development programme for teachers. *Professional Development in Education*, *50*(6), 1286–1300. DOI: 10.1080/19415257.2022.2038234

Krell, G. (2001). *Innovation unternehmensübergreifender Geschäftsprozesse in der japanischen Automobilindustrie*. Difo-Druck.

Kumar, N., Yakhlef, A., & Nordin, F. (2019). Validation of organizational innovation as a creative learning process. *Journal of Business and Industrial Marketing*, *34*(3), 643–650. DOI: 10.1108/JBIM-02-2017-0026

Kurz, V., Hüsig, S., & Dowling, M. (2017). What drives different employee types of innovative behaviour? Development and test of an integrative model of employee-driven innovation in German firms. *International Journal of Entrepreneurship and Innovation Management*, *21*, 1–21.

Lamnek, S. (1995). Qualitative Sozialforschung: Vol. 1. *Methodologie* (3rd ed.). Beltz.

Lee, Y.-N., & Walsh, J. P. (2016). Inventing while you work: Knowledge, non-R&D learning and innovation. *Research Policy, 45*(1), 345–359. DOI: 10.1016/j.respol.2015.09.009

Lemmetty, S. (2024). Real-time and long-term challenges of remote learning and innovation: Cases from police and technology organisations. *Vocations and Learning, 17*(3), 565–587. DOI: 10.1007/s12186-024-09354-1

Li, C., Sun, L.-Y., & Dong, Y. (2018). Innovating via building absorptive capacity: Interactive effects of top management support of learning, employee learning orientation and decentralization structure. *Creativity and Innovation Management, 27*(4), 431–443. DOI: 10.1111/caim.12261

Lin, H.-E., McDonough, E. F.III, Lin, S.-J., & Lin, C. Y.-Y. (2013). Managing the exploitation/exploration paradox: The role of a learning capability and innovation ambidexterity. *Journal of Product Innovation Management, 30*(2), 262–278. DOI: 10.1111/j.1540-5885.2012.00998.x

Lüders, C., & Reichertz, J. (1986). Wissenschaftliche Praxis ist, wenn alles funktioniert und keiner weiß warum – Bemerkungen zur Entwicklung qualitativer Sozialforschung. *Sozialwissenschaftliche Literatur Rundschau, 12*, 90–102.

Lungstraß, R. (1976). *Der Zweckverband als Planungs- und Finanzinstrument neuer öffentlicher Aufgaben: Erläutert am Beispiel eines Abwasserzweckverbands in Nordrhein-Westfalen*. Westdeutscher. DOI: 10.1007/978-3-322-88586-9

Macharzina, K. (1970). *Interaktion und Organisation: Versuch einer Modellanalyse*. Universitätsbibliothek.

Machkour, B., & Abriane, A. (2025). The rise of artificial intelligence in educational management: A prospective analysis on the role of the virtual educational director. *Procedia Computer Science, 257*, 1233–1238. DOI: 10.1016/j.procs.2025.03.165

MacVaugh, J., & Schiavone, F. (2010). Limits to the diffusion of innovation: A literature review and integrative model. *European Journal of Innovation Management, 13*(2), 197–221. DOI: 10.1108/14601061011040258

Marquardt, M. (2020). *Optimizing the power of action learning: Real-time strategies for developing leaders, building teams and transforming organizations* (3rd ed.). Nicholas Brealey.

Martínez-Ros, E., & Orfila-Sintes, F. (2012). Training plans, manager's characteristics and innovation in the accommodation industry. *International Journal of Hospitality Management, 31*(3), 686–694. DOI: 10.1016/j.ijhm.2011.09.004

Mayring, P. (1990). *Einführung in die qualitative Sozialforschung*. Psychologie-Verlag-Union.

Muehlemann, S. (2025). Artificial intelligence adoption and workplace training. *Journal of Economic Behavior & Organization, 238*, 107206. DOI: 10.1016/j.jebo.2025.107206

Nonaka, I., & Konno, N. (1998). The concept of "Ba": Building a foundation for creating knowledge. *California Management Review, 40*(3), 40–54. DOI: 10.2307/41165942

Nonaka, I., & Takeuchi, H. (1995). *The knowledge-creating company: How Japanese companies create the dynamics of innovation*. Oxford University Press. DOI: 10.1093/oso/9780195092691.001.0001

Nonaka, I., & Toyama, R. (2003). The knowledge-creating theory revisited: Knowledge creation as a synthesizing process. *Knowledge Management Research and Practice, 1*(1), 2–10. DOI: 10.1057/palgrave.kmrp.8500001

Nonaka, I., Toyama, R., & Konno, N. (2000). SECI, Ba and leadership: A unified model of dynamic knowledge creation. *Long Range Planning, 33*(1), 5–34. DOI: 10.1016/S0024-6301(99)00115-6

O'Connor, G. C. (2008). Major innovation as a dynamic capability: A systems approach. *Journal of Product Innovation Management, 25*(4), 313–330. DOI: 10.1111/j.1540-5885.2008.00304.x

OECD. (2023). *Skills outlook 2023: Enabling lifelong learning for all.* OECD Publishing. DOI: 10.1787/14d2c4b9-

Olfert, K., & Steinbuch, P. A. (1999). *Personalwirtschaft* (8th ed.). Kiehl.

Pansera, M., & Shanker, D. (2014). Social construction of innovation narratives: Implications for management studies. *IIM Bangalore Research Paper No. 457.* DOI: 10.2139/ssrn.2422759

Piekkari, R., Welch, C., & Paavilainen, E. (2009). The case study as disciplinary convention: Evidence from *International Business Journal. Organizational Research Methods, 12*(3), 567–589. DOI: 10.1177/1094428108319905

Pieler, D. (2000). *Weiterbildungscontrolling: Eine systemorientierte Perspektive*. DUV. DOI: 10.1007/978-3-322-97808-0

Radel, T. (1997). Die Formatierung horizontaler Netzwerke: Ein Rahmen für Innovationsprozesse? In Heidelhoff, F., & Radel, T. (Eds.), *Organisation von Innovation: Strukturen, Prozesse, Interventionen* (pp. 105–126). Rainer Hampp.

Ragin, C. C. (1997). Turning the tables: How case-oriented research challenges variable-oriented research. *Comparative Social Research, 16*, 27–42.

Rammert, W. (2008). Technik und Innovation. In Maurer, A. (Ed.), *Handbuch der Wirtschaftssoziologie* (pp. 291–319). VS. DOI: 10.1007/978-3-531-90905-9_15

Remenyi, D., Money, A., Price, D., & Bannister, F. (2002). The creation of knowledge through case study research. *Irish Journal of Management, 23*(2), 1–17.

Ritala, P., Hurmelinna-Laukkanen, P., & Nätti, S. (2012). Coordination in innovation-generating business networks – The case of Finnish mobile TV development. *Journal of Business and Industrial Marketing, 27*(4), 324–334. DOI: 10.1108/08858621211221698

Rogers, E. M. (2003). *Diffusion of innovations* (5th ed.). Free Press.

Saunders, M., Lewis, P., & Thornhill, A. (2016). *Research methods for business students* (7th ed.). Pearson.

Schmelzer, F. (2014). Innovative Innovationsberatung. In *Mut zu Innovationen: Impulse aus der Forschung, Beratung und Ausbildung* (pp. 131–150). Springer. DOI: 10.1007/978-3-642-40227-2_11

Schmid, G. (1970). Niklas Luhmanns funktional-strukturelle Systemtheorie: Eine wissenschaftliche Revolution. *Politische Vierteljahresschrift, 11*(2–3), 186–218.

Schwarz, R., & Ewaldt, J. W. (2008). Über den Beitrag systemdynamischer Modellierung zur Abschätzung technologischer Evolution. In Möhrle, M. G., & Isenmann, R. (Eds.), *Technologie-Roadmapping: Zukunftsstrategien für Technologieunternehmen* (pp. 409–425). Springer. DOI: 10.1007/978-3-540-74755-0_20

Schwarz, R., & Ewaldt, J. W. (2008). *Innovationsorientiertes Bildungsmanagement: Hochschulentwicklung durch Sicherung der Nachhaltigkeit von eLearning*. VS.

Tushman, M., Smith, W. K., Woody, R. C., & Westerman, G. (2010). Organizational designs and innovation streams. *Industrial and Corporate Change, 19*(5), 1331–1366. DOI: 10.1093/icc/dtq040

Umesi, D. A. (2024). The role of educational management in enhancing effective teaching and learning in 21st century schools. *Brock Journal of Education, 12*(3), 66–75.

Vahs, D., & Brem, A. (2013). *Innovationsmanagement: Von der Idee zur erfolgreichen Vermarktung* (4th ed.). Schäffer-Poeschel.

Van de Ven, A. H., Polley, D. E., Garud, R., & Venkataraman, S. (1999). *The innovation journey*. Oxford University Press.

von Au, D. (2010). *Strategisches Innovationsmanagement: Eine empirische Analyse betrieblicher Innovationssysteme in der spezialchemischen Industrie in Deutschland*. Gabler.

Wang, J., Hussain, Y., Mao, C., & Jiang, F. (2025). Effective educational management strategies: Enhancing institutional performance and student success. *Journal of Education, Humanities, and Social Research*, *2*(2), 1–12. DOI: 10.71222/yqw52v02

Weber, W. (1985). *Betriebliche Weiterbildung: Empirische Analysen betrieblicher und individueller Entscheidungen über Weiterbildung*. Poeschel.

Weigel, S., & Hadwich, K. (2019). Erfolgsfaktoren von Dienstleistungsnetzwerken im Kontext der Servicetransformation – Eine qualitative Analyse. *Schmalenbachs Zeitschrift fur Betriebswirtschaftliche Forschung = Schmalenbach Journal of Business Research*, *71*(1), 1–43. DOI: 10.1007/s41471-019-00062-4

Wengenroth, U. (2010). Innovationsprozesse in Wirtschaft und Gesellschaft – Vorbemerkung. In Hof, H., & Wengenroth, U. (Eds.), *Innovationsforschung* (pp. 1–5). LIT.

Wigger, L. (2013). Argumentationsanalyse als erziehungswissenschaftliche Forschungsmethode. In Friebertshäuser, B., Langer, A., & Prengel, A. (Eds.), *Handbuch Qualitative Forschungsmethoden in der Erziehungswissenschaft* (4th ed., pp. 351–364). Beltz.

World Economic Forum. (2023). *Future of jobs report 2023*. Geneva: WEF.

Yin, R. K. (2003). *Case study research – Design and methods* (2nd ed.). Sage.

Yin, R. K. (2013). *Case study research: Design and methods* (5th ed.). Sage.

Zabich, C., & Breßler, J. (2016). Anforderung und Vermittlung von Innovationskompetenzen in der Automobilindustrie. *Working Papers of the Chair for Innovation Research and Technology Management, TU Chemnitz*,06-01.

Zehrer, A., & Muskat, B. (2016). Der Treiber Innovation in touristischen Unternehmen. In Siller, H., & Zehrer, A. (Eds.), *Entrepreneurship und Tourismus: Unternehmerisches Denken und Erfolgskonzepte aus der Praxis* (2nd ed., pp. 29–46). Linde International.

Zhao, J., Li, Y., & Liu, Y. (2016). Organizational learning, managerial ties and radical innovation: Evidence from an emerging economy. *IEEE Transactions on Engineering Management*, *63*(4), 489–499. DOI: 10.1109/TEM.2016.2597290

ADDITIONAL READING

Billett, S., Harteis, C., & Gruber, H. (Eds.). (2014). *International handbook of research in professional and practice-based learning* (Vol. 1). Springer. DOI: 10.1007/978-94-017-8902-8

Fuller, A., & Unwin, L. (2011). Workplace learning and the organization. The SAGE handbook of workplace learning, 46-59. DOI: 10.4135/9781446200940.n4

KEY TERMS AND DEFINITIONS

Educational Management: The strategic coordination of learning initiatives within organizations, including planning, implementing, and evaluating educational measures to foster employee development and innovation.

Formal Learning: Refers to structured learning activities that are typically planned, institutionalized, and lead to recognized certifications or qualifications. These forms of learning occur within established education and training systems and follow a predefined curriculum.

Informal Learning: Unstructured, non-institutionalized learning that occurs spontaneously through daily work interactions, social exchange, or self-directed exploration.

Innovation Process: A structured or emergent sequence of actions through which new ideas are developed, refined, and implemented within an organization to create added value.

Knowledge Management: The systematic process of capturing, sharing, and applying organizational knowledge to improve decision-making, performance, and innovation outcomes.

Learning Episodes: Learning episodes describe discrete units or situations in which individuals engage with new content, skills, or reflective processes. They can occur in both formal and informal settings and are characterized by their temporal and contextual boundaries, often shaped by organizational or individual learning needs.

Workplace Learning: Learning that occurs in or through the work environment, encompassing formal training programs, informal knowledge exchange, and experiential learning activities.

Chapter 6
The Ethics of Creativity: Can Innovation Be Morally Neutral?

Sooraj Kumar Maurya
https://orcid.org/0000-0002-6974-5508
Zakir Husain Delhi College (Evening), University of Delhi, India

Aditya Kumar Gupta
https://orcid.org/0000-0001-9347-0367
University of Delhi, India

Vikash Ranjan Singh
https://orcid.org/0009-0006-9130-6997
Zakir Husain Delhi College (Evening), University of Delhi, India

Sapna Tiwari
Zakir Husain Delhi College (Evening), University of Delhi, India

ABSTRACT

The issue of creativity is a long-debated tool of progress, innovation, and culture change, but which creates exceptional moral predicaments. The chapter reflects on how creativity may (or may not) become morally neutral, highlighting its modality as both productive and disruptive. It examines conflicts involving radical freedom moral responsibility, and unintended consequence using Nietzschean, Kantian, and utilitarian understandings. According to Nietzsche, creativity is an act of the will to power, and it has frequently gone beyond the norms of conventional morality, whereas in Kant, creativity fits within the confines of duty and the universality of principles. Utilitarianism makes judgements on creative acts, however, on their benefits towards

DOI: 10.4018/979-8-3373-2742-6.ch006

society and so runs the risk of defining art merely in terms of consequences. The chapter posits that ethically responsible creativity should be contextual, deliberate, and considerate of implications to persons and collectives.

INTRODUCTION

With creativity having been hailed as one of the most revolutionary forces in human history, it is the driving force behind multiple technological breakthroughs, scientific discoveries, artistic masterpieces, and social revolutions. It is commonly accepted as a virtue promoting development, enhancing innovation, solving issues, and enriching cultural life. The creative act has long been seen as a motivating factor for human growth and development. Indeed, creativity fuels economic expansion, enables artistic expression, and opens new horizons in human potential (Csikszentmihalyi, 1996). However, despite its positive aspects, creativity has a fairly serious ethical dilemma: should it always be perceived as something good, or it can also be morally neutral and even bad?

Conventionally, creativity has been linked with enlightenment, scientific development and cultural prosperity. The Renaissance, for instance, transformed European thought through artistic and scientific advances, laying foundations for modern Western civilization. Similarly, during the Industrial Revolution, creativity was valorized for addressing technological challenges and sustaining economic prosperity (Mokyr, 2018). However, creativity is not invariably benign. It has generated life-saving innovations such as vaccines and medical devices, while simultaneously producing destructive technologies, manipulative propaganda, and powerful surveillance systems (Bostrom, 2014). This duality begs the question whether being creative can be a morally neutral practice. Is the moral relevance of it limited to its use or does the process of creativity have ethical relevance? The morality of creativity is tied to the results, so unless projected but not yet realized results are included, creativity is morally neutral. However, when creativity is inseparably connected with considering ethical aspects, it means that any creation becomes a responsibility. These tensions, between progress and peril, freedom and accountability, shape the ethical question addressed by this chapter, what it means to be ethical as a creative being, and in just what ways people are thus creatively hazardous.

The Ethical Paradox of Innovation

Innovation occurs when creativity transforms into practical applications—new products, services, or processes (West, 2002). Although a widely commemorated concept of innovation as a beneficial force that could resolve issues and drive social advancements, it is ethically indifferent never. Not all of the consequences of innovations are equally far-reaching, and some can completely change whole societies, posing significant ethical questions on what they will mean to the people, societies, and the environment. Artificial intelligence (AI) illustrates this duality. AI has revolutionized healthcare, communication, and transportation. It enhances efficiency and accessibility but simultaneously threatens privacy, embeds algorithmic bias, and risks diminishing human agency (Zuboff, 2019). Similarly, advances in genetic engineering, particularly CRISPR gene-editing, promise cures for hereditary diseases while igniting debates over human enhancement, genetic discrimination, and the unforeseen effects of altering life's code. Nuclear technology provides another stark example: nuclear energy offers a clean and efficient power source, yet nuclear weapons remain among the gravest existential threats (Rhodes, 1986). These illustrations demonstrate the moral ambivalence of innovation, its ability to promote well-being or increase harm. Therefore, the question to societies is: what is the line between innovation in the service of the common good and innovation that is hazardous? How do we make creativity governable in a manner that will maximize progressive desirable consequences, minimizing harmful risks?

The philosophical reflection has always struggled with these questions weighing in terms of moral responsibility, ethical limitations and the consequences of artistic expression. Three main standpoints, the concept of the *will to power* presented by Nietzsche, the *categorical imperative* introduced by Kant and the consequentialist approach to utilitarianism, have different and clear explanations of the relationship between creativity and innovation with ethical considerations. Friedrich Nietzsche defined creativity as an expression of the *will to power*, the fundamental drive toward self-overcoming and excellence (Nietzsche, 1886/1966). For Nietzsche, creativity arises when individuals transgress traditional moral boundaries to establish their own values. The most important creators, artists, scientists, visionaries bend the norms of their societies in order to determine their own ethical courses of action. Within this framework, the creativity is self-determination, the process of becoming and overcoming. However, given that they are released of all moral restrictions, can innovation justify devastating or injurious consequences? Nietzsche denied the ordinary morality and stressed the importance of individual freedom, yet misuse becomes a possibility. The Nazi distortion of the *Übermensch* concept to justify racial supremacy and genocide exemplifies how Nietzsche's philosophy, when co-opted, leads to ethical relativism and nihilism (Safranski, 2002).

By contrast, Immanuel Kant argued that creativity must be bound by rational moral principles and duty. According to his Categorical Imperative, an action is morally permissible only if it can be willed as a universal law, applying equally to all (Korsgaard, 2010). Therefore creativity ought not to have selfish or destructive ends as it should be in regard to universal responsibilities to have regard to human dignity. Therefore, innovators, artists, and scientists have moral responsibility towards social impacts of their actions. However, Kantian ethics does pose practical questions: is the reasoning that one can use stricter universal rules to judge all the creative actions? Are radical experimentation and the creative breakthroughs based on this premise of strict adherence to duty dangerous? According to Kant, the moral constraint guarantees the common good; to his opponents, the constraint limits the freedom of innovation.

A third framework, utilitarianism, takes a consequentialist approach. For thinkers like Jeremy Bentham and John Stuart Mill, the value of any act—including innovation—lies in its outcomes, aiming to maximize happiness and minimize suffering (Mill, 1863/2001). In this perspective creative innovations like medical advances, renewable energy, and social entrepreneurship are examples of ethical positivity when promoting the maximum good to the maximum number. Nonetheless, utilitarianism is not an exemption: what is good to the greatest number might be detrimental to marginalized groups or can destabilize set ups. For instance, automation and AI have a chance to boost efficiency and save costs, but it also can lead to displacement of workers, which disproportionally impacts low-income communities. This makes it ethically challenging on who must pay the price of innovation and how the society can maintain efficiency and equity.

Collectively, these frameworks shed light on several aspects of the ethical paradox of innovation. Nietzsche particularly focuses on autonomous and extreme freedom, yet there is a threat of justifying the creative destruction. Kant places paramount emphasis on duty and responsibility, yet perhaps at the cost of boundary-crossing innovation. Utilitarianism takes advantage of consequences and social good, yet it might overlook wicked alternatives of moral trade or forswear personal achievement that has a creative worth in itself. We live in the more complicated technological world, and it is essential to factor in more than creative, innovation, and the moral responsibilities when applying them in the tension they created. Through it, we can come up with ethical models that will protect society against evil as well as encourage innovations that will actually enrich communal living.

NIETZSCHE: CREATIVITY AS A FORCE BEYOND MORALITY

Friedrich Nietzsche stands as one of the most influential and controversial philosophers in the discourse on creativity, autonomy, and morality. His thinking repudiates the traditional models of morality and places creativity outside the scope of moral considerations. For Nietzsche, creativity is not merely the presentation of new ideas or aesthetic expressions; it is the fertile Will to Power, the fundamental force of human existence. Unlike Kantian deontology, which grounds creativity within universal moral laws and duties, Nietzsche views it as an act of self-overcoming—a transformative process in which individuals seek to expand their strength, vision, and individuality (Reginster, 2009). This kind of creativity is disruptive to the norms and conventions, and results into something radically new and in many cases uncomfortable.

The *will to power*, in the interpretation put upon it by Nietzsche, cannot be put in the category of a wish to have pleasure, to survive: the underlying impulse is the impulse to be the Lord of the situation, and to remake the world and revalue it. Creativity therefore becomes an active response of being and not a passive accommodation. As he declares: "The noble type of man experiences itself as value-creating; it does not need approval; it knows itself to be that which first accords honor to things; it is value creating" (Nietzsche, 1887/2007, p. 260). In this case, the authenticity of creativity lies in the self-determination as opposed to outside validation, which Nietzsche believed a creator should be the sole backgrounder of value. Unlike Kant (1785/1997, p. 65), who anchors creativity within universal duties, Nietzsche insists that the artist or innovator must liberate themselves from moral constraints in order to realize their unique vision.

This philosophy culminates in Nietzsche's portrayal of the *Übermensch* in *Thus Spoke Zarathustra*. The *Übermensch* is the master of human creativity, one who does not accept any codes of morality that have been inherited but that he/she is to create new values and realities. As Nietzsche asserts, "Man is something that shall be overcome." The *Übermensch* is the ideal of the creative man who has outgrown all the bonds of morality and fellow feeling and conformity, and reinterpreted humanity. In that respect, creativity is essentially amoral, that is to say, it is creative because it is morally transgressive, because the innovation lies exactly in the incursion into moral boundaries. One of the most significant aspects of Nietzsches outlook is his critical view of Christian and Kantian morals, which he thought were systems aimed at suppressing human potential and imposing order by destroying any signs of life. By rejecting these moral codes, Nietzsche defended creative autonomy—the power to transgress boundaries, oppose norms, and generate new values independent of prevailing ethical standards (Schacht, 1983). Creativity, as Nietzsche conceives it, thus has nothing to do with moral obligation but with self-overcoming and decompressing oneself and the culture she or he belongs to by liberating both the self and the culture of self-imposed bondage.

The Case for Unrestricted Creativity

The sense of moral freedom that is implied by Nietzsche is provocative: is creativity to have no moral boundaries? This idea has worked on artists, writers, and musicians who have tried to break taboos and shatter conventions in the name of freedom of art. Nietzschean themes of transgression, self-creation, and rejection of moral codes resonate in avant-garde movements such as surrealism, expressionism, and postmodernism (Nehamas, 1987). The so-called the free spirit refers to a concept in Nietzsche, which gives a logical explanation to artistic experimentation and artistic rebellion. Yet unbounded creativity also carries risks. Provocative art could inspire critical discussion but it also could enforce maladaptive idea, propagate stereotypes or celebrate violence. Globalized entertainment in the form of books, movies, music, or other works that normalize exploitation, hate speech, or institutional violence is how artistic freedom, without moral consideration, can hurt communities. Such a strain poses the ever-troubling question: should the process of creative expression be an unmonitored activity, or should it be neutralized by the principle of ethical boundaries when its results attack honor as well as health?

Beyond the Arts: Scientific and Technological Innovation

Although Nietzschean system is commonly argued on the arts, it is applicable to science as well as to technology. Revolutionary fields such as genetic engineering, artificial intelligence, and quantum computing carry immense potential for progress while posing grave ethical risks (Bostrom, 2014). One example is AI-enhanced surveillance that ensures effectiveness but poses a danger to privacy and self-determination. The CRISPR technology promises cures to genetic diseases raising questions in regards to human enhancement and the risks of editing life. The truth is that scientific creativity is ethically ambiguous like artistic: it can make break-throughs that are transformative but can also have a disastrous effect. The question arises then, how much can scientists and innovators get away with in a world in which they are relieved of ethical responsibility, as Nietzsche encouraged them to be. History knows cases of radical innovators who did not conform to existing trends. Galileo Galilei even faced threat of religious condemnation to pursue the heliocentric view, which transformed science defying dogma. In the arts, Cubism, innovated by Pablo Picasso challenged precedents of representation and redefined visual expression. By denouncing religious morality himself, Nietzsche created the trend in existentialism and post-modernism that emphasized authorial meaning in a godless universe. Such personalities are paradigmatic of the Nietzschean spirit of creativity: norm-transgressive, transgressive by boundaries, and world-transformative. However, as later abuses of his philosophy have tragically shown, especially in the Nazi misappropriation of the Ubermensch the cultural prosperity lies as much within the dynamics of radical freedom as does the spread of murderous movements.

The Dangers of Amoral Creativity

However, although Derrida argues that unrehearsed creativity urged by him is much more about openness and play, in the vision shared by Nietzsche, there is an unnerving ethical danger to it. Does creatively exercised without accountability mean there is nothing in the way of moral restraint to exploitation or harm? History offers sobering lessons: art has been weaponized in Nazi propaganda, and creativity has fueled unethical medical experiments. These cases highlight the dangers of using innovation without considering ethics. The current advances in biotechnology and artificial intelligence are modern examples of such threats. Technologies like gene editing examples for this profoundly confront identity, equity, and unintended effects of manipulating human genetic material. Artificial intelligence, though promising efficiency and accessibility, also poses threats of algorithmic bias, privacy invasion, and the manipulation of public opinion (Zuboff, 2019). It is also, in a parallel way, through political ideologies informed by distorted uses of Nietzschean thought that authoritarianism and elitism have either been justified outright or used in this fashion as in the case of the Nazi propagandists in borrowing his thought distortion.

The Nazi Misuse of Nietzsche's Ideas: A Cautionary Tale

The most notorious perversion of Nietzsche philosophy was in the Nazi doctrine. Adolf Hitler and his regime misinterpreted Nietzsche's concept of the *Übermensch* as a justification for racial superiority, militarism, and genocide (Safranski, 2002). However, Nietzsche himself was never an anti-Semite, nor a nationalist, and his texts were directed at the self-overcoming of individuals, rather than state-sponsored tyranny. Nazi chose and distorted his ideas to reflect the *Übermensch* as a subject of Aryan superiority and right to subjugate of degenerate races, like the Jews and the Roma. In reality, Nietzsche's *Übermensch*, presented in *Thus Spoke Zarathustra*, was a philosophical figure of self-transcendence, one who created new values beyond conventional morality. The Nazi rewriting turned this imagination of creativity into a politics of subordination, oppression and violence. Seeing the necessity of the value-creation, which Nietzsche proclaimed, as an authoritarianism of ruthless violence, they employed his philosophy in the justification of refuting the value called humanitarianism ethics, equality, and humanity. The noble end was the fact that the grand idea of Nietzsche, creative freedom was weaponized into a genocidal defense. This misrepresentation points to the risks of the division of creativity into a neutral domain and ethical liability: unconstrained invention may be put to disastrous use. In stark contrast, Immanuel Kant insisted that creativity, like all human activity, must be bound by moral duty and rational principles. His ethics is focused on duty, reason and universality of ethical laws. Whereas Nietzsche celebrated creativity as autonomous expression and self-assertion (Reginster, 2009), Kant argued that its legitimacy rests on adherence to universal principles of morality. To Kant, the value of any action cannot be determined by its outcomes; instead, the value of any action is whether it adheres to rational duty. This deontological theory bases creativity on responsibility and once it is practiced it must be within dignity and fairness and not ambition or innovation per se.

The Categorical Imperative: Universal Moral Laws

At the heart of Kant's ethics lies the Categorical Imperative: individuals must act only according to maxims they could will as universal laws (Kant, 1785/1997). When applied to creativity this means that artistic or scientific creativity must be defendable as morally permissible to all rational beings. In a second formulation, Kant asserts: "Act in such a way that you always treat humanity, whether in your own person or in the person of any other, never simply as a means but always at the same time as an end" (Kant, 1785/1997, p. 429). Creativity, in turn, should not be thrust upon the exploitation of others or the deception and instrumentalization of others but should confirm the dignity of the other.

According to Kant, creativity as a form of creative expression has moral value based on motivation rather than results. The art which is inspired not by profit or acclaim, or striving to achieve something, but rather is driven by a sense of duty holds a moral integrity. This is an ethic of responsibility that expects artists, scientists and innovators to make sure that what they do is in line with universal definitions of fair play and respect, acceptable or not, within society. To illustrate, an AI system that is developed by a Kantian based ethics precept would place emphasis on the need of transparency, fairness, and safeguarding human integrity even when a utilitarian approach may wish to present a few evils in order to deliver greater significance to society. In contrast to utilitarian consequentialism, which balances costs and benefits, Kant held that ethical motive and treatment of persons is most important.

Kant's Take on Creative Ethics

The philosophical approach proposed by Kant offers valuable ethical framework to understand creativity but leaves certain questions open, such as the question of ethics during creativity, or the boundary of free artistic expression, and ethics in technological innovation. In the system of Kant, the moral worth of an action does not lie in the consequence of the action but in the motive of doing it. It is the intention of duty, he claims, which renders an act a moral action, not its outward fortunate consequence. This focus on intention has important consequences in assessing creativity. In another instance, a Kantian interpretation of the concept of moral duty would have an architect planning a sustainable house to impede environmental degradation as morally upright, even though there are practical challenges the project is likely to encounter. On the other hand, a company that manipulates its products in an advertisement campaign, though it increases profits, will infringe under Kantian ethics since it will undermine truth and justice.

Kantian ethics therefore puts the intentionality and the principle of the creative work at account. Creation is not to be assessed only on the strength or popularity of the work but of whether the underlying intentions are within universal moral laws? For instance, an artist or innovator who exploits, defrauds, or otherwise hurts others, is acting immorally, no matter how culturally appraised or commercially successful his or her work is. This begs the question--should any creative endeavor be balanced against a universal ethical framework? How do we evaluate art or innovation that consciously breaches the norms, provokes outrage or challenges established values? For instance, politically charged art—such as Ai Weiwei's critiques of authoritarianism—may offend some sensibilities while simultaneously advancing social justice (Nochlin, 1989). Is there room in the Kantian model to accommodate this kind of fertile creativity or will it become a menace to freedom in art? Though this theory by Kant claims that creativity must not jeopardize human dignity, it is not always evident when this should be applied in various cultural and political settings. What are seen as ethically acceptable in one community cannot be viewed that way in all others, and where there is a conflict between moral obligation and the right to express themselves? Creativity therefore lies between two poles where there is the obligation to maintain dignity and fairness on one hand and the desire to break up the status quo on the opposite hand.

Kantian principles also have clear applications in technological innovation. Renewable energy initiatives, such as solar power or electric vehicles, embody duty-driven innovation by promoting sustainability for present and future generations (Sachs, 2015). Likewise, artificial intelligence development poses acute moral requirements. According to Kantian views, fairness, transparency, and accountability are ethical requirements, which have to be imbibed in algorithms. Companies such as OpenAI and Google DeepMind increasingly adopt ethical frameworks to ensure that their technologies respect human rights rather than exploit individuals. This subsumes the Kantian imperative that humans should not be used as a human means but as an end in and of themselves. The one consistent criticism of Kantian creative ethics is its inflexibility. Kant neglects that ethical standards vary in every culture, industry, and time because he demands that moral laws should be applied universally. What is ethical in a case of a Western and the democratic society can vary a great deal in collectivist societies in the East. It is in this respect that Kantian universalism may seem untenable, as able to find no room to maneuver in the contextual positioning of creative practice that is all too frequently needed when addressing so-called complex and culture specific creative enterprises.

The Limits on Artistic Expression and Innovation

The issue of artistic freedom and scientific innovation and how Kantian ethics may be discouraging such ventures is a recurrent issue. It runs the risk of suppressing the innovative breakthroughs and blurring of boundaries required by creativity through confining creativity to narrow principles of the right and the wrong. Are films that highlight violence, injustice or certain taboo social issues allowed to be censored, in light of the commands of Kantian duties? Can the genetic modification or human enhancement, as promising of the medical innovations, be limited only on the ethical grounds? These questions bring out the conflict that exists between the ethical imperative to uphold human dignity and the innovative impulse to innovate, to subvert, and to seek new artistic or scientific frontiers. Although the framework provided by Kant is a good moral compass, it tends to be so inflexible as to keep pace with the swiftly developing creative and technology fields.

Kantian ethics presupposes that there are moral laws which are fixed and enforceable to everyone. However, creative/ innovative activities often require contextual reasoning. The innovations of today are realized in dynamic and unpredictable contexts and flexibility and responsiveness are essential. In that regard, Kantian universalism fails to capture the triangles of real-life dilemmas, because it gives first consideration to the principles than to the situation. As Rawls (1argued, ethical reasoning often requires situational adaptation, weighing principles within the complexities of particular contexts rather than applying rigid universals.

MODERN IMPLICATIONS OF KANTIAN CREATIVE ETHICS

These concerns are particularly relevant today in the context of the modern revival of artificial intelligence. If AI systems are designed through a Kantian lens, they must embed principles of fairness, transparency, and accountability to ensure that individuals are treated as ends in themselves and never merely as means (Floridi & Taddeo, 2016). The programmers are thus morally bound to engineer technologies that favour humanity by not abusing human beings who are their clients. For Kant (1785/1997), morality depends not on outcomes but on intentions and conformity with universal duty. It means that artists, scientists, innovators or other creative individuals should rest their efforts on the moral but not on fortunes, social acceptance, and aspirations. To artists, it involves applying the power of art to assert dignity, create empathy and eradicate social injustices. Politically charged art, for instance, carries a responsibility not to perpetuate harm but to cultivate solidarity and moral awareness (Nochlin, 1989). Not even provocative or controversial works should be exploitive or abusive, as the moral duty of the artist is to further moral and intellectual development, not popularity or gain.

In the same way, scientists and innovators have the moral right and duty to create technologies that benefit humanity without denying their rights or welfare. Integrity is critical: to breakthroughs in medicine, biotechnology and AI must benefit human rights, not undermine them. For example, AI systems should be built with safeguards against bias, manipulation, and exploitation, ensuring that long-term impacts remain consistent with the Kantian imperative to treat humanity as an end in itself (Kant, 1785/1997). By doing so, Kantian morality questions those who live creative lives, in any discipline, to think of their work not merely as a demonstration of talent or ambition but as a sense of duty, a contribution to human progress. By guiding creativity through respecting dignity, equity, and integrity, the creators are in a position to make sure that innovation becomes beneficial to the rights of the individuals and the general wellbeing of the society.

Utilitarianism: Creativity for the Greatest Good

Utilitarianism, one of the most influential ethical theories, was developed by Jeremy Bentham and John Stuart Mill. It is a consequentialism theory which judges the morality of actions not based on intentions but on the outcome. Rooted in the "greatest happiness principle," utilitarianism holds that ethical actions are those which maximize well-being for the greatest number.

The hedonistic calculus posited by Bentham was an attempt to measure pleasure and pain to identify a moral value, and it provided a measurable, policy-based system of ethics. Mill subsequently developed this formulation by differentiating between pleasures of a higher and a lower type. To Mill, moral, intellectual, and artistic pleasures were more valuable than physical pleasure. Therefore, artistic outputs which add value to knowledge, culture, or even moral knowledge possess more ethical value, as they yield long-term societal benefits. This differentiation brought intellect and artistic creativity to a new level regarding moral philosophy. Utilitarianism is a practical theory, which can be translated into an effective method of assessing artistic expression and innovation. The ethical concerns of creative works are determined by whether they are personally more harmful than useful. Examples of creativity that will maximize long term societal well-being include lifesaving medical innovations, including vaccines or gene therapies or renewable energy like solar power. However, utilitarianism also recognizes complexity: there are numerous innovations with their advantages as well as disadvantages.

The ethical trade-off dilemma is evident in disruptive technologies. Artificial intelligence (AI) and automation can increase productivity, but they also displace workers in vulnerable sectors. The social media facilitate worldwide conversation but misinform, polarize and broadcast harmful information. Equally, the pharmaceutical industry has made life-saving medicines, as well as monopolistic prices against low-income groups. The cases are an example of utilitarian conflict between the greater good and individual harm. In practice, applying utilitarian ethics to creativity is challenging. The measurement of well-being is notoriously hard and innovations are mixed. As an illustration, a novel technology might increase the efficiency of industry but also trigger mass unemployment. It requires balancing cost in the short-term profits against detriments in the long run, but this is usually unpredictable. Utilitarian assessment is risky due to the intricacy of measuring net effects.

The other constraint is the conflict between economic incentive and ethical responsibility. The motive of profit therefore prevails over social good in a market driven economy. It causes a problem in pharmaceutical pricing: the saved lives because of the medical innovative developments are limited due to profit-maximizing behavior. From utilitarian perspective, ethical quality is based on a fair outcome of benefits which are frequently thwarted by lack of balance within economic arrangements. Globalization further complicates utilitarian ethics. The same innovation, which is considered beneficial at all in one culture, might be regarded as harmful in another one. Digital services, such as, have different ethical norms in various societies. Relying on the same utilitarian calculus, such a pluralistic situation threatens to homogenize values and cultural sensitivities.

Notwithstanding these challenges, utilitarianism is valuable in evaluating the ethical aspect of creativity. It brings to the fore the social role of artists, scientists, and innovators, reminding us that artistic or scientific innovation should not necessarily be gauged in terms of novelty or ambition but can also be judged by how it affects the common good. Nevertheless utilitarian ethics would also need safeguards and accountability mechanisms to address the issue of inequality, safeguarding vulnerable populations as well as assuring that creativity works to advance long term human flourishing. However, it is important to balance innovation and responsibility in case creativity can receive its transformative power in the way that would positively affect everyone.

Virtue Ethics: Creativity as Character and Flourishing

Virtue ethics differs with the deontological school of thought of Kant and utilitarianism school of consequence. Virtue ethics does not focus on rules or outcomes, but rather on the development of good character and the enhancement of moral virtues. Rooted in Aristotle's *Nicomachean Ethics* (350 BCE/2009), virtue ethics highlights the pursuit of eudaimonia—often translated as "flourishing" or "living well." To Aristotle, eudaimonia is the supreme goods of a human being which is attained not by material things but through the virtue as a matter of habit. In contrast to disembodied universal rules, virtues are practised habits that orient individuals towards acts of excellence in specific situations.

The ethical framework by Aristotle is particularly relevant when considering creativity due to his considerations towards the practical and situated human action. Creativity often involves navigating uncertainty, novelty, and tension. Unlike Kantian rules, which may be too rigid, or utilitarian calculations, which may be too reductive, virtue ethics acknowledges that moral wisdom (phronesis) is essential to judging what counts as responsible creativity in diverse circumstances (MacIntyre, 1981/2007). The Aristotelian tradition was later taken up and adapted by Thomas Aquinas, who integrated virtue ethics into a Christian theological framework by emphasizing the cardinal virtues (prudence, justice, temperance, fortitude) and theological virtues (faith, hope, charity). In modern moral philosophy, virtue ethics was revived by thinkers such as Elizabeth Anscombe, Alasdair MacIntyre, Rosalind Hursthouse, and Julia Annas. These researchers pointed out that virtues are not personal performances but actions in communities and cultures and traditions. This lends itself to virtue ethics as a fertile framework or conceptualization of creativity, because creative work is personal and yet socially situated.

Creativity as an Expression of Virtue

Virtue ethics does not consider creativity as a morally indifferent talent but as an activity that has a disposition. The question is not simply whether an act of creation obeys universal duties (as in Kant) or maximizes good outcomes (as in utilitarianism), but whether the act is performed with the right intention, in the right way, and for the right reasons. The attributes of a strong creator include imagination, courage, and humility, responsibility, etc. A good creator will strive to reflect these within their work. The example of virtue is the act of a scientist who makes medical breakthroughs due to his or her compassion toward patients. An architect designing sustainable housing for future generations demonstrates prudence and justice by balancing present needs with long-term responsibilities (Sachs, 2015). An artist who uses their work to expose injustice or foster empathy embodies courage and integrity, even if their work provokes discomfort or controversy. These examples demonstrate that creativities can be a source of virtues and as such can lead to not only innovation but also to moral and cultural prosperity.

On the other hand, any form of creativity that is generated by vices like being vain, greedy, or reckless into themselves could potentially end up in harmful results despite their novelty. As an example, the artists performing the violence in order to get the money or the corporations focusing on the more exploitative technology can be considered the vice-driven creativity. In virtue ethics, the question is not merely whether creativity is novel, but whether it emerges from and cultivates the virtues necessary for a flourishing life (Hursthouse, 1999).

Phronesis and the Moral Judgement of Creativity

At the heart of virtue ethics is that of phronesis, the practical wisdom or moral discernment. Creativity is usually acted out in situations with dubious morals where inflexible provisions are unable to help. The development of phronesis allows innovators to balance conflicting values, judge appropriateness of innovations, and judge with moral sensitivity. This can mean that, when creating artificial intelligence, engineers will have to make trade-offs between efficiency and fairness, innovation and privacy. A virtue ethicist would argue that such dilemmas cannot be resolved by abstract rules alone; instead, they require wise judgment shaped by virtues such as honesty, humility, and justice (Floridi & Cowls, 2019). This focus on evaluating judgment characteristics harkens virtue ethics to apply to the assessment of creativity in complex and changeable situations. In contrast to the Kantian strict universality or calculative treatment of utilitarianism, virtue ethics is instead more context-specific and situational. This fluidity is reflective of the volatile and experimental nature of the creativity itself.

With regard to the arts, virtue ethics stresses the importance of creativity both in the development of the moral character of the artist and the community. One thing that artistic people struggle with is whether their creative expression needs to be bound by some ethical thing. A Kantian may discuss the existence of universal duties, and a utilitarian might compare harms with social benefits. Virtue ethics instead poses the following question: what type of individual does a given artistic practice make, does it lead to the happiness of society?

For instance, avant-garde art movements that challenge taboos can be virtuous if they encourage critical reflection, empathy, or resilience (Nehamas, 1987). On the one hand, creative works that praise hatred, exploitation or violence can be devious reflections and contributions to malice even though the works are technically creative. Virtue ethics thus is able to offer a subtle judgement on questionable art: it does not necessarily require censorship but underlines the task of the artists of embodying positive values in the creative process. In science, traits discussed in virtue ethics are intellectual honesty, humility and perseverance. Scientific creativity thrives when scientists nourish virtues that boost truth-searching and integrity. On the other hand, corruption of creativity by arrogance, fraud, or greed negatively affects the science and society. To give an example, once inventive research or poorly considered experimentation can be creative in its manifestation yet evil in nature.

In the field of biotechnology, virtue ethics stresses modesty faced with the complexity of life and compassion to future generations. Gene-editing technologies such as CRISPR may hold the potential to cure diseases, but they also raise profound ethical questions about human identity and equity. Before it is too late, a virtue ethicist would urge prescient, just and humane pursuit of such technologies not because of money or fame but with a view towards wisdom. Technological innovation places great emphasis on virtues, i.e. prudence, justice and responsibility. Artificial intelligence, for example, can enhance efficiency but also risks perpetuating biases, undermining privacy, and eroding human agency (Zuboff, 2019). The moral philosophy of virtue would involve shaping of the ethical nature of computer programmers and companies so that the innovativeness in AI is informed by virtuous qualities such as fairness, honesty, and respect to human dignity. This perspective also applies to sustainability and environmental innovation. Renewable energy projects such as solar and wind power reflect virtues of prudence and justice by balancing present needs with future responsibilities (Sachs, 2015). In comparison, those technologies whose sole interest is immediate profit without regard to future evils represent a lapse in the moral character of those technologies and not lack of creativity.

Despite its strengths, virtue ethics faces important criticisms. One is that it seems to lack criteria of clear decision making. As opposed to Kantian duty or a utilitarian calculus, virtue ethics does not give an answer to the question of the morality of a creative act as ruled by any specific procedure. Critics argue this vagueness makes it difficult to resolve disputes, particularly in pluralistic societies with diverse values (Kristjánsson, 2018). Another limitation is cultural relativity. The meaning of virtues can vary in different societies, which begs the question of universally valid norms in virtue ethics. What may be considered to be a virtuous creativity in a certain culture will be looked at as vice in another. To use an example, artistic performances that oppose authority might be appreciated in a liberal democracy but punished in an authoritarian one.

Even so, virtue ethicists claim that the relative flexibility is also what makes it strong. The flexibility facilitated by an emphasis on character instead of strict rules makes virtue ethics applicable in many different contexts, without losing attention to moral responsibility. It does not substitute other ethical approaches, being complementary to them, providing a human perspective of creativity moral assessment. Virtue ethics has enhanced the discussion since it introduced a character-based approach to the argument of creativity and morality. Nietzsche highlighted absolute freedom and self-overcoming, but was at risk of ethical relativism. Kant emphasized the concept of duty and responsibility to all but this came at the cost of being less flexible. Utilitarianism put an emphasis on consequences and benefit to the society but it fell short of oversimplification and inequalities. Virtue ethics, in its turn, sites greater emphasis on the ethical maturity of the creator and the building of virtues to lead an exciting life.

In this respect, virtue ethics helps seal the loophole between hypothetical universalism of Kant and outcome-based utilitarian ethics and it softens the radicalism of freedom described by Nietzsche by stressing responsibility and quality of character. It implies that there is not only a freedom in creativity, or creational rules, or expected outcomes, but the kind of beings we become when we are engaged in the practice of creating, and the sort of community we grow towards through our creative habits.

CREATIVITY AND ETHICAL RESPONSIBILITY IN THE DIGITAL AGE

In today's digital age, where technology develops at a rapid pace, the rise of artificial intelligence (AI), social media, genetic engineering and biotechnology has completely transformed the creative landscape, bringing forth serious ethical issues. One of these has been creativity; once something only humans did, it is something that can now be achieved by sophisticated algorithms that produce music, create art, and even make critical decisions in areas such as medicine, finance, and entertainment (Floridi & Cowls, 2019). Despite these innovations enhanced efficiency and augmented human capability, they have also posed authorship, intellectual property, and data privacy dilemmas and difficult questions about the broader societal implications (Zuboff, 2019). The more technology is used in the creative process as well as in decision making process the more the issues seem to appear and in reality, a two edged sword is what it is behind it, causing large leaps in human ingenuity and abilities, it has on the one hand, yet on the other, a source of anxiety over fear of ethical responsibility, undermining of human creativity and the fear of allowing unreasonable technological advances.

The division between human and machine-made art is crumbling with AI-generated works of art proving to be problematic when it comes to the way we approach the concept of authorship and the nature of our ethical responsibility in the era of AI developers and companies. In addition, digital platforms have influenced the delivery of information and have created a space for misinformation to spread at an unmatched rate while raising ethical issues of accountability and content moderation (Tufekci, 2018). Additionally, in the discipline of biotechnology, breakthroughs in genetic engineering have radicalized medicine and human health while simultaneously generating ethical concerns about genetic inequality, biohacking and the possible long adverse effects of editing genes. The emerging of these developments necessitates a framework that not only encourages technological creativity but also works simultaneously with the ethical responsibilities that protective advances undergo lags in their moral decor.

Artificial intelligence (AI) and automation are transforming the landscape of creative industries, reshaping the role of human creativity in unprecedented ways. Algorithms now compose symphonies, write poetry, generate paintings, and even craft journalistic articles (Boden, 2016). The advance of these technologies poses basic ethical concerns pertaining to originality, authorship, human agency, and the definition of creativity itself in digital age. Although involving AI can deliver performative value and extends artistic creation to novel possibilities, it also produces fears of discrimination, responsibility, and visibility, as well as worry about throwing human inventiveness away. The moral deed, then, is to will a way to understand whether technologically-induced creativity can improve human flourishing, or will imperil it, and to develop guidelines to balance innovation and responsibility.

Can Artificial Intelligence Generated Creativity Substitute Human Ingenuity?

The ability of the AI systems to generate art and literature has been improved immensely. Algorithms such as Google's DeepDream, OpenAI's DALL·E, and similar deep-learning models generate aesthetically complex images, music, and text at speeds unmatched by humans (Elgammal et al., 2017). These innovations challenge traditional conceptions of creativity by raising the question: can machines be truly creative, or do they merely recombine existing patterns from human-generated data? The issue of authorship is central. When an AI is used to create a track of music, or a work of visual art, who should get credit: the programmer who generated the algorithm, the person who trained or prompted the AI, or the AI itself? The existing law defining ownership is usually attached to either the developers or the users but this does not eliminate root philosophical concerns regarding originality. Creativity is traditionally viewed as an attempt of human beings to behave in a game of intentionality, imagination and morality. Kantian ethics would suggest that because AI lacks autonomous moral reasoning, it cannot qualify as an ethical creator (Kant, 1785/1997). In this respect, AI can only simulate creativity but not possess it.

However, utilitarianism offers a contrasting interpretation. If AI-generated art increases social welfare by democratizing access to cultural goods—making literature, art, and music more widely available—it may be ethically acceptable (Brynjolfsson & McAfee, 2014). To give an example, text-to-image technology enables non-artists to generate digital illustration, making them more included in the creative industries. The utilitarianism approach implies the value of consequences: in the case of AI improving the well-being by increasing access and reducing prices, creativity can be justified in ethical dimensions irrespective of the issues regarding originality.

However, critics claim that this kind of framing introduces the danger of turning art into a commodity, with its value dropping to the calculable social payback. Art frequently causes reflection, contests expectations, and creates cultural changes that cannot be measured in utilitarian terms. However artificially intelligent content can be as efficient as it can be relatively lacking the serendipitous, explorative and disruptive that human creativity has. The ethical issue is in the judgment as to whether style and form reproduced by technologies could replace the richness of human purpose and cultural meaning.

The Moral Responsibility of AI Developers in Algorithmic Decision-Making

The ethical issues of AI are far beyond creative arts and cover the activities of other spheres of social life. AI systems are playing an ever-larger role in making important decisions in employment, policing, healthcare and governance. Moral responsibility of the corporations and especially AI developers is pressing as such systems continue to become widespread.

Biased hiring algorithms, for example, have excluded candidates from minority backgrounds due to historical inequities encoded in training data, perpetuating systemic discrimination (West et al., 2019). Facial recognition technologies, widely deployed for surveillance, have been linked to racial profiling and violations of privacy (Zuboff, 2019). Predictive policing tools, heralded as objective, frequently reproduce existing social biases, disproportionately targeting marginalized communities and reinforcing structural injustice. These cases show that AI systems, without considering their ethical risks, may end up exacerbating disparities and jeopardizing the most essential rights. According to a Kantian view, these types of applications are profoundly problematic as they would regard persons as means rather than ends in themselves. To manipulate, exclude, or surveil people through opaque algorithms violates the categorical imperative's demand to respect human dignity (Kant, 1785/1997). The Kantian approach to ethics would entail the guidelines of fairness, respect and honesty as central outputs of the design of AI systems, irrespective of the consequences.

Utilitarianism- As in utilitarian perspective, efficiency or minimisation of harm to the greatest number of people justifies algorithmic decision-making. Utilitarianism, however, also reveals the trade-offs in such systems: more efficiency in the process of hiring employees because of the method of hiring can lead to greater inequality; predictive policing can be more energy-efficient and streamline the distribution of resources, however, it can also encourage unfairness to continue. These trade-offs reveal the limitations of utilitarian calculus, as quantifying the "greatest good" in diverse and plural societies is fraught with uncertainty and prone to oversimplification (Floridi & Taddeo, 2016). Virtue ethics provides an additional lens. It does not dwell solely on rules or need to face the consequences, but on the moral nature of developers and institutions. AI systems should be created with virtues such as honesty, prudence, fairness, and responsibility, fostering technologies that reflect moral integrity rather than profit-driven expedience (MacIntyre, 2007). It focuses on the development of ethical culture of technology development instead of focusing on compliance with external regulations.

Value Assignment, Accountability, and Ethical Ambivalence

The issue of value assignment is one of the core ethical problems of AI-generated creativity. The worth of art, literature and innovation is difficult to measure: art may speak to the culture, subjectivity or only time may reveal its value. Utilitarianism is ill-suited to this challenge, being that it too may prioritize quantifiable results and underemphasize the immeasurable, revolutionary strengths of creativity. To give an illustration, a computer-generated painting can become a great success with a vast audience, yet its role in human reflection, empathy, or cultural critique might be minor in comparison with an obnoxious art piece created by a human. Similarly, assigning responsibility in AI systems remains complex. Who takes responsibility of an algorithm making a discriminatory decision: the developers, the data curators or the institution deploying the algorithm? This accountability framework tends to be vague, giving corporations a way to clumsily dismiss responsibility due to its technical or market impassivity. The lack of obvious accountability risks normalizing harms created by AI: prejudice, exclusion, surveillance, and others are bad costs that come with such and such progress. This is a corollary of the ambivalence of creativity, which the reviewer identified as the possible risks of harm or immense potential in social benefits in AI-driven innovations. The moral duty is to develop structures that would bring maximum good, and to minimize harm, not in a theoretical sense but within practicable protections.

Cultural Sensitivity and Global Perspectives

The consideration of morality of AI cannot disengage culture. What to one people is considered a useful innovation is a harmful thing to another. For example, facial recognition technologies are embraced in some countries as tools of security, while in others they are condemned as instruments of authoritarian control (Zuboff, 2019). The acceptability of AI-generated art is also different among cultural traditions with varying beliefs about originality, imitation, and authorship. Rawls's emphasis on contextual moral reasoning is particularly relevant here. The universality of Kantian ethics threatens to be rigid, whereas the utilitarian threatens to homogenize the different (and unequal) values under one scale of utility. Rawlsian approach to justice implies that it has to be sensitive to pluralism, where ethical models on AI can allow themselves to be malleable in various cultures in maintaining the basic promises of justice and equality.

TOWARD ETHICAL SAFEGUARDS IN AI DEVELOPMENT

The most burning question pertains to the fact whether AI should be creative enough or not, but the question that arises was how the societies can create a stable authority regarding the creativity of AI and ethical usage of it. Several safeguards are necessary. First, the algorithmic systems have to be designed in such a way that they provide transparency that allows the process of decision making to be scrutinized. Second, responsibility should be directed clearly to developers, corporations and institutions. Third, fairness and non-discrimination must be embedded in design, requiring deliberate auditing of training data and outcomes (Floridi & Taddeo, 2016). Fourth, the process should be open to the society so that the ethical discussions include various cultural values and democratic participation. There is a role to be played by policymakers in institutionalizing such safeguards by way of regulatory frameworks, ethics, and cross-cultural collaboration. Technological innovation and ethical responsibility can be bridged through professional codes of conduct, corporate responsibility commitments and interdisciplinary oversight boards. The emergence of AI and automation in the realm of creativity and decision-making is a metaphor of the ambivalence of any modern-day innovation. On the one hand, AI can democratize creativity and efficiency; it can create benefits to society. On one hand, it threatens to cause discredit to human dignity, systemic biases, and culture commercialization. Kantian ethics emphasises how human beings should be respected as ends, not as a means, and this form of ethics requires AI to respect dignity and fairness. Utilitarianism emphasizes the prospects of delivering social benefits to the utmost but demonstrates the complexity of optimizing trade-offs and counting on intangible cultural assets. Virtue ethics would focus on virtuousness of developers and establishments, with the culture being one that upholds responsibility, honesty and prudence in technological development. Lastly, Rawls points out that context and pluralism should be taken into account as far as globally used technologies are concerned; it is essential to apply culturally informed methods of assessment. Finally, ethics of AI and automation is not a single model. Rather, they demand a balanced view where the clash of freedom and responsibility, innovation and harm, and creativity and accountability are recognized. The only way through which societies can ensure that the creativity of AI contributes to the flourishing of humanity instead of an undermining factor is to incorporate safeguarding measures and develop more virtuous practices as well as through critical and pluralistic reflection.

Social Media and the Ethics of Digital Expression

The interconnection of the world using the social media platforms has revolutionized communication, political engagement, and cultural engagement. Platforms such as Facebook, Twitter (now X), Instagram, and TikTok allow individuals to share ideas, mobilize movements, and democratize creativity at an unprecedented scale. Yet, alongside these benefits, social media has amplified misinformation, enabled data exploitation, deepened political manipulation, and raised profound ethical concerns (Tufekci, 2018). The question now becomes how to strike a balance between freedom of expression which is one of the biggest values in democratic societies and the demand to regulate content on platforms to make sure that creativity is put forth in the digital space to enhance a sensible discussion instead of causing misinformation and polarisation.

The Spread of Misinformation and Digital Accountability

Among the most pressing ethical challenges of social media is the proliferation of misinformation, disinformation, and the rise of deepfake technologies (Zuboff, 2019). The interface design of social media platforms focuses on encouraging communication, whereby algorithms promote the content that is most probable to get clicks and shares and to form reactions. This often means privileging sensational, polarizing, or misleading narratives over accurate but less engaging information. Causing confusion over what is true and what is not, misinformation can travel rapidly, and it has real-life implications as to elections, health, and societal bonds. These developments raise critical questions of accountability. Are social media companies supposed to be accountable by what they accelerate? Or is it the case that those subject to responsibility are mostly the users eating and sharing information? Tighter regulation poses the risk of violating the freedom of speech but in the absence of control there are possibilities of manipulation and exploitation. From a Kantian perspective, content moderation must follow universal duties: knowingly spreading false or harmful information violates the imperative to treat humanity with respect and honesty (Kant, 1785/1997). Appreciation of untruth creates havoc to human dignity through the use of people as objects where the bottom line is to gain profit or ideology.

Utilitarianism, however, frames the issue in terms of consequences. Alignment of harmful misinformation could boost the general social up-lift of populations, particularly guardianship of democratic institutions and the security of public health.

Yet utilitarian reasoning also reveals tensions: content moderation could stifle legitimate dissent, curtail minority perspectives, or privilege dominant narratives (Mill, 1863/2001). The issue of ethics is the creation of mechanisms that decrease the harmful factor without ending pluralism, so that freedom of expression is provided, but with a minimum destructive impact is achieved. Virtue ethics provides another lens, emphasizing the cultivation of virtues such as honesty, responsibility, and integrity among both platform designers and users (Hursthouse, 1999). A moral social media environment would not make sensationalism and lying lucrative but it would motivate knowledgeable discussion and understanding. Similarly, Rawls's emphasis on fairness and context-sensitive reasoning reminds us that regulations must respect pluralism while ensuring equal access to truthful and reliable information (Rawls, 1971).

Beyond Misinformation: Biotechnological Parallels

Even though social media and biotechnology may appear unrelated to each other, they are both illustrations of the situation where innovation is ahead of regulation. Genetic engineering, particularly CRISPR-Cas9, holds promise for curing hereditary diseases but also raises questions about genetic inequality, identity, and human dignity. In this case, the comparison of the social media is informative: unusual opportunities provided by technologies can both increase inequality or introduce harm as long as not controlled. From a utilitarian perspective, gene editing is justified if it reduces suffering and promotes health outcomes for the greatest number. However, Kantian ethics cautions against commodifying human life or undermining its inherent dignity (Habermas, 2003). In a similar fashion, social media can democratize the communication process but when social media is manipulative, when it abuses data, and when it destroys the civic trust it contravenes the ethical imperative to regard human beings as ends and not as a means. The two realms demonstrate that ethical controls, disclosure and responsibility agents are urgently required to carve abuse of this nature as well as foster creativity.

Ethical Frameworks for Digital Creativity

The paradoxes of social media are an indication of the larger issue concerning the conflict between creative technological thinking on the one hand and moral accountability on the other hand. Digital spaces facilitate self-expression, but also reveal weaknesses there: violation of privacy, addictive loops of use, online bullying and narrow-minded communities. Addressing these challenges requires integrating ethical frameworks into governance. Kant ethics places emphasis on the elements of honesty, transparency and human dignity in the digital society. The following engines are helpful to tackle the issue from a normative point of view:

- Utilitarian ethics demands evaluation of harms and benefits. Risk-reduction policies designed to prevent misinformation can have social benefits at the cost of possible free-speech restrictions.
- Virtue ethics focuses on the development of responsibility, empathy, and fairness on both the producers and the consumers of digital media.
- Rawlsian fairness highlights the importance of context-sensitive reasoning and equitable access to trustworthy information in pluralistic societies (Rawls, 1971).

Toward Safeguards and Global Regulation

Since social media goes across borders, national controls are not enough. Responsible governance must be interstate, inter-corporate, and inter-civil society, moreover, with global implications. The following unified framework can be used for digital ethics grounded in transparency, accountability, fairness, and respect for human rights:

- Algorithmic transparency – allowing social media to be scrutinized on how content is prioritised and amplified.
- Accountability systems - definition of responsibility, clear attribution of harms related to misinformation or harmful content.
- Cross-cultural sensitivity - that the laws must take into consideration cultural variances without neglecting universal moral binding on dignity and impartiality.
- An Interdisciplinary governance: bringing ethicists, technologists, policymakers and communities in to formulate standards with regards to digital expression.

Social media epitomizes the ambivalence of digital creativity. It has the potential to support those marginalized, to democratize the information, and bring the solidarity across the world. Simultaneously, it has the potential to misinform, introduce disharmony, and undermine democratic faith. It is the moral challenge to satisfy freedom of expression and responsibility so that that digital creativity can be an enabling form rather than a manipulating one. Kantian ethics requires that the creators of digital products and corporations share an obligation to truth and honor; utilitarianism points to the necessity of determining communal gains and damages; virtue ethics focuses on developing accountability and compassion; performing justice across cultural backgrounds is stressed by Rawls. Collectively, these frameworks can provide a more detailed basis of ethical policy development and guidance to corporate practice and user responsibilities. Transparency, accountability, and international collaboration will be key to keeping a digital future ethical. Societies can only expect digital creativity to be a force that spurs human flourishing and not lead to increased crises of trust, inequality, and manipulation by way of embedding moral protections in the craft and management of social media.

Creativity as the ability to innovate is lauded as a driver in all aspects of progress, artistic representation, and technological development, though the ethics of this process is not only ambiguous but also limited within its context. As this chapter has shown, creativity can be constructive or destructive depending on who exercises it, how it is employed, and the circumstances surrounding its use (Gaut, 2010). Nietzschean creative freedom presents a stimulating vision of boundless innovation, but when left unchecked, it risks moral irresponsibility and harm to society (Reginster, 2009). By contrast, Kant's deontological framework guarantees ethical responsibility in artistic and scientific endeavors, though its emphasis on rigid and universal duties may at times inhibit the very freedom and innovation it seeks to guide (Kant, 1785/1997). Utilitarianism, with its pragmatic aim of maximizing well-being, provides a useful framework for evaluating creative ethics, but it often struggles to balance competing interests and ethical trade-offs (Mill, 1863/2001).

The creativity judgment is getting more intricate and multidisciplinary in an age defined by the globalization process, digital culture, and the development of new technologies. Creativity is not inherently moral or immoral; its significance lies in intent, impact, and application (Gaut, 2010). For example, CRISPR gene-editing technologies hold promise for curing genetic disorders but simultaneously raise concerns about human enhancement, genetic inequality, and bioengineering risks. The same can be said of artistic creativity, which can carry social change and political activism or may easily fall to the misinformation, propaganda and psychological manipulation. Therefore, ethics approach to creativity should go further to declare an act good or bad. It requires a contextual assessment of the creator's intent, the societal effects of their innovations, and the potential ethical trade-offs involved (Boden, 2016). Unless it is approached with such reflective attentiveness, then creativity is treated as an uncertain power- it can send man and nature into cooperative processes, which elevate the overall well-being of mankind, or it can send man down the paths of self-destruction.

CONCLUSION

Nietzsche's conception of creativity, in which the *Übermensch* breaks free of conventional morality, provides a seductive though morally suspect model (Nietzsche, 1883/2005). He has inspired generations of artists, scientists, and innovators to break tradition, reject norms, and follow their own creative destinies (Pippin, 2010). Nonetheless, the supposed freedom for unchecked creativity to do harm insured by Nietzsche's abnegation of moral constraints raises a problem of creative autonomy morally legitimating behaviors that are unethical or destructive (Schacht, 1983). An outstanding example is the distortion of Nietzsche's philosophy by Nazi ideology, which usurped the notion of the *Übermensch* to defend racial superiority, militarism, and eugenics (Safranski, 2002). The distortion leads to the illustration of the risks that uncontrolled creative autonomy entails when it exists outside of ethical responsibility, in particular when applied to creative work which is decontextualized. The absence of a moral responsibility does allow the use of creativity to be at the service of other oppressive, violent or exploitative purposes.

Kant's Deontological Safeguards in Creative Endeavors

The rigorous moral framework provided by Kantian ethics ensures respect for human dignity and upholds universal ethical principles (Kant, 1785/1997) in the appreciation of creative endeavor. According to the Categorical Imperative, if an act of creativity cannot be willed as universal moral law it is unethical. Innovation is therefore ensured of working in tandem with the ethical responsibility so that there is no exploitation, fraud or injury in the creative spheres. The Kantian inflexible moral framework, does in fact, pose a problem to artists and scientists. While Kantian ethics require strict moral justification of creative actions (Guyer, 2012), creativity often thrives on disruption, controversy, and challenges to moral norms—conditions increasingly common in the digital age. As a case in point, must provocative or controversial art be curtailed so as not to offend the existing moral values? Or is scientific research on stem cell and artificial intelligence to be limited by invariably defined ethical responsibilities? Kantian ethics therefore provide an ethical protective factor against destructive creativity, but probably to the detriment of artistic freedom, intellectual dissidence and technological adventurism.

Utilitarian Pragmatism and Creative Trade-offs

Utilitarianism, supported by Mill's outlook, approaches creativity in a practical, outcomes-focused manner, prioritizing endeavors that maximize societal well-being (Mill, 1863/2001). It enables scientific breakthroughs, technological innovations, and social changes that yield the most happiness with the least suffering (Driver, 2012). Yet utilitarian ethics also reveal persistent trade-offs. AI automation increases efficiency but displaces workers, generating economic inequalities (Brynjolfsson & McAfee, 2014). Social media enhances connectivity and activism but also spreads misinformation and fosters digital addiction, undermining trust in public discourse (Tufekci, 2018). Drug discoveries have the potential of saving lives and eliminating disparities in health, but company-driven profit goals limit access to drugs. These examples underscore utilitarianism's challenge of balancing benefits against harms so that progress does not privilege some groups at the expense of others (Sinnott-Armstrong, 2018).

Virtue Ethics and the Character of the Creator

Contrary to the strict standards or cost and benefit approach to ethics that Kant and the utilitarians prescribed respectively, virtue ethics pays more attention to the moral integrity and motives of the producer. Rooted in Aristotle's philosophy, virtue ethics argues that good creativity emerges from cultivating virtues such as wisdom, courage, honesty, and empathy (Aristotle, trans. 2009; Hursthouse, 1999). An example of this is that an artist with empathy and a sense of righteousness will not play into creating a propaganda that is damaging to society but a scientist who uses intellectual integrity and humility will not be manipulative to gain a certain benefit. Virtue ethics does not primarily ask "what rule must I follow?" (As in Kant) or "what outcome will this maximize?" (As in utilitarianism), but rather "what kind of person should I be while creating?" (MacIntyre, 2007). This model puts creativity in the context of a lifetime course of moral character development, which will imply that disruptive innovations will be based on integrity and social accountability. In contemporary terms, virtue ethics is especially relevant in AI development, where coders and designers must embody virtues of fairness and responsibility to avoid embedding systemic biases (Floridi & Cowls, 2019). By focusing on the character of creators, virtue ethics provides a human-centered anchor to creativity that neither dismisses freedom (as Kant sometimes does) nor reduces morality to outcomes (as utilitarianism risks).

An interdisciplinary ethical framework must address creativity's evolution across philosophy, law, science, technology, and art (Floridi & Cowls, 2019). Creative ethics can neither be strictly philosophical nor purely technological; it requires dialogue between ethical theory, artistic integrity, human rights, and policy (Raworth, 2017). For instance, algorithmic decision-making reflects systemic biases unless checked by ethical scrutiny (O'Neil, 2016). Artists and media creators grapple with dilemmas of misinformation, manipulation, and content moderation (Zuboff, 2019). Gene editing and human enhancement raise profound bioethical questions requiring regulation to safeguard dignity and equity. All these issues prove that creativity should be influenced by a comprehensive number of ethical points of view. Freedom of Nietzsche is the liberation of innovation and needs protection against abuse. Kantian duty can offer form but cannot be too strict because it could not adapt to the disruptive nature of creativity. Utilitarian calculations also show the benefit to the society at large but has to implement a balance pro of the benefits. Finally, virtue ethics is focused on the moral quality of the innovator and judge's creativity on the basis of the creativity being responsible, modest, and morally upright.

Ultimately, whether we are artists, scientists, or innovators, we inhabit a universe that is both commonsensical and creative, both moral and creative, with the interface between these two domains being directional in human civilization. The ethical course has to be steered because, to leverage the power of creativity as a force of change, the latter has to be ethically guided. Creativity does not simply influence individuals who are creators but also the society, environment, and posterity. It carries the power to generate injustice and inequalities that may continue into a future; or it can help realize righteousness, compassion and thriving. To have an ethically sound sense of novelty, Nietzsche, Kant, Mill and Aristotle have to be brought together in terms of freedom, duty, utility, and virtues. It is only then, that creativity can stay innovative and ethically responsible to sustain a hope that human ingenuity is instead constructive than destructive, protective as opposed to exploitive and transnationally accountable to a better and more just tomorrow.

REFERENCES

Anscombe, G. E. M. (1958). Modern moral philosophy. *Philosophy (London, England), 33*(124), 1–19. DOI: 10.1017/S0031819100037943

Aristotle, . (2009). *Nicomachean ethics* (Ross, W. D., Trans.). Oxford University Press. (Original work published 350 BCE)

Boden, M. A. (2016). Creativity and artificial intelligence. *Artificial Intelligence, 103*(1-2), 347–356. DOI: 10.1016/S0004-3702(98)00055-1

Bostrom, N. (2014). *Superintelligence: Paths, dangers, strategies.* Oxford University Press.

Bostrom, N., & Yudkowsky, E. (2014). The ethics of artificial intelligence. In Frankish, K., & Ramsey, W. M. (Eds.), *The Cambridge handbook of artificial intelligence* (pp. 316–334). Cambridge University Press. DOI: 10.1017/CBO9781139046855.020

Brynjolfsson, E., & McAfee, A. (2014). *The second machine age: Work, progress, and prosperity in a time of brilliant technologies.* W. W. Norton.

Csikszentmihalyi, M. (1996). *Creativity: Flow and the psychology of discovery and invention.* HarperCollins.

Driver, J. (2012). *Consequentialism.* Routledge.

Elgammal, A., Liu, B., Elhoseiny, M., & Mazzone, M. (2017). CAN: Creative adversarial networks, generating "art" by learning about styles and deviating from style norms. *arXiv preprint arXiv:1706.07068.* https://arxiv.org/abs/1706.07068

Floridi, L., & Cowls, J. (2019). A unified framework of five principles for AI in society. *Harvard Data Science Review, 1*(1), 1–15. DOI: 10.1162/99608f92.8cd550d1

Floridi, L., & Taddeo, M. (2016). What is data ethics? *Philosophical Transactions. Series A, Mathematical, Physical, and Engineering Sciences, 374*(2083), 20160360. DOI: 10.1098/rsta.2016.0360 PMID: 28336805

Gaut, B. (2010). The philosophy of creativity. *Philosophy Compass, 5*(12), 1034–1046. DOI: 10.1111/j.1747-9991.2010.00351.x

Guyer, P. (2012). *Kant on freedom, law, and happiness.* Cambridge University Press.

Habermas, J. (2003). *The future of human nature.* Polity Press.

Hursthouse, R. (1999). *On virtue ethics.* Oxford University Press.

Kant, I. (1997). *Groundwork for the metaphysics of morals* (Gregor, M. J., Trans.). Cambridge University Press. (Original work published 1785)

Korsgaard, C. M. (2010). *The sources of normativity*. Cambridge University Press.

Kristjánsson, K. (2018). *Virtuous emotions*. Oxford University Press. DOI: 10.1093/oso/9780198809678.001.0001

MacIntyre, A. (2007). *After virtue: A study in moral theory* (3rd ed.). University of Notre Dame Press. (Original work published 1981)

Mill, J. S. (2001). *Utilitarianism*. Hackett Publishing. (Original work published 1863)

Mokyr, J. (2018). *A culture of growth: The origins of the modern economy*. Princeton University Press.

Nehamas, A. (1987). *Nietzsche: Life as literature*. Harvard University Press.

Nietzsche, F. (1966). *Beyond good and evil: Prelude to a philosophy of the future* (W. Kaufmann, Trans.). Vintage Books. (Original work published 1886).

Nietzsche, F. (2005). *Thus spoke Zarathustra: A book for all and none* (G. Parkes, Trans.). Oxford University Press. (Original work published 1883).

Nietzsche, F. (2007). *On the genealogy of morals* (Johnston, I., Trans.). Dover Publications. (Original work published 1887)

Nochlin, L. (1989). *The politics of vision: Essays on nineteenth-century art and society*. Harper & Row.

O'Neil, C. (2016). *Weapons of math destruction: How big data increases inequality and threatens democracy*. Crown Publishing.

Pippin, R. B. (2010). *Nietzsche, psychology, and first philosophy*. University of Chicago Press.

Rawls, J. (1971). *A theory of justice*. Harvard University Press. DOI: 10.4159/9780674042605

Raworth, K. (2017). *Doughnut economics: Seven ways to think like a 21st-century economist*. Chelsea Green Publishing.

Reginster, B. (2009). *The affirmation of life: Nietzsche on overcoming nihilism*. Harvard University Press.

Rhodes, R. (1986). *The making of the atomic bomb*. Simon & Schuster.

Sachs, J. D. (2015). *The age of sustainable development*. Columbia University Press. DOI: 10.7312/sach17314

Safranski, R. (2002). *Nietzsche: A philosophical biography*. W. W. Norton & Company.

Schacht, R. (1983). *Nietzsche's critique of morality*. Routledge.

Sinnott-Armstrong, W. (2018). *Think again: How to reason and argue*. Oxford University Press.

Tufekci, Z. (2018). *Twitter and tear gas: The power and fragility of networked protest*. Yale University Press.

West, S. M., Whittaker, M., & Crawford, K. (2019). *Discriminating systems: Gender, race, and power in AI*. AI Now Institute.

Zuboff, S. (2019). *The age of surveillance capitalism: The fight for a human future at the new frontier of power*. PublicAffairs.

Chapter 7
Ethical Leadership in Social Creativity:
Effect on OCB Mediating Role of Organization Culture Integrated Healthcare in Ethiopia

Wako Jio
Bule Hora University, Ethiopia

Shashi Kant
https://orcid.org/0000-0003-4722-5736
Lovely Professional University, India

Hirut Assegid
https://orcid.org/0009-0003-6192-459X
Bule Hora University, Ethiopia

Zerihun Kinde Alemu
https://orcid.org/0000-0002-8546-2882
Ethiopian Civil Service University, Ethiopia

ABSTRACT

The research focuses on understanding how ethical leadership impacts social creativity as well as resulting organizational citizenship behavior (OCB) in integrated healthcare facilities of Ethiopia. A total of 390 healthcare employees participated in the study that used statistical approaches like Kaiser-Meyer-Olkin (KMO) as well as confirmatory factor analysis (CFA) to prove construct validity. SEM analysis through AMOS software operates as the research methodology to evaluate the proposed connections among ethical leadership, social creativity, organizational

DOI: 10.4018/979-8-3373-2742-6.ch007

culture, as well as OCB. The study discovers that ethical leadership produces enhanced social creativity that positively affects OCB. Organizational culture serves as a mediator that intensifies the impact of ethical leadership on social creativity while boosting its influence over OCB according to this analysis. Organizations must dedicate resources to develop ethical leadership approaches as well as build powerful organizational cultures because this combination results in innovative employee behaviors.

INTRODUCTION

Ethical leadership stands as a crucial organizational element because of global interconnection especially in healthcare institutions (Taamneh et al., 2024). Through ethical leadership organizations develop environments that support innovation along through collaboration as well as achieve transparency as well as integrity through accountability (Jio et al., 2025a). The research examines the influence of ethical leadership on social creativity as well as its consequences for organizational citizenship behavior (OCB) in Ethiopian integrated healthcare facilities (Jio et al., 2025b). The principles of ethical leadership stem from research in moral philosophy as well as organizational behavior which emphasizes proper ethical choices as well as leader examples for decision-making (Sugiono & Nurhasan, 2025). Various research studies demonstrate that ethical leadership creates positive effects on multiple organizational results that involve employee engagement as well as trust as well as operational performance (Şengüllendi et al., 2024). Most studies about ethical leadership took place in Western areas although researchers have failed to understand developing nation's distribution specifically in Africa (Azhar et al., 2025). Ethiopian healthcare faces several practical obstacles due to insufficient resources as well as high labor shifts as well as cultural elements which could affect leader success rates as well as staff conduct (Jio et al., 2025b). The situation emphasizes the necessity of developing scientific studies that guide decision-making processes. Research exploring the mediating impact of organizational culture on relations among ethical leadership as well as social creativity toward OCB remains insufficient for this context in particular (Taamneh et al., 2024).

The objective of this chapter involves obtaining empirical data through a research sample of 390 healthcare employees in Ethiopia. Through confirmatory factor analysis as well as structural equation modeling the study will uncover how ethical leadership as well as social creativity jointly relates to the outcome of OCB. This study's main research question is: *How does organizational citizenship behavior as well as social creativity in integrated healthcare settings get influenced by ethical leadership, as well as how does organizational culture mediate these relationships?*

In addition to advancing scholarly knowledge, answering this question will provide useful information for decision-makers as well as healthcare executives working to increase organizational efficacy in Ethiopia as well as comparable settings.

BACKGROUND OF THE STUDY

The research setting establishes ethical leadership as fundamental for organizational functioning particularly through in the essential healthcare sector (Jio et al., 2025b). Ethical leadership places value on maintaining integrity together through fairness while making moral decisions in order to develop trust as well as teamwork among personnel (Azhar et al., 2025). Healthcare venues that conduct life-saving work need ethical leadership to maintain optimal patient outcomes because decision-making consequences remain significant. Various case reports depict the obstacles which arise during healthcare ethical leadership implementation (Taamneh et al., 2024). South African investigators found that ethical guidelines did not prevent many leaders from failing to maintain these principles since systemic results including resource restrictions as well as bureaucratic workload challenges highly influenced their decision-making. Healthcare leaders dealt through difficult situations where ethical needs conflicted through operational requirements leading to possible ethical standards deterioration. Nigerian research findings documented that insufficient training in ethical decision-making among healthcare leaders produced inconsistent ethical practice implementation that intensified the workplace trust deficit as well as employee engagement problems (Jio et al., 2025a). The healthcare system at Ethiopia has achieved a lot in the last 10 years mainly through programs including the Health Extension Program (HEP) whose objective is to enhance access to the basic health services in the rural regions. By 2023 the percentage had risen to approximately 70 percent with the population living within five kilometers of a health facility; thus, increased access. This has improved maternal health with the mother mortality ratio standing at 676 to 100,000 of live births in 2010 and currently to about 401 in 2021. On the same note, infant mortality rate has also decreased by 123 to 88 per 1,000 live births due to efforts made to specifically address this issue, such as the Maternal and Child Health (MCH) Initiative. Nevertheless Taamneh et al., 2024), Ethiopia continues to struggle with the communicable diseases especially HIV/ AIDS, which is afflicting approximately 0.9 percent of the adult population, and malaria, which is endemic in most parts. The nation has approximately 4,800 health centers and 3,000 hospitals mainly government-owned, yet there is still a lack of resources in the country, and shortage of healthcare professionals. Such programs as the Community-Based Health Insurance (CBHI) have increased coverage and lowered financial impediments to access. Although this has been achieved to a commendable extent, more efforts are needed to combat disparities and improve healthcare outcomes nationally (Jio et al., 2025b) .

Ethiopia faces intensified problems because of its economic conditions which block resource availability as well as lead to heavy staff departures as well as traditional customs that contrast Through Western moral codes (Sugiono & Nurhasan, 2025). Healthcare managers in this example select their operational requirements ahead of ethical considerations thus establishing a pattern that damages staff loyalty as well as work commitment. The vertical hierarchy of Ethiopian organizational culture prevents employees from freely sharing concerns or innovative solutions because employees feel they lack the authority to do so (Şengüllendi et al., 2024). These real-world difficulties highlight the need for a sophisticated comprehension of how moral leadership might be successfully incorporated into the particular setting of Ethiopian healthcare (Jio et al., 2025b). This study intends to offer practical insights that can assist healthcare leaders in navigating these complications as well as promoting a more moral as well as involved workplace by analyzing the interactions among ethical leadership, social creativity, as well as organizational citizenship behavior (Taamneh et al., 2024). In the end, resolving these issues is essential to improve patient care results in Ethiopia's healthcare system as well as organizational performance (Jio et al., 2025a).

STATEMENT OF THE PROBLEM

Many integrated healthcare facilities in Ethiopia as well as other locations worldwide show a substantial gap among the theoretical ideal of ethical leadership practices which improve organizational outcomes together through worker participation as well as actual observed implementations (Jio et al., 2025b). Leadership in the ideal state requires constant display of ethical standards together through developing team trust as well as inspiring social creativity (Sugiono & Nurhasan, 2025). Numerous research findings demonstrate conflicting results about ethical leadership because practical obstacles such as resource constraints as well as cumbersome bureaucracies along through cultural patterns which oppose transparency as well as responsibility systems work against ethical leadership practices (Jio et al., 2025a). Research findings have shown that researchers still need to clarify how key structures function in the healthcare system of Ethiopia (Taamneh et al., 2024). Numerous research papers demonstrate that ethical leadership creates positive relationships among employee engagement as well as OCB yet additional research results face ambiguity when studying organizational culture's mediation capabilities (Azhar et al., 2025). The majority of theoretical work originates from Western perspectives which fall short in understanding the true nature of Ethiopian organizational behavior (Jio et al., 2025b). Research challenges investigators to determine effective methods for implementing ethical leadership across diverse cultural environments as well as also poses problems because study results struggle to translate findings from one territorial region to another (Jio et al., 2025a). The practical implementation of ethical leadership becomes complicated because of two primary issues: high employee turnover together through deficient training for ethical decision-making (Taamneh et al., 2024). Organizations face both development limitations for supportive cultures as well as reduced employee morale together through negative patient care results because of these challenges (Şengüllendi et al., 2024).

There are a number of ethical issues and crises that confront healthcare leaders in Ethiopia in their decision-making and resource management. There is the problem of limited resources, especially in the rural regions where the healthcare centers are underfunded and understaffed. Leaders have to balance between the ethical issues of delivering fair care to all populations and devoting resources to high-impact interventions (Taamneh et al., 2024). Also, cultural dominance of traditional medicine brings a dilemma of ways to combine culturally accepted practices with evidenced based medical care, whereby the leader must be able to strike a balance between upholding cultural beliefs and the scientific rigor. Besides, corruption and transparent problems in the healthcare system may undermine ethics, causing unfair service access. Lastly, the current pressure of communicable diseases, including HIV/AIDS and malaria, contributes to the exacerbation of ethical issues since the leaders must focus on the most urgent social demands and guarantee the rights and dignity of patients are prioritized in care provision (Jio et al., 2025a). By offering actual data on the connections among OCB, social creativity, as well as ethical leadership in the Ethiopian hospital setting, this study seeks to close these gaps. This study will shed light on how organizational culture mediates these associations using a large sample size as well as sophisticated statistical techniques, providing knowledge that may guide theory as well as practice. Future scholars wishing to investigate the intricacies of moral leadership in many contexts as well as politicians hoping to put into practice successful leadership techniques that boost organizational effectiveness as well as increase healthcare delivery will find value in the results. The ultimate goal of this research is to close the current knowledge gaps as well as advance a more thorough comprehension of moral leadership in integrated healthcare systems.

THEORETICAL FOUNDATION

Transformational Leadership Theory: Leaders who implement transformational leadership deliver motivational power which enables followers to surpass their personal goals by working for organizational advancement. Researcher James

MacGregor Burns applied these two distinct leadership approaches against each other in his late 1970s work. Transformational leaders enable workplaces that promote innovative approaches by making employees participate in organizational procedure development. The healthcare setting greatly benefits from leaders who show transformational behaviors because these leaders motivate their team members to combine ethical practices through teamwork for better patient outcomes (Eaton et al., 2024).

Social Exchange Theory: Social exchange theory developed by George Homans and Peter Blau defines social behavior patterns as outcomes from exchanges which seek maximum gains against minimum expenses. Ethical leadership in organizations triggers employees to return ethical conduct through positive behaviors which includes OCB. Trust together through social bonds represents an essential element which demonstrates the value of mutual relationships through in work environments. Knowledge of these exchanges provides leaders in healthcare through tools to build an employee base that seeks active participation (Luo et al., 2025).

Organizational Culture Theory: The shared values beliefs plus norms which generate organizational behavior patterns constitute the core focus of this theory. Organizational culture theory described by Edgar Schein explains that organizational culture shapes employee perceptions about what their roles entail. Organization culture through positive qualities boosts employee dedication along through motivation creating better outcomes for the entire entity. Patient care receives enhanced benefits from a healthcare supportive culture when this culture matches ethical leadership because it promotes social creativity together Through OCB (Sindakis et al., 2024).

Ethical Leadership Theory: Ethical leadership theory places great significance on ethical conduct along through moral principles throughout leadership practices. According to moral philosophical foundations this theory shows how ethical leadership of leaders impacts what followers do as well as how they think. Ethical leaders maintain integrity combined through fairness as well as a dedication to performing the right actions. This theory establishes key knowledge about how ethical leadership produces social creativity while encouraging healthcare citizenship behaviors thus being very appropriate for this study context (Shiundu, 2024).

The main theoretical foundation of this study derives from ***Ethical Leadership Theory*** because it specifically examines ethical practices in healthcare organizations. The theory outlines basic principles about how ethical leadership creates social creativity as well as OCB thus guiding this study to investigate these connections in the Ethiopian context (Shiundu, 2024).

DEFINITION AND ORIGIN OF TERMS

Ethical Leadership: The principle of ethical leadership consists of showing good behavior through personal conduct as well as building mutual relationships through supporters along through leading people to show the same appropriate ethical actions. Leaders in organizations require modeling ethical behavior which builds trust as well as organizational integrity according to the concept that emerged from ethical theory combined through leadership studies (Azhar et al., 2025).

Social Creativity: Social creativity describes group as well as individual capabilities to develop fresh ideas as well as creative solutions by working together in collaborative settings. The concept emerged from organizational behavior as well as social psychology disciplines to show that organizational success as well as creative problem-solving arises from different perspectives (Perry-Smith, 2024).

Organizational Citizenship Behavior (OCB): The concept of OCB defines additional employee actions which are voluntary yet productive for the organization above standard work expectations. Organ introduced the concept during the 1980s which underscores how unapproved additional employee actions serve the fundamental operational requirements of organizations (Worku & Debela, 2024).

Organizational Culture: Organizational culture represents the collective teachings as well as work traditions as well as group perceptions which define an organizational identity. In the 1980s Edgar Schein made organizational culture popular by explaining how it affects employee conduct while impacting business success. A solid organizational culture helps employees grow more committed as well as brings improved performance levels for the organization (Sindakis et al., 2024).

EMPIRICAL LITERATURE REVIEW

Ethical Leadership in Social Creativity and Organizational Citizenship Behavior

Numerous studies exploring the connections among ethical leadership as well as social creativity as well as organizational citizenship behavior (OCB) have expanded across different organizational settings (Jio et al., 2025b). Organizations following ethical leadership principles create workplaces which inspire employees to perform extra duties as well as appreciate them in their functions (Taamneh et al., 2024). Research shows that ethical leaders possessing integrity as well as transparency as well as fairness enable trust-based collaboration that boosts social creativity in organizations. A research proved that leaders promoting ethical practices create better employee performance rates because they build an ethical as well as socially-responsible work environment. The climate enables staff members to participate actively in innovative problem-solving because they believe their ideas will be protected from any consequences. Ethical leaders become better at acknowledging as well as recognizing creative accomplishments so they can successfully build creativity through in their organization through recognition programs. The essential nature of innovation in healthcare requires leaders to exhibit ethical leadership so they can handle complicated ethical situations as well as stimulate team solidarity as well as creative problem-solving (Jio et al., 2025b). A literature review provides the findings with a solid base of other research works that investigate the essence of the constructs in the research topic. As an example, the reports on universal health coverage issued by World Health Organization (WHO) offer the necessary information about the access to healthcare, highlighting the significance of the equal distribution of services. Research into the social determinants of health has brought to light the extent that socioeconomic status has a significant impact on health outcomes, and thus it is important to assert that there is a critical relationship between income, education and health disparities (Taamneh et al., 2024. In addition, the Health Extension Program implemented in Ethiopia and reviewed by other researchers depicts the successful community-based intervention in promoting maternal and child health. A study highlights the connection between economic growth and improvement of health, which supports the fact that sustainable investments on health infrastructure have to be made. Combining these preliminary studies, the literature review does not only place the existing research findings into a perspective but also forms a solid theoretical framework that guides the further research direction in healthcare systems and policy making (Jio et al., 2025b).

Searchers found a straight connection among ethical leadership strategies as well as OCB which demonstrates ethical leaders help create conditions that motivate workers to contribute positively to their team members as well as company operations (Jio et al., 2025a). The healthcare sector requires OCB as collective work leads to enhanced patient success together through improved organizational effectiveness. Organizations experience better performance because people working under ethical leadership tend to show more compassion alongside courteous attitudes as well as civic merit (Taamneh et al., 2024). The mediating function of organizational culture in these interactions is further supported by empirical data. A supportive workplace culture, for example, enhances the beneficial benefits of moral leadership on OCB, according to a research. Employees are more likely to participate in social creativity as well as demonstrate civic activities in environments that appreciate as well as encourage ethical conduct. This emphasizes the significance of both moral leadership as well as the requirement for an ethical company culture (Şengüllendi et al., 2024).

H1: Ethical leadership in Social Creativity and organizational citizenship behavior having empirical association

Ethical Leadership in Social Creativity and Organization Culture

Academic research investigating the ethical leadership interaction through social creativity together through organization culture has intensified because businesses understand challenges in finding creative solutions in complex situations (Jio et al., 2025a). Organizations experience substantial influence on team creative capabilities from leaders who prioritize ethical values as well as standards known as ethical leaders. The research shows that ethical leadership enables an environment which promotes open communication as well as trust along through teamwork because these elements serve as critical conditions for social creativity. Ethical leadership builds a positive organizational culture which protects employee psychological well-being to create areas where creativity flourishes according to research findings (Şengüllendi et al., 2024). Workers who observe ethical leadership behavior from their superiors will actively share their innovative concepts as well as take acceptable risks as they feel protected from detrimental consequences (Taamneh et al., 2024). The connective environment plays a fundamental role in activating social creativity since it helps coworkers unite their thoughts to create innovative solutions that boost organizational performance. Studies have found that organizational culture functions as a mediator which connects ethical leadership through social creativity (Jio et al., 2025a). The research demonstrates ethical leaders who build organizational environments based on ethics lead workers to participate more often in creative work activities. Organizations Through embedded ethical standards create an environment where staff members demonstrate enhanced creativity because they understand their work associates through the organizational purpose. The alignment enhances creativity levels while strengthening employee belonging as well as concurrently increases their engagement together through productivity rates (Jio et al., 2025b).

Healthcare organizations specifically depend on ethical leadership to strengthen their organizational culture because adaptability as well as innovation represents top priorities for this sector (Şengüllendi et al., 2024). Healthcare organizations operated by ethical leaders develop stronger abilities to collaborate as well as innovate according to research findings. These companies are more capable of handling problems as well as coming up through innovative solutions, which eventually enhances patient care as well as organizational effectiveness. Despite these realizations, the majority of the research to date has been on Western contexts, leaving a significant knowledge vacuum about the ways in which corporate culture as well as ethical leadership interacts to foster social innovation across culturally varied situations (Jio et al., 2025a). By examining these processes inside Ethiopian healthcare companies, where certain cultural as well as contextual factors may affect how well ethical leadership fosters social creativity, this chapter aims to close this gap

(Jio et al., 2025b). The project intends to make significant additions to the body of knowledge on organizational culture as well as ethical leadership by investigating this link, providing information that may guide practice as well as policy in a variety of contexts (Taamneh et al., 2024).

H2: Ethical leadership in Social Creativity and organization Culture behavior having empirical association

Organization Culture and Organizational Citizenship Behavior

The examination of organizational culture impacts on organizational citizenship behavior (OCB) stands central in organizational behavior research because standard values among team members produce significant voluntary workplace conduct (Şengüllendi et al., 2024). A workplace setting determined by organizational culture will either support organizational citizenship behavior to thrive or will prevent its development. Empirical evidence establishes that organizations through positive cultures produce high levels of OCB because positive cultures inspire employees to perform acts that benefit organizational success. Historical studies developed OCB understanding by showing how cultures built on trust as well as respect together through workplace belongingness help workers exceed set duties (Sugiono & Nurhasan, 2025). Research findings showed organizations practicing team-based cultural approaches achieve increased levels of OCB from their employees. Organizational effectiveness improves when workers experience support from their work environment because they then demonstrate altruistic team-related conduct such as assisting colleagues. Additional research demonstrates how particular cultural attributes including innovative conduct through an open climate as well as ethical standards produce substantial impacts on OCB. The cultural practice of innovation enables organizations to drive employee initiative because workers feel openly enabled to make creative contributions to their groups. Employees display enhanced citizenship behaviors when they work in an environment that values ethical conduct because such cultures establish a proper moral framework which motivates employees to prioritize organizational as well as workmate interests (Şengüllendi et al., 2024).

The effects of corporate culture on OCB are especially noticeable in the healthcare industry. Research has shown that improved OCB among healthcare workers is correlated through a strong, positive organizational culture, which is essential for guaranteeing high-quality patient care (Sugiono & Nurhasan, 2025). Healthcare workers are more likely to act in ways that promote team dynamics as well as patient outcomes in settings that prioritize cooperation as well as support. Even though research shows that organizational culture as well as OCB are positively correlated, little is known about how these dynamics function in various cultural contexts, particularly in developing nations (Şengüllendi et al., 2024). The complexity of organizational culture as well as OCB in varied contexts may not be well captured by the majority of the research that has been done so far, which has mostly been done in Western settings. By investigating these interactions Through in Ethiopian healthcare institutions, this study seeks to close this knowledge gap as well as offer insights that may guide theory as well as practice in a variety of cultural contexts. In the end, better organizational performance as well as more successful management techniques may result from an awareness of how organizational culture affects OCB in this situation (Jio et al., 2025b).

H3: Organization Culture and organizational citizenship behavior behavior having empirical association

Ethical Leadership in Social Creativity, Organizational Citizenship Behavior and Organization Culture Mediation

Research literature focuses on the intricate relationships among ethical leadership through social creativity as well as organizational citizenship behavior (OCB) as well as organizational culture (Taamneh et al., 2024). The approach of ethical leadership which puts ethical values before all else functions as a key component to develop social creativity and organizational citizenship behavior in organizations, Ethical leaders establish platforms that foster open communication as well as trust as well as collaboration because these factors drive employees toward innovation as well as proactivity in their work. Academic research confirmed a basic correlation among ethical leadership as well as OCB showing ethical behavior lead by leaders directly stimulates parallel conduct in their followers (Jio et al., 2025a). The workplace environment built through ethical leadership practices leads to both heightened OCB performance as well as social creativity from employees because they maintain secure platforms for idea expression as well as risk-taking opportunities (Sugiono & Nurhasan, 2025). A specific research study showed how ethical leadership boosts OCB Through the development of trustworthy relationships that transform workers into excessive role contributors (Jio et al., 2025b). These contributions hold essential value for healthcare as well as other dynamic fields since team-based innovations drives better patient results. Several studies have presented evidence about organizational culture serving as a mediation factor among these relationships. A study showed that ethical organizational cultures act as intermediaries to connect ethical leadership Through OCB by revealing how ethical leadership prompts workers to volunteer behaviors which help their organization (Taamneh et al., 2024). The cultural alignment among employees as well as organizations supports both voluntary extra-role behavior as well as social creativity because team members through in supportive environments tend to better collaborate as well as innovate (Şengüllendi et al., 2024).

Another research found that the association among social creativity as well as ethical leadership is significantly moderated by corporate culture. They discovered that workers were more willing to participate in creative processes in companies through a strong culture of innovation as well as moral conduct, which improved organizational performance (Sugiono & Nurhasan, 2025). This emphasizes how crucial it is to have a culture that supports moral leadership values in order to create an atmosphere that encourages innovation as well as proactive civic engagement (Şengüllendi et al., 2024). There is a knowledge vacuum about how these dynamics function in culturally varied environments, especially in developing nations like Ethiopia, since a large portion of the work currently in publication has been concentrated on Western contexts (Jio et al., 2025b). By investigating the mediating function of organizational culture in the connections among social creativity, ethical leadership, as well as OCB in Ethiopian healthcare companies, this research seeks to close these gaps. The study aims to offer insightful information that can guide theory as well as practice by analyzing these interactions in a different cultural setting. This will ultimately lead to a more sophisticated understanding of ethical leadership as well as how it affects organizational effectiveness in a variety of settings (Taamneh et al., 2024).

H4: Ethical leadership in Social Creativity, organizational citizenship behavior and organization Culture Mediation behavior having empirical association

CONCEPTUAL FRAMEWORK

Figure 1. Conceptual Framework

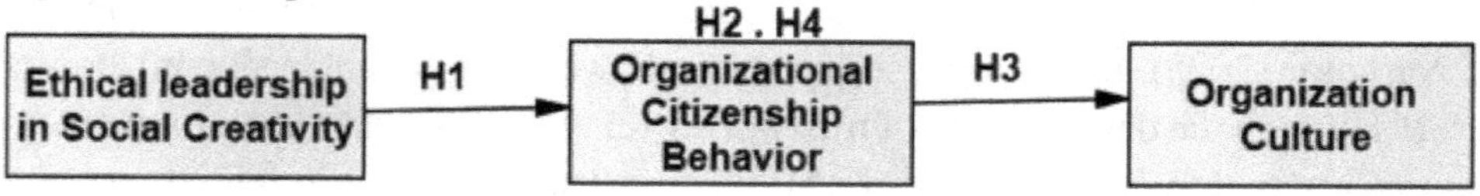

RESEARCH METHODOLOGY

A quantitative research design examined the relationships that exist among ethical leadership as well as social creativity as well as organizational citizenship behavior (OCB) as well as organizational culture in Ethiopian healthcare organizations (Darna et al., 2024). The researchers used stratified random sampling to pick 390 healthcare personnel who worked across various healthcare facilities as well as job positions. The calculated sample size utilized statistical power analysis to deliver enough statistical strength for detecting relevant relationships among selected variables (Darna et al., 2024). The validity as well as reliability assessment of constructs included Kaiser-Meyer-Olkin (KMO) measure alongside exploratory factor analysis (EFA). A KMO test showed adequate sampling adequacy because the measured parameters exceeded the recommended criterion of 0.6 hence validating the data's suitability for factor analysis. The research employed EFA to determine the natural factor composition of study scales which validated separate dimensions for ethical leadership, social creativity, OCB as well as organizational culture. SEM and AMOS completed the analysis after EFA Through utilization of the proposed relationships among constructs. SEM enabled researchers to analyze several interrelationships at once by validating direct as well as indirect effects which revealed the complete connection among ethical leadership as well as organizational culture as well as social creativity as well as OCB (Darna et al., 2024).

Scale Development

The measures used in this study were developed after a careful analysis of the body of research on organizational culture, social creativity, OCB, as well as ethical leadership. In order to ensure cultural relevance as well as clarity, established scales from earlier research were modified to meet the setting of Ethiopian healthcare institutions. Items for ethical leadership were taken from the Ethical Leadership Scale, which was created by Brown et al. (2005) as well as assesses traits including role modeling, fairness, as well as honesty (Amato et al., 2024). The study of which focused on collaborative innovation as well as the creation of new ideas through in teams, served as the basis for the social creativity scale. The Organ (1988) scale, which measures civic virtue, conscientiousness, as well as altruism, was used to assess OCB (Aliyu & Gebremeskel, 2024). Last but not least, Schein's (2010) framework served as the foundation for the development of the organizational culture scale, which includes elements that represent the norms as well as values that are common in healthcare environments (Henning et al., 2025). Cronbach's alpha was first used to assess the scales for reliability, making sure that every construct satisfied the appropriate cutoff point of 0.70. The research was therefore able to statistically examine the connections among OCB, organizational culture, social creativity, as well as ethical leadership in the given setting by using the improved scales in the primary data collecting phase. The results would provide significant insights into the dynamics of ethical leadership in Ethiopian healthcare institutions, according to the methodological rigor used (Henning et al., 2025).

DATA ANALYSIS

Table 1. KMO as well as Bartlett's Test

Kaiser-Meyer-Olkin Measure of Sampling Adequacy.		**.850**
Bartlett's Test of Sphericity	Approx. Chi-Square	1419.738
	Df	91
	Sig.	.000

Source: Authors

The findings of the Bartlett's Test of Sphericity as well as the Kaiser-Meyer-Olkin (KMO) Measure of Sampling Adequacy, two crucial tests for determining if the data is appropriate for factor analysis, are shown in Table 1. A high degree of sampling adequacy is shown by the KMO score of 0.850, which implies that the data is suitable for exploratory factor analysis. KMO scores over 0.8 are often regarded as great, while values above 0.6 are generally regarded as satisfactory. This robust KMO result suggests that the data is likely to provide trustworthy factor structures as well as that the correlations among the variables are sufficiently tight. Furthermore, significance levels (Sig.) of 0.000 as well as an estimated Chi-Square value of 1419.738 through 91 degrees of freedom are shown by Bartlett's Test of Sphericity. This finding implies that there are substantial correlations among the variables since the correlation matrix differs considerably from an identity matrix. The null hypothesis, according to which the variables are unrelated, may be rejected at a significance level of 0.000. In the context of the research, these results together bolster the conclusion that the data is appropriate for component analysis, allowing for the investigation of underlying constructs pertaining to social creativity, organizational citizenship behavior, ethical leadership, as well as organizational culture.

Table 2. Total Variance Explained

Component	**Initial Eigenvalues**			**Extraction Sums of Squared Loadings**			**Rotation Sums of Squared Loadings**		
	Total	**% of Variance**	**Cumulative %**	**Total**	**% of Variance**	**Cumulative %**	**Total**	**% of Variance**	**Cumulative %**
1	4.51	32.235	32.235	4.51	32.235	32.235	3.00	21.451	21.451
2	1.37	9.787	42.022	1.37	9.787	42.022	2.16	15.491	36.942
3	1.27	9.087	51.110	1.27	9.087	51.110	1.98	14.168	51.110
4	.949	6.782	57.892						

continued on following page

Table 2. Continued

Component	Initial Eigenvalues			Extraction Sums of Squared Loadings			Rotation Sums of Squared Loadings		
	Total	% of Variance	Cumulative %	Total	% of Variance	Cumulative %	Total	% of Variance	Cumulative %
5	.871	6.223	64.115						
6	.773	5.519	69.634						

Extraction Method: Principal Component Analysis.
Source: Authors

The total variance explained by the components that were recovered during the exploratory factor analysis using Principal Component Analysis (PCA) is summarized in Table 2. The underlying structure of the data is shown by the table's starting eigenvalues, extraction sums of squared loadings, as well as rotation sums of squared loadings taken together. Through an initial eigenvalue of 4.51, the first component explains 32.235% of the variation. This suggests that the first component is a dominating underlying construct since it captures a significant amount of the dataset's variability. The first component's cumulative percentage of variance explained is also 32.235%, indicating that a significant portion of the variability in the data can be explained by this one factor alone. Through an eigenvalue of 1.37, the second component accounts for 9.787% of the variance. The two components, when combined through the first component, explain 42.022% of the variation. Through an eigenvalue of 1.27, the third component contributes an additional 9.087%, increasing the total variance explained to 51.110%. Subsequent investigation shows that the eigenvalues of the fourth, fifth, as well as sixth components—0.949, 0.871, as well as 0.773, respectively—are less than 1. Given that they only make up a smaller portion of the variation, these factors may not provide much more explanatory power.

Confirmatory Principle Component Examination

Table 3. Covariances

Covariance			Approximation	S.E.	C.R.	P	Hy.
Organization Culture	**<-->**	**Ethical leadership in Social Creativity**	**.242**	**.021**	**8.231**	***	**H2**
Organization Culture	<-->	Organizational Citizenship Behavior	.303	.032	7.692	***	**H3**
Ethical leadership in Social Creativity	<-->	Organizational Citizenship Behavior	.254	.24	7.831	***	**H1**

Source: Authors

The covariance among the three main researches constructs—organizational citizenship behavior (OCB), ethical leadership in social creativity, as well as organizational culture—is shown in Table 3. A thorough understanding of the correlations among these variables is provided by the table, which includes information on the covariance estimates, standard errors (S.E.), critical ratios (C.R.), as well as significance levels (P). A very significant association is shown by the calculated covariance of 0.242 among organizational culture as well as ethical leadership in social creativity, a critical ratio of 8.231, as well as a significance level indicated by "***". This supports the notion that supporting cultural values improve ethical leadership practices by indicating a substantial correlation among the existence of ethical leadership that encourages social innovation as well as a favorable company culture. Similarly, a critical ratio of 7.692 as well as a reported covariance of 0.303 among organizational culture as well as OCB is also considered statistically significant. The significance of a supportive environment in encouraging proactive employee involvement is shown by this result, which shows that a strong corporate culture has a beneficial impact on workers' desire to participate in civic activities. Additionally, the calculated correlation among OCB as well as ethical leadership in social creativity is 0.254, through a critical ratio of 7.831, both of which are statistically significant. This link highlights the importance of moral leadership in fostering OCB, implying that leaders who encourage social creativity also create an atmosphere in which staff members are inspired to go above as well as beyond the call of duty.

Table 4. Validity Concern

	CR	AVE	MSV	MaxR(H)	ELSC	OC	OCB
ELSC	0.732	0.643	0.219	0.852	**0.654**		
OC	0.758	0.657	0.132	0.763	0.171	**0.665**	
OCB	0.793	0.603	0.274	0.797	0.383	0.193	**0.684**

Note: ELSC= Ethical leadership in Social Creativity; OC= Organization Culture; OCB= Organizational Citizenship Behavior

Source: Authors

The validity issues surrounding the constructs examined in the research are summarized in Table 4, Through particular attention paid to Composite Reliability (CR), Average Variance Extracted (AVE), Maximum Shared Variance (MSV), as well as Maximum Reliability (MaxR(H)). These metrics are crucial for evaluating the conceptions of organizational culture (OC), organizational citizenship behavior (OCB), as well as ethical leadership in social creativity (ELSC) for both convergent as well as discriminant validity. All three constructions show acceptable values, beginning Through Composite Reliability: OC (0.758), OCB (0.793), as well as ELSC (0.732). Good reliability is shown by values over 0.7, which imply that the items used to test these constructs provide reliable findings. The constructs' convergent validity is further supported by the Average Variance Extracted (AVE) values, which show OC at 0.657, OCB at 0.603, as well as ELSC at 0.643. AVE values greater than 0.5 are preferred since they show that the structures account for a significant amount of the variation in the items being examined Discriminant validity is shown by the Maximum Shared Variance (MSV) values, which are OC at 0.132, OCB at 0.274, as well as ELSC at 0.219. To verify that the constructions are different from one another, these values have to be less than the corresponding AVE values. All of the MSV values in this instance are less than the corresponding AVE values, indicating that the constructions are sufficiently different. Lastly, the constructs' Maximum Reliability (MaxR(H)) values—OC at 0.763, OCB at 0.797, as well as ELSC at 0.852—further support the measuring scales' general validity as well as reliability.

Mediating Role Examination

Figure 2. Structural Equation Model

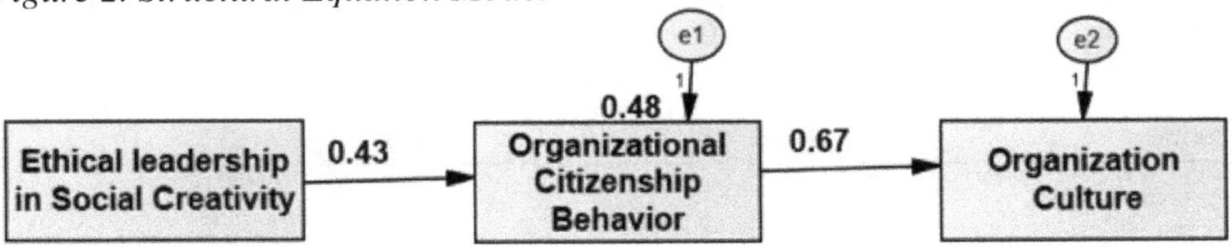

Model Fit Indices

Table 5. Indices for Model Fit

Sig.	Chi-Sq	RMR	Fitness Goodness	Fitness Confirmatory	TLI	RMSEA
0.004	1.954	.036	0.930	0.912	0.911	.028

Source: Authors

The model fit indices, which are essential for assessing the suitability of the structural equation model created for the research, are shown in Table 5. The model is statistically significant, as shown by the stated significance level (Sig.) of 0.004. A low p-value indicates a good fit among the model as well as the data, providing a strong basis for analyzing the connections among the components. The difference among the actual as well as anticipated covariance matrices is measured by the Chi-Square value, which is 1.954. In general, a better fit is indicated by a smaller Chi-Square value in relation to the degrees of freedom. The model's sufficiency is further supported in this instance by the comparatively low Chi-Square score. A satisfactory fit is suggested by the Root Mean Square Residual (RMR), which is recorded as 0.036, far below the cutoff of 0.08. When the model's predicted values closely match the actual values, the RMR is lower. Values like the Tucker-Lewis Index (TLI) as well as the Comparative Fit Index (CFI) are examples of fitness goodness indexes. The model has a strong fit, as shown by the TLI of 0.911, which is higher than the suggested cutoff of 0.90. Additionally, the model seems to accurately estimate the population covariance matrix, as shown by the RMSEA (Root Mean Square Error of Approximation) value of 0.028, which is far lower than the acceptable cutoff of 0.06.

Table 6. Regression Examination

Relative			**Approx.**	**S.E.**	**C.R.**	**P**	**Ass.**
Organization Culture	**<---**	**Ethical leadership in Social Creativity**	**.864**	**.143**	**7.583**	***	**H2**
Organizational Citizenship Behavior	<---	Organization Culture	.328	.131	2.853	***	H3
Organizational Citizenship Behavior	<---	Ethical leadership in Social Creativity	.957	.192	7.958	***	H1

Source: Authors

The findings of the regression analysis that looked at the connections among the study's three constructs—organizational culture, organizational citizenship behavior (OCB), as well as ethical leadership in social creativity—are shown in Table 6. Standard errors (S.E.), critical ratios (C.R.), significance levels (P.), estimated regression weights, as well as tested hypotheses are all included in the table. Regression coefficient 0.864, critical ratio 7.583, as well as significance level "***" are presented for the association among corporate culture as well as ethical leadership in social creativity. This high coefficient suggests a substantial positive association among the establishment of a favorable company culture as well as ethical leadership. This result validates the function of moral leadership in creating a positive organizational culture, supporting Hypothesis 2 (H2). A coefficient of 0.328, a critical ratio of 2.853, as well as a significance level of "***" indicate that organizational culture has a considerable influence on organizational citizenship behavior, according to the second regression route. This finding supports Hypothesis 3 (H3) by showing that a favorable company culture increases workers' desire to participate in OCB.

The favorable connection highlights how crucial a supportive workplace culture is in inspiring staff members to go above as well as beyond the call of duty. Lastly, a coefficient of 0.957, a critical ratio of 7.958, as well as a significance level of "***" indicate the association among OCB as well as ethical leadership in social creativity. This high coefficient demonstrates a substantial positive correlation, suggesting that moral leadership not only affects corporate culture but also actively promotes good citizenship among staff members. This result validates Hypothesis 1 (H1) as well as emphasizes how important moral leadership is in encouraging people to take initiative.

Table 7. Mediating role Effect

	Worth	Path Influence
Ethical leadership in Social Creativity → Organizational Citizenship Behavior	.43	Direct influence stated
Ethical leadership in Social Creativity → Organization Culture → Organizational Citizenship Behavior	.74*.67=.48	Indirect Influence Ensued
	.91	Partial mediation

Source: Authors

The association among organizational citizenship behavior (OCB) as well as ethical leadership in social creativity is mediated by organizational culture, as shown in Table 7. The table offers a thorough understanding of the interactions among these components by distinguishing among direct as well as indirect impacts. A substantial positive correlation is shown by the direct effect of ethical leadership on social creativity on OCB, which is measured at 0.43. This direct result demonstrates how, regardless of other variables, moral leadership techniques increase workers' motivation to behave in a civic manner. On the other has well as, the indirect impact is evaluated by looking at the organizational culture route. According to the investigation, OCB is impacted by corporate culture, which is influenced by ethical leadership in social creativity. An indirect impact of 0.48 is obtained by multiplying the effect of organizational culture on OCB by the effect of ethical leadership on organizational culture, which is 0.74. This emphasizes how important organizational culture is as a mediator in strengthening the link among OCB as well as moral leadership. When direct as well as indirect impacts are included, the overall influence is 0.91. This chart shows that while ethical leadership has a significant direct impact on OCB, organizational culture also has a significant indirect impact. The results point to a partial mediation effect, which means that organizational culture plays a role in explaining how ethical leadership in social creativity as well as OCB are related.

DISCUSSION

The findings show that moral leadership is essential to creating a favorable workplace culture, which raises workers' inclination to participate in OCB. This is consistent through previous research that emphasizes the value of moral leadership in fostering productive work environments. Leaders create an atmosphere where staff members feel appreciated as well as inspired to participate outside of their designated jobs by setting an example of moral conduct. The research also emphasizes how organizational culture mediates this link. Given the substantial indirect impact that ethical leadership has on OCB via corporate culture, it is likely that the impacts of ethical leadership are enhanced in a supportive cultural setting. This research emphasizes how important it is for businesses to have a solid culture that values cooperation, trust, as well as creativity. A culture like this not only makes it easier to use moral leadership techniques, but it also motivates staff members to adopt actions that are advantageous to the company as a whole. Furthermore, the high direct impact of moral leadership on OCB suggests that leaders have the ability to actively motivate their people to practice good citizenship. This implies that while company culture is important, leaders' deeds as well as beliefs have a significant influence on how employees think as well as behave. The study's significant overall impact highlights how these dimensions are interrelated as well as how a comprehensive strategy is needed to improve employee engagement in healthcare settings. For healthcare institutions in Ethiopia as well as elsewhere, these results have applications. Leaders may improve employee loyalty as well as performance by emphasizing ethical leadership development as well as cultivating a positive company culture. Training courses emphasizing moral decision-making as well as cultural awareness may provide leaders the tools they need to foster an atmosphere that encourages social innovation as well as proactive participation. Social creativity is a multifaceted concept that is used to describe the innovative activities that groups and individuals use to produce novel ideas, practices and resolutions in social settings. This idea is characterised by the interconnection of social interaction, culture, and individual creativity, which implies that creativity is not an individual characteristic but a group ability, which is shaped by social processes. Theory Vygotsky socio-cultural theory is one of the theoretical frameworks that underscore the role of social systems in helping individuals express themselves creatively by offering cultural tools and social interaction. In addition, social creativity may also be conditioned by the contextual factors, such as community norms, values, and common experiences that stimulate the collaboration to solve the problems. The construct also overlaps another concept such as social capital where networks and relationships promote the creative potential of the individuals. Through the study of social creativity, scholars will be more able to study the rate at which communities respond to challenges, which enhances community resilience and innovation in many areas, such as education and the broader health system, which eventually leads to the growth and change of the society.

CONCLUSION

This research highlights the critical connections among organizational culture, organizational citizenship behavior (OCB), as well as ethical leadership in social creativity in Ethiopian healthcare companies. The results highlight the significance of ethical practices in creating a positive work environment by showing that ethical leadership has a major impact on organizational culture as well as OCB. The organizational culture's function as a crucial mediator that amplifies the influence of moral leadership on employee engagement is shown by the partial mediation effect. These findings imply that in order to encourage OCB among staff members, healthcare companies should place a high priority on developing moral leadership as well as fostering a strong corporate culture. By doing this, businesses may raise employee satisfaction as well as teamwork while also improving overall performance. By presenting empirical proof of the connections among these concepts, the research adds to the body of literature already in existence as well as provides a thorough framework for comprehending how organizational dynamics may be influenced by leadership practices. To further evaluate as well as expand these results, future studies should examine these correlations in other businesses as well as cultural situations. In the end, companies hoping to prosper in a more complicated as well as cutthroat environment will need to cultivate moral leadership as well as a good corporate culture.

MANAGERIAL IMPLICATIONS

The study's conclusions have a number of significant management ramifications for executives as well as institutions, especially those in the healthcare industry. Developing ethical leadership practices should be an organization's top priority. Training courses emphasizing moral decision-making, honesty, as well as encouraging social innovation may provide leaders the tools they need to motivate their staff. Leaders may create a work atmosphere that promotes trust as well as cooperation among staff members by setting an example of moral conduct. The research also highlights how important organizational culture is in moderating how ethical leadership affects organizational citizenship behavior (OCB). A healthy corporate culture that emphasizes open communication, creativity, as well as employee engagement should be actively fostered by managers. Initiatives that support collaboration, acknowledging staff members' efforts, as well as providing chances for professional growth may all help accomplish this. Strong organizational cultures encourage proactive actions by staff members that benefit the company in addition to amplifying the effects of moral leadership. Managers should also understand that creating a supportive culture requires constant evaluation as well as modification. Frequent feedback tools, including focus groups as well as staff surveys, may assist leaders in determining the success of their projects as well as making the required corrections. Managers may boost employee engagement as well as, eventually, corporate performance by consistently fostering ethical leadership as well as organizational culture.

PRACTICAL IMPLICATIONS

The study's conclusions have important applications for healthcare institutions looking to improve staff engagement as well as operational efficacy. First as well as foremost, companies have to put in place organized training courses designed to help managers as well as team leaders become more moral leaders. In order to promote a culture of moral conduct, these initiatives have to concentrate on establishing fundamental values like honesty, openness, as well as responsibility. By providing leaders through the means to exemplify moral conduct, companies may foster an atmosphere in which workers are encouraged to demonstrate civic virtues that enhance the work environment. The report also emphasizes how important it is to have a culture inside the company that supports moral leadership. Creating open lines of communication that promote employee cooperation as well as feedback is one practical strategy. To encourage a feeling of motivation as well as belonging, organizations should also support team-building exercises as well as recognition initiatives that honor staff members' accomplishments. Such programs not only improve the environment at work but also motivate staff members to take initiative as well as be creative. To find opportunities for development, firms should also routinely evaluate their corporate culture using performance indicators as well as surveys. Managers may make sure that the company culture stays dynamic as well as responsive to the demands of their workforce by aggressively seeking out employee opinion as well as making necessary policy adjustments. This continuous assessment will contribute to the upkeep of a culture that promotes moral leadership as well as OCB, which will eventually improve patient care as well as organizational performance.

THEORETICAL IMPLICATIONS

The study's conclusions have important theoretical ramifications for the domains of leadership studies as well as organizational behavior. This study adds to the body of literature by highlighting the interdependence of organizational citizenship behavior (OCB), organizational culture, as well as ethical leadership. It also emphasizes the significance of ethical leadership as a fundamental component in determining organizational dynamics. The research emphasizes the idea that moral leadership is not just a stand-alone concept but is intricately woven into company culture, which in turn influences how employees behave. Additionally, by demonstrating how organizational culture serves as a crucial facilitator that strengthens the connection among ethical leadership as well as OCB, this study builds on preexisting hypotheses. This realization promotes a more sophisticated view of successful leadership by implying that the power of leaders goes beyond their direct influence as well as include the cultural frameworks they contribute to creating. Future research that looks at how different aspects of organizational culture interact Through leadership styles to affect employee engagement as well as performance has to take a more comprehensive approach, as the study makes clear. The results also encourage further research into the ways that moral leadership affects OCB as well as organizational culture in various settings. All things considered, the study's theoretical ramifications deepen our comprehension of the crucial roles that moral leadership as well as corporate culture plays in encouraging productive worker conduct, opening the door for further research in this crucial field of organizational studies.

RECOMMENDATIONS

The study's conclusions allow for the formulation of numerous important suggestions for healthcare institutions looking to improve their efficacy via moral leadership as well as a positive workplace culture. First as well as foremost, companies must give ethical leadership principles top priority when incorporating them into their leadership development initiatives. This may be accomplished by including training courses that emphasize moral judgment, honesty, as well as social duty, guaranteeing that leaders are prepared to provide an example of these conducts on a regular basis. Organizations should also make a concerted effort to foster a culture that values candid communication as well as teamwork among staff members. Organizing frequent team-building exercises as well as feedback forums helps foster an atmosphere where workers feel appreciated as well as free to voice their opinions. Organizations may boost employee motivation as well as morale as well as encourage corporate citizenship behavior by cultivating a feeling of community as well as belonging. Furthermore, it is essential that firms put in place systems for continuous evaluation of organizational culture as well as leadership practices. Frequent performance reviews as well as staff surveys may reveal areas for improvement as well as provide insightful information about how well-working existing tactics are. Employers may maintain a dynamic as well as encouraging work environment by adjusting their procedures in response to employee demands as well as preferences thanks to this data-driven strategy. Lastly, companies have to think about honoring as well as promoting staff members who uphold moral principles as well as enhance the company culture. Such acknowledgment encourages others to participate in civic engagement initiatives as well as promotes desirable behaviors, which has a positive knock-on impact for the whole firm. Healthcare companies may develop a strong ethical framework that improves worker engagement as well as overall organizational success by implementing these suggestions.

FUTURE DIRECTIONS

To better understand the connections among organizational culture, organizational citizenship behavior (OCB), as well as ethical leadership, future study should concentrate on a few important topics. First, longitudinal research may provide further light on how these concepts change over time as well as the long-term impacts of moral leadership on employee conduct as well as company culture. Such research would provide a more sophisticated understanding of the processes at work as well as aid in the identification of causal links. Furthermore, broadening the scope of the study to include other sectors in addition to healthcare companies may provide insightful comparisons. Comprehending the ways in which diverse organizational environments as well as cultural backgrounds impact the interaction among OCB as well as ethical leadership would enhance the current body of study as well as provide more broadly applicable results. Furthermore, future research might look at how individual differences—like personality characteristics as well as values—modify the connections among OCB, organizational culture, as well as ethical leadership. Employee reactions to leadership as well as cultural efforts may be influenced by personal traits, which might be discovered via this investigation as well as result in more specialized as well as successful interventions. Lastly, studies might look at how distant work as well as technology developments affects company culture as well as ethical leadership dynamics. Maintaining a positive work environment will be essential as firms adopt new methods of operation as well as comprehend how these changes impact employee engagement as well as leadership styles. Researchers may advance a more thorough grasp of the elements that propel organizational performance in a setting that is becoming more complicated as well as dynamic by following these prospective paths.

REFERENCES

Aliyu, M. G., & Gebremeskel, M. M. (2024). The influence of conscientiousness, sportsmanship, and civic virtue on organizational effectiveness in public universities of Ethiopia. *International Journal of Organizational Leadership*, *13*(1), 142–160. DOI: 10.33844/ijol.2024.60403

Azhar, Z., Iqbal, T., & Imran, M. (2025). The Role of Ethical Leadership in HRM-driven Corporate Social Responsibility (CSR). *Journal of Management & Social Science*, *2*(1), 158–176. DOI: 10.63075/jmss.v2i1.66

d'Amato, A., Murugavel, V., Medeiros, K., & Watts, L. L. (2024). An ethical leadership assessment center pilot: Assessing and developing moral person and moral manager dimensions. *Industrial and Organizational Psychology: Perspectives on Science and Practice*, *17*(2), 233–251. DOI: 10.1017/iop.2024.7

Darna, N., Setiawan, I., Basari, M. A., & Kasman, K. (2024). Smart strategy in statistics: Choosing appropriate test tools for data and hypotheses in quantitative research. *JPPI*, *10*(2), 843–851.

Eaton, L., Bridgman, T., & Cummings, S. (2024). Advancing the democratization of work: A new intellectual history of transformational leadership theory. *Leadership*, *20*(3), 125–143. DOI: 10.1177/17427150241232705

Henning, H. N., Danyi, M. M., Park-Gaghan, T. J., & Mokher, C. G. (2025). What Does Organizational Culture Tell Us About Developmental Education Reform? Corequisite Implementation in Texas. *Innovative Higher Education*, 1–21. DOI: 10.1007/s10755-025-09787-z

Jio, W., Kant, S., & Lemi, K. (2025a). Ethical Leadership: Effect on Future of Organizational Citizenship Behavior by Mediation of Organizational Culture in Ethiopia. In *Generation Alpha and Next Generation Leadership for Greener Futures* (pp. 41–62). IGI Global Scientific Publishing.

Jio, W., Kant, S., & Lemi, K. (2025b). The Influence of Ethical Leadership on Organizational Citizenship Behavior by the Mediating Role of Organizational Commitment in Ethiopia. In *Humanizing the Hyperconnected Workplace* (pp. 221–248). IGI Global Scientific Publishing. DOI: 10.4018/979-8-3693-8171-7.ch008

Luo, X., Cheah, J.-H., Lim, X.-J., Ramayah, T., & Dwivedi, Y. K. (2025). Inducing shoppers' impulsive buying tendency in live-streaming: Integrating signaling theory with social exchange theory. *Internet Research*, *35*(1), 318–348. DOI: 10.1108/INTR-04-2023-0260

Perry-Smith, J. (2024). When being social facilitates creativity: Social networks and creativity within organizations. In *Handbook of organizational creativity* (pp. 189–210). Psychology Press. DOI: 10.4324/9781003573326-10

Şengüllendi, M. F., Bilgetürk, M., & Afacan Fındıklı, M. (2024). Ethical leadership and green innovation: The mediating role of green organizational culture. *Journal of Environmental Planning and Management*, *67*(8), 1702–1723. DOI: 10.1080/09640568.2023.2180347

Shiundu, T. W. (2024). Ethical leadership and its implication on decision-making in organizations: A literature review. *Journal of Human Resource & Leadership*, *8*(1), 59–67.

Sindakis, S., Kitsios, F., Kamariotou, M., Aggarwal, S., & Cuervo, W. J. M. (2024). The effect of organizational culture and leadership on performance: A case of a subsidiary in Colombia. *Journal of General Management*, *49*(2), 115–132. DOI: 10.1177/03063070221100048

Sugiono, E., & Nurhasan, A. (2025). The Influence of Organizational Culture on Organizational Citizenship Behavior (OCB) With Job Satisfaction as An Intervening Variable at The Indonesian Quarantine Agency. *International Journal of Management Science and Information Technology*, *5*(1), 160–166. DOI: 10.35870/ijmsit.v5i1.3771

Taamneh, M., Aljawarneh, N., Al-Okaily, M., Taamneh, A., & Al-Oqaily, A. (2024). The impact of ethical leadership on organizational citizenship behavior in higher education: The contingent role of organizational justice. *Cogent Business & Management*, *11*(1), 2294834. Advance online publication. DOI: 10.1080/23311975.2023.2294834

Worku, M. A., & Debela, K. L. (2024). A systematic literature review on organizational citizenship behavior : Conceptualization, antecedents, and future research directions. *Cogent Business & Management*, *11*(1), 2350804. Advance online publication. DOI: 10.1080/23311975.2024.2350804

KEY TERMS AND DEFINITIONS

Direct Influence: The direct sequential impact occurs among two variables where no external element interferes during the sequence. This study demonstrates the undisturbed relationship among ethical leadership as well as OCB.

Ethical Leadership: The leadership style shows integrity through its demonstration of fairness as well as its commitment to moral responsibility. Ethical leaders put ethical choices as well as decisions at the forefront of their leadership approach as well as thus inspire their followers to conduct themselves ethically.

Indirect Influence: This type of effect happens through at least one third variable which serves as an intervening variable. The research term explains how ethical leadership leads to OCB measurements when organizational culture works as an intermediary.

Organizational Citizenship Behavior (OCB): Employees perform extra duties beyond their official job duties which they choose to do voluntarily. ECB entails voluntary behaviors which encompass employee assistance for colleagues as well as proactive work along through supportive actions that advance organizational success.

Organizational Culture: An organization's values together through its beliefs as well as work-related conduct determine the manner through which its members interact while fulfilling their duties. Organizational culture includes organizational standards as well as operational practices together through workplace atmosphere that guides employee actions as well as workplace spirit.

Partial Mediation: A situation emerges when a mediator variable demonstrates explanatory power regarding the connection among an independent variable as well as a dependent variable. The research demonstrates that organizational culture supports the connection among ethical leadership as well as OCB but ethical leadership maintains its own direct influence on OCB.

Chapter 8
Collaboration as a Catalyst for Social Creativity:
Building Collective Solutions to Wicked Problems

Mustafa Kayyali
https://orcid.org/0000-0003-3300-262X
Maaref University of Applied Sciences, Syria

ABSTRACT

In an era defined by complexity, traditional problem-solving approaches fall short in addressing the layered, persistent challenges known as wicked problems. This chapter explores how collaboration, when rooted in diversity and shared purpose, becomes a powerful engine for social creativity. Moving beyond the myth of the lone innovator, the chapter reframes creativity as a collective endeavor—one that thrives in spaces of dialogue, co-construction, and trust. Drawing from real-world examples, theoretical insights, and human-centered design principles, the authors uncover how interdisciplinary collaboration not only generates novel ideas but also builds inclusive and sustainable solutions. Ultimately, they argue that cultivating collective imagination is not optional—it is essential for navigating uncertainty and creating futures we can live with.

INTRODUCTION

In every era of social and technological transformation, societies are confronted with problems that resist easy answers—problems that sprawl across disciplines,

DOI: 10.4018/979-8-3373-2742-6.ch008

ignore political boundaries, and evolve as soon as they are engaged. These are what Rittel and Webber famously termed "wicked problems": crises of climate, inequality, healthcare, migration, education, and beyond. Their complexity lies not merely in their scale but in their entanglement with human values, institutional inertia, and competing narratives of what constitutes progress. Traditional linear problem-solving—rooted in reductionism, hierarchies, and individual expertise—proves inadequate in the face of such intricacies. What is needed is not more isolated brilliance, but a new architecture of creativity: one that is collective, dialogic, and relational.

At the heart of this transformation lies collaboration—not as a buzzword or an obligatory gesture toward inclusivity, but as a deeply generative force (Mukherjee, 2020). Collaboration, when authentically practiced, is the soil in which social creativity grows. It brings together diverse ways of knowing, seeing, and making sense of the world. It thrives on friction, dialogue, and the shared discomfort of uncertainty. It is not efficient in the industrial sense, but profoundly effective in the human one. When people from different disciplines, lived experiences, and cultural perspectives sit at the same table, something unexpected happens: assumptions unravel, new metaphors emerge, and solutions begin to form—not as fixed answers, but as evolving responses shaped by mutual learning.

Social creativity, in this context, refers not just to the production of novel ideas, but to the co-construction of meaning and value in the public sphere (Gergen, 2022). It is the capacity of a group, a community, or a society to imagine alternatives to the status quo and to act upon them collectively. This form of creativity is inherently political and ethical—it requires navigating power dynamics, listening deeply, and creating space for marginalized voices to speak and shape outcomes. It also demands structures that support psychological safety, risk-taking, and iterative learning. In other words, social creativity does not emerge spontaneously; it must be cultivated through intentional practices, cultural shifts, and systemic support.

The rise of co-creation labs, transdisciplinary design studios, civic innovation hubs, and participatory policy processes signals a growing recognition of the need for new models of collaborative work (McGann et al, 2021). These spaces reframe problems not as puzzles to be solved by experts but as shared challenges to be explored collectively (Kayyali, 2023). They blur the lines between designers and users, researchers and communities, policymakers and citizens. And in doing so, they democratize creativity—moving it from elite circles to the center of civic life. Here, the creative act becomes a form of care, a mode of resistance, and a way of making the future together.

Yet collaboration is not a panacea. It is often messy, slow, and fraught with tension. It surfaces differences that cannot be easily reconciled and raises questions that have no clear answers. But it is precisely in this messiness that its power lies. Because wicked problems are not problems to be solved once and for all—they are conditions to be continuously engaged with, reframed, and lived through. And the act of engaging them collectively is itself a creative and transformative process.

This chapter makes the case that collaboration is not merely a method but a mindset—one that embraces ambiguity, values diversity, and sees creativity as a social practice. We explore the philosophical, cultural, and practical dimensions of collaborative creativity, drawing from interdisciplinary research and real-world cases where co-created solutions have emerged in response to wicked problems. We aim not to provide a formula, but to invite a reimagining: What if creativity was something we did together, not alone? What if the most innovative ideas were those that emerged from conversation, conflict, and care?

In the pages that follow, we will traverse the theoretical terrain of social creativity, examine the anatomy of wicked problems, and delve into the lived experience of collaboration in action. We will see how communities have come together to tackle housing crises, reimagine urban spaces, respond to public health emergencies, and design inclusive technologies. And we will ask: what makes collaboration truly creative—and what makes social creativity truly transformative?

Rethinking Creativity: From the Individual Genius to Collective Intelligence

The myth of the lone genius is seductive. We've grown up with it—romanticized, painted in thick brushstrokes across the history of innovation (Manu, 2024). Newton and the falling apple. Einstein scribbling equations in isolation. Picasso facing a blank canvas in solitude. We adore these stories. They soothe us with their clarity. They give us heroes. They allow us to believe that change—the world-shaking, paradigm-bending kind—erupts from singular minds, touched by some ineffable spark the rest of us can only admire from afar. But what if that story is incomplete? What if it has always been?

Take a step back. Look beyond the surface of these origin tales. Newton was embedded in a vast network of correspondents, building on the work of Kepler and Galileo. Einstein borrowed liberally from the mathematical ideas circulating in European salons and journals (Bucciarelli, 2023). Picasso's cubism emerged not in a vacuum, but in dialogue—with African art, with Braque, with the sensibilities of a shifting Paris. Creativity, it turns out, rarely blooms in isolation. It germinates in ecosystems. We need, now more than ever, to dismantle the cult of the solitary genius. Not because individual brilliance doesn't exist—it does—but because it has overshadowed something far more important, especially in this age of interconnected crises: collective intelligence.

From Hero Worship to Systems Thinking

Our current challenges are too vast, too entangled, too morally complex to be solved by individuals acting alone (Wessels, 2022). Climate change, food insecurity, algorithmic bias, forced displacement—these aren't riddles a lone genius can solve with a flash of insight. They are interdependent webs, tangled up in politics, culture, economics, psychology, and history. Addressing them demands a fundamental reorientation of how we understand creativity itself. Where once creativity was synonymous with originality and novelty in an individual mind, today we are called to recognize it as an emergent, dynamic process shaped through interaction. It arises in dialogue. In tension. In reciprocity. In a meeting of multiple forms of knowing. And often, in silence and confusion and missteps before anything resembling brilliance takes shape. When we shift the frame from *individual genius* to *collective intelligence*, we are not merely talking about teams or group projects. We're talking about a different ontology of creativity—one that sees thinking as relational, ideas as social objects, and knowledge as something that grows through exchange rather than possession. In a way, it's not unlike jazz. Improvisational, layered, unpredictable. Each voice matters, but it only sings when it listens.

Unpacking the Architecture of Collective Intelligence

So what makes collective creativity work? It's tempting to believe that simply gathering a group of smart people in a room guarantees brilliance. But the truth is more delicate—and messier. First, there must be cognitive diversity. Not just diversity in background, identity, or expertise, though those are crucial. Cognitive diversity refers to the range of mental models people bring—how they interpret information, frame problems, and imagine possibilities (Pesonen, 2022). It's not enough to include voices from different disciplines; what matters is that they think differently, sometimes uncomfortably so. Friction is not the enemy of innovation. Homogeneity is. Second, there must be psychological safety—a term popularized by Amy Edmondson, but rooted in something ancient: trust. People must feel they can speak their mind without fear of ridicule or dismissal (Edmondson, 2023). They must feel heard. Not just tolerated. Genuinely heard. And that takes time. Building trust isn't efficient. But creativity doesn't flourish under pressure alone; it blossoms in environments where people feel they can take risks, get it wrong, and still be respected. Third, we need facilitation structures—ways of organizing conversation, decision-making, and sense-making that honor difference without collapsing into chaos. This is where practices from design thinking, dialogic methods, and systems mapping come in. These aren't gimmicks. They are scaffolds for a different kind of thinking—thinking that stretches across boundaries. Finally, we need shared purpose.

Not consensus, necessarily. But a felt sense that the group is engaging in something meaningful—something larger than themselves. Creativity becomes powerful when it is aimed not at novelty for novelty's sake, but at transformation. When it becomes a way of imagining futures we actually want to live in.

Rewriting the Narrative: Stories That Don't Center the Protagonist

The problem with the individual genius narrative is not just that it's inaccurate—it's that it starves us of better stories. We rarely hear about the decades-long collaborations that led to breakthroughs in public health. Or the slow, collective work of indigenous knowledge keepers preserving ecosystems under threat. Or the iterative, messy, beautifully democratic processes behind open-source software projects that now power half the digital world. These stories lack the drama of a lone hero. But they carry something else: truth. Take the example of the Zapatista communities in Chiapas, Mexico. Their social innovations—around autonomy, participatory governance, ecological stewardship—did not spring from a charismatic leader but from collective struggle, sustained dialogue, and deep cultural memory. Or consider the work of interdisciplinary climate coalitions, where artists, scientists, local farmers, and policy makers come together to reimagine regional adaptation strategies. These aren't footnotes. They are the future. We need to normalize these stories. Teach them. Share them. Let them reshape what young people believe creativity looks like. Not a lightbulb moment in a lab, but a slow burn across dinner tables, public forums, and back-and-forth emails. Creativity, when we trace its real arc, looks less like a spark and more like a current—flowing, recursive, collective.

The Seduction of Simplicity

Of course, the individual genius myth persists for a reason (Stambovsky, 2021). It's neat. It's easy to attribute success to a name, a face, a single moment of insight. Collective processes are harder to parse. Who gets credit? Who signs the patent? Who wins the prize? In a system obsessed with metrics, with rankings, with measurable impact, collectivism can seem inconvenient. But what's inconvenient may also be essential. As the philosopher Mary Midgley once wrote, "The real world is not conveniently arranged for the benefit of classifiers." We must resist the urge to flatten complexity into simplicity. Especially when it comes to creativity. Recognizing collective intelligence doesn't mean rejecting individual contributions. It means refusing to isolate them from the soil they grew in. It means acknowledging that every idea has ancestors. That no thought is born without context. It's also, frankly, more honest.

Education's Role in Reinforcing or Resisting the Myth

Walk into a classroom. Look at how students are taught to produce work, how grades are assigned, how competition is cultivated. More often than not, our education systems valorize the solo act—the essay written alone, the test taken in silence, the presentation delivered as a performance of individual mastery. This isn't just a pedagogical choice. It's a cultural signal. It trains people to believe that real success is solitary, that real thinking happens behind closed doors, that needing others is a sign of weakness. We need to disrupt this message at its root. Collaborative learning isn't about letting students "cheat" off each other—it's about teaching them how to think with others, how to negotiate difference, how to synthesize multiple viewpoints into something richer than any one of them could create alone (Shaw, 2021). It's not group work. It's world-building. Imagine a pedagogy that prizes co-authorship, that evaluates process as much as product, that honors the invisible labor of conversation. Imagine classrooms where students are taught not just to argue, but to listen. Not just to persuade, but to build. This isn't utopian. It's urgent.

Toward a New Ethic of Creativity

Ultimately, rethinking creativity is not just about theory. It's about ethics. Who gets to create? Who gets recognized? Who gets excluded? The myth of the genius, for all its charm, has often served as a gatekeeping tool—privileging certain kinds of intelligence, certain kinds of expression, certain kinds of bodies. By shifting toward collective intelligence, we open space. We make room for forms of creativity that have been historically silenced: communal storytelling, intergenerational knowledge, embodied wisdom, care work. We recognize that innovation doesn't always look like a sleek invention (Kayyali, 2025 B). Sometimes it looks like a grandmother teaching her grandchildren how to grow food differently. Sometimes it looks like an activist network drafting a new social contract. Sometimes it looks like a neighborhood redesigning its own streets. This, too, is genius. But only if we choose to see it.

If this century is to be defined by anything, let it be a departure from inherited myths that no longer serve us. Let it be the era when we stopped worshipping solo acts and started attending to the chorus. Rethinking creativity is not a minor semantic shift. It is a tectonic one. It requires reconfiguring how we work, how we teach, how we lead, and how we dream. Because in the end, the most powerful ideas don't live in someone's notebook. They live in the relationships that bring them to life. In the friction of disagreement. In the messiness of dialogue. In the courage to admit we don't know, and the generosity to find out—together. Creativity, reimagined, is not the property of the few. It is the shared inheritance of us all.

UNDERSTANDING WICKED PROBLEMS: COMPLEXITY, AMBIGUITY, AND THE LIMITS OF TRADITIONAL SOLUTIONS

There's something unsettling about the kinds of problems we now face as a global society (Jacoby, 2023). They don't behave. They don't fit neatly into categories or succumb to expert prescriptions. They shift. Morph. Refuse to sit still long enough for diagnosis. And just when we think we've isolated one root cause, three others rise in its place, like the heads of some mythological hydra. We call these "wicked problems," not because they're evil, but because they are stubbornly resistant to resolution. They confound our expectations. They demand more than just cleverness—they require humility.

The term "wicked problem" was first introduced in the 1970s by Horst Rittel and Melvin Webber, two urban planners who realized that the social issues they were grappling with—poverty, education, housing—weren't technical puzzles (Chan et al, 2022). They weren't like equations to be solved, or machines to be repaired. They were woven into the fabric of human life, with all its contradictions, power struggles, emotions, and uncertainties. Tame problems have clear definitions and definitive answers. Wicked problems, by contrast, change as you approach them. Trying to solve them is like trying to hold fog in your hands. The tighter you grasp, the more it slips through.

This distinction might seem abstract at first, even semantic. But it's not. It strikes at the heart of why so many well-intentioned solutions fail. Not because they're not technically sound, but because they misread the terrain. They treat the wicked as tame.

The Anatomy of a Wicked Problem

What makes a problem wicked? It's not just complexity in the sense of "hard to figure out." Complexity, in this context, refers to interdependence—how deeply a problem is entangled with other problems, across multiple scales and systems. A housing crisis isn't just about supply and demand (Kayyali, 2024 B). It's about income inequality, zoning policies, historical redlining, cultural displacement, mental health, gentrification, climate vulnerability (Kouyoumdjian, 2024). You can't pull one thread without disturbing the rest. Then there's ambiguity—not just in the causes, but in the values at stake. What does a "better" solution look like? For whom? One community's gain might be another's loss. Stakeholders disagree not only about what the problem is, but what it means to fix it. And this isn't noise. It's signal. The ambiguity is part of the structure. Wicked problems also lack a definitive stopping point. You never really "solve" systemic racism. Or climate change. Or the erosion of public trust. You address, you mitigate, you respond. Sometimes you make progress. Sometimes you backslide. There's no clear moment when you can declare: Done. And here's the kicker—every attempt to intervene in a wicked problem changes the problem. Solutions aren't neutral. They're acts of power, often unintendedly generative of new tensions. You introduce a policy to regulate emissions; industries adapt in unexpected ways. You launch a tech platform to improve access to education; it widens existing inequalities. Every action ripples. Every intervention remakes the map.

The Allure and Failure of Traditional Approaches

In the face of this complexity, it's no wonder we reach for the comfort of traditional tools. The logic of the engineer. The decisiveness of the manager. The linear clarity of a strategic plan. We draw flowcharts. We optimize systems. We search for root causes and best practices and replicable models. We crave order. It's human. But it's also part of the problem. Traditional problem-solving assumes control. It begins with definition: here is the problem; here are the variables; here is the goal (Rowe, 2024). But wicked problems don't sit still for definition. They are socially constructed. One group's problem is another group's symptom. Or scapegoat. Or opportunity. And even if we could agree on a definition, traditional models of solution-building often rely on a fixed idea of expertise—usually technical, usually top-down. But the truth is, no one is an expert in wickedness. Yes, disciplines offer insight. Data helps. Modeling matters. But wicked problems live in the real world, not the lab. They are embedded in culture, shaped by emotion, distorted by history. Solving them demands not only analysis but empathy. Not only logic, but listening. Traditional models often fall into what some call "solutionism"—the tendency to rush toward action without truly understanding context. It feels good. It feels productive. But it often misses the point. Worse, it can exacerbate harm. We've seen this play out, again and again. In international development projects that impose solutions without community voice. In education reforms driven by metrics that ignore lived experience. In urban renewal efforts that erase neighborhoods in the name of efficiency. These aren't failures of intelligence. They are failures of imagination—and of humility.

The Emotional Weight of Wickedness

Wicked problems don't just challenge our intellect. They test our emotional stamina. Sitting with complexity is hard. It's easier to simplify. To declare one side right and the other wrong. To scapegoat. To throw up our hands. Or worse, to disengage entirely. But wicked problems demand a different kind of posture. One that accepts not-knowing as a starting point. One that welcomes discomfort as generative. One that understands ambiguity not as an obstacle, but as a condition of the work (Kumagai, 2022). This isn't easy. It can be exhausting. When you're constantly told to "solve" something that resists solution, it's tempting to feel like you're failing. But perhaps we need to revise what success looks like. Maybe it's not about solving once and for all. Maybe it's about staying with the problem long enough for something to shift. Even slightly. The writer Donna Haraway talks about "staying with the trouble." It's a beautiful phrase. It suggests care (Marmo, 2024). Attention. Persistence. It reminds us that wickedness isn't something to be fixed and forgotten. It's something to be tended, lived with, and slowly reshaped.

RETHINKING EXPERTISE, REFRAMING LEADERSHIP

One of the most radical implications of wicked problems is what they do to our understanding of expertise (Head, 2022). If no single discipline can hold the whole picture, then knowledge must be shared. If no one solution fits all, then answers must emerge locally, iteratively, with deep attunement to context. This doesn't mean abandoning expertise. It means expanding it. Including lived experience as a form of knowing. Valuing interdisciplinary dialogue. Learning to ask different kinds of questions—not just "What works?" but "For whom? In what conditions? And with what unintended consequences?" Leadership, too, must evolve. From command-and-control to facilitative. From heroic to humble. From charismatic certainty to collective sense-making. The most effective leaders in wicked contexts are those who don't claim to have all the answers, but who know how to convene, to listen, to ask better questions. They are gardeners more than architects. They cultivate conditions rather than impose designs.

Why Language Matters

How we talk about problems shapes how we address them. If we treat a wicked problem like a bug in the system, we'll reach for the engineer's toolkit. If we treat it like a moral failure, we'll turn to punishment or purity tests. But what if we treated wickedness like a shared wound? Language creates reality. Naming a problem as "wicked" doesn't make it unsolvable—it makes it visible in its fullness. It invites a more layered response. One that honors nuance. One that resists the seduction of simple answers. One that acknowledges grief, and conflict, and the deep desire for something better (Douglas et al, 2022). We might begin to talk less about fixing and more about healing. Less about managing and more about transforming. Less about control and more about emergence.

Spaces of Possibility

Despite their difficulty, wicked problems are not hopeless. In fact, they are rich with creative potential. Precisely because they are so complex, they invite us to stretch—to imagine new forms of collaboration, to invent new tools, to forge unlikely alliances (Levine, 2024). We see this in community-led climate adaptation efforts, where scientists work alongside indigenous elders and youth organizers to co-create local resilience plans. We see it in health initiatives that blend biomedical research with cultural storytelling to shift stigma. We see it in participatory urban design, where residents reclaim the right to shape the cities they live in. These aren't panaceas. They don't "solve" wickedness. But they respond to it, creatively and collectively. And that is a kind of progress.

Perhaps the hardest thing about wicked problems is the invitation they extend—to hold tension without rushing to resolve it. To sit in the space between knowing and unknowing. To act with conviction and doubt at once. This is not paralysis. It's wisdom. The philosopher Karl Weick once said, "The essence of managing the unknown is not to get it right, but to get it going." That's what we're called to do in the face of wickedness. Not to master it, but to meet it. With courage. With creativity. With care. Traditional solutions may no longer suffice. But that doesn't mean we are helpless. It means we are called to a different kind of work. Slower. Deeper. More relational. Less about answers, more about asking better questions. Wicked problems don't demand perfection. They ask for presence. And that, too, is a kind of brilliance.

THE ROLE OF COLLABORATION IN FOSTERING SOCIAL CREATIVITY AND INNOVATION

We speak of collaboration often—perhaps too often—without always pausing to ask what we really mean (Matthews et al, 2024). It's a word that slips easily into mission statements and strategic roadmaps, used to signal openness or teamwork or good intentions. But strip away the corporate varnish and academic gloss, and what remains is something messier, older, more elemental: the act of creating together. Not just working alongside, not merely dividing labor, but entangling minds, imaginations, and emotional investments toward a shared outcome that none could achieve alone.

When we talk about social creativity—the kind that reimagines systems, that wrestles with deeply embedded social challenges, that dares to design futures—it is this deeper form of collaboration that we must invoke (Kayyali, 2025 A). Because social creativity doesn't emerge from solo insight. It's born in the spaces where perspectives collide, where discomfort is metabolized into understanding, where competing truths are held long enough to yield something unexpected. It is, at its core, relational. And it's in these relations—these unpredictable, textured, sometimes tense human entanglements—that innovation finds its roots.

A Shift in the Creative Paradigm

For centuries, we've framed creativity as a solitary act. The genius in the attic. The poet scribbling through sleepless nights. The eccentric inventor tinkering in silence. It's a narrative that flatters the ego and simplifies the story. But it fails to account for the social conditions that shape creative thought—the mentors, the collaborators, the critics, the context. Creativity, especially the kind that aspires to social transformation, isn't isolated. It is social by design (Massari et al, 2023). And collaboration, when understood as a process of mutual sense-making and collective imagining, becomes not just helpful but essential. Why? Because no single person can hold the full complexity of a wicked problem. Because diverse perspectives don't just add variety—they reveal blind spots. They complicate easy narratives. They stretch the imaginative range of what's possible. Think of collaboration not as a means of coordination, but as a site of tension. And tension, in the right conditions, is a generative force.

Trust, Tension, and the Creative Friction Zone

There's a moment in every truly collaborative process when things get uncomfortable. When disagreements surface, when worldviews clash, when assumptions are dragged into the light. It's tempting to back away at that point. To smooth things over. To default to consensus. But that moment—that uncomfortable, edge-of-your-seat tension—is often where creativity lives. Social psychologist Keith Sawyer refers to this as the "collaborative emergence" of creativity: the idea that creative breakthroughs don't reside in any one person, but emerge through the interaction itself (Ritella & Hakkarainen, 2021). The dialogue is the source. The back-and-forth, the give-and-take, the pauses, the missteps, the breakthroughs—they are the architecture of innovation. But that emergence doesn't happen automatically. It needs the right conditions. And the first among them is trust. Not the superficial kind where everyone smiles in meetings and avoids conflict, but the deeper, earned trust that allows people to disagree constructively, to risk vulnerability, to admit uncertainty. Trust is what makes friction bearable. It turns conflict into dialogue, divergence into possibility. And ironically, it's built not by avoiding tension, but by moving through it together.

Figure 1. Waterfall of Capability Levers Driving Collaborative Breakthroughs

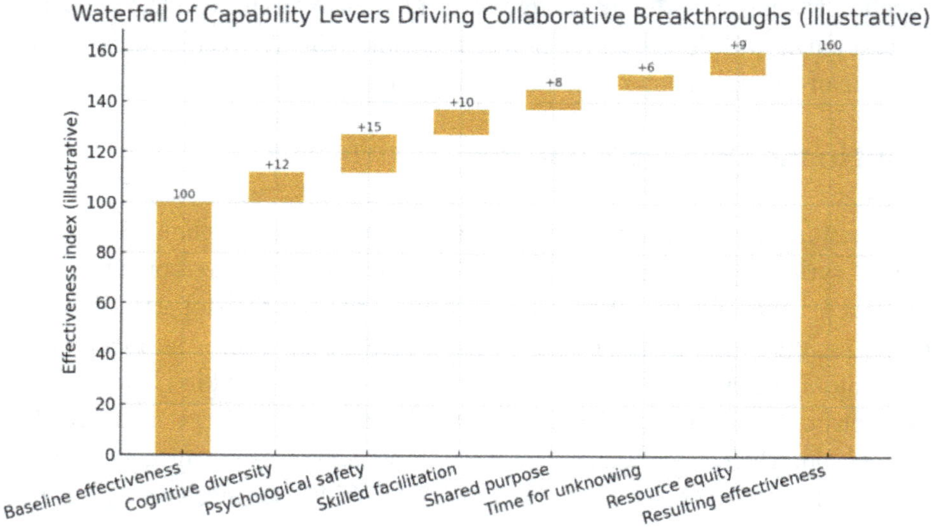

Collaboration as a Space of Translation

When people from different domains come together—artists and engineers, policymakers and activists, scientists and storytellers—they bring with them different languages. Not just different vocabularies, but different ways of framing reality, different metaphors, different logics. Collaboration, then, becomes an act of translation (Weisz et al, 2021). Not just linguistic, but conceptual and cultural. It's the process of learning to see through someone else's lens without abandoning your own. It's slow. Often frustrating. Full of "Wait, what do you mean by that?" moments. But it's precisely in this space—this liminal zone between shared understanding and stubborn difference—that new ideas take shape. Not because one perspective wins, but because something new is forged in the in-between. It's the poet helping the data scientist make the invisible legible. The urban planner learning to read the emotional cartography of a neighborhood. The policy analyst absorbing the subtle, quiet wisdom of lived experience. When collaboration works, it doesn't flatten differences. It honors them. It uses them. It allows them to *do work*—to produce something richer than any single perspective could alone.

Beyond Efficiency: The Value of Slowness

There's a prevailing assumption—especially in sectors driven by deadlines and deliverables—that collaboration is slower than working alone. And that's true. It is slower. But that slowness isn't a bug. It's a feature. Slowness allows space for reflection, for iteration, for emotional processing. It gives time for trust to form, for assumptions to be questioned, for meaning to be negotiated. Social creativity isn't efficient in the way factory production is efficient (Souto, 2022). It's recursive. It loops back on itself. It demands time to wander, to get lost, to argue, to reconcile. But in that meandering, something crucial happens: people begin to care. About each other. About the work. About the impact. And that care, once kindled, fuels the creative process in ways no deadline ever could.

Invisible Labor, Emotional Labor, Collective Labor

Much of what makes collaboration possible is invisible. It's the emotional labor of checking in, of holding space, of mediating tension. It's the cognitive labor of translation, of framing, of contextualizing. It's the logistical labor of scheduling, of facilitating, of synthesizing (Massey, 2021). This labor is often feminized, often underappreciated, often unacknowledged. But it is not ancillary. It is not extra. It is the **scaffolding** of collaborative creativity. We need to name it. To value it. To reward it. Because without it, the whole structure crumbles. Innovation isn't just a product. It's a process. And that process is built on a foundation of relationships, many of which are held together by the quiet, often uncredited work of care.

Innovation as a Social Act

When collaboration works—really works—it doesn't just lead to better ideas. It changes people (Marion & Fixson, 2021). It changes how they think, how they listen, how they see the world. It cultivates empathy, flexibility, intellectual humility. And that, in turn, reshapes the innovation itself. It makes it more responsive. More inclusive. More rooted in the messy realities of the people it's meant to serve. Social innovation doesn't emerge from creativity in a vacuum. It emerges from relationships. From contexts. From contradictions. It is social not just in its impact, but in its making. This means that if we want more socially creative solutions, we must invest not just in tools or strategies, but in cultures of collaboration. In the norms, practices, and environments that make true co-creation possible.

Figure 2. Sites of Social Creativity and Co-Creation

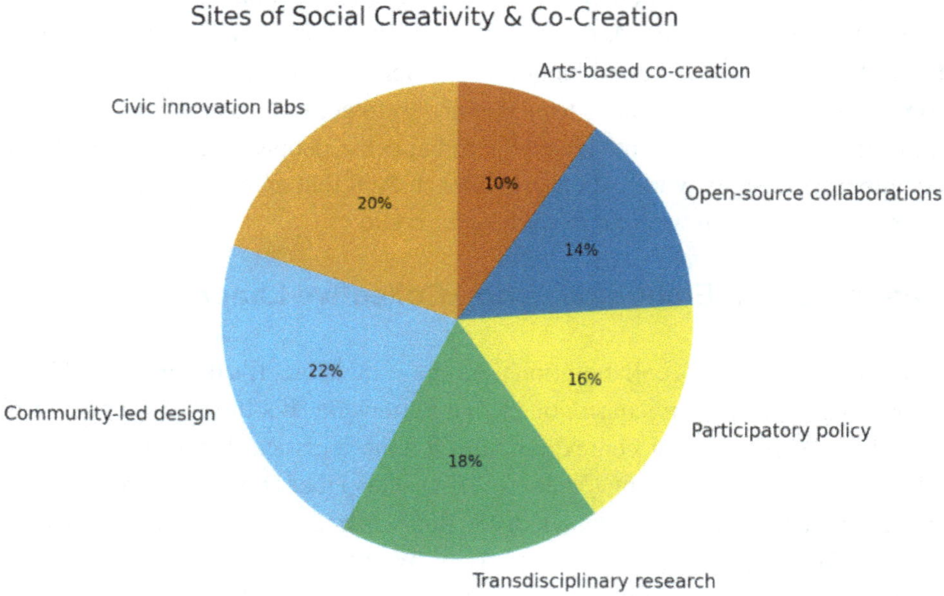

Case in Point: Listening as a Creative Act

A few years ago, I sat in on a workshop where a group of designers, community organizers, and health workers were trying to co-design an intervention for maternal care in underserved communities. The initial sessions were awkward. People talked past each other. Some deferred. Some dominated. The designers wanted data. The organizers told stories. But over time—through dinners, long walks, silent pauses, and tearful conversations—a rhythm began to emerge. People started listening not just to reply, but to understand. The language changed. So did the solutions. The final outcome wasn't flashy. It wasn't what anyone had predicted. But it worked. Not because it was clever, but because it was co-created by people who had come to trust one another, to challenge each other, and to hold the stakes of the problem together. That's what collaboration can do. It can turn listening into design. Grief into strategy. Conflict into possibility.

Barriers to Collaboration—and What We Can Do About Them

Of course, this isn't easy. Real collaboration is vulnerable, time-consuming, and sometimes exhausting. There are barriers—structural, cultural, psychological

(Šmite et al, 2021). Hierarchies inhibit voice. Scarcity breeds competition. Bias shuts down trust. Institutional norms reward individual achievement over collective process. But none of these are immutable. They are cultural artifacts. And culture can be changed. We can design processes that decentralize power. We can reward collaboration in our evaluation systems. We can teach facilitation as a core skill. We can make space—for listening, for unknowing, for emergence. We can build spaces where collaboration isn't a last resort, but the first instinct.

In the face of rising complexity and existential uncertainty, we need more than innovation. We need social innovation. And that means we need to treat collaboration not as a tactic, but as a way of being. We need to let go of the idea that the best ideas come from lone minds. We need to stop pretending that solutions can be engineered from above. We need to step into the slow, awkward, beautiful dance of thinking together. Because when we collaborate well—when we show up with openness, with patience, with curiosity—we don't just generate ideas. We build the kinds of relationships that can hold those ideas through conflict, through change, through failure. Collaboration, at its best, is not about agreement. It's about coherence. A shared sense of direction, held loosely, with room for difference. It's messy. It's nonlinear. It's deeply human. And in that humanity, we find not just the seeds of creativity—but the roots of transformation.

CASE STUDIES IN CO-CREATION: WHEN DIVERSE MINDS BUILD SHARED SOLUTIONS

There's something both disarming and deeply human about watching a group of people try to solve something together—not in a performative way, not as a box-ticking exercise, but as a sincere, messy, urgent act. Co-creation, in its truest form, is not about consensus or even about harmony. It's about the will to remain at the table—through confusion, frustration, contradiction—long enough for something new to emerge (Stembert, 2024). This section looks closely at four case studies in co-creation across different contexts. These are not "success stories" in the neat, celebratory sense. Rather, they are living archives of struggle, adaptation, tension, and genuine transformation. They show what happens when diverse minds not only meet, but build—and how the architecture of that building reflects not only what is made, but how people are changed in the making.

1. **Urban Design from the Ground Up: Medellín's Participatory Transformation:** Once known as the most dangerous city on Earth, Medellín, Colombia, is now studied around the world as a model for participatory urban innovation. But what makes the Medellín story remarkable isn't just its crime

statistics or infrastructure. It's how the city chose to design with rather than design for its people. In the early 2000s, Medellín's government, facing widespread violence, inequality, and institutional distrust, shifted its approach. Instead of delivering top-down solutions, it began inviting residents—especially those in marginalized barrios—to become co-designers of their own neighborhoods. Architects, sociologists, urban planners, and community elders came together in what were called "Urban Laboratories," informal spaces for dreaming, debating, disagreeing. One of the first tangible outputs was the Metrocable—a cable car system that connected the isolated hillside communities to the city's economic and cultural core. But the real innovation wasn't the cable cars. It was the process: open meetings, design charrettes, walking audits, kitchen-table conversations. No one actor owned the solution. Every detail—from the location of the stations to the murals that adorned the buildings—was shaped collectively. The logic was not efficiency. It was dignity. The changes didn't come without friction. Engineers clashed with artists. Local leaders had to translate policy into poetry. Timeframes ballooned. But in that slow churn, a new kind of city emerged—one that saw infrastructure not just as physical connectivity, but as social glue. A city that recognized co-creation as not just a means of making things, but a way of healing.

2. **Digital Justice in Practice: The Data for Black Lives Movement:** Data is supposed to be neutral. But we know better. Behind every dataset is a story—about who collected it, how, and for what purpose. The Data for Black Lives (D4BL) movement began as a recognition of this reality (Destine, 2023). Founded by Yeshimabeit Milner, a data scientist raised in Miami's Black communities, D4BL set out to shift the narrative: from data as surveillance to data as liberation (Bui, 2025). From the outset, the movement understood that technical knowledge alone would not suffice. Coders, organizers, artists, public health experts, policy wonks—people with radically different ways of knowing—came together around a single provocation: *What if data served the people it has historically harmed?* One powerful project was a collaboration between formerly incarcerated individuals and tech researchers to redesign predictive policing algorithms from the inside out. Not just to audit or critique them—but to rebuild them based on values of community safety, rather than carceral control. The process was fraught. Language barriers emerged—not linguistic, but epistemic. Engineers spoke in probabilities; organizers spoke in lived pain. But they kept showing up. They ate meals together. Traded books. Brought their grandmothers into the workshops. And over time, the work deepened—not just technically, but relationally. The resulting algorithm wasn't perfect. It wasn't meant to be. What mattered more was what it disrupted: a system where tools were imposed on communities, instead of emerging from them. D4BL didn't just create a tool.

It reimagined the politics of toolmaking. That's co-creation—not just shared output, but shared ownership of the process itself.

3. **Climate Adaptation in Vanuatu: Weaving Indigenous and Scientific Knowledge:** The Pacific Island nation of Vanuatu faces the looming threat of climate collapse—rising seas, intensified storms, vanishing coastlines. For many, the impulse would be to rush in with technical solutions. Sea walls. Evacuation plans. Renewable grids. But the people of Vanuatu have a different relationship to change—one that's slower, story-bound, rooted in ancestral rhythm. In 2018, a team of climate scientists partnered with Ni-Vanuatu elders, youth leaders, weavers, and land stewards to imagine what a culturally grounded adaptation strategy might look like. The goal wasn't to "translate science into local language." It was to listen differently. The meetings took place not in sterile conference rooms, but under banyan trees, during communal meals, amid dances and oral storytelling. Scientists were asked not just to present graphs, but to share where they were from, what they feared, who their ancestors were. In return, they heard creation myths that encoded flood cycles, migration patterns, herbal pharmacology. At first, the two ways of knowing seemed irreconcilable. But slowly, metaphors formed bridges. Ancestral stories were layered with geospatial maps. Weaving patterns became visual models of ecosystem resilience. The plan that emerged was neither "traditional" nor "modern." It was hybrid. Alive. Rooted in both evidence and memory. This wasn't just co-creation. It was co-reverence. A shared act of imagination across worldviews, where the line between science and spirituality was not erased, but held delicately in tension. And that tension produced something more durable than policy: mutual regard.
4. **Reimagining Public Health: A Transdisciplinary Response to Mental Health in Refugee Camps:** In the refugee camps of Northern Jordan, mental health is both urgent and invisible. Traumas accumulate—war, displacement, dislocation—but the resources are few, and the stigma is vast. In 2020, a team of researchers, artists, and camp residents began a year-long participatory design initiative to address the crisis. The idea wasn't to import therapy models. It was to co-invent pathways of care. The process began with story circles. No agendas. Just space. Refugees—many of them women and teens—shared stories not of war, but of small resilience: cooking with borrowed spices, planting stolen seeds in soda bottles, singing lullabies to block out the drones. From these fragments, the team noticed recurring symbols—rooftops, seeds, lullabies. An artist from Amman transformed these symbols into participatory murals. A psychologist designed group exercises based on traditional songs. Teen boys, previously withdrawn, began organizing rooftop film nights. Slowly, what emerged wasn't a mental health "program," but a fabric of small, interconnected rituals of belonging. The team didn't walk away with a toolkit. They walked away with relationships. The

kind that continue beyond funding cycles. The kind that make healing possible. This is the quiet power of co-creation: not spectacle, not speed—but shared presence in the face of pain.

What Makes These Cases Matter?

Across these cases, certain patterns echo:

- **Co-creation is slow.** Nothing unfolds on schedule. And yet, the slowness is what allows trust to grow roots.
- **Knowledge is plural.** No single framework is sufficient. Answers emerge in the weaving of many threads.
- **Emotion matters.** Not just ideas, but feelings—grief, joy, fear—shape the process and must be honored.
- **The process is the product.** Even when tangible outcomes are achieved, what endures most is the transformation of the people involved.

Table 1. Collaboration Pattern Matrix

Pattern	Core practices	Benefits	Risks	Enablers
Co-creation lab	Multistakeholder workshops; prototyping sprints	Novel options; shared language	Tokenism risk; facilitation load	Open calls; resident stipends; rotating roles
Participatory policy	Deliberative forums; citizensâ€™ juries	Legitimacy; context-fit	Capture by elites; fatigue	Clear mandates; feedback loops; childcare
Transdisciplinary studio	Artists+scientists+community briefs	Translation across domains	Jargon walls; timeline drift	Boundary spanners; bilingual briefs
Open-source coalition	Distributed contribution & review	Scalable collaboration	Burnout; governance disputes	Code of conduct; maintainer rotation
Community research	Local researchers; lived-experience data	Trust; relevance	Extractive habits; privacy	MOUs; data sovereignty tags
Civic imagination hub	Story circles; speculative prototyping	Future orientation; cohesion	Perceived impracticality	Seed funds; narrative archives

Perhaps the most radical insight from these stories is this: co-creation is not just a method. It's a worldview. It asks us to show up differently. To let go of control. To stay with tension. To believe that the future is not something we inherit passively—but something we must build, together, even when the bricks are unfamiliar, and the mortar uncertain. We often seek new language to capture the spirit of co-creation. Words like emergence. Entanglement. Holding space. These aren't just poetic flourishes. They reflect a deeper truth: that building shared solutions is not a linear act. It's not a transaction. It's a relational unfolding. In an age that prizes scale and replicability, these stories remind us of something older, and maybe wiser: that the most lasting innovations are often small in footprint but vast in resonance (Kayyali, 2024 A). Not because they solve the whole problem, but because they change how the problem is held. Who gets to name it. Who gets to shape the response. Co-creation, then, is not a guarantee of success. It doesn't promise ease. But it does offer something else—something rarer. A glimpse of what it looks like when we refuse to abandon complexity. When we stay. Together. In the hard work of making a world we don't yet know how to name.

TOWARD A CULTURE OF COLLECTIVE IMAGINATION: FRAMEWORKS FOR FUTURE PRACTICE

Let's begin with a question that resists easy answers: *What do we mean when we talk about imagining together?* Not just thinking in groups, not brainstorming over sticky notes or echoing one another in a polished workshop (Förster, 2023). But *imagining*—as in conjuring, envisioning, feeling forward into realities that don't yet exist, and doing so not in solitude, but in synchrony (Kayyali, 2024 C). A culture of collective imagination is not merely a luxury in times of crisis; it is a necessity, a survival instinct, an act of resistance against the inertia of what is. And yet, we live in a time where imagination has been steadily privatized, professionalized, and in many ways, policed. We outsource vision to futurists. We commodify dreaming in branded design thinking sprints. We treat imagination as something to be monetized, or worse, as something naïve. But look closely. Beneath the surface of every uprising, every social movement, every unlikely alliance of citizens reshaping their own futures—you'll find it. That quiet, stubborn pulse. The shared capacity to *imagine otherwise*. To cultivate a culture of collective imagination is to design for that pulse. To create the conditions—cultural, institutional, emotional—where it can be protected, practiced, and passed on. Not once, but continuously. Not by a few, but by all.

WHY IMAGINATION MATTERS (NOW, MORE THAN EVER)

We often hear that we're living in an age of acceleration. Technological change, ecological breakdown, institutional collapse—it all moves faster than our stories can keep up with. And in the wake of this speed, there's a kind of imaginative fatigue. We begin to recycle futures. Dystopia becomes default. Even our utopias feel mass-produced—green cities glowing with drone delivery systems and vertical farms, populated by diverse avatars in diversity-themed ads. But genuine collective imagination doesn't work like that. It's not predictive. It's speculative. Messy. Relational.

Rooted in the *how* as much as the *what if*. It doesn't serve the logic of optimization or scalability. It moves differently—more like a river than a roadmap. In a culture of collective imagination, the future is not a destination to be engineered. It's a terrain to be navigated together, across differences, uncertainties, contradictions. And crucially, it's a terrain that can only be reached by feeling as much as by thinking. Imagination here is not fantasy. It's muscle. It's memory and desire and story, woven into the body of a community. It's political. And yes, it's personal.

Figure 3. Institutional Readiness for Collective Imagination

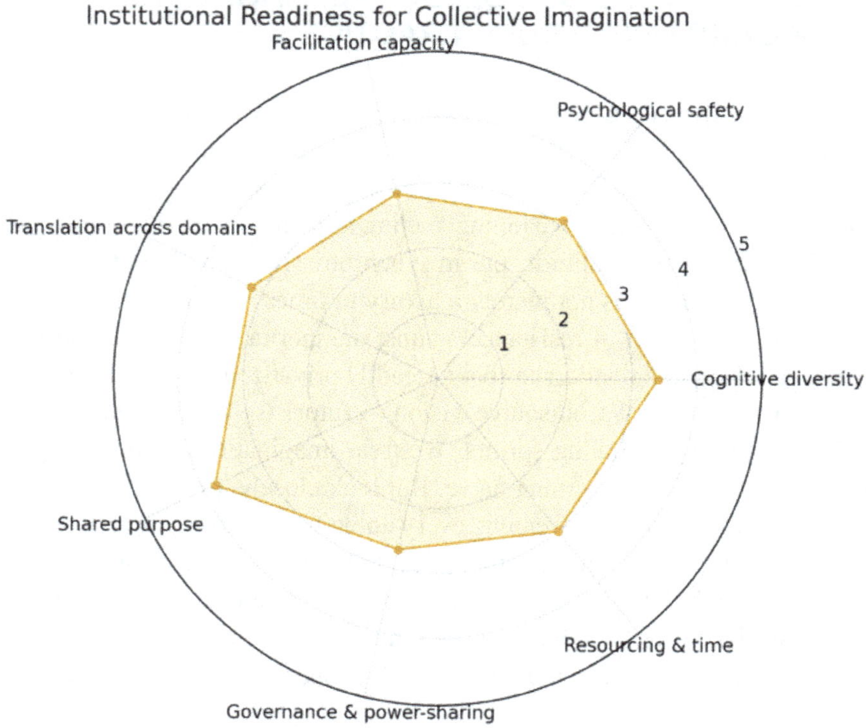

The Erosion of Imagination: How Did We Get Here?

Before we can rebuild, we have to reckon. How did imagination become so rare, so brittle, so easily dismissed? Start with education. Most of us are trained early on to value answers over questions, repetition over invention. Risk-taking is discouraged. Deviations from the script are penalized. Imagination becomes extracurricular, not foundational. Then look at governance. Bureaucracies reward what can be measured. The future gets reduced to projections, forecasts, budgets

(Newman et al, 2022). Creativity is siloed in "innovation units" that are often too removed from lived realities to spark meaningful change. Even in activism, where imagination should thrive, exhaustion has crept in. Burnout has replaced vision. Urgency has squeezed out possibility. Hope begins to feel like a luxury. And yet—paradoxically—it's precisely in these moments of rupture that imagination becomes most vital. Not because it offers escape, but because it keeps us tethered to the idea that something else is possible. That possibility is the seed of all transformation. And it doesn't grow in isolation.

WHAT DOES A CULTURE OF COLLECTIVE IMAGINATION LOOK LIKE?

It doesn't begin with blueprints. It begins with practice. With a commitment to cultivating spaces—physical, digital, emotional—where people can think together differently. Imagine a community center that doesn't just offer services but hosts storytelling nights where elders and youth dream out loud about futures they've never seen. Picture a city hall where planning documents are co-authored not just by experts, but by artists, janitors, gardeners, and historians. Visualize a university where the final project isn't a thesis but a *provocation*, judged not on polish but on its capacity to disturb, to evoke, to open. These aren't fantasies. They're fragments from real places—pilot programs, pop-up collectives, artistic residencies, alternative schools—where the culture is shifting, slowly and deliberately, toward co-creative futurity. The question is: how do we take these fragments and make them foundations?

Frameworks Without Rigidity: Guiding Principles for Collective Imagination

Let's resist the urge to create another ten-step model. Instead, what follows are not rules, but patterns—rhythms, orientations, postures—that support the cultivation of collective imagination across contexts.

1. Make Time for Unknowing: Imagination thrives in liminality—in the space between certainty and surprise. But our systems are designed to minimize ambiguity. Metrics. Timelines. KPIs. These are useful, yes. But they also constrict. So we must carve out intentional time—"slow time," some call it—for exploration, for divergence, for dreaming without immediate utility. This is not wasted time. It is sacred.
2. Center the Margins: The most radical futures are often born at the edges—among those who have had to imagine alternatives just to survive. Queer communities,

Indigenous nations, diasporic networks, disabled artists—these are the cartographers of possibility. A culture of collective imagination listens here first. Not to extract. But to learn. To honor. To amplify.

3. Treat Conflict as Creative Material: Disagreement is not a design flaw. It's fuel. Imagination is not consensus—it's polyphony. Frameworks for collective imagination must allow for difference to be held, explored, even celebrated. This means developing tools—not to suppress conflict, but to navigate it generatively. To let the friction spark new forms.
4. Design for Resonance, Not Replication: Scalability is the dominant paradigm of innovation. But collective imagination moves differently. It's not about copying and pasting solutions. It's about resonance—creating something so alive in one place that it echoes elsewhere, not through replication, but through adaptation. Think mycelial networks, not franchises.
5. Value the Invisible: Emotional labor. Listening. Holding space. Tending relationships. These are the roots of co-creative cultures. And yet they're rarely seen, let alone resourced. A robust framework for collective imagination must make the invisible visible. Must build structures that recognize, reward, and redistribute the labor of care.
6. Tell Better Stories: Imagination needs language. Needs narrative. Needs art. Without stories, ideas float. But stories ground. They bind memory to possibility. So invest in narrative infrastructure: community archives, oral histories, speculative fiction labs. Train not just designers or strategists—but *storytellers of systems*.

The Role of Institutions: Can Systems Host Imagination?

It's easy to romanticize the grassroots. But the truth is, institutions matter. They set conditions. Allocate resources. Shape norms. The question isn't whether institutions can host imagination—but how.

Some already are. The Civic Imagination Office in Bologna, Italy. The Participatory City initiative in London. The "Imaginings" project by the US-based Center for Artistic Activism. These aren't perfect. But they're trying. Experimenting with rituals, rules, and rhythms that allow for emergence. That don't smother imagination in red tape, but hold it gently. For institutions to truly support a culture of collective imagination, they must learn to be permeable. To let the outside in. To host ambiguity. To fund ideas that don't come with neat ROI. To reward *questions*, not just answers. This is slow work. Cultural work. But it's possible.

Table 2. Collective Imagination KPI Dashboard

KPI	Definition	Baseline (2024)	Target (2027)	Owner
Participation diversity index	Breadth of stakeholder representation per project	0.46	0.75	Project office
Psychological safety (1"5)	Avg team score on candor & voice	3.1	4.2	Facilitators; HR
Idea resonance rate (%)	Ideas adopted or adapted by other teams/cities	14	40	Network leads
Time-to-first-prototype (days)	From team formation to testable artifact	45	25	Design leads
Translation events (#/qtr)	Cross-domain translation sessions held	6	18	Boundary spanners
Governance participation (%)	Decisions made with community voting/input	22	60	Steering group
Care labor recognition (%)	Projects budgeting for facilitation/care work	18	70	Finance; PMO

Imagination, when practiced deeply, also invites grief. Because to imagine otherwise is to see what is—and what isn't (Lear, 2022). What was promised and never delivered. What was lost. What might never be. We cannot build a culture of collective imagination without making room for sorrow. Not as a weakness. But as a wellspring. Grief, when held collectively, can become generative. It can forge bonds. Ground vision in love, not illusion. To imagine together is also to mourn together. And to find, in that mourning, a kind of hope that is fierce, not fragile.

A culture of collective imagination isn't about aesthetics. It's not about whimsical futures or quirky workshops (van Lente & Peters, 2022). It's about power. About who gets to dream, and whose dreams shape the world. It's about transforming the very way we think about thinking—away from isolation, toward entanglement. Away from prediction, toward possibility. Away from ownership, toward stewardship. And it's about remembering that every future we build is first a story we tell. The work ahead isn't easy. It asks us to unlearn. To listen differently. To slow down when everything screams for speed. To risk vulnerability in spaces that don't always feel safe. But this work, as hard as it is, is also joyful. Because there is joy in making things together. In imagining lives we haven't lived. In seeing your vision reflected in someone else's eyes—and knowing it matters. So we begin. Again and again. With stories. With questions. With small rituals of care. And with a refusal to accept that the future is already written. Because it's not. We're writing it now. Together.

CONCLUSION

By the time we reach the end of a collaborative journey, something has shifted—within the individuals involved, the community they represent, and the system they sought to change. The solution itself, if one emerges, may not be perfect. It may be provisional, contingent, or incomplete. But the process—of listening across difference, of holding complexity, of daring to imagine together—leaves behind something more enduring than any single innovation. It leaves behind a sense of shared authorship and mutual responsibility. It builds social fabric. It plants seeds for a different kind of future.

The kind of future we face today—one marked by ecological instability, mass displacement, systemic inequality, and the erosion of public trust—demands more than technical fixes. It demands a reorientation toward collective meaning-making and shared imagination. Wicked problems are not just about facts and policies; they are about values, fears, hopes, and histories. To engage them is to engage ourselves—not just as problem-solvers but as co-creators of the worlds we wish to inhabit. In this light, collaboration is not a luxury or a strategy—it is a necessity, a moral and creative imperative.

Yet collaboration, as we have seen, is not always comfortable. It requires patience, humility, and a willingness to relinquish control. It asks us to sit with discomfort, to stay open to change, and to trust in processes whose outcomes we cannot predict. It is slow, nonlinear, and often frustrating. But it is also deeply human. And perhaps that is its greatest strength. In an age of algorithmic speed and technocratic solutions, collaboration brings us back to the core of what it means to be human: to connect, to care, to imagine, and to build together.

Social creativity is the art of navigating the unknown—of sensing what is possible even when nothing seems certain. It is born in the spaces between us, where difference becomes not a barrier but a bridge. It arises when we stop asking "Who has the answer?" and start asking "What can we create—together?" In this way, social creativity is not just a way of solving problems; it is a way of becoming. A way of becoming more attuned, more responsive, and more alive to the possibilities of collective life.

As we look ahead, the challenge is not merely to scale collaborative initiatives, but to embed their ethos into the very structures of society—into how we teach, govern, design, and live. This means rethinking education to value co-learning over competition. It means reshaping institutions to support distributed leadership and shared agency. It means designing technologies that amplify connection, not division. And it means reweaving the social contract—not around markets or mandates, but around mutual flourishing. The road is long, and the terrain is uncertain. But the path forward will not be forged by solitary visionaries. It will be shaped by communities who dare to imagine together, who meet complexity with creativity, and who understand that the solutions to our most intractable problems do not lie in individual genius—but in our collective capacity to listen, to learn, and to create anew.

REFERENCES

Bucciarelli, L. (2023). Spreading the word: practices of discipleship in early modern natural philosophy (Doctoral dissertation, University of Oxford).

Bui, M. (2025). Data and/as activism: Community-based racial justice data repertoires. *New Media & Society*, *27*(4), 2127–2145. DOI: 10.1177/14614448231206118

Chan, J. K. H., & Xiang, W. N. (2022). Fifty years after the wicked-problems conception: Its practical and theoretical impacts on planning and design. *Socio-Ecological Practice Research*, *4*(1), 1–6. DOI: 10.1007/s42532-022-00106-w PMID: 35308020

Destine, S. L. (2023). The importance of intersectionality in evaluating the surveillance and protest politics of the Movement for Black Lives (M4BL). In Research Handbook on Law, Movements and Social Change (pp. 254-267). Edward Elgar Publishing.

Douglas, J., Alisauskas, A., Bassett, E., Duranseaud, N., Lee, T., & Mantey, C. (2022). 'These are not just pieces of paper': Acknowledging grief and other emotions in pursuit of person-centered archives. *Archives & Manuscripts*, *50*(1), 5–29. DOI: 10.37683/asa.v50.10211

Edmondson, A. C. (2023). *Right kind of wrong: The science of failing well*. Simon and Schuster.

Förster, T. (2023). Imagining Together: The Social Dimension of Imagination. In *In Tandem–Pathways towards a Postcolonial Anthropology| Im Tandem–Wege zu einer postkolonialen Ethnologie* (pp. 231–258). Springer Fachmedien Wiesbaden. DOI: 10.1007/978-3-658-38673-3_13

Gergen, K. J. (2022). An invitation to social construction: Co-creating the future. Academic Press.

Head, B. W. (2022). *Wicked problems in public policy: Understanding and responding to complex challenges*. Springer Nature. DOI: 10.1007/978-3-030-94580-0

Jacoby, B. (2023). Facing the unsettled questions about service-learning. In *The future of service-learning* (pp. 90–105). Routledge. DOI: 10.4324/9781003447825-8

Kayyali, M. (2023). Promoting Entrepreneurship and Innovation in Higher Education. *Online Submission*, *2*(1), 1–26.

Kayyali, M. (2024). A). Career development in higher education: Best practices and innovations. In *Advancing student employability through higher education* (pp. 1–19). IGI Global. DOI: 10.4018/979-8-3693-0517-1.ch001

Kayyali, M. (2024 B). Crisis Response and Higher Education: Social Innovations in Times of Global Challenges. In Social Innovations in Education, Environment, and Healthcare (pp. 1-17). IGI Global.

Kayyali, M. (2024). C). Design thinking and creativity in entrepreneurial innovation. In *Applying Business Intelligence and Innovation to Entrepreneurship* (pp. 155–170). IGI Global Scientific Publishing. DOI: 10.4018/979-8-3693-1846-1.ch008

Kayyali, M. (2025a). Cross-Border and Cross-Industry Collaboration: Open Innovation Strategies for Effective Competitive Advantage. In Open Innovation Strategies for Effective Competitive Advantage (pp. 25-58). IGI Global Scientific Publishing.

Kayyali, M. (2025b). Understanding Innovation in Higher Education: Challenges and Future Directions. In Cultivating Creativity and Navigating Talent Management in Academia (pp. 117-138). IGI Global Scientific Publishing.

Kouyoumdjian, A. (2024). Rising Scholar: The Long-term Effects of Redlining on Climate Vulnerability and Food Insecurity. *International Social Science Review, 100*(4).

Kumagai, A. K. (2022). Discomfort, doubt, and the edge of learning. *Academic Medicine, 97*(5), 649–654. DOI: 10.1097/ACM.0000000000004588 PMID: 35020611

Lear, J. (2022). *Imagining the end: Mourning and ethical life*. Harvard University Press.

Levine, A. S. (2024). *Collaborate Now!: How Expertise Becomes Useful in Civic Life*. Cambridge University Press. DOI: 10.1017/9781009411882

Manu, A. (2024). The Myth of the Creative Genius. In *Transcending Imagination* (pp. 119–131). Chapman and Hall/CRC. DOI: 10.1201/9781003450139-13

Marion, T. J., & Fixson, S. K. (2021). The transformation of the innovation process: How digital tools are changing work, collaboration, and organizations in new product development. *Journal of Product Innovation Management, 38*(1), 192–215. DOI: 10.1111/jpim.12547

Marmo, L. (2024). An investigation into puppetry as sympoiesis in relation to Marta Cuscunà's work with reference to Staying with the Trouble by Donna Haraway. Academic Press.

Massari, S., Galli, F., Mattioni, D., & Chiffoleau, Y. (2023). Co-creativity in living labs: Fostering creativity in co-creation processes to transform food systems. JCOM: Journal of Science Communications, 22(3).

Massey, G. (2021). Re-framing conceptual metaphor translation research in the age of neural machine translation: Investigating translators' added value with products and processes. Training. *Language and Culture*, *5*(1), 37–56.

Matthews, K. E., Sherwood, C., Enright, E., & Cook-Sather, A. (2024). What do students and teachers talk about when they talk together about feedback and assessment? Expanding notions of feedback literacy through pedagogical partnership. *Assessment & Evaluation in Higher Education*, *49*(1), 26–38. DOI: 10.1080/02602938.2023.2170977

McGann, M., Wells, T., & Blomkamp, E. (2021). Innovation labs and co-production in public problem solving. *Public Management Review*, *23*(2), 297–316. DOI: 10.1080/14719037.2019.1699946

Mukherjee, A. S. (2020). *Leading in the digital world: How to foster creativity, collaboration, and inclusivity*. MIT Press. DOI: 10.7551/mitpress/12584.001.0001

Newman, J., Mintrom, M., & O'Neill, D. (2022). Digital technologies, artificial intelligence, and bureaucratic transformation. *Futures*, *136*, 102886. DOI: 10.1016/j.futures.2021.102886

Pesonen, R. (2022). Argumentation, cognition, and the epistemic benefits of cognitive diversity. *Synthese*, *200*(4), 295. DOI: 10.1007/s11229-022-03786-9

Ritella, G., & Hakkarainen, K. (2021). Knowledge Practices. *Theoretical Investigations: Philosophical Foundations of Group Cognition*, *18*, 149–167. DOI: 10.1007/978-3-030-49157-4_7

Rowe, H. A. (2024). *Problem solving and intelligence*. Taylor & Francis. DOI: 10.4324/9781032636696

Shaw, A. (2021, January). Teaching or cheating? Using collaboration and technology to support student learning. In International Journal on E-Learning (pp. 47-58). Association for the Advancement of Computing in Education (AACE). DOI: 10.70725/703731kdsrzb

Šmite, D., Moe, N. B., & Gonzalez-Huerta, J. (2021). Overcoming cultural barriers to being agile in distributed teams. *Information and Software Technology*, *138*, 106612. DOI: 10.1016/j.infsof.2021.106612

Souto, J. E. (2022). Organizational creativity and sustainability-oriented innovation as drivers of sustainable development: Overcoming firms' economic, environmental and social sustainability challenges. *Journal of Manufacturing Technology Management*, *33*(4), 805–826. DOI: 10.1108/JMTM-01-2021-0018

Stambovsky, P. (2021). *Myth and the Limits of Reason* (Vol. 39). Brill.

Stembert, N. (2024). Co-creation. In *Springer Handbook of Internet of Things* (pp. 841–864). Springer International Publishing. DOI: 10.1007/978-3-031-39650-2_35

van Lente, H., & Peters, P. (2022). The future as aesthetic experience: Imagination and engagement in future studies. *European Journal of Futures Research, 10*(1), 16. DOI: 10.1186/s40309-022-00204-8

Weisz, J. D., Muller, M., Houde, S., Richards, J., Ross, S. I., Martinez, F., & Talamadupula, K. (2021, April). Perfection not required? Human-AI partnerships in code translation. In *Proceedings of the 26th International Conference on Intelligent User Interfaces* (pp. 402-412). DOI: 10.1145/3397481.3450656

Wessels, K. R. (2022). *Pedagogy of entanglement: A response to the complex societal challenges that permeate our lives.* Springer Nature. DOI: 10.1007/978-3-031-15787-5

KEY TERMS AND THEIR DEFINITIONS

Cognitive Diversity: Intentionally mixing different mental models and ways of knowing to surface blind spots and expand solution space.

Collective Imagination: Sustained, communal practice of envisioning alternative futures and building narrative/relational infrastructure to reach them.

Collective Intelligence: Creativity emerging from interaction, translation across perspectives, and reciprocity rather than isolated insight.

Facilitation Structures: Dialogic, design, and systems-mapping practices that turn friction into generative collaboration.

Psychological Safety: Norms of trust that let participants voice dissent, risk error, and learn together without retaliation or ridicule.

Social Creativity: Group capacity to co-construct meaning and generate shared responses that are ethical, contextual, and transformative.

Wicked Problems: Complex, evolving challenges with contested values and no single "right" solution, requiring ongoing, collective engagement.

Chapter 9
From Peer-to-Peer to Meta-Platforms:
The Evolution of the Sharing Economy

Anja Herrmann-Fankhänel
https://orcid.org/0000-0002-6158-392X
Chemnitz University of Technology, Germany

ABSTRACT

This chapter is about the sharing economy as an example how people and their social creativity has changed resource allocation and hence can be viewed as a transformative innovation in different sectors towards more sustainable futures. With a conceptual approach, definitions and features of the sharing economy are used to outline how sharing economy organizations vary. About 1,000 examples are used to ground this variety. By comparing theoretical concepts and empirical data, innovations for society and organizations are outlined. The sharing economy is discussed as a concrete outcome of social creativity—a process through which individuals and communities collectively reimagined economic participation beyond traditional market logics. It is shown that social creativity materializes in diverse organizational models, from peer-driven, idealistic platforms to hybrid and commercialized ventures. The chapter argues that social creativity is not only a foundational force but the ongoing driver of the sharing economy's structural, normative, and technological diversification.

DOI: 10.4018/979-8-3373-2742-6.ch009

1 INTRODUCTION

The demand for economy and society to act in a resource-aware manner, is up to date. A recent phenomenon, with a changed resource usage among people, is the Sharing Economy (Gerwe & Silva, 2018). The Sharing Economy is focussed on how access to and usage of existing resources can be enhanced among people through digital technologies (Botsman & Rogers, 2010). Moreover, the Sharing Economy seems to be fruitful in terms of the demand for sustainable development (Plewnia & Guenther, 2018).

Since its beginning in around 2007, the Sharing Economy has been said to contribute to social welfare (Heinrichs & Grunenberg, 2012). Within this particular kind of the economy, individuals interact without business intermediates on online platforms, which makes it an equal peer-to-peer process with less asymmetry in information and with fewer capitalistic motivations (Notz, 2010). This normative perspective in particular, and the associated positive value around the Sharing Economy, has caught and is still catching the interest of people and motivates them to use and build Sharing Economy organisations, create sharing occasions, or rethink ownership and resource access (Fitzmaurice et al., 2020; Hamari et al., 2016). In consequence, business actors try to benefit from this positive wave of the Sharing Economy and build business models that they label as 'sharing' (Ciulli & Kolk, 2019). This seems to be a logical development. But the participation of traditional businesses has tackled the concept and especially the normative assumptions about the Sharing Economy (MacDonald, 2018; Martin, 2016; Murillo et al., 2017).

Besides the normative debate, further fields of tension have accompanied the Sharing Economy since its rise. The Sharing Economy has attracted attention through headlines such as "The sharing economy: a whole new way of living" (Silver, 2013), "The end of consumerism" (Acey, 2013), and "How the Sharing Economy can help developing nations" (Feeney, 2014), as well as with "The Sharing Economy undermines workers' rights" (Morozov, 2013), "Why hotel industry lobbyists want a global crackdown on Airbnb" (Edwards, 2013), and "Uber vs. the law" (Diamandis, 2014) in its early days. Although all of these media titles are between ten years and older, they still show why the Sharing Economy is of interest theoretically and empirically as the topics of these titles are present in recent academic publications. First, the Sharing Economy is said to improve the lives of individuals or even nations or particular sections of a population (Pandey et al., 2021). Second, it is argued that is illegal and controversial from, for instance, the perspective of labour (Geissinger et al., 2021). Third, consumption may changes generally because of the Sharing Economy (Morewedge et al., 2021), which, fourth, seems to force traditional business sectors and actors to react (Chang & Sokol, 2022). Notwithstanding this perspective (consumers or producers), the Sharing Economy was, and still is, described in both as positive and negative terms for individuals as well as businesses in media and academia (Pérez-Pérez & Benito-Osorio, 2025).

Moreover, it is considered a dynamic and new field of research as well as a new way of doing business. With its raise after the financial crisis since 2008, it continues to undergo development (De las Heras et al., 2021). Investigations about the Sharing Economy are thus taking place in a dynamic field of growing literature as well as in a constantly evolving field of a multitude of various cases besides 'airbnb' and 'uber'. Meanwhile, academic investigations aid in understanding the Sharing Economy in more detail in terms of its definitions, business cases, and impacts on the economy on the individual, organisational, and the macroeconomic level. But, although Sharing Economy considerations have remained similar over time, it is still of interest to figure out which kinds of economic activity are a part of the Sharing Economy and which are not (Pouri & Hilty, 2021), as, for instance, a commonly agreed definition is still lacking (Botsman, 2013; Gerwe & Silva, 2018; Markman et al., 2021). The methods and results of academic investigations may have changed over time as the body of research has been developing, but empirical investigations in particular are still required (Agarwal & Steinmetz, 2019).

In conclusion, the research interests of this chapter are: What is the Sharing Economy? How does the Sharing Economy differ from traditional business? How has the Sharing Economy evolved since 2008 and how will it develop in future? To answer these research questions, the first section serves as an introduction to the Sharing Economy. The underlying questions are: What are related terms? Which Sharing Economy definitions exist? What are the constituting features of Sharing Economy organisations? What is discussed to outline the Sharing Economy's particularity? What are the challenges in the scholarly discussion about the Sharing Economy? Is the Sharing Economy anything different to traditional business? If so, what makes the Sharing Economy a distinguishable phenomenon within economy?

An empirical consideration that is linked to the major take aways from the theoretical discussion follows. The research question of this part is: How can the Sharing Economy be described empirically? Based on a large sample of about 1,050 cases, which proclaim their affiliation to the Sharing Economy in the business database Crunchbase[1], empirical data are summarised. The contemplation of cases serves to outline theoretically discussed features in their practical accomplishment. On the one hand, theoretical aspects aided in structuring this part of the chapter. On the other hand, the comparison between theoretical considerations and empirical data shows discrepancies. There are kinds of organisations that think about and communicate their affiliation with the Sharing Economy but do not fit with the (narrow) definitions and their combination of constituting features of the scholarly term 'Sharing Economy'. The challenge points to a mismatch between theoretical and empirical considerations.

The Sharing Economy can be conceptualized as an innovation-driven model that has redefined traditional business paradigms. Based on Schumpeterian perspectives on innovation (Schumpeter, 1931) and Vahs & Brem's, (2015) classification of overlapping innovation types, this chapter will examine how Sharing Economy platforms serve as incubators for service innovation and servitization (Vandermerwe & Rada, 1988). The technological enablers, including Web 2.0, mobile connectivity, and algorithmic matchmaking have allowed individuals and organizations to establish new forms of digital marketplaces (Herrmann-Fankhaenel & Huesig, 2020).

2 THEORETICAL PERSPECTIVES

2.1 Social Creativity

"Creative activity grows out of the relationship between an individual and the world ..., and the ties between an individual and other human beings." (Fischer et al., 2004)

Creativity, understood as an individual competence (Amabile, 2012), is a prerequisite for social creativity, as these forms of creativity are not entirely separable (Fischer et al., 2005). Social creativity encompasses creative processes that occur through interactions between individuals and artifacts, embodying the collective knowledge and ethos of peer groups. The socio-cultural context in which social creativity occurs significantly influences both the process and its outcomes (Engeström, 2001). Moreover, it is embedded within a broader system comprising a domain of action and a peer group that collaboratively generates new solutions (Csikszentmihalyi, 2014). These systems may include groups, organizations, institutional environments, and markets (Watson, 2007).

In digital contexts, social creativity is also conceptualized as computational social creativity, wherein 'curious design agents' generate, evaluate, reject, or reconstruct novel artifacts (Saunders & Gero, 2001). An individual's contribution to an artificial social (digital) group through knowledge-sharing is a fundamental aspect of social creativity, as these artifacts are ultimately human-evaluated (Saunders & Bown, 2015). The Sharing Economy organizations are said to be one example of computational social creativity (Richardson, 2015).

2.2 Sharing Economy

The Sharing Economy is defined as an economic interaction among people who share products and services predominantly with the help of the Internet (Cambridge University Press, 2018). From an economic or business perspective, the term

'Sharing Economy' points to technology-enabled enterprises for access (Bardhi & Eckhardt, 2012; Belk, 2014b) to products or services that is not primarily based on ownership (Botsman & Rogers, 2010; Bucher et al., 2016; Davidson et al., 2018). In this sense, the focus is on how access is created by means of online platforms to enable an on-demand economy (Botsman, 2013; Cockayne, 2016; Owyang, 2016). Business-to-consumer online platforms, also called the platform economy (Schor & Attwood-Charles, 2017), are associated with the Sharing Economy as well (Demary, 2015; Fraiberger & Sundararajan, 2015). Furthermore, sharing is sometimes conducted for monetary reward and sometimes not (Belk, 2014a; Botsman & Rogers, 2010). Differentiations are also made between for-profit (Kung & Zhong, 2017; Latitude, 2015; Nash, 2015) and non-profit (Böcker & Meelen, 2017; Martin et al., 2015) organisations.

Sharing Economy is a conceptual term (Ranjbari et al., 2018), largely referring to making resources available online. Botsman portrayed the scope of the Sharing Economy phenomenon by explaining different related terms already in use in 2013: collaborative economy — distributed networks rather than centralized institutions are important; collaborative consumption — this involves access rather than ownership and changes in consumption patterns; Sharing Economy — this involves sharing underutilised assets (from space to skills) for monetary or non-monetary purposes; and peer economy — which refers to person-to-person marketplaces built on peer trust. These terms are offering a wide scope of what is associated with the Sharing Economy.-Often Sharing Economy and collaborative consumption are terms used synonymously (Codagnone & Martens, 2016).

Investigations have tried to visualise linkages and overlaps of these terms. Interestingly, Sharing Economy is positioned as the core in Figure 1 and Figure 2 between the terms that lack clear boundaries (Görög, 2018). Both visualisations have an economic perspective and outline particular fields of the economy that differ in their focus. Both figures refer to the fields of the access and the platform economy as well as to the community or crowd economy. While Acquier et al. (2017) investigate the overlaps of the different economies, Görög (2018) organises the different fields of economy from the most focussed (Sharing Economy) to the least focussed (digital economy). Hence, the outer parts include all the inner parts. Moreover, Görög (2018) embedded the Sharing Economy in a larger scope of digital economy, product-service systems, and second-hand platforms. Based on these considerations, the Sharing Economy is viewed as the core of a field of economy that is sourced by the concepts of platforms, access, on demand, and a community or crowd interacting digitally for products and services. Boundaries between the related terms and the Sharing Economy are less clear. This is the first challenge in grasping the Sharing Economy. However, the Sharing Economy seems to represent the core of these related concepts as it includes their various concepts in combination.

Figure 1. Terms Related to Sharing Economy Based on a Literature Review (Görög, 2020)

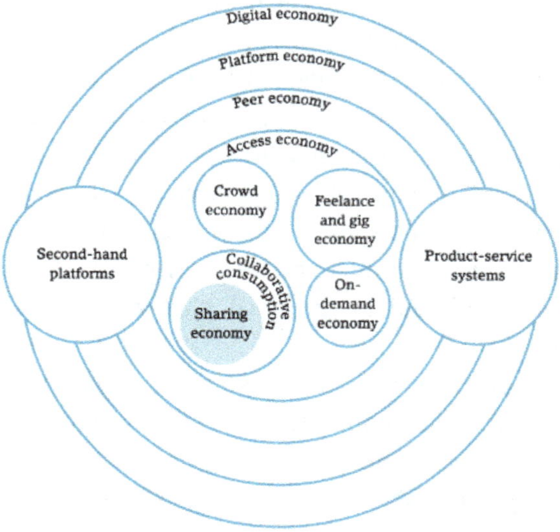

Figure 2. A Conceptual Organisation of Terms (Acquier et al., 2017)

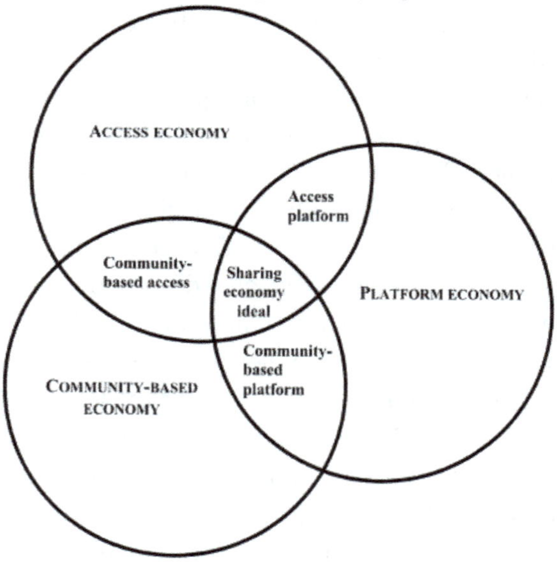

In terms of time, the Sharing Economy has experienced some technological and societal drivers since 1978, when the term collaborative consumption was used at first by Felson and Spaeth (1978) (Figure 3). Although, the Sharing Economy is based on economic activity, such as bartering, which is as old as humanity, its raise started when digital innovations became available to the public in 1990 (Siuskaite et al., 2019). Thus, the origin of the success and growth of the Sharing Economy is technology and its application for the purposes of communication and interaction, such as with Web 2.0 (Belk, 2014b). Technology is used to organize the exchange of products or services in multiple ways and in numerous industrial sectors based on digital, social networks (Oh & Moon, 2016). Having been observed and researched for years as e-business (Kenney & Curry, 1999), it is now perceived to be a new step or level because of the melding of the roles of the customer and the producer (Ritzer et al., 2012).

2.3 Understanding the Sharing Economy as enabled by social creativity

According to Tajfel et al. (1979) social creativity is not an individualistic endeavor but rather a group strategy. People identify as members of distinct groups, which differentiate themselves through unique social positions (Lemaine, 1974). Within the Sharing Economy individuals emphasized their unity and strength as peers to distinguish from traditional businesses (Botsman & Rogers, 2010). Consequently, they have developed alternative forms of interaction that enable resource access beyond conventional business models. This shift has been driven by a shared ethos that transforms communities through social creativity (Bilton, 2016). People developed first sharing models based on a non-capitalistic ethos for exchanging resources (Notz, 2010). By maintaining and reinterpreting these models as intergroup relations, participants reinforced their social identity, which is itself an element of social creativity (Van Bezouw et al., 2021).

Figure 3. Enablers of the Sharing Economy (Adapted from Siuskaite et al., 2019)

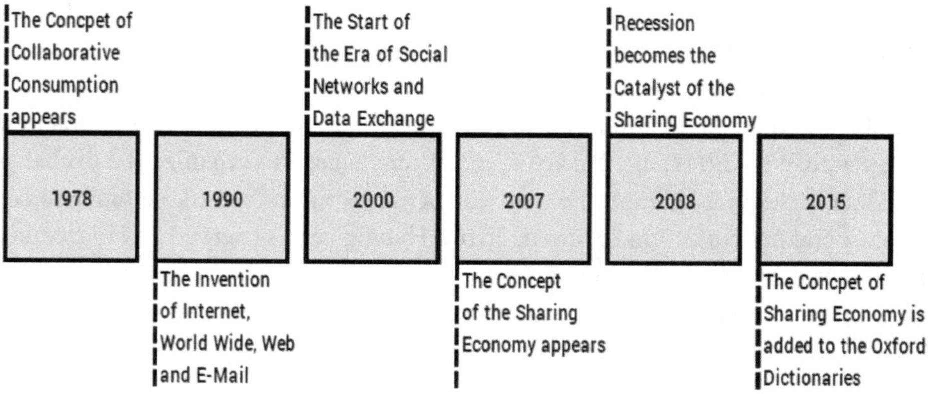

Knowledge-sharing is integral to social creativity, as it fosters innovation (Fischer et al., 2005). Especially the design of, for instance, a new service is formed by social creativity (Villari, 2018) and so was the design of new resource allocation within the Sharing Economy. Rather than solely purchasing goods, individuals facilitated access by lending possessions, increasing donations, and prioritizing reduced ownership (Bardhi & Eckhardt, 2012). The process of creating new artifacts typical for a group (Saunders & Gero, 2001) is also understood as co-creation within a socio-technical environment (Giaccardi, 2004). This principle underpins the Sharing Economy, in which digital platforms serve as artifacts enabling the exchange of goods and services (Kyprianou, 2018). From the perspective of social creativity the communities of peers is the frame in which new forms of economy participation was facilitated, today understood as the Sharing Economy (Richardson, 2015). Furthermore, the Sharing Economy is widely discussed in relation to sustainable futures (Evans et al., 2017), in particular to social sustainability (Böcker & Meelen, 2017), which is itself a product of social creativity (Watson, 2007).

In conclusion, it was the social creativity of individuals who identified themselves as different to capitalistic conviction, and jointly found new ways for resource allocation and established own initiatives and businesses with a non-capitalistic ethos. Since the widely acknowledged emergence of the Sharing Economy in 2008, it has continued to evolve through processes of adaptation and maintenance. As individuals can participate in multiple groups and domains, knowledge and sharing concepts have been transferred across contexts (Saunders & Bown, 2015), leading to the proliferation of sharing models. Consequently, the Sharing Economy has undergone a significant evolution, now encompassing diverse forms of resource exchange.

2.4 Definitions

As a result of a transparent and comprehensive research process, considering a wide span of previous conceptual and empirical studies, and published at a high level at the Academy of Management Perspectives, Sharing Economy is defined as "… a socioeconomic system that allows peers to grant temporary access to their underutilised physical and human assets through online platforms" (Gerwe & Silva, 2018, p. 13). This definition is used in this chapter.

In academic publications there are a variety of definitions (Ranjbari et al., 2018), which can be assigned to broader and narrower understandings (Table 1). Acquier et al. (2017) differentiated between narrow and broad perspectives when focussing on the essence of the Sharing Economy definitions, the aspects remain similar but are formulated from different angles (macro versus micro).The broad definitions seem to have a macroscopic point of view by addressing the Sharing Economy in its entirety as a collection of organisations or initiatives. For instance, it is referred to as a continuum (Habibi et al., 2017), an economic model (Botsman, 2013), a socio-economic system (Muñoz & Cohen, 2017), or the ways products or services are shared (Schor, 2016). The narrow definitions seem to focus on the level of a platform (Cockayne, 2016), the individual exchange of goods by consumers (Belk, 2014a; Frenken & Schor, 2017; Stephany, 2015) or the process of interaction (Bardhi & Eckhardt, 2012; Benkler, 2004). Table 1 includes the aspect of 'essence': what did the authors outline to define the Sharing Economy's essence? Obviously, there are two or more aspects as a combination that constitute the Sharing Economy, such as online access, no ownership transfer, and underutilised assets (Stephany, 2015).

Table 1. Narrow and Broad Sharing Economy Definitions (Adapted from Acquier et al, 2017)

Examples of Narrow Definitions		Essence
Benkler, 2004	**Refers to 'sharing goods' as 'a class of resources or goods that are amenable to being shared within social sharing systems rather than allocated through markets' (p. 356).**	**- Amenable resources allocated through - Social systems not markets**
Bardhi & Eckhardt, 2012	'The access economy, [...] also known as the sharing, or peer-to-peer, economy, [...] provides temporary access to consumption resources for a fee or for free without a transfer of ownership' (p. 210).	- Temporary access - Consumption resources - For fee or free - Without ownership transfer
Belk, 2014a	'Sharing is an alternative to the private ownership that is emphasized in both marketplace exchange and gift-giving' (p. 10).	- An alternative to the private ownership in - Markets and by gifting
Cockayne, 2016	'The on-demand or 'sharing' economy is a term that describes digital platforms that connect consumers to a service or commodity through the use of a mobile application or website' (p. 73).	- Digital access - To service or products - For consumers
Stephany, 2015	'The sharing economy is the value in taking underutilized assets and making them accessible online to a community, leading to a reduced need for ownership of those assets' (p. 9).	- Online access - Without ownership to - Underutilized assets
Frenken & Schor, 2017	Define the sharing economy as 'consumers granting each other temporary access to underutilized physical assets ('idle capacity'), possibly for money' (pp. 4–5).	- Temporary access to - Underutilized, idle physical assets
Examples of Broad Definitions		
Botsman, 2013	'An economic model based on sharing underutilized assets from spaces to skills to stuff for monetary or non-monetary benefits' (n.p., online article).	- Economic model - Underutilised assets - With or without fees
Schor, 2016	'Sharing economy activities fall into four broad categories: recirculation of goods, increased utilization of durable assets, exchange of services, and sharing of productive assets' (p. 2).	- Recirculation, - Increased utilisation, - Service exchange, - Sharing productive assets
Habibi et al., 2017	'[We] suggest a sharing-exchange continuum that helps distinguish the degree to which actual sharing is being offered' (p. 115).	- Continuum of sharing
Muñoz & Cohen, 2017	'A socio-economic system enabling an intermediated set of exchanges of goods and services between individuals and organizations which aim to increase efficiency and optimization of sub-utilized resources in society' (p. 2).	- Socio-economic system - Exchanges of goods - Between individuals and organisations

2.5 Features

To address definition-related challenges, different investigations such as Petrini et al. (2017) and Wruk et al. (2019), collected and compared previous studies and the features considered to constitute Sharing Economy organisations. These structured overviews sheds light on the main features and particular characteristics from the viewpoint of Sharing Economy organisations (Table 2 and Table 3). In doing this, conceptual and empirical investigations about the Sharing Economy are mixed up by both author teams.

Table 2. Characteristics and their Occurrence in the Sharing Economy according to Petrini et al., 2017

Characteristics	Occurrence	References
Platform Type	Interfering	Botsman & Rogers, 2010; Hamari et al., 2015
	Intermediary	
Sharing Model	Access	Belk, 2010; Botsman & Rogers, 2010; Bardhi & Eckhardt, 2012
	Transfer	
Sharing Type	Renting	Belk, 2010; Botsman & Rogers, 2010; Corciolani & Dalli, 2014; Hamari et al., 2015
	Lending	
	Swapping	
	Donating	
	Gifting	
	Purchasing used goods	
Market Structure	Peer-to-peer	Schor, 2014
	Business-to-peer	
Sharing Nature	Experimental	Bardhi &Eckhardt, 2012
	Functional	
Financial Transaction	Present	Bardhi & Eckhardt, 2012; Schor, 2014; Hamari et al., 2015
	Absent	
Sharing Duration	Short Term	Bardhi & Eckhardt, 2012
	Long Term	
Consumer Anonymity	Possible	Bardhi & Eckhardt, 2012
	Impossible	
Consumer Involvement	Low	Bardhi & Eckhardt, 2012
	High	
Political Influence	Low	Bardhi & Eckhardt, 2012; Laamanen et al., 2015
	High	
Collective Innovation	Oriented	Kozinets et al., 2008
	Concentrated	

Table 3. Discussed Features of the Sharing Economy (Adapted from Wruk et al., 2019)

	Dimensions Debated in Categorisation Efforts											
	Characteristics of Exchanged Products and Activities		Relevance of an Online Platform		Transaction Characteristics				Regional Scope of Organisations		Types of Interaction Partners	
Reference	Tangible products	Services/ non-tangible	Online models	Offline models	No transfer of ownership	Exchange of ownership	Non-monetary	Monetary	Locally bound	Globally active	Peer-to-peer	Business-to-consumer
Botsman & Rogers, 2010												
Frenken & Schor, 2017												
Voytenko Palgan et al., 2017												
Cohen & Kietzmann, 2014												
Gerwe & Silva, 2018												
Codagnone & Martens, 2016												
Schor, 2016												
Kenny & Zysman, 2016												
Cohen & Muñoz, 2016												
Hamari et al., 2016												
Belk, 2014b												

	Feature is used in provided definitions and categorisations. This is this emphasised as a key feature characterising sharing organisations.
	Feature is explicitly discussed as characterising sharing organisations.
	Feature is not named as an inclusion criterion, but from the author's argumentation or base on provided examples of sharing organisations, it becomes clear, that it is a relevant feature.
	Feature is explicitly discussed as exclusion criterion.
	Feature is not a characteristic for sharing organisations. This conclusion can be drawn from the author's argumentation.
	Indicates that authors do neither discuss this feature nor do they provide examples indicating whether it is relevant or not form them.

Neither of these investigations do claim to include or exclude certain feature characteristics as not being sharing, despite repeated previous studies on this matter. In consequence, both investigations outline a plenty of characteristics that differ partially when compared. For instance, both refer to the transfer of ownership, which can or cannot take place, and the focus on consumers, which leads to the Sharing Economy being business-to-consumer and consumer-to-consumer as well. Furthermore, both collections of characteristics outline the difference in either having non-monetary or monetary and thus financial transactions or not. In spite of this, Wruk et al. (2019) also consider the regional scope of a Sharing Economy organisation. This is not reflected upon in the investigation of Petrini et al. (2017). Additionally, Petrini et al (2017) outline the sharing types, including, for instance, renting and donating. That is not part of the study by Wruk et al. (2019).

2.6 Maps, Frameworks, and Types of Sharing Organisations

On the level of feature combinations, scholars outline frameworks of the Sharing Economy (Richter et al., 2017), or delineable sharing business models (Muñoz &

Cohen, 2018; Täuscher & Laudien, 2018). While Muñoz and Cohen (2018) and Täuscher and Laudien, (2018) focus on business models from the viewpoint of an organisation and its features, which can be investigated with, for instance, a business model canvas (Osterwalder & Pigneur, 2010), Richter et al. (2017) build a framework including requirements, drivers, sharing types, and goals (Figure 4).

Richter et al. (2017) followed the broad, macroscopic views within the definitions. Besides the organisational perspective of having three different types of sharing (digital content, physical goods, and in the context of social projects), there are aspects outside of a Sharing Economy organisation itself that matter. For instance, Richter et al. (2017) indicate societal drivers such as urbanity and the requirement for prosumers (Heinrichs & Grunenberg, 2012).

Figure 4. Framework of the Sharing Economy (Adapted from Richter et al., 2017)

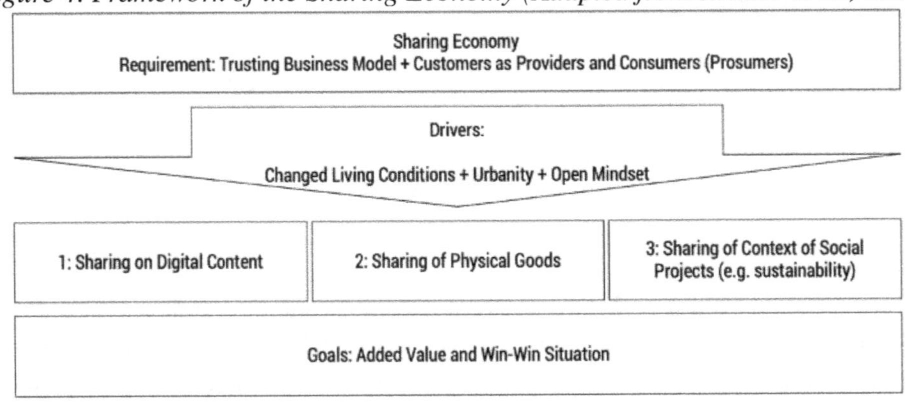

The narrow perspectives investigate the Sharing Economy on an organisational or an individual level, to which Muñoz and Cohen (2018) and Täuscher and Laudien, (2018) contributed to. Muñoz and Cohen (2018) developed the sharing business model compass (Figure 5) with a multitude of combination options on the basis of six main features (e.g. technology, shared resources) and concluded there were three dominant business models: platform corporation, platform cooperative, and hybrid sharing models. In contrast, Täuscher and Laudien, (2018) outline six basic business models within the Sharing Economy that derive from five main features (e.g. platform type, revenue model). An adaption of their results is noted in Table 4.

Figure 5. Sharing Economy Business Model Compass (Muñoz & Cohen, 2018)

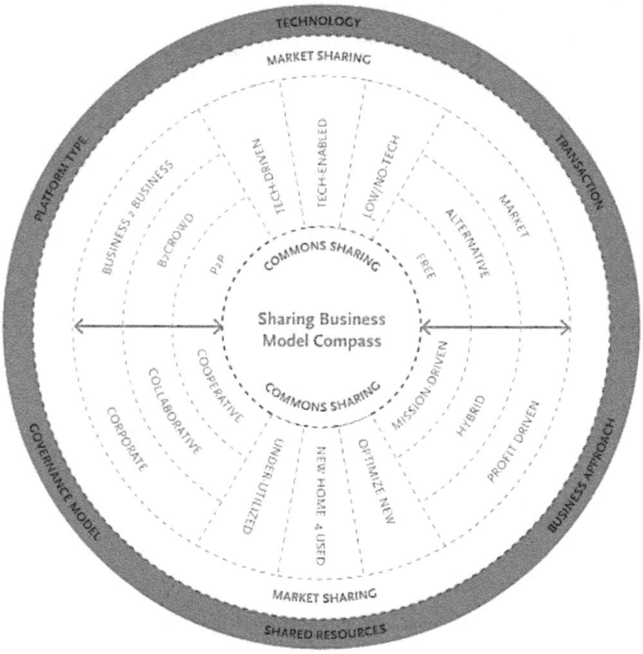

Interestingly, Muñoz and Cohen (2018) and Täuscher and Laudien (2018) focus on similar aspects such as shared resources but outline different operationalisations. While Muñoz and Cohen (2018) refer to the resources' characteristics of being new, underutilised, or used, Täuscher and Laudien (2018) differentiate between goods that have an online, offline, or physical nature as well as between dealing with services and products. Moreover, when looking at the platform type, which is considered by both investigations, they refer to different aspects of the Sharing Economy organisations. In the study of Muñoz and Cohen (2018), the platform type differentiates the business concept based on interacting parties: business, crowd, and peers. Contrarily, Täuscher and Laudien (2018) investigated whether it is a web- or mobile-based platform or both when discussing the platform type. Furthermore, Täuscher and Laudien (2018) also include the aspect of offline interaction within the sphere of Sharing Economy businesses. Although, the Sharing Economy is said to be an online phenomenon, investigations also outline the offline dimension of accomplishing online-initiated exchange or interaction (Fitzmaurice et al., 2020; Reischauer & Mair, 2018). Additionally, the business model compass by Muñoz and Cohen (2018) displays the aspects of mixed or hybrid features as well. There is a hybrid option in the business approach between mission- and profit-driven and an alternative type of transaction between market and free transaction. It opens the perspective of feature overlaps in the Sharing Economy, which is referred to as 'hybridity' (Reischauer & Mair, 2018).

Table 4. Business Models of the Sharing Economy according to Täuscher and Laudien, 2018 (Adaption)

Focus of Business Model	Platform type	Platform partici-pants	Value proposition (to demand side)	Trans-action type & good	Revenue model	Example
Efficient Product Transactions	Web-based platform	C2C, B2B	Large product variety	Physical products	Commission fee, subscription fee (mostly supply side	Beepi (eBay for used cars)
Digital Product Community	Web-based platform	C2C	Being part of a primary non-commercial community	Digital products; physical products	Commission fee; supply side, demand side	Sellfy (connecting 'neighbours' to share durable goods with each other)
Product Aficionados	Web-based & mobile platform	B2C, C2C	Exchanging knowledge about niche products with community of like-minded people	Physical products	Commission fee; supply side	hobbyDB (eBay meets IMDB/ Wikipedia" for hobbies & collectibles)
On-demand Offline Services	Web-based & mobile platform	B2C	Accessing large service variety in a novel form	Offline services	Commission fee, subscription fee; mostly supply side	StyleSeat (connecting beauty salons & consumers)
Online Services	Web-based platform	C2C, B2C	Providing novel online services with social networking	Online services	Commission fee, subscription fee; mostly supply side	iTalki (connecting language learners with teachers for 1-to-1 online lessons)
Peer-to-Peer Offline Services	Web-based & mobile platform	C2C	Providing novel services with community feeling within & outside digital platform	Offline services	Commission fee (demand & supply side), subscription fee (third parties)	Airbnb (connecting people to list, discover, and book private accommodations)

2.7 Hybridity – Blending of Features

Scholars describe the blending or overlapping of features within the Sharing Economy, known as hybridity (Reischauer & Mair, 2018; Scaraboto, 2015). Hybridity refers to distinct or contrasting characteristics that exist in parallel at one organization, such as enabling renting as well as buying on one online platform (Muñoz & Cohen, 2018; Reischauer & Mair, 2018). Hybridity also refers to the side-by-side existence of different organisations under the umbrella term sharing or hybrid economy (Görög, 2018; Scaraboto, 2015).

2.7.1 Consumers and Producers

Users are peers or consumers and thus users' roles are producers and consumers within the Sharing Economy (Gerwe & Silva, 2018; Heinrichs & Grunenberg, 2012).

Users within the Sharing Economy are either consume or produce or both, while 'both' points to the blending of the aspect of users' roles, making them 'prosumers' (Ertz et al., 2025; Reischauer & Mair, 2018) (Table 5, in grey). Furthermore, participants within the Sharing Economy are divided into users and operators of an online platform, which may be individuals, organizations, or initiatives (Benoit et al., 2017; Wruk et al., 2019). The notion of having peers as users is referred to as sharing activities carried out solely among individuals. Hence, formal organizations, as in business-to-consumer and business-to-business models, are sometimes excluded from the term's definition (Gerwe & Silva, 2018). However, many scholars include organizations as participants of the Sharing Economy and even describe the business-to-business Sharing Economy (Benoit et al., 2025). In conclusion, users' roles within the Sharing Economy are often hybrid as they are both producers and consumers.

Table 5. User Roles and Types of Businesses in the Sharing Economy

Users referring to both sides of the market		**Producers**	
		Individuals	**Organisations**
Consumers	Individual	Consumer-to-Consumer *'Prosumers' as 'Hybrid Business'*	Business-to-Consumer *'Traditional Business'*
	Organisations	Consumer-to-Business *'Undescribed in literature'*	Business-to-Business *'Traditional Business'*

2.7.2 Online and Offline User Interaction

There is the involvement of online platforms in user interaction enabling online interaction. Nevertheless, offline interaction is often required when realising a service such as sharing a car ride (Schor, 2016; Reischauer & Mair, 2018). The involvement of technology in user interaction addresses the integration of online platforms within the Sharing Economy in particular (Belk, 2014b). First, technological progress thereby helps offline sharing concepts to move beyond stationary exchange, by expanding to the online dimension (Schor, 2016). Second, Sharing Economy participants experience an online and an offline part of the interaction of particular sharing concepts (Reischauer & Mair, 2018). Therefore, a distinction has to be made regarding the initiation and execution of sharing activities (Table 6). While online sharing models make use of platforms for both (the set 'Online Sharing

Businesses' in Table 6), offline sharing models show a digital presence in terms of providing general information such as opening hours on a website ('Offline Sharing Businesses' in Table 6). But they do not depend on digital platforms to initiate or execute the sharing as they are offline initiatives (Acquier et al., 2017; Muñoz & Cohen, 2017; Wruk et al., 2019). Hybrid models refer to ride-sharing for instance, where the initiation to share a ride is online but is realised offline when driver and user are in the car (in grey in Table 6) .

Table 6. Online Platform Integration in User Interaction within the Sharing Economy

<table>
<tr><th colspan="2" rowspan="2">Accomplishment of Users' Interaction has two Dimensions</th><th colspan="2">Initiation</th></tr>
<tr><th>Online</th><th>Offline</th></tr>
<tr><td rowspan="2">Execution</td><td>Online</td><td>Online Sharing Businesses</td><td>Hybrid Interaction – undescribed in literature</td></tr>
<tr><td>Offline</td><td>Hybrid Sharing Business</td><td>Offline Sharing Business</td></tr>
</table>

2.7.3 Non-Market and Market Logics

There is the blending of non-market and market logics or non-profit and for-profit orientations (Fitzmaurice et al., 2020; Scaraboto, 2015). The blending of non-market and market logic goes back to the investigation of Scaraboto in 2015. As a hybrid economy, the Sharing Economy can include traditional market logics as well as community or non-market logics in an organisation or initiative at once. Conclusions about the non-market and market logic are deduced from particular features specifications. For instance, non-pecuniary interaction is associated with non-market logics and pecuniary interaction with market logics. Sharing concepts, ranging between non-market and market orientation, are understood as a hybrid. They received different terms such as 'hybrid economy' that have a communal orientation but are organized based on, for example, pecuniary interaction (Scaraboto, 2015); 'new business models' (Petrini et al., 2017), or 'commercial peer-to-peer' (Siuskaite et al., 2019), which both have a for-profit orientation but are organized as consumer-to-consumer. The aspects of market and non-market logics derive from financial transfers and are linked to the normative debate about the Sharing Economy being idealistic.

Figure 6. Sharing Economy Core's Differentiation by Siuskaite, 2019

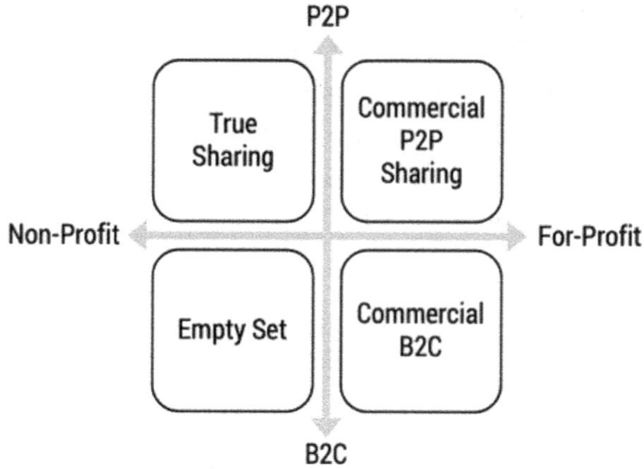

2.8 Idealistic Orientation

Some of the Sharing Economy organisations are said to have idealistic goals (Albinsson et al., 2019; Barbu et al., 2018; Belk, 2014a; Fitzmaurice et al., 2020; Herrmann-Fankhaenel & Huesig, 2016; Ozanne & Ballantine, 2010; Wruk et al., 2019). To tackle the issue of idealistic goals, investigations made various differentiations between an idealistic and a commercial orientation (Table 7) or idealistic orientations based on integrated kinds of users (Figure 6 and Figure 7).

Table 7. Financial Equivalents for an Idealistic Intention of Sharing Economy Organisations

Reference	Idealistic Orientation	Commercial Orientation
Scaraboto, 2015	Non-market logic	Market logic
Benkler, 2017	Communal sharing with intrinsic motivation	*No named counterpart*
Dobusch, 2019	Commons-based models	Market-based models
Fitzmaurice et al., 2020	Non-profit	For-profit
Akin et al., 2021	Non-pecuniary	Pecuniary

When addressing the financial equivalents to outline an idealistic orientation, these differentiations are made with reference to an organisation having a non-market logic, a commons-based model, or a non-profit orientation. Financial aspects such as a for-profit or a non-profit orientation of an organisation have been used to outline a differentiation of Sharing Economy organisations that exist side-by-side (Siuskaite et al., 2019). However, the Sharing Economy's idealistic or communal connotation experienced criticism as soon as monetary transactions became paradigmatic and a commercial understanding of sharing was developed as well (Gerwe & Silva, 2018). Thus, the idealistic intention deduced from financial issues hence seems to be a discussion against the background of the Sharing Economy development.

On the other hand, authors refer to the interaction of users as being non-pecuniary when being idealistic. An idealistic intention is subsumed of a Sharing Economy organisation if it addresses individuals, consumers, or peers (idealistic) instead of organisations or businesses, which have a commercial orientation (Gruszka, 2017). Considering the financial and the peer aspect in combination, theoretically leads to four different sharing types (Figure 6 and Figure 7): (1) the ideal or true sharing is characterised by peers sharing for a non-profit purpose or in a non-profit organisation or in a non-pecuniary manner, (2) redesigned or commercial businesses that are for-profit or with financial business-to-peer transactions, (3) and the new business or for-profit peer-to-peer sharing with financial transactions (Codagnone & Martens, 2016; Petrini et al., 2017; Siuskaite et al., 2019). Finally, scholars conclude (4) an empty set in a matrix of four sets. This empty set stands for non-profit or the absence of financial transactions with a business-to-peer alignment. This is said to be empty or non-existent in the Sharing Economy.

The given names true sharing (Siuskaite et al., 2019) and sharing by ideal (Petrini et al., 2017) from set (1) indicate the idealistic, real, or core intention of the Sharing Economy, where individuals act with each other without business intermediates and without money. Furthermore, in set (2) these frameworks also include business-to-consumer models as a part of the Sharing Economy. These are not viewed as idealistic as they include financial interference or for-profit orientations. Hence, the frameworks include one idealistic and one commercial set of Sharing Economy organisations.

Moreover, individuals also revealed interaction without businesses but with monetary transfer with each other (set 3). Here, the challenge to consider is whether these interactions are still idealistic as individuals do not share products or services because of good-will solely but also for a transfer of money (Kuzminska et al., 2025). One issue of idealistic orientation (individuals) is given, one issue of idealistic orientation (financial aspects) is not given. It thus can be seen as hybrid regarding the idealistic and commercial orientation. These refer to the options the Sharing Economy developed after the financial crisis in 2008 (Botsman & Rogers, 2010): individuals looking for alternatives of private interaction without business intermediates but not without financial benefits.

A similar or hybrid consideration would be required if the fourth set were not be empty. There are non-profit or non-pecuniary business-to-consumer organisations, where the financial aspect would indicate an idealistic intention while the aspect of business-to-individuals would refer to a commercial instead of an idealistic intention, such as social entrepreneurship.

Figure 7. Sharing Economy Core's Differentiation by Pertini et al., 2017

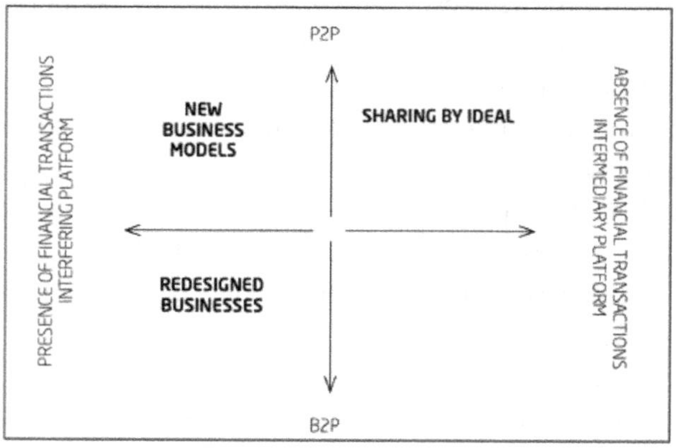

Interestingly, the literature reveals a tendency for idealistic examples of the Sharing Economy to be present primarily when there is a predominantly offline (Albinsson et al., 2019), or local orientated (Wruk et al., 2019), or if there is a community-oriented interaction (Dobusch, 2019). Within the context of a toy library (offline interaction only), users reported the motivation to do something better for themselves or the community and avoid typical for-profit markets (Ozanne & Ballantine, 2010). In sharing events in communities (offline interaction only), non-market logics such as non-pecuniary interaction and resource allocation are dominant (Albinsson et al., 2019). Moreover, the integration of financial payments in sharing between neighbours (offline interaction only) revealed a distancing of particular participants as it does not fit into this community logic (Akin et al., 2021). In contrast, online interactions are mostly associated with traditional economies, such as a for-profit orientation. There are redesigned businesses that are digital, business-to-consumers, and for-profit (Petrini et al., 2017) or are called 'platform-based organisations' showing for-profit orientations (Wruk et al., 2019). However, an idealistic intention is also followed in online or hybrid formats within the Sharing Economy (Herrmann-Fankhaenel & Schell, 2022).

2.9 Conceptual challenges of the Sharing Economy

So far, definitions, features, and types of Sharing Economy organisation have been outlined. However, there are conceptual challenges which have to be addressed for a proper investigation of cases.

In essence, the Sharing Economy is a part of the economy that is based on combinations of features that derive from, and are embedded in, concepts such as access, community, peer and platforms in general. The Sharing Economy is based on old economic activities such as bartering and swapping, which received a boost because of digital technology and applications for time- and space-independent resources-related communication and interaction. Within these concepts, the Sharing Economy receives a core position as it combines aspects of all these concepts. Moreover, there is a 'true Sharing Economy' that refers to a combination of features where online platforms help individuals to exchange products and services with each other (without financial benefits). This is concluded from idealistic considerations about types of sharing organisations.

Linked to the concept of a true Sharing Economy are the wider and narrow definitions. Narrow and broader understandings or narratives of the Sharing Economy exist side-by-side (Netto & Tello-Gamarra, 2020). They created awareness for missing boundaries between the Sharing Economy and traditional business from a phenomenological perspective and made a limited contribution to the grasping the particularity of the Sharing Economy. Hence, the level of organisational characteristics or features were outlined, which led to options for considering the Sharing Economy's particularity.

When following a broad understanding, which includes narrower perspectives, there are plenty of characteristics that aid in describing Sharing Economy organisations. However, the features used in different investigations sometimes share their name but vary in their operationalisation when comparing different studies. Therefore, certain features, such as idealistic orientation and kinds of user, were analysed regarding their realization to show their variety. Moreover, based on feature combinations, organisational types are concluded. Maps and frameworks aid in understanding the wide span of the Sharing Economy phenomenon based on varying organisational features that appear in different combinations. Despite these issues, the perspective of features and their combinations on the one hand allows addressing the plenty of organisational sharing types without the exclusion of particular, for instance, particular business models and without an upfront exclusion of features and thus particular cases.

When the Sharing Economy is discussed as a hybrid economy, it is obvious that this relates to the aspects of users, technology involvement, and the basic logic. The Sharing Economy in a broad sense represents many possible forms of (economic) interaction between individuals or organisations with the help of the Internet on a continuum between commercial, hybrid, and idealistic models. The blending of features and feature overlaps contribute to the understanding of the Sharing Economy's hybridity and thus particularity: within the Sharing Economy, distinct spheres such as individuals versus organisations, online versus offline as well as non-profit versus for-profit logics unite. First, this is possible from a meta-perspective of the Sharing Economy as an umbrella term grasping the whole phenomenon. Second, it is also possible at one organisation that features mix such as having users as producers and consumers.

2.10 Theoretical Frame for the Sharing Economy

Taking the unclear boundaries of related terms, the definitions being broad or narrow, different concepts of relevant features as well as the different operationalisation of these constituting features in considerations requires an open understanding of the Sharing Economy for the contemplation of cases. The literature review did not enable a clear set of boundaries for a definition, exclusion of features, or feature combination (types). Thus, with a broad understanding, a wide range of features, and the perspective of various types existing side-by-side, enables a frame for investigating cases from a broad perspective and outlining kinds of particularities, different concepts of narrow understandings as well as hybridity and idealistic accomplishments.

For investigating cases of the Sharing Economy in the following part Table 8 summarises the first section and outlines relevant features. The definition by Gerwe and Silva (2018) addressed five main features in combination to outline what the term Sharing Economy broadly means. Moreover, it became obvious that the definition of the Sharing Economy needs an operationalisation of its constituting features to investigate Sharing Economy organisations in detail. Additionally, the assignment of particular features' operationalisations to a traditional business perspective, to a normative connotation as well as to the aspect of hybridity allows the Sharing Economy's particularity to be discussed.

Table 8. Summary – Main Features and Operationalisation Including their Assignment to an Idealistic or a Commercial Connotation and to Hybridity

Main Features of the Definition by Gerwe and Silva (2018)	Operationalisation			
	General	Idealistic Connotation	Commercial Connotation	Hybrid Options
A Socio-economic System	Multi-Sided Markets: Triadic System between Operator and Users	Individuals as Operators and Users	Organisations as Operators and Users	Individuals as Producers and Consumers as Users
That Allows Peers	User Focus	Individuals	Organisations	Individuals as Producers and Consumers
To Grant Temporary Access	Kinds of Consumption and Transfer of Ownership	No Transfer of Ownership enabled through - Renting - Lending - Swapping - Donating	Transfer of Ownership enabled through - Sale - Resale	More Options on one Online Platform
	Monetary Transaction	No	Yes	Both on one Online Platform
To their Underutilized Physical and Human Assets	Services or Products	Underutilized Assets	All Kinds of Assets	Mix of Physical, Human, and Digital assets
Through Online Platforms	Online Platforms	Online Platforms as Multi-Sided Markets	Interactive Websites and Multi-Sided Markets	Mix of Online Initiation and Offline Execution

3. CONTEMPLATION OF CASES

3.1 Description of the Sharing Economy Organisations' Features

For this chapter, I am working with a sample of about 1,050 international Sharing Economy organisations. This represents a broad perspective as it includes all organisations of the sample (comprehensive survey) that claim to be part of the Sharing Economy based on their self-conception (Acquier et al., 2017).

In Crunchbase, a worldwide business database, organisations can list, edit, and describe themselves based on categories such as sectors. 'Sharing Economy' is listed as an option of the category sectors, that an organisation can choose in Crunchbase to classify their sector of business. Crunchbase listed about 1,050 organisations when filtered with the category Sharing Economy for industry. This collection of cases serves as a sample to assess empirical data about the Sharing Economy. To do so, the main features deduced in the former section served as orientation for the data gathering (Table 9).

It was possible to ascertain each main feature based on the variables. This was possible predominantly in the expected different characteristics of each variable. The socio-economic system and the online platforms were investigated similarly. The focus of the socio-economic system was the multi-sided market and the focus of the online platform consideration was the fact of being online. As all cases are online accessible but not a platform, the deliberation about being a platform and thus a multi-sided marked was of more importance. Thus, the outlined quantity of these two main features is similar. Furthermore, the variable users are required to include governmental actors as well besides the expected individuals and organisations. Additionally, kinds of consumption raised awareness for having more than one type of consumption one Sharing Economy organisation. This is linked to the reflection of products or services in the Sharing Economy as well as the issue of transfer of ownership.

When looking at the quantities of the variables and their specific characteristics, some mismatches are obvious. Not all cases are multi-sided markets and thus about a third does not represent a socio-economic system. Although all cases are online, about 30% are no platforms but (online) organisations with websites. Furthermore, a minority were detected as being for individuals or peers (less than 10%). Finally, transfer of ownership exemplifies a minority but not an exclusivity in the sample. First, there is a dominance of services, where transfer of ownership is not of importance. Second, for products the kinds of consumption are for transfer of ownership in about 11%.

However, literature about the Sharing Economy indicates that the essence and particularity of the Sharing Economy results from the combination of features. Therefore, the following parts include a discussion on data gathered from, for instance, cross-tabulations. The aims are to describe the cases close to the argumentation from the previous part and to recognize specifics beyond theoretical deliberation.

Table 9. Sample Description Based on the Definition by Gerwe and Silva, 2018

Main Features of the Definition by Gerwe and Silva (2018)	Operationalisation		Sample Data	
	Variable	**Characteristics**	**Quantity**	**Percentage**
A Socio-economic System	Multi-Sided-Markets	Yes No	715 339	68% 32%
That Allows Peers	User Focus	Individuals	94	9%
		Organisations	133	13%
		Individuals & Organisations	804	77%
		Government	8	1%
To Grant Temporary Access	Kinds of Consumption *(multiple choices were necessary)*	Sale & Resale Swapping Donating Renting Lending *Paying for Services**	99 6 3 333 26 *848*	9% 0.5% 0.3% 32% 3% *67%*
	Transfer of Ownership	Transfer	119	11%
		No Transfer	324	31%
		Both	15	1%
		*Services (No Transfer)***	*598*	*57%*
To their Underutilized Physical and Human Assets	Products or Services	Services Products Both	542 207 306	51% 20% 29%
Through Online Platforms	Online Platforms	Yes No	715 339	68% 32%

* In the case of services as shared asset, kinds of consumption does hardly apply. As services are intangible, paying for a service, which creates the access to the service, is the sole option. There is no differentiation such as lending or sale. As there are 542 cases that have services as shared assets and 306 that have services and products as shared assets in 848 cases payment for a service is the kind of consumption.

** 306 cases offer additional services to their basic products or services offered. 56 are additional services to the services offered, thus, 598 cases solely offer services at all, where transfer of ownership does not apply.

3.2 Peers and Other User Groups on Online (Platform) Organisations

While the discussion on peers and consumers, who can be producers and consumers at once was carried out, the issue of having organisations as users was also noted. But when gathering the data about the Sharing Economy organisations, the categories for users needed extension. All in all, there are three different kinds of users, which emerge in four combinations (Table 10).

Interestingly, there are organisations associating themselves with the Sharing Economy that exclude individuals by only allowing organisations. These cases represent a minority of about 13% being exclusively a business-to-business Sharing Economy organisation.

Moreover, there are governmental organisations that are open to all kinds of users that feel a proximity to the Sharing Economy. The governmental actors require a consideration of the triadic system (Benoit et al., 2017) or the aspect of the Sharing Economy being multi-sided markets or platforms (Rochet & Tirole, 2003). Governmental actors build organisations as platforms or traditional government-to-consumer or government-to-business organisations where they are the operators. Furthermore, governmental organisations participate as users in Sharing Economy online platforms or traditional businesses. They are in a minority of less than 1%.

The majority of about 80% allows individuals and organisations as users. This is in line with the literature about the broad understanding of the Sharing Economy. However, it is beyond the true or ideal of the Sharing Economy as it is based on individuals interacting without each other.

Table 10. Users of the Sharing Economy Organisations According to their Status of Being a Platform or Not

Users	Platform	No Platform	In Total
Individuals Only	78	16	94
Organisations Only	47	86	133
Individuals and Organisations	577	227	804
Individuals, Organisations, and Governmental Actors	5	3	8
In Total	707	332	1,039

3.3 Underutilised Physical and Human Assets and Transfer of Ownership

Assets or resources shared can be physical or human, digital, money and non-physical within the Sharing Economy (Gerwe & Silva, 2018). Although some researchers suggested restrictions to physical assets and thus products instead of any kind of services (Frenken & Schor, 2017), predominantly the Sharing Economy in a broad perspective is not limited in this matter. All in all, when investigating the organisations offering services or products, about 44% of the organisations can be aligned to offering physical products and thus 56% to offering services. Complementarily, 29% of all organisations offer services in addition to the basic product or service (Figure 8).

When considering the aspect of transfer of ownership and thus the issue of access to resources, the differentiation is becoming more complex than focussing on products or services. Services and their characteristic of being immaterial do not allow to consider a transfer of ownership but a consumption by usage. Hence, more than 50% of all cases do not enable the access to resources in the first instance. In a second instance, this may indicate an increase of services around physical products as an alternative or supplement to product sale such as product renting (servitization (Vandermerwe & Rada, 1988)). This could also be interpreted as an implication of making resources available without the necessity of ownership.

In contrast, products, which are physical by nature, enable a differentiation of the transfer of ownership, such as through the forms of consumption. Product-related organisations enable a transfer of ownership in about 37% of the cases, which is deduced from the type of consumption being (re)sale, donation, or swapping. Organisations that are product-related and focus on lending or renting are understood as not enabling transfer of ownership (63%).

Additionally, because of the digital nature of Sharing Economy businesses, the focus on products and services receives a further dimension. The question arises as to whether the Sharing Economy is related to a physical product and/or service in the physical world or refers to digital products or digital services or a combination.

The awareness was created by the characteristic of online platforms and the hybridity of online initiation and offline execution of Sharing Economy businesses. Form this point of view, the Sharing Economy organisations include six different options in different quantities as outlined in Figure 9. While the terms 'physical' and 'non-physical' relate to the offline instead of the digital world, digital products and services occur online solely. No differentiation is made explicitly about an asset within the Sharing Economy of either being a digital service or a digital product (Hui & Chau, 2002). However, a minority does not seem to include digital services or products within the Sharing Economy as the business is based on a service, a product, or a combination of both in the offline world solely (three dark sets in the circle of Figure 9). The majority supplements their products and/or services with online services or products (three light sets in the circle of Figure 9). The requirement to be considered a digital service or product was if the organisation acts beyond the aspect of informing users as this would apply for each Sharing Economy organisation. The largest group with approximately half of the Sharing Economy organisations is services in the offline world combined with online products or services (white set with black dots in Figure 9). It should to be noted that the borders between online and offline products and services are blurred.

A final remark is given to the aspect of transfer of ownership. When focussing on the online platforms for individuals only, which are 93 of all included Sharing Economy organisations, 44 of these 93 are aligned to services and 42 to products where no transfer of ownership takes place. This applies for more than 90% of Sharing Economy organisations restricted to individuals as users from the viewpoint of individuals who try to make resources available without ownership transfer. This is linkable to the Sharing Economy ideal by Acquier et al. (2017), which is defined as an economy based on a crowed acting on a platform to enable access to resources. This is applicable for about 8% of the entire investigated sample[2].

3.4 The Ideal Sharing Economy Represented by Cases

Referring to the 'true Sharing Economy', when analysing these about 1,050 organisations as a basic population, about 68% are online platforms and 8% are online platforms that are exclusively for individuals as users. Thus, more than 90% of these organisations in Crunchbase do not represent the theoretical concept of the 'true Sharing Economy', which is based on online platforms for individuals. In other words, the Sharing Economy in practice is rather different to what is attempted to be conceptualised as the Sharing Economy theoretically.

Figure 10. Layers of Sharing Economy Organisations

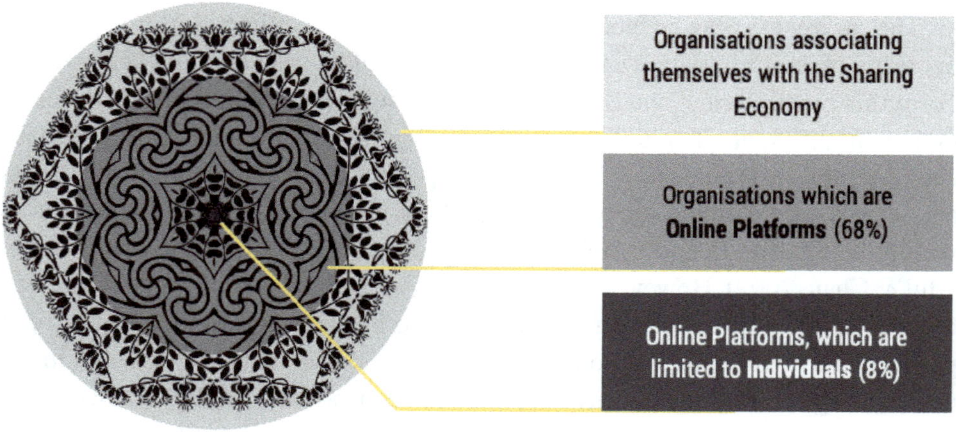

Figure 10 illustrates the Sharing Economy in practice and its obscure and growing nature. In the centre, there are cases that fulfil the requirement of online platforms and the restriction of users to individuals. It has been argued, that this is the true, ideal, or the core of the Sharing Economy. This core was once the basic idea after the financial crisis in 2008: individuals unite digitally to explore labour options, resource resale or swap or lend without intermediates such as capitalistic businesses: What's mine is yours! (Botsman & Rogers, 2010). The second layer of cases in Figure 10 includes all online platforms. Besides the online platforms for individuals, many cases allow business as well as individual users. About 60% of the basic population fulfil this criterion. These may possibly have evolved out of the core idea. The reason could be, that this is necessary as otherwise the online platforms would run out of users, as the users become businesses by permanently offering cars, homes, goods, or services on a platform (Herrmann-Fankhaenel & Huesig, 2020). Another assumption is, that this is not that important internationally as the law and regulations are less strict in comparison to Germany. In the USA, for instance, there is a tax form to record such private interactions that are accompanied by an income without making them business-people.

The third layer of cases in Figure 10 includes all organisations associating themselves with the Sharing Economy that are not online platforms (about 30%). These organisations have websites but do not act as the operator of a platform as they offer their own products and/or services and not the users. All in all, there is no criterion of the Sharing Economy that applies here. However, they think they belong to the Sharing Economy (Acquier et al., 2017). On closer inspection, these organisations often offer services or products that are required in the Sharing Economy, such as digital management and marketing tools for hosts at airbnb, digital rating solutions or background checks of users, or software to enter cars, homes, or other physical resources. Their associations derives from their felt proximity to the Sharing Economy as they help the Sharing Economy to work as expected by users meanwhile. This aspect led the organisations choose 'Sharing Economy' as their 'sector' in Crunchbase.

From a theoretical point of view, these layers result from the professionalisation and evolution of the Sharing Economy as a niche phenomenon from alternative to mainstream business for the rest of the world (Grieco, 2021). This perspective of the Sharing Economy having developed from the core idea to organisations in the periphery, which differs a lot from the core, may be supported by the average ages of the organisations. Online platforms for individuals were on average (mean) seven years old. Online platforms for any users are on average five years old. All organisation of the outer layer are on average between eight and nine years old. This descriptive fact supports the assumption of the development of online platforms for individuals to any users. However, organisations lacking the criteria of the Sharing Economy are on average the oldest and include 10% of the organisations older than 15 years. This may indicate the transition of existing organisations (incumbents) towards the Sharing Economy through, for instance, business model innovation (Ciulli & Kolk, 2019), or product or service innovations. Notwithstanding these aspects, it may also simply demonstrate that positioning oneself as part of the 'good' Sharing Economy is fanciful and profitable today (share washing (Habibi, 2019)).

In conclusion on the cases of the Sharing Economy, Figure 10 is understood as symbolizing an on-going process of development. There are some established characteristics that form what academia thinks the Sharing Economy is, such as the 'lines' in the layer of online platforms. These clear structures are not totally left out towards the outside but receive 'leaves' that make the picture fuzzier. These 'leaves' are standing for the ever-growing ideas of what is associated with the Sharing Economy practically and that it is still evolving towards unknown areas of business. In other words, the Sharing Economy is fanciful, has melded with the mainstream economy but keeps a small core of alternative business options for individuals digitally.

This part raised awareness of international organisations associating themselves with the Sharing Economy from an empirical point of view. While the first part enabled a frame to be set to investigate the cases by focussing on several features, the contemplation of cases increased the variety of these features' realisation. This has two implications. First, when investigating the Sharing Economy, single cases do not represent the Sharing Economy in its variety of options. Moreover, different cases are able to fulfil the narrow definition of being online platforms for individuals, which vary widely in their other features. Second, the Sharing Economy as a phenomenon reaches different parts of the economy that are debatable as being sharing such as business-to business online platforms from a perspective of time. Thus, delineations are still of importance to distinguish Sharing Economy organisations from (traditional) digital business organisations to outline innovation for society and economy enabled by social creativity.

4. DISCUSSION

4.1 Developmental Aspects of the Main Features of Sharing Economy Organizations

4.1.1 Socio-economic System as Multi-Sided Markets

A socio-economic system was understood and outlined as multi-sided markets or marketplaces (Rochet & Tirole, 2003) in this chapter. The ratio of multi-sided markets and non-multi-sided markets from the contemplation of cases revealed about 30% of the cases that are not a multi-sided market but associate themselves with the Sharing Economy (Crunchbase). Having a platform or a multi-sided market, where supply and demand can meet, is one main feature that distinguishes Sharing Economy organisations from non-sharing ones. This is in line with the literature, which positioned the Sharing Economy as a core between platform and crowd or community economy and the definitions having the platform aspect included. The simple differentiation between platform operators who are or are not offering their own products or services would enable an easy way to distinguish sharing and non-sharing in a first step. The second step to investigate whether or not the users are limited to individuals.

4.1.2 Individuals as Users

From the descriptive results, the peer aspect cannot be outlined as being a feature with the majority of the sample. Thus, the concept of multi-sided markets for individuals was assigned to a minority. Although, the feature of users, in particular a limitation to individuals, is less easy to judge it is of importance when addressing the intension of sharing and the early initiatives and organisations and for instance discussing the 'true Sharing Economy'. Aspects that contribute to the concept of individuals as sole users is twofold: the Sharing Economy being the core of a community or crowd economy; and individuals that are producers and consumers at once, which contributes to the concept of hybridity of the Sharing Economy.

Contrarily, there are three aspects against the limitation of individuals as users: first having Sharing Economy organisations that run out of users if they do not allow business users; second, strict boundary between business and individuals, including customer protection, etc.; third, having individuals interacting is in line with the basic and idealistic concept of the Sharing Economy close to the beginning more than ten years ago (Belk, 2014b; Botsman & Rogers, 2010). Meanwhile, the Sharing Economy went through a development where individuals may have changed their status towards business, which is also in line with the literature on new life styles through the Sharing Economy (Botsman & Rogers, 2010).

Based on this argumentation, individuals as a constituting feature, to distinguish the Sharing Economy from traditional businesses, is hard to decide. One suggestion here is to differentiate between generations of Sharing Economy organisations and consider the development of the Sharing Economy phenomenon. Another suggestion is to consider the status of the resources participants bring into a Sharing Economy organisation. Are the shared resources privately owned before participating or have the resources been purchased to be shared in a socio-economic system of a Sharing Economy organisation?

4.1.3 Resources of Individuals or Organisations

Differentiating between the status of a resource of either being there before or being newly purchased brings awareness of different intentions to participate in the Sharing Economy. A user is either reflecting on what to create access to that is already in one's ownership or what can be purchased additionally to the current resources with the aim of creating access to. Both can in consequence enhance the resources of a particular community but the second one would require a traditional economic activity before contributing to the Sharing Economy. Both can take place because of idealistic purposes – the first one to let others benefit from their own resources while the second one, the extra purchase, enlarges the resources of a community if it may not have the financial means to create access to required resources. But the second one could be financially motivated as well to gain money for the access to a resource. This in fact would be beyond the idealistic concept of the Sharing Economy, firstly because of the required purchase before the real participation on an online platform and secondly, because of the financial motivation. This could lead to individuals that create new lifestyles through the options of the Sharing Economy (opportunistic) and individuals becoming businesses in the small-scale value chains of a highly specified economy. However, in both cases the focus is on private individuals' resources that can be distinguished from business resources.

Moreover, sector-related investigations are viewed as interesting from theoretical perspectives such as platforms, sector life cycles (Cusumano et al., 2006; Peltoniemi, 2011), and dominant design (Suarez & Utterback, 1993). The dates of foundation of cases in a sector, such as mobility or accommodation over time shows a particular development. There is a development from a physical resource such as a car (to rent) to services such as a car ride to digital accompanying services. This was derived from the features product and/or services of the Sharing Economy cases and if there is a link to a physical product or service. This, for instance, allows the cases to be differentiated by product organisations, service organisations, or digital services organisations. Thus, an investigation about this development in sectors is viewed as being fruitful for further research.

4.1.4 Temporary and Permanent Access to Resources

The feature access over ownership, requires multiple considerations as argued, such as products and services, digital and offline spheres and accompanying services. Within the Sharing Economy services seem to play a vital role, although early investigations saw a limitation of the Sharing Economy as it refers to physical resources only. Moreover, additional services that accompany the basic product or service of a Sharing Economy are provided by a majority of Sharing Economy organisations (about 80%).

In terms of time, it is becoming obvious that online platforms founded before 2010 proportionally decided more often to found online platforms that enable renting (44.12%). More recently founded online platforms more often enable (re)sale (65.39%) proportionally. Linking the service or product issue to the foundations of Sharing Economy organisations shows a decrease in the number of online platforms enabling product access in 2013, which ended in 2015 with zero. Organisations focussing on services had their peak of foundations in 2013. This can also be seen in the ages of organisations. The age peak is six for service-based organisations and seven years for product-based organisations.

This may imply the declining importance of the concept of sharing in the sense of renting and lending. While after the financial crisis of 2008 people searched for options to jointly use their physical resources and organised them digitally, these options of the Sharing Economy are of less importance and the accomplishment of sharing underwent a development. Over time, the feature temporary access, deduced from types of consumption, shows a growing importance of product (re)sale and payment for services. Services seem to increase, which contributes to the concept of access to resources instead of ownership such as paying a driver instead of renting a car to drive oneself. Contrarily, the growing number of options for resource sale does not fit with the concept of access over ownership but the current concept of the circular economy and keeping resources in streams by for instance prolonging their usage (MacArthur, 2013).

All in all, the descriptive data indicates the importance of the Sharing Economy as being linked to the concept of the access economy. Access, therefore, can refer to a temporary usage of physical products, or a permanent transfer of ownership of physical products if not needed anymore, or access to services. However, as regards the question of access over ownership being a disqualifying criterion for Sharing Economy organisations, the suggestion is to understand it more openly from the viewpoint of access – firstly because of the described development of this feature.

4.1.5 Five Sharing Economy Generations

In this chapter, especially features of Sharing Economy organisations were outlined in relation to time. Taking these findings leads to considering generations of the Sharing Economy (Figure 11). The basic features to describe the Sharing Economy generations are taken from the definition of the Sharing Economy and extended by the intention, and the differentiation between physical and digital products and services.

Individuals searched for alternatives to exchange physical resources in a first instance to save money by renting them from others or by offering, for instance, personal services to make some extra money (First Generation: the Idealists such as 'couchsurfing'). Individuals participated in Sharing Economy organisations with private resources or gained further resources (such as extra apartments to rent at 'airbnb') permanently and thereby became business actors (Second Generation: the Opportunists such as 'uber'). These two generations form the 'true Sharing Economy' with an importance of individuals as users who follow an idealistic or private purpose and share privately owned products or services. The following three Sharing Economy generations do not belong to the 'true Sharing Economy'. However, these generations represent options for business development and innovation and proclaim their affiliation with the Sharing Economy.

Businesses took the concept of sharing and access to resources and offer their own resources, such as short-term rentals. These businesses are not conceptualised as online platforms or multi-sided markets. Their felt proximity to the Sharing Economy derives from the concepts of rentals and thus access over ownership (Third Generation: the Businesses such as 'nextbike'). Afterwards, meta businesses emerged that include all solutions to a problem such as all mobility options in one particular space at a particular time (Fourth Generation: the Meta Business such as 'gotoglobal'). This development finally led to the emerging of accompanying services for the management of Sharing Economy organisations. Examples are software to enter cars by mobile phone such as 'zipcar', management software for 'airbnb' listings such as 'guesty', and apps for payment by phone such as 'redshare'. Moreover, software enables the easy setting up of platforms to create a multi-sided market such as 'ecocar' (Fifth Generation: the Periphery Business). These three generations are based on economic purposes, do not limit their customers, and offer their own business resources. Some are conceptualised as multi-sided markets such as the meta businesses, others are interactive websites but not a multi-sided market. Within these three generations, there is an importance of additional and digital services as well as a focus on access. In particular, generation five plays a special role as these can be interpreted as new services in a reverse innovation cycle (Barras, 1986).

From a developmental perspective, generations four and five did not emerge one after another. This can take place in parallel (partially). Moreover, the argumentation of the Sharing Economy generations is done from a meta-perspective, the Sharing Economy phenomenon. When investigating the development of the Sharing Economy in sectors it is assumed that Sharing Economy organisations from different Sharing Economy generations emerged one after another.

Based on what is described about the development so far, future development scenarios are suggested. When focussing on sectors two pathways are arguable. First, in sectors where Sharing Economy organisations entered a while ago and have some or all of the Sharing Economy generations, a market clearing will take place. Only a few Sharing Economy organisations will survive as seen in the mobility sector. Once, there was 'Drive Now' (BMW) and 'Car2Go' (Daimler). They united to 'ShareNow' in 2019. In 2020 they left the North-American market but still act in Europe. Today, 'ShareNow' is a meta-platform for urban mobility delivering car rentals of different values including luxury-class rentals. Second, it is possible that further parts of society and economy try to benefit from the establishment of digital platforms to bring together supply and demand (new sectors).

Figure 11. Generations of the Sharing Economy

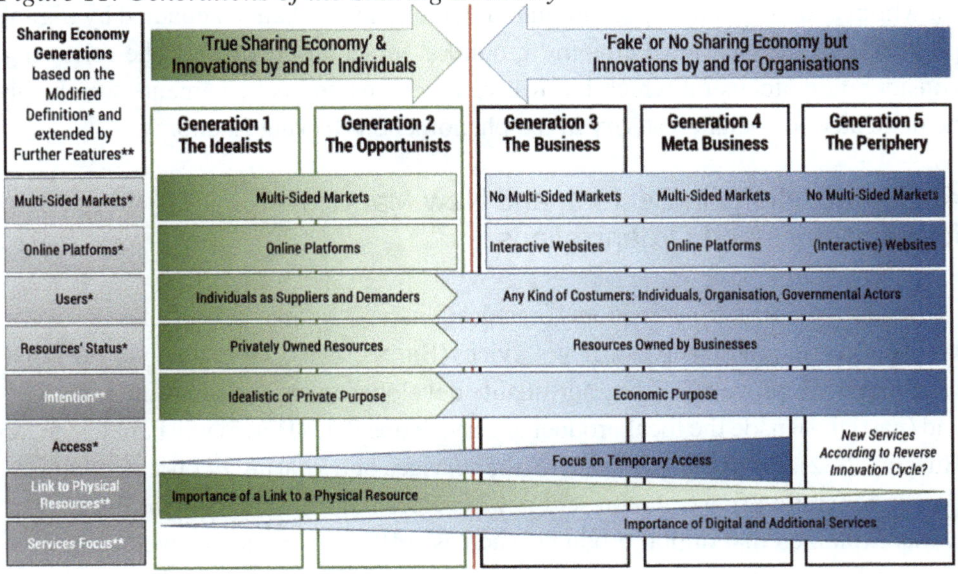

4.2 Innovations initiated by Social Creativity within the Sharing Economy Phenomenon

4.2.1 Kinds of Innovations

Sharing Economy is often outlined as new or innovative (Belezas & Daniel, 2023). Schumpeter's list, the first collection of kinds of innovations, is still of importance as it is discussed as basic understanding (Reichert, 2021): there are five cases of novelty in the sense of new combinations: new products or services, new means of production, new markets, new sources of resources, or new organisations (1931). Meanwhile, concepts distinguish between technological, organisation, and business innovation, too (Zahn & Weidler, 1995), kinds of innovation the Sharing Economy is associated with (Muñoz & Cohen, 2018). Moreover, Sharing Economy organisations are discussed as social innovation (Herrmann-Fankhaenel & Huesig, 2016) which understands new products and services social in its ends and means (Mulgan et al., 2007; Thom, 1980) and transformative innovation as society changing (Margolis, 2024).

For investigating novelty or innovation in the Sharing Economy two aspects are to be considered: what is new in comparison to a previous state and for whom (Hüsig, 2006). When arguing the aspect of for whom it is new, this can be linked to the perspective of individuals or to related entities, such as a organisations, sector, a nation, or humanity (Hauschildt & Salomo, 2011). That will help in discussing for whom and in which way (economic) interaction was changed enabled by digital platforms of the Sharing Economy grounded in social creativity. The following considerations focus on which innovative outcomes and achievements which can be dedicated to social creativity in the phenomenon Sharing Economy.

4.2.2 Innovations in Sectors, and New Markets for Individuals and Organizations

Sectors where Sharing Economy organisations have entered, seem to pass a reverse innovation cycle ending up with new services (Barras, 1986). Over time, services that were used to improve efficiency and quality developed towards a stand-alone service and (partially) made the focal product or service obsolete (Herrmann-Fankhaenel & Huesig, 2022). From this perspective, the services of a Sharing Economy organisation of generation five can represent new services in a particular sector. Moreover, it was explained that digital products, such as software were also developed in the Sharing Economy, such as software to manage 'airbnb' listings. Both examples of new services support the assumption of the Sharing Economy as a pool for service innovations and contributing to servitization (Vandermerwe & Rada, 1988).

New markets, in the sense of finding new customers, as an option for innovation may not, in the first instance, apply for the Sharing Economy from the viewpoint of incumbents. However, in a second instance, new markets offer interesting perspectives about innovation in the Sharing Economy for individuals. Digital platforms are easy to establish nowadays. Hence, creating an online platform where supply and demand can meet is brought up fast. The technology of online platforms and in particular Sharing Economy online platforms, enables new digital markets. Before the interactive options to trade resources online, the scope of such marketplaces was limited by space and time. With the Sharing Economy these online platforms were discovered and used by individuals to create their own markets. Thus, for individuals, new markets have been established and can be understood as an innovation in the sense of having options to offer and obtain privately owned resources. In comparison to former times, individuals now have easier ways to trade resources.

However, over time, these marketplaces, driven by individuals, led to new markets for business organisations as well. First, most online platform operators are business organisations today. At the beginning, operators were also identified as individuals but that is not the case anymore. Second, there are new markets, that are integrated into an existing business, where platform-like services are offered for customers to meet. Third, there are meta platforms that create access to each option to solve a problem such as in mobility (taxi, bus, Uber, train, bike) in one app (Generation 4). And fourth, there is the option for accompanying services that are important to the management of a Sharing Economy participation on both sides of the markets such as software (Generation 5). These may represent innovations for incumbents in the sense of having new customers or markets.

4.2.3 New Sources of Resource

The Sharing Economy revealed a new source of resources: privately owned resources and their (re)integration into resource streams. From this perspective, the Sharing Economy shed light on the digital options to access resources that were unused beforehand. Sharing Economy platforms in general may thus also be viewed as infrastructure innovation for resource streams. Having digital platforms facilitates trading any kind of resources. And the Sharing Economy has contributed to our understanding of the circumstances under which people are willing to trade privately owned resources, when actually acting from a privileged situation, when they do not have to but want to do it. This may solve different challenges in times of resource scarcity and constraints when the Sharing Economy platforms are used to force people to share their resources with others.

The requirement of context considerations or the embeddedness of the Sharing Economy was discussed. The Sharing Economy, as outlined in the introductory section, is dominated by research done in developed or industrialised countries. The Sharing Economy requires a differentiation as it is done because of basic needs, as a part of daily living to survive or as a luxury option besides other options of resource access. In comparison, either access is created to individuals' beforehand unused resources (industrialised countries) or access to relevant, not unused resources is created within a community (developing countries). Both ways are leading to the resource itself, but only the first one has the idea of an add-on, while the second one is daily life. Anyhow, both perspectives contribute to the circulation of resources and the enhanced access to, and improvement in usage of, resources.

If access to unused resources is created by the Sharing Economy as it is done in the industrialised context, it represents a new way of bringing (back) privately owned resources into resource streams. Of course, this is based on voluntary participation at the moment and often linked to a particular community or for private benefit. However, from a community point of view, what could be transferred to improve resource access and usage if, for instance, there are resource constraints or restrictions in private ownership? Will people in industrialised contexts under resource constraints start to use technology, such as digital platforms as it occurs in daily life in developing contexts? Furthermore, the Sharing Economy revealed the options of how to bring privately owned resources into a community. Will that be used to force people to do that in future by government, for instance?

4.2.4 New Organisations and Business Model Innovations

Besides the plenty of (new) business activity outlined before, Sharing Economy organisations can get described as new organisations as well. Sharing Economy organisations are assigned to digital platforms, which are well known (Berger et al., 2018). From this point of view, Sharing Economy organisations are not interpreted as new organisational forms. However, with the aspects of online platforms for individuals, the Sharing Economy of the first and second generation can be understood as a new form of organisation for individuals to exchange privately owned resources.

Considering the form of organisation in the sense of business model innovation (Chesbrough, 2007) that accompanies a technological artefact is also of interest. The development of the Sharing Economy and its spread around sectors can be understood as a business model transfer from one sector to another (Vahs & Brem, 2015). Multi-sided markets for individuals first appeared in the second-hand field such as 'ebay' (goods), followed by 'airbnb' (accommodation) and 'uber' (mobility), which enabled the letting of private flats and the sharing of car rides. Later on, general private resources including individual skills in the sense of services, such as teaching (education) were considered to be shared with the help of the technology online platform. The step-by-step appearance of Sharing Economy online platforms for individuals to interact can be discussed as business model innovation around sectors.

4.2.5 Technological Innovations

As Sharing Economy organisations are online or digital platforms, it is necessary to consider digital technology innovations. Online or digital platforms are understood as one archetype of digital technologies besides others where technology acts as an infrastructure for bidirectional human interaction to transmit information digitally (Berger et al., 2018). As a digital technology, an online platform of the Sharing Economy refers to its modular architecture and can provide services, content, and a network as well as a device (Yoo et al., 2010).

Innovation is understood as a new combination of ends and means that is new in a particular context, was developed in a process, and reached a market (Hüsig, 2006). Because of the digital nature of online platforms of the Sharing Economy, the definition of digital innovation – "... the creation or adoption, and exploitation of an inherently unbounded, value-adding novelty (e.g., product, service, process, or business model) through the incorporation of digital technology" – is considered as well (Hund et al., 2021, p. 6).

Sharing Economy organisation are understood as online platforms, which makes them a digital technology. The understanding of technology here is based on the definition of Burgelman et al. (2008) which is "the theoretical and practical knowledge, skills, and artifacts that can be used to develop products and services as well as their production and delivery system". In particular, within the Sharing Economy the addressed products or services are (online) platforms as multi-sided markets (Rochet & Tirole, 2003). Thus, theoretical concepts such as multi-sided markets as well as the transfer or accomplishment of the technology (Sharing Economy organisations as means to solve a particular problem) are of interest (Specht et al., 2002).

Sharing Economy organisations are hence viewed as human-made artefacts created by social groups which today show a variety of design options for resource allocation in the favour of individuals or organisations or both. The Sharing Economy investigations show how to strategically conceptualise a digital multi-sided markets routed in processes of interacting people to design those different kinds of digital artifacts to distinguish from other kinds of consumption.

4.2.6 Social and Transformative Innovations

Access to resources is one of the major aspects within the Sustainable Development Goals as many people world-wide lack access to important resources such as water, education, and food (United Nations, 2015). The Sharing Economy is relevant for the global demand to act in a resource-aware manner by uniting the concepts of the access economy, crowd concepts and the platform economy. Conceptually and empirically it was shown that access to resources is access to physical or digital resources and access to services, such as resources usage within the Sharing Economy. Thus, the Sharing Economy can be described as an advanced concept for resource-aware (economic) activities. When sticking to the narrow definition, which means having an (online) platform for individuals to share resources with the aim of creating different means of access to offer and to obtain resources, this refers to resource access improvement for individuals (Generation 1 and 2). When addressing organisations this is also arguable for any kind of organisation (Generations 3-5).

Investigations outlined particular examples as socially innovative when they addressed a social problem successfully with the means of the Sharing Economy (Herrmann-Fankhaenel & Huesig, 2016; Qureshi et al., 2021). Particular cases hence shows how particular social challenges are addressed. From an phenomenological perspective the Sharing Economy can be viewed as a source of transformative innovations to contribute to sustainable futures. Hence, all the outlined kinds of innovation together enable this macro perspective long-term change.

4.2.7 Innovations for People

From the viewpoint of individuals, the Sharing Economy showed individuals how to trade their private resources. Thus, the Sharing Economy is an enabler of individuals' economic empowerment when there is no need but a free decision to do so. By learning from the contexts of sharing because of constraints, this freedom of choice may also help to broaden the ideas of where to accomplish sharing additionally. This, in a larger perspective, would help to enrich the field of application of the concept of the Sharing Economy for resource-aware behaviour. And as individuals use their privately owned resources they may get into better or more powerful positions if they have scarce resources (Pfeffer & Salancik, 2003).

In contrast, maybe individuals will get forced to share their scarce resources as Sharing Economy online platforms are considered as reliable institutional technology (Porter & Scully, 1995) by, for instance, government. First indicators of such a development are governmental users in the Crunchbase-sample. Moreover, such a duty of sharing resources can also hit businesses. For instance, maybe businesses are forced to take back sold products, such as cars to ensure the recycling of the inherent resources. Notwithstanding this perspective, the categorisation of Sharing Economy online platforms as institutional technology is understood as one more reason why the Sharing Economy underwent the development from an individual's way to exchange resources to a number of innovations in economy.

For deeper and theoretically driven investigations on these resources-related considerations in the Sharing Economy the concepts of resource ownership, usage, access, and enforcement and regulation from the resource dependence approach could be fruitful (Pfeffer & Salancik, 2003). Therewith, the following questions could get addressed: To whom does a resource belong to and what kind of power over a resource leads to power on Sharing Economy online platforms? Online platforms act as multi-sided markets to simulate a larger resource volume by moderating supply and demand of its users, despite not being the owner of these resources. With the help of the four levels of power over recourses from the resource dependent approach this may offer deeper insights into business model innovation based on considerations about power over resources deriving from individual as well as organisational sources.

Why is 'Sharing Economy' the wrong term to point to anything new? Sharing implies that there are people that jointly use something. This can be the case if they have a joint ownership of something. This can be the case if someone allows another to possess items for a particular time. This can be the case if an organisation rents items within their business model. None of these cases are new. They are only new in our focus because of the scope that technology enables today for these scenarios and because of the hybridity of features. Moreover, in the international context it leads to misunderstandings. Nonetheless, the findings in this section can be understood as manifestations of social creativity, as defined by Fischer et al. (2005): they illustrate how individuals, through interaction and shared digital infrastructures, co-create alternative economic arrangements that depart from ownership-based, market-driven paradigms.

4.3 Contribution

This chapter defined the Sharing Economy and it investigated its constituting features theoretically and empirically. This was done for the international context as well as from the perspective of time. In particular, the main features were investigated based on the definition by Gerwe and Silva (2018). Besides these essential and theoretical considerations, the chapter has a strong focus on investigating the Sharing Economy based on a multitude of associated cases besides 'uber' and 'airbnb'.

Sharing Economy generations are suggested in this chapter. The first and the second generation enable cases to be distinguished from traditional businesses and therewith attention to be paid to the 'true Sharing Economy', which also fulfils a normative or idealistic requirement. Non-sharing businesses could be detected and communicated not as a part of the idealistic Sharing Economy but a later generation.

The theoretical and empirical considerations in combination aided in understanding it in a broad sense and to detect particularities. Awareness was created for practical challenges where theoretical explanations and guidance are needed (Kornmeier, 2007). The Sharing Economy required and helped with the development of the granularity of people's interaction between the spheres of idealistic and commercial intentions as well as between offline and online (hybridity). Besides the endings of both continuums of offline versus online and communal versus commercial interaction, hybrid models were revealed under the umbrella term of the Sharing Economy. With detailed considerations of the meanings of commercial and idealistic as well as hybrid interaction more delineable facets of the Sharing Economy appeared. In consequence, the discussable idealistic core of the Sharing Economy became more substantial.

Although a minority of cases of the sample fit with the (narrow) definitions of the Sharing Economy, the broad sample led to advantages when focussing on the following question: How would the findings change when shrinking the sample according to the narrow understanding? First of all, it would no longer represent the practical accomplishment of the Sharing Economy of the real world. Second, cases would have been excluded upfront that are interesting new cases of doing business on online platforms. Third, because of the complexity and thus the variety of required variables quantitative methods could become impossible nor non-representative or would miss a variance in the sample to outline. Fourth, without the extensive sample, this chapter would not have been able to outline the evolution and how the accomplishment of features may have changed during the existence of the Sharing Economy.

Like every investigation, this one is also limited by the investigated cases, by the theoretical perspectives set and the time frame when accomplished. There was a concentration on business perspectives. Thus, sociological and anthropological perspectives are missing in this chapter. However, economic anthropology in particular is viewed as fruitful to investigate the possibilities and boundaries of the Sharing Economy.

5. FUTURE RESEARCH

The chapter brought awareness of the variety of concepts for supply and demand ranging between business-to-costumers, costumers-to-costumers, business-to-business, and costumers-to-business. While business-to-costumers, costumers-to-costumers, and business-to-business are described in literature, costumers-to-business is less outlined. The option of individuals to act as suppliers and possibly interact with businesses who are demanders is given. Regrettably, there are neither descriptive data within this chapter nor in other investigations regarding this aspect. Thus, it is an interesting research gap to investigate as well as an interesting consideration from a practical view point: does this take place at all? What challenges arise from consumer protection? Does this align with a private or business consumption? Who has which rights and obligations?

Hybridity is one particularity of the Sharing Economy. This was done by outlining the numbers of individuals as sole users. Basic market or non-market logics as well as online and offline initiations and executions were not included int the empirical section and thus are regarded as interesting further investigation. If hybridity is one of the Sharing Economy's particularities, how can hybridity beyond the consumer perspective be quantitatively described based on technology involvement and its basic market logics?

Especially quantitative investigations are viewed as a requirement to contribute to the research field of the Sharing Economy in future. Studies on the basis of the Crunchbase-sample with adequate exclusions of cases, such as non-platforms are viewed as fruitful investigations to estimate whether the Sharing Economy represents a particular kind of economy or if existing concepts make it possible to grasp what the Sharing Economy is, how it is developing and if it may disrupt sectors (Chang & Sokol, 2022).

The Sharing Economy is often linked to discussion about labour (Gerwe & Silva, 2018). This chapter did not include considerations about that and thus is limited in regard to findings about working conditions, changes of jobs or lifestyles in the Sharing Economy. The only perspective that is included is the second generation of the Sharing Economy, when people take advantage of Sharing Economy online platforms to establish their own business. Deeper investigations about their change in life and labour would be interesting to follow, especially from the viewpoint of how Sharing Economy users contribute to value chains as micro participants with privately owned resources.

Finally, from a more practical perspective, it would be interesting to investigate different countries and how the Sharing Economy can be described there. A comparison of countries could also contribute to understanding the development of the Sharing Economy and maybe with the Sharing Economy generations a forecast will be possible. If the Sharing Economy reached the country later on, what can be deduced from finding only Sharing Economy organisations from generation one and two, a forecast about meta-platforms and services would be possible.

6. CONCLUSION

The interactive Internet brought change in numerous ways for many tasks of the daily life. The Sharing Economy represents one perspective of what Internet applications and online platforms can enable for the particular realisation of resource exchange between individuals (and organisations) today initiated by social creativity.

This chapter about the Sharing Economy aimed at understanding alternative and new options of (economic) interaction. Therefore, it was required to use a broad perspective and to depict new and traditional kinds of economic activity from each other – first, because of their coexistence under one umbrella called the 'Sharing Economy' and second, to outline new ways of interacting individually as well as alternative means of organisational businesses to contribute to improved resource usage and access.

Would all the described novelties or innovations for society and economy be possible without the Sharing Economy? My answer is: No! The Sharing Economy in the narrow sense of online platforms for individuals, as it was always a minority, enabled light to be shed on what technology can make possible. But it was the beginning of the Sharing Economy that led to the process of acquisition (or appropriation) by businesses. If only business organisations had made use of online platforms, the idealistic concept of sharing resources voluntarily, for free, with strangers or as a new lifestyle would may not have been discovered. From there, we can now consider accessing unused resources under circumstances in which people are willing to participate. Furthermore, it pushed economy into establishing new digital products and services to organise resource access, usage, control, and regulation and enforcement what led to new business fields for incumbents and new organisations. Of course, the Sharing Economy today, is not primarily idealistic but contributes to sustainable development by making the world aware that acting in a resource-aware manner is possible and can reach new heights based on digital technology because of social creativity.

The Sharing Economy is a part of the current melding of distinct spheres, which is forcing people to overcome mental boundaries and existing conceptions. First, there is the differentiation of individuals as non-business actors versus organisations, although there are concepts such as self-employment and freelancers. The Sharing Economy enables new kinds of businesses for individuals without needing to think of them as traditional business actors. Resources, no matter whether they are physical, digital, or human, are submitted to value chains by their owners when required and beneficial for the owners regardless of their status of being an individual or an organisation. A second boundary lies in the distinction between non-profit and for-profit behaviour. Organisations act either for profit and serve capitalistic principles or act non-profit and serve social or environmental purposes. However, the concept of social entrepreneurship shows that the combination of for-profit means with the aim of tackling social challenges thus is bridging the gap between these both worlds. Under the umbrella term "Sharing Economy" social creativity enabled the melding of those spheres because people wanted to cross boundaries.

This is of interest for economic anthropology as it enhances the knowledge of technologically-based interaction globally or in the specific context of a country. This has two dimensions: the options that exist and the boundaries the realised options face in different regulation and enforcement environments. In consequence, both dimensions require discussion regarding: What kind of (economic) interaction can in fact be revealed within a particular environment and what features and changes does an environment need to foster particular (economic) interaction? Sharing Economy can be a frame for people to socially create, try, and establish answers to these questions.

REFERENCES

Acey, M. (2013, June 5). The end of consumerism? *CNN*. https://www.cnn.com/interactive/2013/06/world/sharing-economy/index.html

Acquier, A., Daudigeos, T., & Pinkse, J. (2017). Promises and paradoxes of the sharing economy: An organizing framework. *Technological Forecasting and Social Change*, *125*, 1–10. DOI: 10.1016/j.techfore.2017.07.006

Agarwal, N., & Steinmetz, R. (2019). Sharing Economy: A Systematic Literature Review. *International Journal on Management of Innovation & Technology*, *16*(06), 1–17. DOI: 10.1142/S0219877019300027

Akin, D., Jakobsen, K. C., Floch, J., & Hoff, E. (2021). Sharing with neighbours: Insights from local practices of the sharing economy. *Technology in Society*, *64*, 101481. DOI: 10.1016/j.techsoc.2020.101481

Albinsson, P. A., Perera, B. Y., Nafees, L., & Burman, B. (2019). Collaborative Consumption Usage in the US and India: An Exploratory Study. *Journal of Marketing Theory and Practice*, *27*(4), 390–412. DOI: 10.1080/10696679.2019.1644956

Amabile, T. (2012). Componential theory of creativity [Harvard Business School Working Paper No. 12-096]. *Encyclopedia of Management Theory*. Cambridge, MA: Sage.

Barbu, C. M., Bratu, R. Ş., & Sîrbu, E. M. (2018). Business Models of the Sharing Economy. *Review of International Comparative Management / Revista de Management Comparat International*, *19*(2), 154–166. DOI: 10.24818/RMCI.2018.2.154

Bardhi, F., & Eckhardt, G. M. (2012). Access-based consumption: The case of car sharing. *The Journal of Consumer Research*, *39*(4), 881–898. DOI: 10.1086/666376

Barras, R. (1986). Towards a theory of innovation in services. *Research Policy*, *15*(4), 161–173. DOI: 10.1016/0048-7333(86)90012-0

Belezas, F., & Daniel, A. D. (2023). Innovation in the sharing economy: A systematic literature review and research framework. *Technovation*, *122*, 102509. DOI: 10.1016/j.technovation.2022.102509

Belk, R. (2014a). Sharing Versus Pseudo-Sharing in Web 2.0. *The Anthropologist*, *18*(1), 7–23. DOI: 10.1080/09720073.2014.11891518

Belk, R. (2014b). You are what you can access: Sharing and collaborative consumption online. *Journal of Business Research*, *67*(8), 1595–1600. DOI: 10.1016/j.jbusres.2013.10.001

Benkler, Y. (2004). *Sharing Nicely: On Shareable Goods and the Emergence of Sharing as a Modality of Economic Production.* https://www.yalelawjournal.org/essay/sharing-nicely-on-shareable-goods-and-the-emergence-of-sharing-as-a-modality-of-economic-production

Benkler, Y. (2017). Peer production, the commons, and the future of the firm. *Strategic Organization, 15*(2), 264–274. DOI: 10.1177/1476127016652606

Benoit, S., Baker, T. L., Bolton, R. N., Gruber, T., & Kandampully, J. (2017). A triadic framework for collaborative consumption (CC): Motives, activities and resources & capabilities of actors. *Journal of Business Research, 79*, 219–227. DOI: 10.1016/j.jbusres.2017.05.004

Benoit, S., Merfeld, K., Tunn, V. S. C., Schaefers, T., & Andreassen, T. W. (2025). The B2B sharing economy: Framework, implications, and future research. *Journal of Business Research, 191*, 115244. DOI: 10.1016/j.jbusres.2025.115244

Berger, S., Denner, M.-S., & Roeglinger, M. (2018). *The Nature of Digital Technologies-Development of a Multi-Layer Taxonomy.* 92.

Bilton, C. (2016). A creative industries perspective on creativity and culture. *The Palgrave Handbook of Creativity and Culture Research*, 661–679.

Böcker, L., & Meelen, T. (2017). Sharing for people, planet or profit? Analysing motivations for intended sharing economy participation. *Environmental Innovation and Societal Transitions, 23*, 28–39. DOI: 10.1016/j.eist.2016.09.004

Botsman, R. (2013). *The Sharing Economy lacks a shared definition. Givin meaning to the terms.* https://www.slideshare.net/slideshow/embed_code/28428767

Botsman, R., & Rogers, R. (2010). *What's Mine Is Yours: The Rise of Collaborative Consumption* (International ed.). HarperBusiness.

Bucher, E., Fieseler, C., & Lutz, C. (2016). What's mine is yours (for a nominal fee) – Exploring the spectrum of utilitarian to altruistic motives for Internet-mediated sharing. *Computers in Human Behavior, 62*, 316–326. DOI: 10.1016/j.chb.2016.04.002

Burgelman, R. A., Christensen, C. M., & Wheelwright, S. C. (2008). *Strategic management of technology and innovation.* McGraw-Hill/Irwin.

Cambridge University Press. (2018). *Sharing economy.* https://dictionary.cambridge.org/dictionary/english/sharing-economy

Chang, H., & Sokol, D. D. (2022). How incumbents respond to competition from innovative disruptors in the sharing economy—The impact of Airbnb on hotel performance. *Strategic Management Journal, 43*(3), 425–446. DOI: 10.1002/smj.3201

Chesbrough, H. (2007). Business model innovation: It's not just about technology anymore. *Strategy and Leadership*, *35*(6), 12–17. DOI: 10.1108/10878570710833714

Ciulli, F., & Kolk, A. (2019). Incumbents and business model innovation for the sharing economy: Implications for sustainability. *Journal of Cleaner Production*, *214*, 995–1010. DOI: 10.1016/j.jclepro.2018.12.295

Cockayne, D. G. (2016). Sharing and neoliberal discourse: The economic function of sharing in the digital on-demand economy. *Geoforum*, *77*, 73–82. DOI: 10.1016/j.geoforum.2016.10.005

Codagnone, C., & Martens, B. (2016). Scoping the sharing economy: Origins, definitions, impact and regulatory issues. *Scoping the Sharing Economy: Origins, Definitions, Impact and Regulatory Issues. Institute for Prospective Technological Studies Digital Economy Working Paper, 1.*

Cohen, B., & Kietzmann, J. (2014). Ride On! Mobility Business Models for the Sharing Economy. *Organization & Environment*, *27*(3), 279–296. DOI: 10.1177/1086026614546199

Cohen, B., & Muñoz, P. (2016). Sharing cities and sustainable consumption and production: Towards an integrated framework. *Journal of Cleaner Production, 134, Part A*, 87–97. DOI: 10.1016/j.jclepro.2015.07.133

Csikszentmihalyi, M. (2014). Society, Culture, and Person: A Systems View of Creativity. In Csikszentmihalyi, M. (Ed.), *The Systems Model of Creativity: The Collected Works of Mihaly Csikszentmihalyi* (pp. 47–61). Springer Netherlands. DOI: 10.1007/978-94-017-9085-7_4

Cusumano, M., Kahl, S., & Suarez, F. F. (2006). Product, process, and service: A new industry lifecycle model. *A Research and Education Initiative at the MIT, Sloan School of Management, Working Paper No, 228.*

Davidson, A., Habibi, M. R., & Laroche, M. (2018). Materialism and the sharing economy: A cross-cultural study of American and Indian consumers. *Journal of Business Research*, *82*, 364–372. DOI: 10.1016/j.jbusres.2015.07.045

De las Heras, A., Relinque-Medina, F., Zamora-Polo, F., & Luque-Sendra, A. (2021). Analysis of the evolution of the sharing economy towards sustainability. Trends and transformations of the concept. *Journal of Cleaner Production*, *291*, 125227. DOI: 10.1016/j.jclepro.2020.125227

Demary, V. (2015). *Competition in the sharing economy* (IW Policy Paper 19/2015). Institut der deutschen Wirtschaft Köln. http://hdl.handle.net/10419/112778

Diamandis, P. (2014, September 8). *Uber vs. The Law (My Money's on Uber)*. Forbes. https://www.forbes.com/sites/peterdiamandis/2014/09/08/uber-vs-the-law-my-moneys-on-uber/

Dobusch, L. (2019). Dynamiken der'Sharing Economy'zwischen Commons und Kommodifizierung. *Momentum Quarterly-Zeitschrift Für Sozialen Fortschritt*, *8*(2), 109–115. DOI: 10.15203/momentumquarterly.vol8.no2.p109-115

Edwards, J. (2013, May 27). *Why Hotel Industry Lobbyists Want A Global Crackdown On Airbnb*. Business Insider. https://www.businessinsider.com/why-hotel-industry-lobbyists-want-a-global-crackdown-on-airbnb-2013-5

Engeström, Y. (2001). Expansive learning at work: Toward an activity theoretical reconceptualization. *Journal of Education and Work*, *14*(1), 133–156. DOI: 10.1080/13639080020028747

Ertz, M., Maravilla, J. M. B., & Cao, X. (2025). Prosumer: A new approach to conceptualisation. *Journal of Innovation & Knowledge*, *10*(1), 100653. DOI: 10.1016/j.jik.2025.100653

Evans, S., Vladimirova, D., Holgado, M., Fossen, K. V., Yang, M., Silva, E. A., & Barlow, C. Y. (2017). Business Model Innovation for Sustainability: Towards a Unified Perspective for Creation of Sustainable Business Models. *Business Strategy and the Environment*, *26*(5), 597–608. DOI: 10.1002/bse.1939

Feeney, M. (2014, August 6). *How the Sharing Economy Can Help Developing Nations*. Cato Institute. https://www.cato.org/blog/how-sharing-economy-can-help-developing-nations

Felson, M., & Spaeth, J. L. (1978). Community structure and collaborative consumption: A routine activity approach. *The American Behavioral Scientist*, *21*(4), 614–624. DOI: 10.1177/000276427802100411

Fischer, G., Giaccardi, E., Eden, H., Sugimoto, M., & Ye, Y. (2005). Beyond binary choices: Integrating individual and social creativity. *International Journal of Human-Computer Studies*, *63*(4–5), 482–512. DOI: 10.1016/j.ijhcs.2005.04.014

Fischer, G., Scharff, E., & Ye, Y. (2004). *Fostering social creativity by increasing social capital. Social Capital and Information Technology*. MIT Press.

Fitzmaurice, C. J., Ladegaard, I., Attwood-Charles, W., Cansoy, M., Carfagna, L. B., Schor, J. B., & Wengronowitz, R. (2020). Domesticating the market: Moral exchange and the sharing economy. *Socio-economic Review*, *18*(1), 81–102. DOI: 10.1093/ser/mwy003

Fraiberger, S. P., & Sundararajan, A. (2015). *Peer-to-Peer Rental Markets in the Sharing Economy* (Working Paper 15–19). NET Institute. https://econpapers.repec.org/paper/netwpaper/1519.htm

Frenken, K., & Schor, J. (2017). Putting the sharing economy into perspective. *Environmental Innovation and Societal Transitions, 23*, 3–10. DOI: 10.1016/j.eist.2017.01.003

Geissinger, A., Laurell, C., Öberg, C., Sandström, C., & Suseno, Y. (2021). The sharing economy and the transformation of work: Evidence from Foodora. *Personnel Review*.

Gerwe, O., & Silva, R. (2018). Clarifying the sharing economy: Conceptualization, typology, antecedents, and effects. *The Academy of Management Perspectives*. Advance online publication. DOI: 10.5465/amp.2017.0010

Giaccardi, E. (2004). Principles of Metadesign: Processes and Levels of Co-Creation in the New Design Space. *Leonardo Electronic Almanac, 12*(10).

Görög, G. (2018). The Definitions of Sharing Economy: A Systematic Literature Review. *Management, 13*(2).

Grieco, C. (2021). Innovating the innovated: Business model innovation process in sharing economy companies. *Creativity and Innovation Management, 30*(4), 860–871. DOI: 10.1111/caim.12457

Gruszka, K. (2017). Framing the collaborative economy—Voices of contestation. *Environmental Innovation and Societal Transitions, 23*, 92–104. DOI: 10.1016/j.eist.2016.09.002

Habibi, M. R. (2019). The Progression and Impact of the Sharing Economy; a Preface. *Journal of Marketing Theory and Practice, 27*(4), 349–354. DOI: 10.1080/10696679.2019.1644959

Habibi, M. R., Davidson, A., & Laroche, M. (2017). What managers should know about the sharing economy. *Business Horizons, 60*(1), 113–121. DOI: 10.1016/j.bushor.2016.09.007

Hamari, J., Sjöklint, M., & Ukkonen, A. (2016). The sharing economy: Why people participate in collaborative consumption. *Journal of the Association for Information Science and Technology, 67*(9), 2047–2059. DOI: 10.1002/asi.23552

Hauschildt, J., & Salomo, S. (2011). Innovationsmanagement. 5., überarb., erg. U. Aktualis. *Aufl. München: Vahlen (Vahlens Handbücher Der Wirtschafts-Und Sozialwissenschaften).*

Heinrichs, H., & Grunenberg, H. (2012). *Sharing Economy—Auf dem Weg in eine neue Konsumkultur?* https://nbn-resolving.org/urn:nbn:de:0168-ssoar-427486

Herrmann-Fankhaenel, A., & Huesig, S. (2016). How much social innovation is behind the online platforms of the sharing economy?: An exploratory investigation and educing of clusters in the German context. *2016 Portland International Conference on Management of Engineering and Technology (PICMET)*, 370–384. DOI: 10.1109/PICMET.2016.7806696

Herrmann-Fankhaenel, A., & Huesig, S. (2020). An Empirical Based View on the Sharing Economy in Germany: More Mainstream Economy than Collaborative Commons? *International Journal of Innovation and Technology Management*. DOI: 10.1142/S0219877020500315

Herrmann-Fankhaenel, A., & Huesig, S. (2022). *Development and Factors of Survival of (New) Business Ideas in the Online Sharing Economy*. 1–18.

Herrmann-Fankhaenel, A., & Schell, E. (2022). Sharing offline and for idealistic purposes in Germany. *International Journal Technology Management, 88*(2/3/4), 270–293.

Hui, K. L., & Chau, P. Y. (2002). Classifying digital products. *Communications of the ACM, 45*(6), 73–79. DOI: 10.1145/508448.508451

Hund, A., Wagner, H.-T., Beimborn, D., & Weitzel, T. (2021). Digital innovation: Review and novel perspective. *The Journal of Strategic Information Systems, 30*(4), 101695. DOI: 10.1016/j.jsis.2021.101695

Hüsig, S. (2006). *Institutionalisierte Vorentwicklung für radikale Innovationen-Dargestellt am Beispiel der Mannesmann Pilotentwicklung und der LKW-Mauttechnik*. WiKu.

Kenney, M., & Curry, J. (1999). e-commerce: Implications for firm strategy and industry Configuration. *Industry and Innovation, 6*(2), 131–151. DOI: 10.1080/13662719900000008

Kenny, M., & Zysman, J. (2016). The Rise of the Platform Economy. *Issues in Science and Technology*, 61–69.

Kornmeier, M. (2007). *Wissenschaftstheorie und wissenschaftliches Arbeiten: Eine Einführung für Wirtschaftswissenschaftler*. Springer-Verlag. DOI: 10.1007/978-3-7908-1919-9

Kozinets, R. V., Hemetsberger, A., & Schau, H. J. (2008). The wisdom of consumer crowds: Collective innovation in the age of networked marketing. *Journal of Macromarketing*, *28*(4), 339–354. DOI: 10.1177/0276146708325382

Kung, L.-C., & Zhong, G.-Y. (2017). The optimal pricing strategy for two-sided platform delivery in the sharing economy. *Transportation Research Part E, Logistics and Transportation Review*, *101*, 1–12. DOI: 10.1016/j.tre.2017.02.003

Kuzminska, A. O., Gasiorowska, A., Kasałka, O., Narkun, M., & Zaleskiewicz, T. (2025). The social currency of sharing economy: How monetary and nonmonetary interactions impact social capital. *Journal of Cleaner Production*, *500*, 145238. DOI: 10.1016/j.jclepro.2025.145238

Kyprianou, C. (2018). Creating Value from the Outside In or the Inside Out: How Nascent Intermediaries Build Peer-to-Peer Marketplaces. *Academy of Management Discoveries*, *4*(3), 336–370. DOI: 10.5465/amd.2017.0081

Laamanen, M., Wahlen, S., & Campana, M. (2015). Mobilising collaborative consumption lifestyles: A comparative frame analysis of time banking. *International Journal of Consumer Studies*, *39*(5), 459–467. DOI: 10.1111/ijcs.12190

Latitude. (2015). *The New Sharing Economy Study Report*. Scribd. https://www.scribd.com/document/38788695/The-New-Sharing-Economy-Study-Report-by-Latitude-and-Shareable-Magazine

Lemaine, G. (1974). Social differentiation and social originality. *European Journal of Social Psychology*, *4*(1), 17–52. DOI: 10.1002/ejsp.2420040103

MacArthur, E. (2013). Towards the circular economy. *Journal of Industrial Ecology*, *2*, 23–44.

MacDonald, C. (2018). The Sharing Economy: The End of Employment and the Rise of Crowd-Based Capitalism. *Business Ethics Quarterly*, *28*(4), 501–505. DOI: 10.1017/beq.2018.31

Margolis, A. (2024). Do All Roads Lead to Rome? How Three Process Pathways Contribute to Transformative Innovation in Cross-Sector Partnerships. *Business & Society*. Advance online publication. DOI: 10.1177/00076503241289929

Markman, G. D., Lieberman, M., Leiblein, M., Wei, L., & Wang, Y. (2021). The distinctive domain of the sharing economy: Definitions, value creation, and implications for research. *Journal of Management Studies*, *58*(4), 927–948. DOI: 10.1111/joms.12707

Martin, C. J. (2016). The sharing economy: A pathway to sustainability or a nightmarish form of neoliberal capitalism? *Ecological Economics, 121*(Supplement C), 149–159. DOI: 10.1016/j.ecolecon.2015.11.027

Martin, C. J., Upham, P., & Budd, L. (2015). Commercial orientation in grassroots social innovation: Insights from the sharing economy. *Ecological Economics, 118*(Supplement C), 240–251. DOI: 10.1016/j.ecolecon.2015.08.001

Morewedge, C. K., Monga, A., Palmatier, R. W., Shu, S. B., & Small, D. A. (2021). Evolution of consumption: A psychological ownership framework. *Journal of Marketing, 85*(1), 196–218. DOI: 10.1177/0022242920957007

Morozov, E. (2013, October 14). The 'sharing economy' undermines workers' rights. *Financial Times.*

Mulgan, G., Tucker, S., Ali, R., & Sanders, B. (2007). *Social Innovation: What it is, why it matters and how it can be accelerated* [Other Working Paper]. https://eureka.sbs.ox.ac.uk/761/

Muñoz, P., & Cohen, B. (2017). Mapping out the sharing economy: A configurational approach to sharing business modeling. *Technological Forecasting and Social Change, 125*(Supplement C), 21–37. DOI: 10.1016/j.techfore.2017.03.035

Muñoz, P., & Cohen, B. (2018). A compass for navigating sharing economy business models. *California Management Review, 61*(1), 114–147. DOI: 10.1177/0008125618795490

Murillo, D., Buckland, H., & Val, E. (2017). When the sharing economy becomes neoliberalism on steroids: Unravelling the controversies. *Technological Forecasting and Social Change, 125*(Supplement C), 66–76. DOI: 10.1016/j.techfore.2017.05.024

Nash, A. (2015). On the Sharing Economy. *Contexts, 14*(1), 12–19. DOI: 10.1177/1536504214567860

Netto, C. de O., & Tello-Gamarra, J. E. (2020). Sharing Economy: A Bibliometric Analysis. *Research Trends and Research Agenda., 15*(2), 16.

Notz, G. (2010). *Theorien alternativen Wirtschaftens: Fenster in eine andere Welt* (1st ed.). Schmetterling Stuttgart.

Oh, S., & Moon, J. Y. (2016). Calling for a Shared Understanding of the 'Sharing Economy'. *Proceedings of the 18th Annual International Conference on Electronic Commerce: E-Commerce in Smart Connected World*, 35:1-35:5. DOI: 10.1145/2971603.2971638

Osterwalder, A., & Pigneur, Y. (2010). *Business model generation: A handbook for visionaries, game changers, and challengers*. John Wiley & Sons.

Owyang, J. (2016). *Honeycomb 3.0: The Collaborative Economy Market Expansion | Web Strategy by Jeremiah Owyang | Digital Business*. https://www.web-strategist.com/blog/2016/03/10/honeycomb-3-0-the-collaborative-economy-market-expansion-sxsw/

Ozanne, L. K., & Ballantine, P. W. (2010). Sharing as a form of anti-consumption? An examination of toy library users. *Journal of Consumer Behaviour*, *9*(6), 485–498. DOI: 10.1002/cb.334

Pandey, M., Bhati, M., Shukla, D. M., & Qureshi, I. (2021). Resourcing and value creation: A case of sharing economy model at the base of the pyramid. In *Sharing Economy at the Base of the Pyramid* (pp. 197–218). Springer. DOI: 10.1007/978-981-16-2414-8_9

Peltoniemi, M. (2011). Reviewing Industry Life-cycle Theory: Avenues for Future Research. *International Journal of Management Reviews*, *13*(4), 349–375. DOI: 10.1111/j.1468-2370.2010.00295.x

Pérez-Pérez, C., & Benito-Osorio, D. (2025). Sharing is not for the weak: A systematic review of the main drawbacks of the sharing economy. *Journal of Management & Organization*, *31*(5), 2555–2571. DOI: 10.1017/jmo.2025.10020

Petrini, M., De Freitas, C. S., & Da Silveira, L. M. (2017). A Proposal for a Typology of Sharing Economy. *Revista de Administração Mackenzie*, *18*(5), 39–62. https://doi.org/DOI: 10.1590/1678-69712017/administracao.v18n5p39-62

Pfeffer, J., & Salancik, G. R. (2003). *The External Control of Organizations: A Resource Dependence Perspective* (Parental Adviso). Stanford Business Classics.

Plewnia, F., & Guenther, E. (2018). Mapping the sharing economy for sustainability research. *Management Decision*, *56*(3), 570–583. DOI: 10.1108/MD-11-2016-0766

Porter, P. K., & Scully, G. W. (1995). Institutional technology and economic growth. *Public Choice*, *82*(1), 17–36. DOI: 10.1007/BF01047727

Pouri, M. J., & Hilty, L. M. (2021). The digital sharing economy: A confluence of technical and social sharing. *Environmental Innovation and Societal Transitions*, *38*, 127–139. DOI: 10.1016/j.eist.2020.12.003

Qureshi, I., Bhatt, B., & Shukla, D. M. (2021). Overview of Sharing Economy at the Base of the Pyramid. In Qureshi, I., Bhatt, B., & Shukla, D. M. (Eds.), *Sharing Economy at the Base of the Pyramid: Opportunities and Challenges* (pp. 1–23). Springer Nature. DOI: 10.1007/978-981-16-2414-8_1

Ranjbari, M., Morales-Alonso, G., & Carrasco-Gallego, R. (2018). Conceptualizing the sharing economy through presenting a comprehensive framework. *Sustainability (Basel), 10*(7), 2336. DOI: 10.3390/su10072336

Reichert, L. (2021). *Evolution und Innovation*. Duncker & Humblot.

Reischauer, G., & Mair, J. (2018). Platform Organizing in the New Digital Economy: Revisiting Online Communities and Strategic Responses', Toward Permeable Boundaries of Organizations. *Research in the Sociology of Organizations, 57*, 113–135. DOI: 10.1108/S0733-558X20180000057005

Richter, C., Kraus, S., Brem, A., Durst, S., & Giselbrecht, C. (2017). Digital entrepreneurship: Innovative business models for the sharing economy. *Creativity and Innovation Management, 26*(3), 300–310. DOI: 10.1111/caim.12227

Ritzer, G., Dean, P., & Jurgenson, N. (2012). The Coming of Age of the Prosumer. *The American Behavioral Scientist, 56*(4), 379–398. DOI: 10.1177/0002764211429368

Rochet, J.-C., & Tirole, J. (2003). Platform competition in two-sided markets. *Journal of the European Economic Association, 1*(4), 990–1029. DOI: 10.1162/154247603322493212

Saunders, R., & Bown, O. (2015). Computational Social Creativity. *Artificial Life, 21*(3), 366–378. DOI: 10.1162/ARTL_a_00177 PMID: 26280077

Saunders, R., & Gero, J. S. (2001). *Artificial creativity: A synthetic approach to the study of creative behaviour. Computational and Cognitive Models of Creative Design V*. Key Centre of Design Computing and Cognition, University of Sydney.

Scaraboto, D. (2015). Selling, Sharing, and Everything In Between: The Hybrid Economies of Collaborative Networks. *The Journal of Consumer Research, 42*(1), 152–176. DOI: 10.1093/jcr/ucv004

Schor, J. (2016). Debating the Sharing Economy. *Journal of Self-Governance and Management Economics, 4*(3), 7–22.

Schor, J., & Attwood-Charles, W. (2017). The "sharing" economy: Labor, inequality, and social connection on for-profit platforms. *Sociology Compass, 11*(8), e12493. DOI: 10.1111/soc4.12493

Schumpeter, J. A. (1931). *Theorie der wirtschaftlichen Entwicklung: Eine Untersuchung über Unternehmergewinn, Kapital, Kredit, Zins und den Konjunkturzyklus.* Duncker & Humblot.

Silver, J. (2013, August 3). The sharing economy: A whole new way of living. *The Observer.* https://www.theguardian.com/technology/2013/aug/04/internet-technology-fon-taskrabbit-blablacar

Siuskaite, D., Pilinkiene, V., & Zvirdauskas, D. (2019). The Conceptualization of the Sharing Economy as a Business Model. *The Engineering Economist, 30*(3), 373–381. DOI: 10.5755/j01.ee.30.3.21253

Specht, G., Beckmann, C., & Amelingmeyer, J. (2002). *F&E-Management–Kompetenz im Innovationsprozess. 2. Überarb. Und erw.* Auflage. Schäffer-Pöschel.

Stephany, A. (2015). *The business of sharing: Making it in the new sharing economy.* Springer. DOI: 10.1057/9781137376183

Suarez, F., & Utterback, J. (1993). Patterns of industrial evolution, dominant designs, and firms' survival. *Research on Technological Innovation. Management and Policy, 5*, 47–87.

Tajfel, H., Turner, J. C., Austin, W. G., & Worchel, S. (1979). An integrative theory of intergroup conflict. *Organizational Identity. REAd (Porto Alegre), 56*(65), 9780203505984–16.

Täuscher, K., & Laudien, S. M. (2018). Understanding platform business models: A mixed methods study of marketplaces. *European Management Journal, 36*(3), 319–329. DOI: 10.1016/j.emj.2017.06.005

Thom, N. (1980). *Grundlagen des betrieblichen Innovationsmanagements.* Peter Hanstein Verlag.

United Nations. (2015). *Transforming our World: The 2030 Agenda for Sustainable Development. Sustainable Development Knowledge Platform.* https://sustainabledevelopment.un.org/post2015/transformingourworld/publication

Vahs, D., & Brem, A. (2015). *Innovationsmanagement: Von der Idee zur erfolgreichen Vermarktung.* Schäffer-Poeschel.

Van Bezouw, M. J., Van Der Toorn, J., & Becker, J. C. (2021). Social creativity: Reviving a social identity approach to social stability. *European Journal of Social Psychology, 51*(2), 409–422. DOI: 10.1002/ejsp.2732

Vandermerwe, S., & Rada, J. (1988). Servitization of business: Adding value by adding services. *European Management Journal*, *6*(4), 314–324. DOI: 10.1016/0263-2373(88)90033-3

Villari, B. (2018). A Service Design Approach to Analyse, Map and Design Sharing Services. In Bruglieri, M. (Ed.), *Multidisciplinary Design of Sharing Services* (pp. 3–24). Springer International Publishing. DOI: 10.1007/978-3-319-78099-3_1

Voytenko Palgan, Y., Zvolska, L., & Mont, O. (2017). Sustainability framings of accommodation sharing. *Environmental Innovation and Societal Transitions*, *23*, 70–83. DOI: 10.1016/j.eist.2016.12.002

Watson, E. (2007). Who or What Creates? A Conceptual Framework for Social Creativity. *Human Resource Development Review*, *6*(4), 419–441. DOI: 10.1177/1534484307308255

Wruk, D., Oberg, A., & Friedrich-Schieback, M. (2019). Quantifying the sharing economy: An approach for measuring the ecological, social, and economic effects. *Gaia (Heidelberg)*, *28*(1), 184–189. DOI: 10.14512/gaia.28.S1.3

Wruk, D., Oberg, A., Klutt, J., & Maurer, I. (2019). The Presentation of Self as Good and Right: How Value Propositions and Business Model Features are Linked in the Sharing Economy. *Journal of Business Ethics*, *159*(4), 997–1021. DOI: 10.1007/s10551-019-04209-5

Yoo, Y., Henfridsson, O., & Lyytinen, K. (2010). Research commentary—The new organizing logic of digital innovation: An agenda for information systems research. *Information Systems Research*, *21*(4), 724–735. DOI: 10.1287/isre.1100.0322

Zahn, E., & Weidler, A. (1995). Integriertes Innovationsmanagement. *Handbuch Technologiemanagement, Stuttgart*, *1995*, 351.

KEY TERMS AND DEFINITIONS

Ideal Sharing Economy: In comparison to a wide understanding of the Sharing Economy, the ideal Sharing Economy or the narrow understanding focusses on online platforms for individuals.

Innovation: New ends and means; novelty in the sense of new combinations: new products or services, new means of production, new markets, new sources of resources, or new organisations combination in a particular context diffused in the market.

Sharing Economy: The Sharing Economy is defined as an economic interaction among people who share products and services predominantly with the help of the Internet (Cambridge University Press, 2018).

Sharing Economy Generations: During the evolution of the Sharing Economy different types of organizations formed which can be viewed as generations when comparing particular main characteristics such as users, intensions and multi-sided markets.

Sharing Economy Main Features: According to relevant definitions five main feature characterize Sharing Economy organization, namely socio-economic system, online platforms, users, access and resources.

Social and Transformative Innovation: New products and services social in its ends and means (Mulgan et al., 2007; Thom, 1980) and transformative innovation as society changing (Margolis, 2024).

Social Creativity: Social creativity encompasses creative processes that occur through interactions between individuals and artifacts, embodying the collective knowledge and ethos of peer groups.

ENDNOTES

1 Crunchbase, Inc., based in San Francisco, is a U.S. commercial database provider and news portal for corporate and business information with a focus on technology companies and investors (www.cruchbase.com)

2 Strictly speaking, when taking the service organisations out of this calculation, as a discussion of ownership transfer when consuming services is difficult, only 42 cases or 4% would apply for this strict definition.

Compilation of References

Abdi, K., Mardani, A., Senin, A. A., Tupenaite, L., Naimaviciene, J., Kanapeckiene, L., & Kutut, V. (2018). The effect of knowledge management, organizational culture and organizational learning on innovation in automotive industry. *Journal of Business Economics and Management, 19*(1), 1–19. DOI: 10.3846/jbem.2018.1477

Acar, O. A., Tarakci, M., & van Knippenberg, D. (2019). Creativity and Innovation Under Constraints: A Cross-Disciplinary Integrative Review. *Journal of Management, 45*(1), 96–121. DOI: 10.1177/0149206318805832

Acar, O., Tarakci, M., & van Knippenberg, D. (2019). Why Constraints Are Good for Innovation. *Harvard Business Review.*

Acey, M. (2013, June 5). The end of consumerism? *CNN.* https://www.cnn.com/interactive/2013/06/world/sharing-economy/index.html

Acquier, A., Daudigeos, T., & Pinkse, J. (2017). Promises and paradoxes of the sharing economy: An organizing framework. *Technological Forecasting and Social Change, 125,* 1–10. DOI: 10.1016/j.techfore.2017.07.006

Adler, H. (2015). *Balanceakt Innovation: Das Management unternehmungsexterner und -interner Entwicklungsverläufe über Proto-Institutionen.* Logos.

Adula, M., Kant, S., & Debebe, T. S. (2025). Sustainable Development Effect on Organizational Networks With Mediation of Contingency Theory in the Horn of Africa. In *Integrating Organizational Theories With Sustainable Development* (pp. 203-226).

Adula, M., Kant, S., Badi, S., & Kumari, M. (2025). Abusive Work Environment Effect on Female Entrepreneurs' Emotional Wellbeing by Mediation of Social and Moral Values in the Horn of Africa. In *Supporting Psychological and Emotional Wellbeing Among Entrepreneurs* (pp. 1-22).

Agarwal, N., & Steinmetz, R. (2019). Sharing Economy: A Systematic Literature Review. *International Journal on Management of Innovation & Technology*, *16*(06), 1–17. DOI: 10.1142/S0219877019300027

Agostini, M. R., Vieira, L. M., Tondolo, R., & Tondolo, V. (2017). An overview of social innovation research: Guiding future studies. *BBR. Brazilian Business Review*, *14*(4), 385–402. DOI: 10.15728/bbr.2017.14.4.2

Ahlin, B., Drnovšek, M., & Hisrich, R. D. (2014). Entrepreneurs' creativity and firm innovation: The moderating role of entrepreneurial self-efficacy. *Small Business Economics*, *43*(1), 101–117. DOI: 10.1007/s11187-013-9531-7

Akin, D., Jakobsen, K. C., Floch, J., & Hoff, E. (2021). Sharing with neighbours: Insights from local practices of the sharing economy. *Technology in Society*, *64*, 101481. DOI: 10.1016/j.techsoc.2020.101481

Albinsson, P. A., Perera, B. Y., Nafees, L., & Burman, B. (2019). Collaborative Consumption Usage in the US and India: An Exploratory Study. *Journal of Marketing Theory and Practice*, *27*(4), 390–412. DOI: 10.1080/10696679.2019.1644956

Al-Fadhali, N. (2024). An AMOS-SEM approach to evaluating stakeholders' influence on construction project delivery performance. *Engineering, Construction, and Architectural Management*, *31*(2), 638–661. DOI: 10.1108/ECAM-09-2021-0780

Aliyu, M. G., & Gebremeskel, M. M. (2024). The influence of conscientiousness, sportsmanship, and civic virtue on organizational effectiveness in public universities of Ethiopia. *International Journal of Organizational Leadership*, *13*(1), 142–160. DOI: 10.33844/ijol.2024.60403

Alshuhumi, S. R., Al-Hidabi, D. A., & Al-Refaei, A. A.-A. (2024). Unveiling the behavioral nexus of innovative organizational culture: Identification and affective commitment of teachers in primary schools. *Journal of Human Behavior in the Social Environment*, *34*(1), 130–152. DOI: 10.1080/10911359.2023.2267600

Amabile, T. (2012). Componential theory of creativity [Harvard Business School Working Paper No. 12-096]. *Encyclopedia of Management Theory.* Cambridge, MA: Sage.

Amabile, T. M. (1996). Creativity and Innovation in Organizations. Harvard Business School Industry and Background Note 396-239.

Amabile, T. (2012). Componential theory of creativity. In *Encyclopedia of Management Theory*. Sage.

Amabile, T. M. (1988). A model of creativity and innovation in organizations. *Research in Organizational Behavior, 10*(1), 123–167.

Amabile, T. M., Conti, R., Coon, H., Lazenby, J., & Herron, M. (1996). Assessing the work environment for creativity. *Academy of Management Journal, 39*(5), 1154–1184. DOI: 10.2307/256995

Amabile, T. M., & Pratt, M. G. (2016). The dynamic componential model of creativity and innovation in organizations: Making progress, making meaning. *Research in Organizational Behavior, 36*, 157–183. DOI: 10.1016/j.riob.2016.10.001

Amit, R., & Zott, C. (2020). *Business model innovation strategy: Transformational concepts and tools for entrepreneurial leaders*. John Wiley & Sons.

Anderson, B. B., & Dees, J. G. (2006). Rhetoric, reality, and research: Building a solid foundation for the practice of social entrepreneurship. *Social Entrepreneurship: New Models of Sustainable Social Change*, 144–168.

Anderson, N., Potočnik, K., & Zhou, J. (2014). Innovation and creativity in organizations: A state-of-the-science review, prospective commentary, and guiding framework. *Journal of Management, 40*(5), 1297–1333. DOI: 10.1177/0149206314527128

Anscombe, G. E. M. (1958). Modern moral philosophy. *Philosophy (London, England), 33*(124), 1–19. DOI: 10.1017/S0031819100037943

Argarwal, D., Bersin, J., Lahin, G., Schwartz, J., & Volini, E. (2018). *The rise of the social enterprise*. Deloitte Insights.

Aristotle, . (2009). *Nicomachean ethics* (Ross, W. D., Trans.). Oxford University Press. (Original work published 350 BCE)

Asbari, M. (2021). From leadership to innovation: managing employee creativity. *Available at SSRN* 4708682.

Asbari, M., Prasetya, A. B., Santoso, P. B., & Purwanto, A. (2021). From Creativity to Innovation: The Role of Female Employees' Psychological Capital. *International Journal of Social and Management Studies, 02*(02), 66–77. https://ijosmas.org/index.php/ijosmas/article/view/18

Assembly, U. N. G. (2015). *Transforming our world: the 2030 agenda for sustainable development, 21 October 2015*. A/RES/70/1.

Audretsch, D. B., Eichler, G. M., & Schwarz, E. J. (2022). Emerging needs of social innovators and social innovation ecosystems. *The International Entrepreneurship and Management Journal, 18*(1), 1–38. DOI: 10.1007/s11365-021-00789-9

Avelino, F., Wittmayer, J. M., Pel, B., Weaver, P., Dumitru, A., Haxeltine, A., Kemp, R., Jørgensen, M. S., Bauler, T., Ruijsink, S., & O'Riordan, T. (2019). Transformative social innovation and (dis) empowerment. *Technological Forecasting and Social Change*, *145*, 195–206. DOI: 10.1016/j.techfore.2017.05.002

Azhar, Z., Iqbal, T., & Imran, M. (2025). The Role of Ethical Leadership in HRM-driven Corporate Social Responsibility (CSR). *Journal of Management & Social Science*, *2*(1), 158–176. DOI: 10.63075/jmss.v2i1.66

Babu, D., & Kushwaha, B. P. (2024). Does transformational leadership influence employees' innovativeness and mediate the role of organisational culture? Empirical evidence. *Int. Res. J. Multidiscip. Scope*, *5*(1), 428–440. DOI: 10.47857/irjms.2024.v05i01.0244

Bahemia, H., Sillince, J., & Vanhaverbeke, W. (2018). The timing of openness in a radical innovation project: A temporal and loose-coupling perspective. *Research Policy*, *47*(10), 2066–2076. DOI: 10.1016/j.respol.2018.07.015

Balasubramanian, S., & Fernandes, C. (2022). Confirmation of a crisis leadership model and its effectiveness: Lessons from the COVID-19 pandemic. *Cogent Business & Management*, *9*(1), 2022824. DOI: 10.1080/23311975.2021.2022824

Bal, M. (1996). *Double Exposures: The Subject of Cultural Analysis*. Routledge.

Bammens, Y. (2016). Employees' innovative behavior in social context: A closer examination of the role of organizational care. *Journal of Product Innovation Management*, *33*(3), 244–259. DOI: 10.1111/jpim.12267

Bank, V. (1997). *Controlling in der betrieblichen Weiterbildung*. Botermann & Botermann.

Banmairuroy, W., Kritjaroen, T., & Homsombat, W. (2022). The effect of knowledge-oriented leadership and human resource development on sustainable competitive advantage through organizational innovation's component factors: Evidence from Thailand's new S-curve industries. *Asia Pacific Management Review*, *27*(3), 200–209. DOI: 10.1016/j.apmrv.2021.09.001

Barbu, C. M., Bratu, R. Ş., & Sîrbu, E. M. (2018). Business Models of the Sharing Economy. *Review of International Comparative Management / Revista de Management Comparat International, 19*(2), 154–166. DOI: 10.24818/RMCI.2018.2.154

Bardhi, F., & Eckhardt, G. M. (2012). Access-based consumption: The case of car sharing. *The Journal of Consumer Research*, *39*(4), 881–898. DOI: 10.1086/666376

Barras, R. (1986). Towards a theory of innovation in services. *Research Policy, 15*(4), 161–173. DOI: 10.1016/0048-7333(86)90012-0

Bass, B. M., & Stogdill, R. M. (1990). *Bass & Stogdill's handbook of leadership: Theory, research, and managerial applications.* Simon and Schuster.

Beckman, S. L., & Barry, M. (2007). Innovation as a learning process: Embedding design thinking. *California Management Review, 50*(1), 25–56. DOI: 10.2307/41166415

Begum, S., Ashfaq, M., Xia, E., & Awan, U. (2022). Does green transformational leadership lead to green innovation? The role of green thinking and creative process engagement. *Business Strategy and the Environment, 31*(1), 580–597. DOI: 10.1002/bse.2911

Belezas, F., & Daniel, A. D. (2023). Innovation in the sharing economy: A systematic literature review and research framework. *Technovation, 122*, 102509. DOI: 10.1016/j.technovation.2022.102509

Belk, R. (2014a). Sharing Versus Pseudo-Sharing in Web 2.0. *The Anthropologist, 18*(1), 7–23. DOI: 10.1080/09720073.2014.11891518

Belk, R. (2014b). You are what you can access: Sharing and collaborative consumption online. *Journal of Business Research, 67*(8), 1595–1600. DOI: 10.1016/j.jbusres.2013.10.001

Benedix, G. (2003). *Innovationsmanagement – Konzepte zur systematischen Gestaltung und Umsetzung*. Technische Universität.

Benkler, Y. (2004). *Sharing Nicely: On Shareable Goods and the Emergence of Sharing as a Modality of Economic Production.* https://www.yalelawjournal.org/essay/sharing-nicely-on-shareable-goods-and-the-emergence-of-sharing-as-a-modality-of-economic-production

Benkler, Y. (2017). Peer production, the commons, and the future of the firm. *Strategic Organization, 15*(2), 264–274. DOI: 10.1177/1476127016652606

Benoit, S., Baker, T. L., Bolton, R. N., Gruber, T., & Kandampully, J. (2017). A triadic framework for collaborative consumption (CC): Motives, activities and resources & capabilities of actors. *Journal of Business Research, 79*, 219–227. DOI: 10.1016/j.jbusres.2017.05.004

Benoit, S., Merfeld, K., Tunn, V. S. C., Schaefers, T., & Andreassen, T. W. (2025). The B2B sharing economy: Framework, implications, and future research. *Journal of Business Research, 191*, 115244. DOI: 10.1016/j.jbusres.2025.115244

Berger, S., Denner, M.-S., & Roeglinger, M. (2018). *The Nature of Digital Technologies-Development of a Multi-Layer Taxonomy.* 92.

Bilton, C. (2016). A creative industries perspective on creativity and culture. *The Palgrave Handbook of Creativity and Culture Research*, 661–679.

Blackmann, J. (2020). Davos calls for Reskilling Revolution as 75% of manufacturers can't fill roles. *Enterprise IoT market segments.*

Blanco, I., & León, M. (2017). Social innovation, reciprocity and contentious politics: Facing the socio-urban crisis in Ciutat Meridiana, Barcelona. *Urban Studies (Edinburgh, Scotland)*, *54*(9), 2172–2188. DOI: 10.1177/0042098016659044

Bliuc, A., & Muntele-Hendre , D. (2025). Narratives of moral superiority in the context of war in Ukraine: Justifying pro-Russian support through social creativity and moral disengagement. *British Journal of Social Psychology*, *64*(2), e12878. DOI: 10.1111/bjso.12878 PMID: 40126340

Bocken, N. M. P., Short, S. W., Rana, P., & Evans, S. (2016). A literature and practice review to develop sustainable business model archetypes. *Journal of Cleaner Production*, *65*, 42–56. DOI: 10.1016/j.jclepro.2013.11.039

Böcker, L., & Meelen, T. (2017). Sharing for people, planet or profit? Analysing motivations for intended sharing economy participation. *Environmental Innovation and Societal Transitions*, *23*, 28–39. DOI: 10.1016/j.eist.2016.09.004

Boden, M. A. (2016). Creativity and artificial intelligence. *Artificial Intelligence*, *103*(1-2), 347–356. DOI: 10.1016/S0004-3702(98)00055-1

Boer, H., Goduscheit, R. C., Schweisfurth, T., & Visser-Groeneveld, J. (2025). The role of creativity and innovation in the quality of our lives, the planet and science. *Creativity and Innovation Management*, *34*(1), 75–77. DOI: 10.1111/caim.12628

Bostrom, N. (2014). *Superintelligence: Paths, dangers, strategies.* Oxford University Press.

Bostrom, N., & Yudkowsky, E. (2014). The ethics of artificial intelligence. In Frankish, K., & Ramsey, W. M. (Eds.), *The Cambridge handbook of artificial intelligence* (pp. 316–334). Cambridge University Press. DOI: 10.1017/CBO9781139046855.020

Botsman, R. (2013). *The Sharing Economy lacks a shared definition. Givin meaning to the terms.* https://www.slideshare.net/slideshow/embed_code/28428767

Botsman, R., & Rogers, R. (2010). *What's Mine Is Yours: The Rise of Collaborative Consumption* (International ed.). HarperBusiness.

Brem, A., & Puente-Díaz, R. (2020). Creativity, innovation, sustainability: A conceptual model for future research efforts. *Sustainability (Basel), 12*(8), 3139. DOI: 10.3390/su12083139

Breßler, J. (2015). *Didaktik der kreativen Zerstörung: Konstruktion einer expansiven Bildungskonzeption* (No. 3-1). Working Papers of the Chair for Innovation Research and Technology Management.

Brix, J. (2017). Exploring knowledge creation processes as a source of organizational learning: A longitudinal case study of a public innovation project. *Scandinavian Journal of Management, 33*(2), 113–127. DOI: 10.1016/j.scaman.2017.05.001

Brocchi, D. (2022). *By Disaster or by Design? Transformative Kulturpolitik: Von der multiplen Krise zur systemischen Nachhaltigkeit*. Springer VS. DOI: 10.1007/978-3-658-38965-9

Brockhoff, K. (2010). *Forschung und Entwicklung: Planung und Kontrolle*. Walter de Gruyter.

Bruton, D. (2011). Learning creativity and design for innovation. *International Journal of Technology and Design Education, 21*(3), 321–333. DOI: 10.1007/s10798-010-9122-8

Bryman, A. (2012). *Social Research Methods* (4th ed.). Oxford University Press.

Brynjolfsson, E., & McAfee, A. (2014). *The second machine age: Work, progress, and prosperity in a time of brilliant technologies*. W. W. Norton.

Bryson, J. J. (2018). Patiency is not a virtue: The design of intelligent systems and systems of ethics. *Ethics and Information Technology, 20*(1), 15–26. DOI: 10.1007/s10676-018-9448-6

Bucciarelli, L. (2023). Spreading the word: practices of discipleship in early modern natural philosophy (Doctoral dissertation, University of Oxford).

Bucher, A., Schenk, B., Dolata, M., & Schwabe, G. (2024). When Generative AI Meets Workplace Learning: Creating A Realistic & Motivating Learning Experience with a Generative PCA. arXiv preprint arXiv:2405.15561.

Bucher, E., Fieseler, C., & Lutz, C. (2016). What's mine is yours (for a nominal fee) – Exploring the spectrum of utilitarian to altruistic motives for Internet-mediated sharing. *Computers in Human Behavior, 62*, 316–326. DOI: 10.1016/j.chb.2016.04.002

Bui, M. (2025). Data and/as activism: Community-based racial justice data repertoires. *New Media & Society, 27*(4), 2127–2145. DOI: 10.1177/14614448231206118

Buonocore, F., Annosi, M. C., de Gennaro, D., & Riemma, F. (2024). Digital transformation and social change: Leadership strategies for responsible innovation. *Journal of Engineering and Technology Management*, *74*, 101843. DOI: 10.1016/j.jengtecman.2024.101843

Burgelman, R. A., Christensen, C. M., & Wheelwright, S. C. (2008). *Strategic management of technology and innovation*. McGraw-Hill/Irwin.

Cambridge University Press. (2018). *Sharing economy*. https://dictionary.cambridge.org/dictionary/english/sharing-economy

Cameron, F., & Kenderdine, S. (Eds.). (2007). *Theorizing Digital Cultural Heritage: A Critical Discourse*. MIT Press. DOI: 10.7551/mitpress/9780262033534.001.0001

Campos, C. R., Nakano, T. D. C., & Ribeiro, W. D. J. (2014). Criatividade e Inovação : uma revisão da produção científica no Brasil. *Revista Faculdades Do Saber,* 168–179.

Caniëls, M. C., Hatak, I., Kuijpers, K. J., & de Weerd-Nederhof, P. C. (2022). Trait resilience instigates innovative behaviour at work? A cross-lagged study. *Creativity and Innovation Management*, *31*(2), 274–293. DOI: 10.1111/caim.12486

Carberry, E. J., Bharati, P., Levy, D. L., & Chaudhury, A. (2019). Social movements as catalysts for corporate social innovation: Environmental activism and the adoption of green information systems. *Business & Society*, *58*(5), 1083–1127. DOI: 10.1177/0007650317701674

Castro-Arce, K., & Vanclay, F. (2020). Transformative social innovation for sustainable rural development: An analytical framework to assist community-based initiatives. *Journal of Rural Studies*, *74*, 45–54. DOI: 10.1016/j.jrurstud.2019.11.010

Caulier-Grice, J. (2012). Defining social innovation. *A Deliverable of the Project: The Theoretical, Empirical and Policy Foundations for Building Social Innovation in Europe (TEPSIE), European Commission 7th Framework Programme/European Commission, DG Research, 18.*

Černe, M., Jaklič, M., & Škerlavaj, M. (2013). Authentic leadership, creativity, and innovation: A multilevel perspective. *Leadership*, *9*(1), 63–85. DOI: 10.1177/1742715012455130

Chang, H., & Sokol, D. D. (2022). How incumbents respond to competition from innovative disruptors in the sharing economy—The impact of Airbnb on hotel performance. *Strategic Management Journal*, *43*(3), 425–446. DOI: 10.1002/smj.3201

Chan, J. K. H., & Xiang, W. N. (2022). Fifty years after the wicked-problems conception: Its practical and theoretical impacts on planning and design. *Socio-Ecological Practice Research, 4*(1), 1–6. DOI: 10.1007/s42532-022-00106-w PMID: 35308020

Chesbrough, H. (2007). Business model innovation: It's not just about technology anymore. *Strategy and Leadership, 35*(6), 12–17. DOI: 10.1108/10878570710833714

Chun, W. H. K. (2008). The Enduring Ephemeral, or the Future Is a Memory. *Critical Inquiry, 35*(1), 148–171. DOI: 10.1086/595632

Ciasullo, M. V., Troisi, O., Grimaldi, M., & Leone, D. (2020). Multi-level governance for sustainable innovation in smart communities: An ecosystems approach. *The International Entrepreneurship and Management Journal, 16*(4), 1167–1195. DOI: 10.1007/s11365-020-00641-6

Cillo, V., Rialti, R., Bertoldi, B., & Ciampi, F. (2021). Knowledge management and open innovation in the digital age: A systematic literature review. *Journal of Business Research, 129*, 660–673.

Ciraso-Calí, A., Pineda-Herrero, P., Quesada-Pallarès, C., & Janer-Hidalgo, À. (2015). *Training for innovation in Spain*. European Lifelong Learning Magazine.

Ciulla, J. B. (2020). Ethics and effectiveness: The nature of good leadership. In *The search for ethics in leadership, business, and beyond* (pp. 3–32). Springer. DOI: 10.1007/978-3-030-38463-0_1

Ciulli, F., & Kolk, A. (2019). Incumbents and business model innovation for the sharing economy: Implications for sustainability. *Journal of Cleaner Production, 214*, 995–1010. DOI: 10.1016/j.jclepro.2018.12.295

Clydesdale, G. (2006). Creativity and competition: The beatles. *Creativity Research Journal, 18*(2), 129–139. DOI: 10.1207/s15326934crj1802_1

Cockayne, D. G. (2016). Sharing and neoliberal discourse: The economic function of sharing in the digital on-demand economy. *Geoforum, 77*, 73–82. DOI: 10.1016/j.geoforum.2016.10.005

Codagnone, C., & Martens, B. (2016). Scoping the sharing economy: Origins, definitions, impact and regulatory issues. *Scoping the Sharing Economy: Origins, Definitions, Impact and Regulatory Issues. Institute for Prospective Technological Studies Digital Economy Working Paper, 1.*

Cohen, B., & Muñoz, P. (2016). Sharing cities and sustainable consumption and production: Towards an integrated framework. *Journal of Cleaner Production, 134, Part A*, 87–97. DOI: 10.1016/j.jclepro.2015.07.133

Cohen, B., & Kietzmann, J. (2014). Ride On! Mobility Business Models for the Sharing Economy. *Organization & Environment*, *27*(3), 279–296. DOI: 10.1177/1086026614546199

Çokpekin, Ö., & Knudsen, M. P. (2012). Does Organizing for Creativity Really Lead to Innovation? *Creativity and Innovation Management*, *21*(3), 304–314. DOI: 10.1111/j.1467-8691.2012.00649.x

Collins, M. (2024). Chat: Creativity, innovation & sustainability. https://chatmtc.com/c/cb7jq1fx177hmxzzqvwfo7nl

Crawford, K. (2021). *Atlas of AI: Power, Politics, and the Planetary Costs of Artificial Intelligence*. Yale University Press.

Creative Denmark. (2023). Creativity as a driver for green transition. https://www.creativedenmark.com

Creative Denmark. (2025). Creativity as a driver for sustainability. https://www.creativedenmark.com/in-focus/creativity-as-a-driver-for-sustainability

Cropley, A. (2006). Creativity: A social approach. *Roeper Review*, *28*(3), 125–130. DOI: 10.1080/02783190609554351

Csikszentmihalyi, M. (2014). The systems model of creativity and its applications. *The Wiley Handbook of Genius*, 533–545. DOI: 10.1002/9781118367377.ch25

Csikszentmihalyi, M., & Csikszentmihalyi, M. (2014). Creativity and genius: A systems perspective. *The Systems Model of Creativity: The Collected Works of Mihaly Csikszentmihalyi*, 99–125.

Csikszentmihalyi, M. (1996). *Creativity: Flow and the psychology of discovery and invention*. HarperCollins.

Csikszentmihalyi, M. (2014). Society, Culture, and Person: A Systems View of Creativity. In Csikszentmihalyi, M. (Ed.), *The Systems Model of Creativity: The Collected Works of Mihaly Csikszentmihalyi* (pp. 47–61). Springer Netherlands. DOI: 10.1007/978-94-017-9085-7_4

Cusumano, M., Kahl, S., & Suarez, F. F. (2006). Product, process, and service: A new industry lifecycle model. *A Research and Education Initiative at the MIT, Sloan School of Management, Working Paper No, 228.*

d'Amato, A., Murugavel, V., Medeiros, K., & Watts, L. L. (2024). An ethical leadership assessment center pilot: Assessing and developing moral person and moral manager dimensions. *Industrial and Organizational Psychology: Perspectives on Science and Practice*, *17*(2), 233–251. DOI: 10.1017/iop.2024.7

Daft, R. L., & Armstrong, A. (2021). *Organization theory and design*. Cengage Canada.

Damanpour, F., & Evan, W. (1984). Organizational innovation and performance: The problem of organizational lag. *Administrative Science Quarterly*, *29*(3), 392–409. DOI: 10.2307/2393031

Danish Government. (2020). A green and sustainable world: The Danish Government's long-term strategy for global climate action. https://um.dk/en/foreign-policy/green-diplomacy

Darna, N., Setiawan, I., Basari, M. A., & Kasman, K. (2024). Smart strategy in statistics: Choosing appropriate test tools for data and hypotheses in quantitative research. *JPPI*, *10*(2), 843–851.

Davidson, A., Habibi, M. R., & Laroche, M. (2018). Materialism and the sharing economy: A cross-cultural study of American and Indian consumers. *Journal of Business Research*, *82*, 364–372. DOI: 10.1016/j.jbusres.2015.07.045

De las Heras, A., Relinque-Medina, F., Zamora-Polo, F., & Luque-Sendra, A. (2021). Analysis of the evolution of the sharing economy towards sustainability. Trends and transformations of the concept. *Journal of Cleaner Production*, *291*, 125227. DOI: 10.1016/j.jclepro.2020.125227

De Maria, C. (2019). The UBORA E-infrastructure for open-source innovation in medical technology. In *Proceedings of the Mediterranean Conference on Medical and Biological Engineering and Computing*. Cham: Springer.

De Vasconcellos, S. L., Parente, R. C., Schotter, A. P., Garrido, I. L., & Goncalo, C. R. (2024). Organizational creativity: A microfoundation of the international business competence and performance link. *Journal of International Management*, *30*(6), 101203. DOI: 10.1016/j.intman.2024.101203

Debebe, T. S. (2024). Sustainable Development Effect on Organizational Networks. *Integrating Organizational Theories With Sustainable Development*, 203.

Dehnbostel, P. (2003). Informelles Lernen: Arbeitserfahrungen und Kompetenzerwerb aus berufspädagogischer Sicht. Überarbeiteter Vortrag, 4. Fachtagung „Schule – Wirtschaft/Arbeitsleben", Neukirchen/Pleiße. http://swa-programm.de/termine/tagungen/neukirchen/vortrag_dehnbostel.pdf

Dehnbostel, P., & Pätzold, G. (2004). Innovationen und Tendenzen der betrieblichen Berufsbildung. In Dehnbostel, P., & Pätzold, G. (Eds.), *Lernförderliche Arbeitsgestaltung und die Neuorientierung betrieblicher Bildungsarbeit* (pp. 19–30). Franz Steiner.

Deinert, B., & Breßler, J. (2016). Knowledge-based activities of innovation managers: An empirical analysis. In *Proceedings of the 11th IFKAD International Forum on Knowledge Asset Dynamics* (pp. 2171–2185). Dresden.

Demary, V. (2015). *Competition in the sharing economy* (IW Policy Paper 19/2015). Institut der deutschen Wirtschaft Köln. http://hdl.handle.net/10419/112778

Deng, C., Gulseren, D., Isola, C., Grocutt, K., & Turner, N. (2023). Transformational leadership effectiveness: An evidence-based primer. *Human Resource Development International, 26*(5), 627–641. DOI: 10.1080/13678868.2022.2135938

Denning, S. (2005). Transformational innovation: A journey by narrative. *Strategy and Leadership, 33*(3), 11–16. DOI: 10.1108/10878570510700119

Dessein, J., Soini, K., Fairclough, G., & Horlings, L. (2015). *Culture in, for and as sustainable development.* European Union/University of Jyväskylä.

Desta, T. (2024). *Reporting Conflicts, Humanitarian Crises and Peace Processes: Cases from Africa.* Cambridge Scholars Publishing.

Destine, S. L. (2023). The importance of intersectionality in evaluating the surveillance and protest politics of the Movement for Black Lives (M4BL). In Research Handbook on Law, Movements and Social Change (pp. 254-267). Edward Elgar Publishing.

Dewey, J. (2005). *Art as Experience* (Neuauflage). New York: Penguin.

Diamandis, P. (2014, September 8). *Uber vs. The Law (My Money's on Uber).* Forbes. https://www.forbes.com/sites/peterdiamandis/2014/09/08/uber-vs-the-law-my-moneys-on-uber/

Dobusch, L. (2019). Dynamiken der'Sharing Economy'zwischen Commons und Kommodifizierung. *Momentum Quarterly-Zeitschrift Für Sozialen Fortschritt, 8*(2), 109–115. DOI: 10.15203/momentumquarterly.vol8.no2.p109-115

Dolejšová, M., Ampatzidou, C., Houston, L., Light, A., Botero, A., Choi, J., Wilde, D., Altarriba Altarriba Bertran, F., Davis, H., & Gonzales Gonzales Gil, F. (2021). Designing for transformative futures: creative practice, social change and climate emergency. *Proceedings of the 13th Conference on Creativity and Cognition*, 1–9.

Dostie, B. (2015). Who benefits from firm-sponsored training? *IZA World of Labor: Evidence-Based Policy Making*, 145.

Douglas, J., Alisauskas, A., Bassett, E., Duranseaud, N., Lee, T., & Mantey, C. (2022). 'These are not just pieces of paper': Acknowledging grief and other emotions in pursuit of person-centered archives. *Archives & Manuscripts*, *50*(1), 5–29. DOI: 10.37683/asa.v50.10211

Dreier, I., & Vinding, A. L. (2007). Searching near and far: Determinants of innovative firms' propensity to collaborate. *Industry and Innovation*, *14*(3), 259–275. DOI: 10.1080/13662710701369205

Dreier, L., Nabarro, D., & Nelson, J. (2019). *Systems leadership for sustainable development: strategies for achieving systemic change*. Harvard Kennedy School.

Driver, J. (2012). *Consequentialism*. Routledge.

Drucker, J. (2009). *SpecLab: Digital Aesthetics and Projects in Speculative Computing*. University of Chicago Press. DOI: 10.7208/chicago/9780226165097.001.0001

Eaton, L., Bridgman, T., & Cummings, S. (2024). Advancing the democratization of work: A new intellectual history of transformational leadership theory. *Leadership*, *20*(3), 125–143. DOI: 10.1177/17427150241232705

Ebers, M. (2017). Organisationsmodelle für Innovation. *Schmalenbachs Zeitschrift fur Betriebswirtschaftliche Forschung = Schmalenbach Journal of Business Research*, *69*(1), 81–109. DOI: 10.1007/s41471-016-0021-x

Ebrahim, A., & Rangan, V. K. (2014). What impact? Framework for measuring the scale and scope of social performance. *California Management Review*, *56*(3), 118–141. DOI: 10.1525/cmr.2014.56.3.118

Edmondson, A. C. (2023). *Right kind of wrong: The science of failing well*. Simon and Schuster.

Edwards, J. (2013, May 27). *Why Hotel Industry Lobbyists Want A Global Crackdown On Airbnb*. Business Insider. https://www.businessinsider.com/why-hotel-industry-lobbyists-want-a-global-crackdown-on-airbnb-2013-5

Egri, C. P., & Herman, S. (2000). Leadership in the North American environmental sector: Values, leadership styles, and contexts of environmental leaders and their organizations. *Academy of Management Journal*, *43*(4), 571–604. DOI: 10.2307/1556356

Eichler, G. M., & Schwarz, E. J. (2019). What sustainable development goals do social innovations address? A systematic review and content analysis of social innovation literature. *Sustainability (Basel)*, *11*(2), 522. DOI: 10.3390/su11020522

Eisenhardt, K. M. (1989). Building theories from case study research. *Academy of Management Review*, *14*(4), 532–550. DOI: 10.2307/258557

Elgammal, A., Liu, B., Elhoseiny, M., & Mazzone, M. (2017). CAN: Creative adversarial networks, generating "art" by learning about styles and deviating from style norms. *arXiv preprint arXiv:1706.07068.* https://arxiv.org/abs/1706.07068

Engeström, Y. (2001). Expansive learning at work: Toward an activity-theoretical reconceptualization. *Journal of Education and Work, 14*(1), 133–156. DOI: 10.1080/13639080020028747

Ertz, M., Maravilla, J. M. B., & Cao, X. (2025). Prosumer: A new approach to conceptualisation. *Journal of Innovation & Knowledge, 10*(1), 100653. DOI: 10.1016/j.jik.2025.100653

Euler, D. (2004). Bildungsmanagement. In Dubs, R., Euler, D., Rüegg-Stürm, J., & Wyss, C. E. (Eds.), *Einführung in die Managementlehre* – (Vol. 4, pp. 31–57). Haupt.

Europa Regina. (2024). Denmark creative industries. https://europaregina.eu

Evans, S., Vladimirova, D., Holgado, M., Fossen, K. V., Yang, M., Silva, E. A., & Barlow, C. Y. (2017). Business Model Innovation for Sustainability: Towards a Unified Perspective for Creation of Sustainable Business Models. *Business Strategy and the Environment, 26*(5), 597–608. DOI: 10.1002/bse.1939

Fargnoli, M., Testa, F., Boiral, O., & Iraldo, F. (2019). The role of design in sustainability transitions: Contributions and research agenda. *Journal of Cleaner Production, 231*, 1145–1158. DOI: 10.1016/j.jclepro.2019.05.286

Farida, I., & Setiawan, D. (2022). Business strategies and competitive advantage: The role of performance and innovation. *Journal of Open Innovation, 8*(3), 163. DOI: 10.3390/joitmc8030163

Farinha, L., Sebastião, J. R., Sampaio, C., & Lopes, J. (2020). Social innovation and social entrepreneurship: Discovering origins, exploring current and future trends. *International Review on Public and Nonprofit Marketing, 17*(1), 77–96. DOI: 10.1007/s12208-020-00243-6

Farr, J. L., & Ford, C. M. (1990). *Individual innovation.* Academic Press.

Faulks, B., Song, Y., Waiganjo, M., Obrenovic, B., & Godinic, D. (2021). Impact of empowering leadership, innovative work, and organizational learning readiness on sustainable economic performance: An empirical study of companies in Russia during the COVID-19 pandemic. *Sustainability (Basel), 13*(22), 12465. DOI: 10.3390/su132212465

Feeney, M. (2014, August 6). *How the Sharing Economy Can Help Developing Nations*. Cato Institute. https://www.cato.org/blog/how-sharing-economy-can-help-developing-nations

Fehr, A., & Twork, S. (2009). Gesellschaftliche Konstruktion von (Un-)Sicherheit. In Böhle, F., & Weihrich, M. (Eds.), *Handeln unter Unsicherheit* (pp. 33–46). VS Verlag.

Felson, M., & Spaeth, J. L. (1978). Community structure and collaborative consumption: A routine activity approach. *The American Behavioral Scientist, 21*(4), 614–624. DOI: 10.1177/000276427802100411

Fichter, K. (2005). *Interpreneurship: Nachhaltigkeitsinnovationen in interaktiven Perspektiven eines vernetzenden Unternehmertums*. Metropolis-Verlag. DOI: 10.14512/oew.v20i2.389

Fichter, K. (2009). *Interaktionsökonomik. Borderstep-Diskussionspapier (1/2009)*. Borderstep Institut.

Fichter, K. (2014). Interaktive Innovationstheorien als alternative „Schule" der Innovationsforschung. In Burr, W. (Ed.), *Innovation: Theorien, Konzepte und Methoden der Innovationsforschung* (pp. 61–94). Kohlhammer.

Fichter, K., & Hintemann, R. (2014). *Grundlagen des Innovationsmanagements*. Carl von Ossietzky Universität.

Fields, Z. (2016). Using creativity and social innovation to create social value and change. In *Incorporating business models and strategies into social entrepreneurship* (pp. 97–112). IGI Global Scientific Publishing. DOI: 10.4018/978-1-4666-8748-6.ch006

Fischer, G. (2004). Social creativity: turning barriers into opportunities for collaborative design. *Proceedings of the Eighth Conference on Participatory Design: Artful Integration: Interweaving Media, Materials and Practices-Volume 1*, 152–161. DOI: 10.1145/1011870.1011889

Fischer, G. (2013). Learning, social creativity, and cultures of participation. In *Learning and Collective Creativity* (pp. 198–215). Routledge.

Fischer, G., Giaccardi, E., Eden, H., Sugimoto, M., & Ye, Y. (2005). Beyond binary choices: Integrating individual and social creativity. *International Journal of Human-Computer Studies, 63*(4–5), 482–512. DOI: 10.1016/j.ijhcs.2005.04.014

Fischer, G., Scharff, E., & Ye, Y. (2004). *Fostering social creativity by increasing social capital. Social Capital and Information Technology*. MIT Press.

Fischer, T., Dietz, J., & Antonakis, J. (2017). Leadership process models: A review and synthesis. *Journal of Management, 43*(6), 1726–1753. DOI: 10.1177/0149206316682830

Fitzmaurice, C. J., Ladegaard, I., Attwood-Charles, W., Cansoy, M., Carfagna, L. B., Schor, J. B., & Wengronowitz, R. (2020). Domesticating the market: Moral exchange and the sharing economy. *Socio-economic Review, 18*(1), 81–102. DOI: 10.1093/ser/mwy003

Floridi, L., & Cowls, J. (2019). A unified framework of five principles for AI in society. *Harvard Data Science Review, 1*(1), 1–15. DOI: 10.1162/99608f92.8cd550d1

Floridi, L., & Taddeo, M. (2016). What is data ethics? *Philosophical Transactions. Series A, Mathematical, Physical, and Engineering Sciences, 374*(2083), 20160360. DOI: 10.1098/rsta.2016.0360 PMID: 28336805

Fluellen, J. E. (2011). *Creating a nation of innovators*. Learning & Brain Conference.

Förster, T. (2023). Imagining Together: The Social Dimension of Imagination. In *In Tandem–Pathways towards a Postcolonial Anthropology| Im Tandem–Wege zu einer postkolonialen Ethnologie* (pp. 231–258). Springer Fachmedien Wiesbaden. DOI: 10.1007/978-3-658-38673-3_13

Fraiberger, S. P., & Sundararajan, A. (2015). *Peer-to-Peer Rental Markets in the Sharing Economy* (Working Paper 15–19). NET Institute. https://econpapers.repec.org/paper/netwpaper/1519.htm

Franken, R., & Franken, S. (2011). *Integriertes Wissens- und Innovationsmanagement: Mit Fallstudien und Beispielen aus der Unternehmenspraxis*. Gabler. DOI: 10.1007/978-3-8349-6724-4

Frederico, R., & Amorim, M. C. S. (2008). Criatividade, inovação e controle nas organizações. *Revista de Ciências Humanas, 42*(1-2), 75–89.

Frenken, K., & Schor, J. (2017). Putting the sharing economy into perspective. *Environmental Innovation and Societal Transitions, 23*, 3–10. DOI: 10.1016/j.eist.2017.01.003

Fry, L. W., & Egel, E. (2021). Global leadership for sustainability. *Sustainability (Basel), 13*(11), 6360. DOI: 10.3390/su13116360

Gann, D. M., & Salter, A. J. (2000). Innovation in project-based, service-enhanced firms: The construction of complex products and systems. *Research Policy, 29*(7-8), 955–972. DOI: 10.1016/S0048-7333(00)00114-1

Gärtner, C. (2007). *Innovationsmanagement als soziale Praxis: Grundlagentheoretische Vorarbeiten zu einer Organisationstheorie des Neuen.* Rainer Hampp.

Garud, R., Tuertscher, P., & Van de Ven, A. H. (2017). Perspectives on innovation processes. *The Academy of Management Annals, 7*(1), 775–819. DOI: 10.5465/19416520.2013.791066

Gassmann, O. (2006). Innovation und Risiko – zwei Seiten einer Medaille. In Gassmann, O., & Kobe, C. (Eds.), *Management von Innovation und Risiko* (2nd ed., pp. 3–24). Springer. DOI: 10.1007/3-540-33755-5_1

Gaut, B. (2010). The philosophy of creativity. *Philosophy Compass, 5*(12), 1034–1046. DOI: 10.1111/j.1747-9991.2010.00351.x

Gede, D. U. (2024). Nexus between Reward System, Employee Commitment and Organizational Performance. *Horn of African Journal of Business and Economics, 7*(2), 93–109.

Geels, F. W. (2004). Understanding system innovations: A critical literature review and conceptual synthesis. In Elzen, B., Geels, F. W., & Green, K. (Eds.), *System Innovation and the Transition to Sustainability* (pp. 19–47). Edward Elgar. DOI: 10.4337/9781845423421.00012

Geissdoerfer, M., Savaget, P., Bocken, N. M., & Hultink, E. J. (2017). The Circular Economy – A new sustainability paradigm? *Journal of Cleaner Production, 143*, 757–768. DOI: 10.1016/j.jclepro.2016.12.048

Geissinger, A., Laurell, C., Öberg, C., Sandström, C., & Suseno, Y. (2021). The sharing economy and the transformation of work: Evidence from Foodora. *Personnel Review.*

Gergen, K. J. (2022). An invitation to social construction: Co-creating the future. Academic Press.

German Federal Government. (2025). Further development of the German Sustainability Strategy: Shaping transformation together and fairly. 2030 Agenda. https://www.2030agenda.de/de/article/weiterentwicklung-der-deutschen-nachhaltigkeitsstrategie-veroeffentlicht

Gerwe, O., & Silva, R. (2018). Clarifying the sharing economy: Conceptualization, typology, antecedents, and effects. *The Academy of Management Perspectives.* Advance online publication. DOI: 10.5465/amp.2017.0010

Giaccardi, E. (2004). Principles of Metadesign: Processes and Levels of Co-Creation in the New Design Space. *Leonardo Electronic Almanac, 12*(10).

Gilson, L. L. (2024). Why be creative: A review of the practical outcomes associated with creativity at the individual, group, and organizational levels. *Handbook of Organizational Creativity*, 303–322.

Glăveanu, V. P. (2020). A sociocultural theory of creativity: Bridging the social, the material, and the psychological. *Review of General Psychology, 24*(4), 335–354. DOI: 10.1177/1089268020961763

Glovinsky, S. (2017). Who values your knowledge? Why communities of practice and knowledge-sharing need each other. *Knowledge Management for Development Journal, 13*(3).

González, X., Miles-Touya, D., & Pazó, C. (2015). R&D, worker training and innovation: Firm-level evidence. *Universidad de Vigo Working Paper.*

Görög, G. (2018). The Definitions of Sharing Economy: A Systematic Literature Review. *Management, 13*(2).

Gregersen, B., & Johnson, B. (2021). The measurement and performance of the Danish innovation system in relation to sustainable development. In Christensen, J. L., Gregersen, B., Holm, J. R., & Lorenz, E. (Eds.), *Globalisation, new and emerging technologies, and sustainable development: The Danish innovation system in transition* (pp. 252–266). Routledge. DOI: 10.4324/9781003037750-18

Grieco, C. (2021). Innovating the innovated: Business model innovation process in sharing economy companies. *Creativity and Innovation Management, 30*(4), 860–871. DOI: 10.1111/caim.12457

Grojean, M. W., Resick, C. J., Dickson, M. W., & Smith, D. B. (2004). Leaders, values, and organizational climate: Examining leadership strategies for establishing an organizational climate regarding ethics. *Journal of Business Ethics, 55*(3), 223–241. DOI: 10.1007/s10551-004-1275-5

Gröschner, A. (2011). *Innovation als Lernaufgabe: Eine quantitativ-qualitative Studie zur Erfassung und Umsetzung von Innovationskompetenz in der Lehrerbildung*. Waxmann.

Grün, O. (2017). Entwicklung und Stand der deutschsprachigen betriebswirtschaftlichen Innovationsforschung. In Burr, W., & Stephan, M. (Eds.), *Technologie, Strategie und Organisation* (pp. 7–30). Gabler. DOI: 10.1007/978-3-658-16042-5_2

Gruszka, K. (2017). Framing the collaborative economy—Voices of contestation. *Environmental Innovation and Societal Transitions, 23*, 92–104. DOI: 10.1016/j.eist.2016.09.002

Guyer, P. (2012). *Kant on freedom, law, and happiness*. Cambridge University Press.

Habermas, J. (2003). *The future of human nature*. Polity Press.

Habibi, M. R. (2019). The Progression and Impact of the Sharing Economy; a Preface. *Journal of Marketing Theory and Practice*, *27*(4), 349–354. DOI: 10.1080/10696679.2019.1644959

Habibi, M. R., Davidson, A., & Laroche, M. (2017). What managers should know about the sharing economy. *Business Horizons*, *60*(1), 113–121. DOI: 10.1016/j.bushor.2016.09.007

Hallikas, J., Karkkainen, H., & Lampela, H. (2009). Learning in networks: An exploration from innovation perspective. *International Journal of Technology Management*, *45*(3-4), 229–243. DOI: 10.1504/IJTM.2009.022650

Hall, S. (1996). Cultural Identity and Diaspora. In Mongia, P. (Ed.), *Contemporary Postcolonial Theory: A Reader* (pp. 110–121). Arnold.

Hamari, J., Sjöklint, M., & Ukkonen, A. (2016). The sharing economy: Why people participate in collaborative consumption. *Journal of the Association for Information Science and Technology*, *67*(9), 2047–2059. DOI: 10.1002/asi.23552

Hansen, J., Hellin, J., Rosenstock, T., Fisher, E., Cairns, J., Stirling, C., Lamanna, C., van Etten, J., Rose, A., & Campbell, B. (2019). Climate risk management and rural poverty reduction. *Agricultural Systems, 172*, 28–46. DOI: 10.1016/j.agsy.2018.01.019

Hansen, J. A., & Pihl-Thingvad, S. (2019). Managing employee innovative behaviour through transformational and transactional leadership styles. *Public Management Review*, *21*(6), 918–944. DOI: 10.1080/14719037.2018.1544272

Hauschildt, J., & Salomo, S. (2011). Innovationsmanagement. 5., überarb., erg. U. Aktualis. *Aufl. München: Vahlen (Vahlens Handbücher Der Wirtschafts-Und Sozialwissenschaften).*

Hauschildt, J., & Salomo, S. (2011). *Innovationsmanagement* (5th ed.). Franz Vahlen.

Head, B. W. (2022). *Wicked problems in public policy: Understanding and responding to complex challenges*. Springer Nature. DOI: 10.1007/978-3-030-94580-0

Heeks, R., Foster, C., & Nugroho, Y. (2014). New models of inclusive innovation for development. *Innovation and Development*, *4*(2), 175–185. DOI: 10.1080/2157930X.2014.928982

Heinrichs, H., & Grunenberg, H. (2012). *Sharing Economy—Auf dem Weg in eine neue Konsumkultur?* https://nbn-resolving.org/urn:nbn:de:0168-ssoar-427486

Heiskanen, T., & Heiskanen, H. (2011). Spaces of innovation: Experiences from two small high-tech firms. *Journal of Workplace Learning*, *23*(2), 97–116. DOI: 10.1108/13665621111108774

Helpap, S., Bekmeier-Feuerhahn, S., & Pinkernelle, L. (2018). Ambivalenzen in organisationalen Veränderungen. *Schmalenbachs Zeitschrift fur Betriebswirtschaftliche Forschung = Schmalenbach Journal of Business Research*, *70*(3), 209–241. DOI: 10.1007/s41471-017-0043-z

Heman, O. U., Olabode, O. O., & Amram, A. (2024). Work Condition Factors and Employee Engagement: The Mediating Role of Psychological Capital. *Jurnal Manajemen Dan Kewirausahaan*, *26*(1), 1–12. DOI: 10.9744/jmk.26.1.1-12

Henning, H. N., Danyi, M. M., Park-Gaghan, T. J., & Mokher, C. G. (2025). What Does Organizational Culture Tell Us About Developmental Education Reform? Corequisite Implementation in Texas. *Innovative Higher Education*, 1–21. DOI: 10.1007/s10755-025-09787-z

Herrera, M. E. B. (2016). Social innovation for bridging societal divides: Process or leader? A qualitative comparative analysis. *Journal of Business Research*, *69*(11), 5241–5247. DOI: 10.1016/j.jbusres.2016.04.119

Herrmann-Fankhaenel, A., & Huesig, S. (2020). An Empirical Based View on the Sharing Economy in Germany: More Mainstream Economy than Collaborative Commons? *International Journal of Innovation and Technology Management*. DOI: 10.1142/S0219877020500315

Herrmann-Fankhaenel, A., & Huesig, S. (2022). *Development and Factors of Survival of (New) Business Ideas in the Online Sharing Economy*. 1–18.

Herrmann-Fankhaenel, A., & Schell, E. (2022). Sharing offline and for idealistic purposes in Germany. *International Journal Technology Management, 88*(2/3/4), 270–293.

Herrmann-Fankhaenel, A., & Huesig, S. (2016). How much social innovation is behind the online platforms of the sharing economy?: An exploratory investigation and educing of clusters in the German context. *2016 Portland International Conference on Management of Engineering and Technology (PICMET)*, 370–384. DOI: 10.1109/PICMET.2016.7806696

Heye, D. (2006). Creativity and innovation: Two key characteristics of the successful 21st century information professional. *Business Information Review*, *23*(4), 252–257. DOI: 10.1177/0266382106072255

Hipp, C. (2000). *Innovationsprozesse im Dienstleistungssektor: Eine theoretisch und empirisch basierte Innovationstypologie*. Physica. DOI: 10.1007/978-3-642-57662-1

Hjort, M. (2023). Aesthetic sustainability and creative practices. In Denmark, C. (Ed.), *Creativity as a driver for green transition* (pp. 38–41). https://www.creativedenmark.com

Hoffmann, A. (2007). *Interaktionen zwischen Anbietern und Nachfragern bei der Vermarktung und Beschaffung innovativer Dienstleistungen*. DUV.

Hofstad, H., Sørensen, E., Torfing, J., & Vedeld, T. (2022). Designing and leading collaborative urban climate governance: Comparative experiences of co-creation from Copenhagen and Oslo. *Environmental Policy and Governance*, *32*(3), 203–216. DOI: 10.1002/eet.1984

Hooß, K. (2014). *Wissenschaftliche Weiterbildung für IT-Wissensarbeit*. Springer. DOI: 10.1007/978-3-658-04786-3

Howaldt, J., Domanski, D., & Kaletka, C. (2016). Social innovation: Towards a new innovation paradigm. *RAM. Revista de Administração Mackenzie*, *17*(6), 20–44. DOI: 10.1590/1678-69712016/administracao.v17n6p20-44

Howaldt, J., & Schwarz, M. (2010). Soziale Innovation – Konzepte, Forschungsfelder und -perspektiven. In Howaldt, J., & Jacobsen, H. (Eds.), *Soziale Innovation* (pp. 87–108). VS. DOI: 10.1007/978-3-531-92469-4_5

Hughes, D. J., Lee, A., Tian, A. W., Newman, A., & Legood, A. (2018). Leadership, creativity, and innovation: A critical review and practical recommendations. *The Leadership Quarterly*, *29*(5), 549–569. DOI: 10.1016/j.leaqua.2018.03.001

Hui, K. L., & Chau, P. Y. (2002). Classifying digital products. *Communications of the ACM*, *45*(6), 73–79. DOI: 10.1145/508448.508451

Hund, A., Wagner, H.-T., Beimborn, D., & Weitzel, T. (2021). Digital innovation: Review and novel perspective. *The Journal of Strategic Information Systems*, *30*(4), 101695. DOI: 10.1016/j.jsis.2021.101695

Hursthouse, R. (1999). *On virtue ethics*. Oxford University Press.

Hüsig, S. (2006). *Institutionalisierte Vorentwicklung für radikale Innovationen-Dargestellt am Beispiel der Mannesmann Pilotentwicklung und der LKW-Mauttechnik*. WiKu.

Hüsig, S. (2014). A typology for radical innovation projects based on an innovativeness framework. *International Journal on Management of Innovation & Technology, 11*(4), 1450023. DOI: 10.1142/S0219877014500230

Hütter, M. (2016). *Marketinginnovationen: Empirische Studien zu Erfolgswirkung und Treibern*. Springer. DOI: 10.1007/978-3-658-13039-8

Hwang, S. Y. (2017). Rethinking creativity: Present in expression in creative learning communities*. *Educational Philosophy and Theory, 49*(3), 220–230. DOI: 10.1080/00131857.2016.1225559

Iqbal, Q., & Piwowar-Sulej, K. (2022). Sustainable leadership in higher education institutions: Social innovation as a mechanism. *International Journal of Sustainability in Higher Education, 23*(8), 1–20. DOI: 10.1108/IJSHE-04-2021-0162

IUCN. (2021). Rights-based approaches must be placed at the heart of conservation efforts. https://iucn.org/news/governance-and-rights/202112/rights-based-approaches-must-be-placed-heart-conservation-efforts

Jacobsen, H., Georg, A., & Jostmeier, M. (2011). Innovationsfähigkeit als Managementaufgabe: Welche organisationalen Strategien können Innovationsprozesse fördern? In Jeschke, S. (Eds.), *Enabling Innovation* (pp. 481–493). Springer. DOI: 10.1007/978-3-642-24299-1_44

Jacoby, B. (2023). Facing the unsettled questions about service-learning. In *The future of service-learning* (pp. 90–105). Routledge. DOI: 10.4324/9781003447825-8

Javed, B., Fatima, T., Khan, A. K., & Bashir, S. (2021). Impact of Inclusive Leadership on Innovative Work Behavior: The Role of Creative Self-Efficacy. *The Journal of Creative Behavior, 55*(3), 769–782. DOI: 10.1002/jocb.487

Jayaratne, T. E. (2024). The value of quantitative methodology for feminist research 1. In *Theories of women's studies* (pp. 140–161). Routledge. DOI: 10.4324/9781003516392-10

Jefferson, M., & Anderson, M. (2017). *Transforming schools: Creativity, critical reflection, communication, collaboration*. Bloomsbury Publishing.

Jeong, I., & Shin, S. J. (2019). High-performance work practices and organizational creativity during organizational change: A collective learning perspective. *Journal of Management, 45*(3), 909–925. DOI: 10.1177/0149206316685156

Jesus, T. (2024). COP 30: For climate action rooted in culture. https://peoplespalaceprojects.org.uk/en/cop-30-for-climate-action-rooted-in-culture/

Jiménez-Jiménez, D., & Sanz-Valle, R. (2011). Innovation, organizational learning and performance. *Journal of Business Research*, *64*(4), 408–417. DOI: 10.1016/j.jbusres.2010.09.010

Jio, W., Kant, S., & Lemi, K. (2025a). Ethical Leadership: Effect on Future of Organizational Citizenship Behavior by Mediation of Organizational Culture in Ethiopia. In *Generation Alpha and Next Generation Leadership for Greener Futures* (pp. 41–62). IGI Global Scientific Publishing.

Jio, W., Kant, S., & Lemi, K. (2025b). The Influence of Ethical Leadership on Organizational Citizenship Behavior by the Mediating Role of Organizational Commitment in Ethiopia. In *Humanizing the Hyperconnected Workplace* (pp. 221–248). IGI Global Scientific Publishing. DOI: 10.4018/979-8-3693-8171-7.ch008

Jones Christensen, L., Mackey, A., & Whetten, D. (2014). Taking responsibility for corporate social responsibility: The role of leaders in creating, implementing, sustaining, or avoiding socially responsible firm behaviors. *The Academy of Management Perspectives*, *28*(2), 164–178. DOI: 10.5465/amp.2012.0047

Jucevičienė, P. (2008). Educational and learning environments as a factor for socioeducational empowering of innovation. *Social Sciences*, *59*(1), 58–70.

Jung, K. B., Kang, S.-W., & Choi, S. B. (2020). Empowering leadership, risk-taking behavior, and employees' commitment to organizational change: The mediated moderating role of task complexity. *Sustainability (Basel)*, *12*(6), 2340. DOI: 10.3390/su12062340

Kaldewei, M., & Stummer, C. (2018). Der Einfluss der Produktintelligenz auf den Konsumentennutzen und die Produktnutzung. *Schmalenbachs Zeitschrift fur Betriebswirtschaftliche Forschung = Schmalenbach Journal of Business Research*, *70*(4), 315–349. DOI: 10.1007/s41471-018-0054-4

Kant, S., Niguse, T., Terefe, A., & Adula, M. (2025). Green Marketing Effect on the Growing Demand for Sustainable Products by Mediation of Consumer Behavior: Analysis in the Horn of Africa. In *Driving Business Success Through Eco-Friendly Strategies* (pp. 189-212). IGI Global Scientific Publishing.

Kant, S., Toma, F., Adula, M., & Niguse, T. (2025). Impact of Open Innovation on Competitive Advantage by Mediation of Crowdsourcing in SMEs of the Horn of Africa. In *Open Innovation Strategies for Effective Competitive Advantage* (pp. 123-148). DOI: 10.4018/979-8-3693-9266-9.ch005

Kant, I. (1997). *Groundwork for the metaphysics of morals* (Gregor, M. J., Trans.). Cambridge University Press. (Original work published 1785)

Karwowski, M., Jankowska, D. M., Brzeski, A., Czerwonka, M., Gajda, A., Lebuda, I., & Beghetto, R. A. (2020). Delving into Creativity and Learning. *Creativity Research Journal*, *32*(1), 4–16. DOI: 10.1080/10400419.2020.1712165

Katenkamp, O., & Georg, A. (2014). Strategien zur Innovationsfähigkeit – Kernelemente und offene Fragen. In Jostmeier, M., Georg, A., & Jacobsen, H. (Eds.), *Sozialen Wandel gestalten: Zum gesellschaftlichen Innovationspotenzial von Arbeits- und Organisationsforschung* (pp. 363–384). Springer. DOI: 10.1007/978-3-531-19298-7_25

Kaul, V., Shah, V. H., & El-Serag, H. (2020). Leadership during crisis: Lessons and applications from the COVID-19 pandemic. *Gastroenterology*, *159*(3), 809–812. DOI: 10.1053/j.gastro.2020.04.076 PMID: 32425233

Kayyali, M. (2024 B). Crisis Response and Higher Education: Social Innovations in Times of Global Challenges. In Social Innovations in Education, Environment, and Healthcare (pp. 1-17). IGI Global.

Kayyali, M. (2025a). Cross-Border and Cross-Industry Collaboration: Open Innovation Strategies for Effective Competitive Advantage. In Open Innovation Strategies for Effective Competitive Advantage (pp. 25-58). IGI Global Scientific Publishing.

Kayyali, M. (2025b). Understanding Innovation in Higher Education: Challenges and Future Directions. In Cultivating Creativity and Navigating Talent Management in Academia (pp. 117-138). IGI Global Scientific Publishing.

Kayyali, M. (2023). Promoting Entrepreneurship and Innovation in Higher Education. *Online Submission*, *2*(1), 1–26.

Kayyali, M. (2024). A). Career development in higher education: Best practices and innovations. In *Advancing student employability through higher education* (pp. 1–19). IGI Global. DOI: 10.4018/979-8-3693-0517-1.ch001

Kayyali, M. (2024). C). Design thinking and creativity in entrepreneurial innovation. In *Applying Business Intelligence and Innovation to Entrepreneurship* (pp. 155–170). IGI Global Scientific Publishing. DOI: 10.4018/979-8-3693-1846-1.ch008

Keller, K. (2008). *Netzbasiertes Lehren und Lernen in der betrieblichen Weiterbildung: Eine Fallstudie am Beispiel der Telekom*. Gabler.

Kenney, M., & Curry, J. (1999). e-commerce: Implications for firm strategy and industry Configuration. *Industry and Innovation*, *6*(2), 131–151. DOI: 10.1080/13662719900000008

Kenny, M., & Zysman, J. (2016). The Rise of the Platform Economy. *Issues in Science and Technology*, 61–69.

Khan, M. K., Sandano, I. A., Pratt, C. B., & Farid, T. (2018). China's Belt and Road Initiative: A global model for an evolving approach to sustainable regional development. *Sustainability (Basel), 10*(11), 4234. DOI: 10.3390/su10114234

Khedhaouria, A., Montani, F., & Thurik, R. (2017). Time pressure and team member creativity within R&D projects: The role of learning orientation and knowledge sourcing. *International Journal of Project Management, 35*(6), 942–954. DOI: 10.1016/j.ijproman.2017.04.002

Kimmel, M., Hristova, D., & Kussmaul, K. (2018). Sources of embodied creativity: Interactivity and ideation in contact improvisation. *Behavioral Sciences (Basel, Switzerland), 8*(6), 52. DOI: 10.3390/bs8060052 PMID: 29882858

Kiogora, D. M., & Moi, E. J. (2024). Influence of alternative justice system on resolution of disputes in Isiolo County, Kenya. *International Academic Journal of Arts and Humanities, 2*(1), 68–88.

Kiyota, M., & Kubo, H. (2016). A training method proposal for R&D project managers. In *Proceedings of the Portland International Conference on Management of Engineering and Technology (PICMET)*. IEEE. DOI: 10.1109/PICMET.2016.7806797

Kolasani, S. (2023). Leadership in business innovation and transformation, navigating complex digital landscapes and enterprise technology ecosystems and achieving sustainable growth in today's rapidly evolving market. *International Journal of Holistic Management Perspectives, 4*(4), 1–23.

Kolk, A., & Lenfant, F. (2015). Cross-sector collaboration, institutional gaps, and fragility: The role of social innovation partnerships in a conflict-affected region. *Journal of Public Policy & Marketing, 34*(2), 287–303. DOI: 10.1509/jppm.14.157

Koppl, R., Kauffman, S., Felin, T., & Longo, G. (2015). Economics for a creative world. In *Journal of Institutional Economics* (Vol. 11, Issue 1). DOI: 10.1017/S1744137414000150

Kornmeier, M. (2007). *Wissenschaftstheorie und wissenschaftliches Arbeiten: Eine Einführung für Wirtschaftswissenschaftler*. Springer-Verlag. DOI: 10.1007/978-3-7908-1919-9

Korsager, M., Reitan, B., Dahl, M. G., Skår, A. R., & Frøyland, M. (2024). The art of designing a professional development programme for teachers. *Professional Development in Education, 50*(6), 1286–1300. DOI: 10.1080/19415257.2022.2038234

Korsgaard, C. M. (2010). *The sources of normativity*. Cambridge University Press.

Kotter, J. P., Akhtar, V., & Gupta, G. (2025). *Change: How organizations achieve hard-to-imagine results in uncertain and volatile times*. John Wiley & Sons.

Kouyoumdjian, A. (2024). Rising Scholar: The Long-term Effects of Redlining on Climate Vulnerability and Food Insecurity. *International Social Science Review, 100*(4).

Kozinets, R. V., Hemetsberger, A., & Schau, H. J. (2008). The wisdom of consumer crowds: Collective innovation in the age of networked marketing. *Journal of Macromarketing, 28*(4), 339–354. DOI: 10.1177/0276146708325382

Krell, G. (2001). *Innovation unternehmensübergreifender Geschäftsprozesse in der japanischen Automobilindustrie*. Difo-Druck.

Kristjánsson, K. (2018). *Virtuous emotions*. Oxford University Press. DOI: 10.1093/oso/9780198809678.001.0001

Kumagai, A. K. (2022). Discomfort, doubt, and the edge of learning. *Academic Medicine, 97*(5), 649–654. DOI: 10.1097/ACM.0000000000004588 PMID: 35020611

Kumar, N., Yakhlef, A., & Nordin, F. (2019). Validation of organizational innovation as a creative learning process. *Journal of Business and Industrial Marketing, 34*(3), 643–650. DOI: 10.1108/JBIM-02-2017-0026

Kung, L.-C., & Zhong, G.-Y. (2017). The optimal pricing strategy for two-sided platform delivery in the sharing economy. *Transportation Research Part E, Logistics and Transportation Review, 101*, 1–12. DOI: 10.1016/j.tre.2017.02.003

Kurz, V., Hüsig, S., & Dowling, M. (2017). What drives different employee types of innovative behaviour? Development and test of an integrative model of employee-driven innovation in German firms. *International Journal of Entrepreneurship and Innovation Management, 21*, 1–21.

Kuzminska, A. O., Gasiorowska, A., Kasałka, O., Narkun, M., & Zaleskiewicz, T. (2025). The social currency of sharing economy: How monetary and nonmonetary interactions impact social capital. *Journal of Cleaner Production, 500*, 145238. DOI: 10.1016/j.jclepro.2025.145238

Kvadrat. (n.d.-a). About us – People and culture. Retrieved June 5, 2025, from https://www.kvadrat.dk/en/about/people-and-culture

Kvadrat. (n.d.-b). Sustainability. Retrieved June 5, 2025, from https://www.kvadrat.dk/en/sustainability

Kyprianou, C. (2018). Creating Value from the Outside In or the Inside Out: How Nascent Intermediaries Build Peer-to-Peer Marketplaces. *Academy of Management Discoveries*, *4*(3), 336–370. DOI: 10.5465/amd.2017.0081

Laamanen, M., Wahlen, S., & Campana, M. (2015). Mobilising collaborative consumption lifestyles: A comparative frame analysis of time banking. *International Journal of Consumer Studies*, *39*(5), 459–467. DOI: 10.1111/ijcs.12190

Lamnek, S. (1995). Qualitative Sozialforschung: Vol. 1. *Methodologie* (3rd ed.). Beltz.

Larraz-Rábanos, N. (2021). Development of creative thinking skills in the teaching-learning process. *Teacher Education-New Perspectives*, 307–322.

Latitude. (2015). *The New Sharing Economy Study Report*. Scribd. https://www.scribd.com/document/38788695/The-New-Sharing-Economy-Study-Report-by-Latitude-and-Shareable-Magazine

Lear, J. (2022). *Imagining the end: Mourning and ethical life*. Harvard University Press.

Lee, Y.-N., & Walsh, J. P. (2016). Inventing while you work: Knowledge, non-R&D learning and innovation. *Research Policy*, *45*(1), 345–359. DOI: 10.1016/j.respol.2015.09.009

Lemaine, G. (1974). Social differentiation and social originality. *European Journal of Social Psychology*, *4*(1), 17–52. DOI: 10.1002/ejsp.2420040103

Lemmetty, S. (2024). Real-time and long-term challenges of remote learning and innovation: Cases from police and technology organisations. *Vocations and Learning*, *17*(3), 565–587. DOI: 10.1007/s12186-024-09354-1

Lévesque, B. (2013). Social innovation in governance and public management systems: toward a new paradigm. *The International Handbook on Social Innovation*, 25–39.

Levine, A. S. (2024). *Collaborate Now!: How Expertise Becomes Useful in Civic Life*. Cambridge University Press. DOI: 10.1017/9781009411882

Li, C., Sun, L.-Y., & Dong, Y. (2018). Innovating via building absorptive capacity: Interactive effects of top management support of learning, employee learning orientation and decentralization structure. *Creativity and Innovation Management*, *27*(4), 431–443. DOI: 10.1111/caim.12261

Lin, H.-E., McDonough, E. F.III, Lin, S.-J., & Lin, C. Y.-Y. (2013). Managing the exploitation/exploration paradox: The role of a learning capability and innovation ambidexterity. *Journal of Product Innovation Management*, *30*(2), 262–278. DOI: 10.1111/j.1540-5885.2012.00998.x

Liu, B. F., Shi, D., Lim, J. R., Islam, K., Edwards, A. L., & Seeger, M. (2022). When crises hit home: How US higher education leaders navigate values during uncertain times. *Journal of Business Ethics*, *179*(2), 353–368. DOI: 10.1007/s10551-021-04820-5 PMID: 34002104

Liu, H. Y., Chang, C. C., Wang, I. T., & Chao, S. Y. (2020). The association between creativity, creative components of personality, and innovation among Taiwanese nursing students. *Thinking Skills and Creativity*, *35*(January), 100629. DOI: 10.1016/j.tsc.2020.100629

Liv, H., Xing, Z., Min, Y., & Liu, G. (2020). Everyone is Creative? Research on the Relationship Between the Work Orientation and Employee Creativity. *DEStech Transactions on Social Science, Education and Human Science,* 514–524. DOI: 10.12783/dtssehs/ssme2019/34817

Loseke, D. (2017). *Thinking about social problems: An introduction to constructionist perspectives*. Routledge. DOI: 10.4324/9781315135601

Lüders, C., & Reichertz, J. (1986). Wissenschaftliche Praxis ist, wenn alles funktioniert und keiner weiß warum – Bemerkungen zur Entwicklung qualitativer Sozialforschung. *Sozialwissenschaftliche Literatur Rundschau*, *12*, 90–102.

Lungstraß, R. (1976). *Der Zweckverband als Planungs- und Finanzinstrument neuer öffentlicher Aufgaben: Erläutert am Beispiel eines Abwasserzweckverbands in Nordrhein-Westfalen*. Westdeutscher. DOI: 10.1007/978-3-322-88586-9

Luo, X., Cheah, J.-H., Lim, X.-J., Ramayah, T., & Dwivedi, Y. K. (2025). Inducing shoppers' impulsive buying tendency in live-streaming: Integrating signaling theory with social exchange theory. *Internet Research*, *35*(1), 318–348. DOI: 10.1108/INTR-04-2023-0260

MacArthur, E. (2013). Towards the circular economy. *Journal of Industrial Ecology*, *2*, 23–44.

MacDonald, C. (2018). The Sharing Economy: The End of Employment and the Rise of Crowd-Based Capitalism. *Business Ethics Quarterly*, *28*(4), 501–505. DOI: 10.1017/beq.2018.31

Macharzina, K. (1970). *Interaktion und Organisation: Versuch einer Modellanalyse*. Universitätsbibliothek.

Machkour, B., & Abriane, A. (2025). The rise of artificial intelligence in educational management: A prospective analysis on the role of the virtual educational director. *Procedia Computer Science*, *257*, 1233–1238. DOI: 10.1016/j.procs.2025.03.165

MacIntyre, A. (2007). *After virtue: A study in moral theory* (3rd ed.). University of Notre Dame Press. (Original work published 1981)

MacVaugh, J., & Schiavone, F. (2010). Limits to the diffusion of innovation: A literature review and integrative model. *European Journal of Innovation Management, 13*(2), 197–221. DOI: 10.1108/14601061011040258

Malik, P. (2024). Individual-focused transformational leadership and change-oriented organizational citizenship behavior: Mediating and moderating mechanisms of job crafting and employee resilience. *Journal of Organizational Effectiveness: People and Performance, 11*(1), 90–113. DOI: 10.1108/JOEPP-05-2022-0120

Manovich, L. (2013). *Software Takes Command.* Bloomsbury. DOI: 10.5040/9781472544988

Manu, A. (2024). The Myth of the Creative Genius. In *Transcending Imagination* (pp. 119–131). Chapman and Hall/CRC. DOI: 10.1201/9781003450139-13

Manzini, E. (2015). *Design, when everybody designs: An introduction to design for social innovation.* MIT Press. DOI: 10.7551/mitpress/9873.001.0001

Margolis, A. (2024). Do All Roads Lead to Rome? How Three Process Pathways Contribute to Transformative Innovation in Cross-Sector Partnerships. *Business & Society*. Advance online publication. DOI: 10.1177/00076503241289929

Mariani, L., Trivellato, B., Martini, M., & Marafioti, E. (2022). Achieving sustainable development goals through collaborative innovation: Evidence from four European initiatives. *Journal of Business Ethics, 180*(4), 1075–1095. DOI: 10.1007/s10551-022-05193-z PMID: 35855697

Marion, T. J., & Fixson, S. K. (2021). The transformation of the innovation process: How digital tools are changing work, collaboration, and organizations in new product development. *Journal of Product Innovation Management, 38*(1), 192–215. DOI: 10.1111/jpim.12547

Markman, G. D., Lieberman, M., Leiblein, M., Wei, L., & Wang, Y. (2021). The distinctive domain of the sharing economy: Definitions, value creation, and implications for research. *Journal of Management Studies, 58*(4), 927–948. DOI: 10.1111/joms.12707

Marmo, L. (2024). An investigation into puppetry as sympoiesis in relation to Marta Cuscunà's work with reference to Staying with the Trouble by Donna Haraway. Academic Press.

Marquardt, M. (2020). *Optimizing the power of action learning: Real-time strategies for developing leaders, building teams and transforming organizations* (3rd ed.). Nicholas Brealey.

Martin, C. J. (2016). The sharing economy: A pathway to sustainability or a nightmarish form of neoliberal capitalism? *Ecological Economics, 121*(Supplement C), 149–159. DOI: 10.1016/j.ecolecon.2015.11.027

Martin, C. J., Upham, P., & Budd, L. (2015). Commercial orientation in grassroots social innovation: Insights from the sharing economy. *Ecological Economics, 118*(Supplement C), 240–251. DOI: 10.1016/j.ecolecon.2015.08.001

Martínez-Ros, E., & Orfila-Sintes, F. (2012). Training plans, manager's characteristics and innovation in the accommodation industry. *International Journal of Hospitality Management, 31*(3), 686–694. DOI: 10.1016/j.ijhm.2011.09.004

Mascareño, J., Rietzschel, E. F., & Wisse, B. (2021). Ambidextrous leadership: Opening and closing leader behaviours to facilitate idea generation, idea promotion and idea realization. *European Journal of Work and Organizational Psychology, 30*(4), 530–540. DOI: 10.1080/1359432X.2021.1872544

Massari, S., Galli, F., Mattioni, D., & Chiffoleau, Y. (2023). Co-creativity in living labs: Fostering creativity in co-creation processes to transform food systems. JCOM: Journal of Science Communications, 22(3).

Massey, G. (2021). Re-framing conceptual metaphor translation research in the age of neural machine translation: Investigating translators' added value with products and processes. Training. *Language and Culture, 5*(1), 37–56.

Matthews, K. E., Sherwood, C., Enright, E., & Cook-Sather, A. (2024). What do students and teachers talk about when they talk together about feedback and assessment? Expanding notions of feedback literacy through pedagogical partnership. *Assessment & Evaluation in Higher Education, 49*(1), 26–38. DOI: 10.1080/02602938.2023.2170977

Ma, X., & Jiang, W. (2018). Transformational leadership, transactional leadership, and employee creativity in entrepreneurial firms. *The Journal of Applied Behavioral Science, 54*(3), 302–324. DOI: 10.1177/0021886318764346

Mayring, P. (1990). *Einführung in die qualitative Sozialforschung*. Psychologie-Verlag-Union.

McGann, M., Wells, T., & Blomkamp, E. (2021). Innovation labs and co-production in public problem solving. *Public Management Review, 23*(2), 297–316. DOI: 10.1080/14719037.2019.1699946

McMillen, S. (2024). *Generational Differences in Perceived and Ideal Organizational Culture*. Point Park University.

Mendenhall, M. E. (2017). Leadership and the birth of global leadership. In *Global leadership* (pp. 3–27). Routledge. DOI: 10.4324/9781315232904-1

Mill, J. S. (2001). *Utilitarianism*. Hackett Publishing. (Original work published 1863)

Ministry of Foreign Affairs of Denmark. (2022). Sustainability strategy and implementation. https://um.dk

Ministry of Foreign Affairs of Denmark. (2024). Denmark: A creative toolbox. https://denmark.dk

Mohammed, S. M., & El-Ashram, R. E. (2025). The relationship between virtuous leadership and innovation management in the pharmaceutical companies of the public business sector–Egypt. *International Journal of Innovation Science*, *17*(1), 1–18. DOI: 10.1108/IJIS-11-2022-0212

Mokyr, J. (2018). *A culture of growth: The origins of the modern economy*. Princeton University Press.

Mongelli, L., & Rullani, F. (2017). Inequality and marginalisation: social innovation, social entrepreneurship and business model innovation: The common thread of the DRUID Summer Conference 2015. *Industry and Innovation*, *24*(5), 446–467. DOI: 10.1080/13662716.2017.1295365

Moran, S. (2010). The roles of creativity in society. *The Cambridge Handbook of Creativity*, 74–90.

Morewedge, C. K., Monga, A., Palmatier, R. W., Shu, S. B., & Small, D. A. (2021). Evolution of consumption: A psychological ownership framework. *Journal of Marketing*, *85*(1), 196–218. DOI: 10.1177/0022242920957007

Morozov, E. (2013, October 14). The 'sharing economy' undermines workers' rights. *Financial Times*.

Morris, M. H., Santos, S. C., & Kuratko, D. F. (2021). The great divides in social entrepreneurship and where they lead us. *Small Business Economics*, *57*(3), 1089–1106. DOI: 10.1007/s11187-020-00318-y

Mørup, M., & Hansen, L. K. (2012). Archetypal analysis for machine learning and data mining. *Neurocomputing*, *80*, 54–63. DOI: 10.1016/j.neucom.2011.06.033

Mostafa, M. (2012). Factors affecting organisational creativity and innovativeness in Egyptian business organisations: An empirical investigation. *Journal of Management Development, 24*(1), 7–33. DOI: 10.1108/02621710510572326

Muehlemann, S. (2025). Artificial intelligence adoption and workplace training. *Journal of Economic Behavior & Organization, 238*, 107206. DOI: 10.1016/j.jebo.2025.107206

Mukherjee, A. S. (2020). *Leading in the digital world: How to foster creativity, collaboration, and inclusivity.* MIT Press. DOI: 10.7551/mitpress/12584.001.0001

Mulgan, G., Tucker, S., Ali, R., & Sanders, B. (2007). *Social Innovation: What it is, why it matters and how it can be accelerated* [Other Working Paper]. https://eureka.sbs.ox.ac.uk/761/

Mulgan, G. (2006). The process of social innovation. *Innovations: Technology, Governance, Globalization, 1*(2), 145–162. DOI: 10.1162/itgg.2006.1.2.145

Mulgan, G. (2019). *Social innovation: How societies find the power to change.* Policy Press.

Mumford, M. D., Mulhearn, T. J., Watts, L. L., Steele, L. M., & McIntosh, T. (2017). Leader Impacts on Creative Teams. *Team Creativity and Innovation*, 131.

Mumford, M. D., Steele, L. M., Mulhearn, T. J., McIntosh, T., & Watts, L. L. (2017). Leader planning skills and creative performance: Integration of past, present, and future. In *Handbook of research on leadership and creativity*. Edward Elgar Publishing. DOI: 10.4337/9781784715465.00009

Muñoz, P., & Cohen, B. (2017). Mapping out the sharing economy: A configurational approach to sharing business modeling. *Technological Forecasting and Social Change, 125*(Supplement C), 21–37. DOI: 10.1016/j.techfore.2017.03.035

Muñoz, P., & Cohen, B. (2018). A compass for navigating sharing economy business models. *California Management Review, 61*(1), 114–147. DOI: 10.1177/0008125618795490

Murillo, D., Buckland, H., & Val, E. (2017). When the sharing economy becomes neoliberalism on steroids: Unravelling the controversies. *Technological Forecasting and Social Change, 125*(Supplement C), 66–76. DOI: 10.1016/j.techfore.2017.05.024

Murray, R. (2010). *The open book of social innovation.* National Endowment for Science, Technology and the Art.

Nakano, T. de C., & Wechsler, S. M. (2018). Creativity and innovation: Skills for the 21st Century. *Estudos de Psicologia (Campinas)*, *35*(3), 237–246. DOI: 10.1590/1982-02752018000300002

Nani, D. A., & Safitri, V. A. D. (2021). Exploring the relationship between formal management control systems, organisational performance and innovation: The role of leadership characteristics. *Asian Journal of Business and Accounting*, *14*(1), 207–224. DOI: 10.22452/ajba.vol14no1.8

Nash, A. (2015). On the Sharing Economy. *Contexts*, *14*(1), 12–19. DOI: 10.1177/1536504214567860

Nehamas, A. (1987). *Nietzsche: Life as literature*. Harvard University Press.

Netto, C. de O., & Tello-Gamarra, J. E. (2020). Sharing Economy: A Bibliometric Analysis. *Research Trends and Research Agenda.*, *15*(2), 16.

New Zero World. (2024). A new era in climate communications – White paper. https://newzeroworld.org

Newman, J., Mintrom, M., & O'Neill, D. (2022). Digital technologies, artificial intelligence, and bureaucratic transformation. *Futures*, *136*, 102886. DOI: 10.1016/j.futures.2021.102886

Newstead, T., Dawkins, S., Macklin, R., & Martin, A. (2020). The virtues project: An approach to developing good leaders. *Journal of Business Ethics*, *167*(4), 605–622. DOI: 10.1007/s10551-019-04163-2

Nietzsche, F. (1966). *Beyond good and evil: Prelude to a philosophy of the future* (W. Kaufmann, Trans.). Vintage Books. (Original work published 1886).

Nietzsche, F. (2005). *Thus spoke Zarathustra: A book for all and none* (G. Parkes, Trans.). Oxford University Press. (Original work published 1883).

Nietzsche, F. (2007). *On the genealogy of morals* (Johnston, I., Trans.). Dover Publications. (Original work published 1887)

Nisula, A.-M., Blomqvist, K., Bergman, J.-P., & Yrjölä, S. (2022). Organizing for knowledge creation in a strategic interorganizational innovation project. *International Journal of Project Management*, *40*(4), 398–410. DOI: 10.1016/j.ijproman.2022.03.011

Noble, S. U. (2018). *Algorithms of Oppression: How Search Engines Reinforce Racism*. NYU Press. DOI: 10.18574/nyu/9781479833641.001.0001

Nochlin, L. (1989). *The politics of vision: Essays on nineteenth-century art and society*. Harper & Row.

Nonaka, I., & Konno, N. (1998). The concept of "Ba": Building a foundation for creating knowledge. *California Management Review, 40*(3), 40–54. DOI: 10.2307/41165942

Nonaka, I., & Takeuchi, H. (1995). *The knowledge-creating company: How Japanese companies create the dynamics of innovation*. Oxford University Press. DOI: 10.1093/oso/9780195092691.001.0001

Nonaka, I., & Toyama, R. (2003). The knowledge-creating theory revisited: Knowledge creation as a synthesizing process. *Knowledge Management Research and Practice, 1*(1), 2–10. DOI: 10.1057/palgrave.kmrp.8500001

Nonaka, I., Toyama, R., & Konno, N. (2000). SECI, Ba and leadership: A unified model of dynamic knowledge creation. *Long Range Planning, 33*(1), 5–34. DOI: 10.1016/S0024-6301(99)00115-6

Notz, G. (2010). *Theorien alternativen Wirtschaftens: Fenster in eine andere Welt* (1st ed.). Schmetterling Stuttgart.

O'Connor, G. C. (2008). Major innovation as a dynamic capability: A systems approach. *Journal of Product Innovation Management, 25*(4), 313–330. DOI: 10.1111/j.1540-5885.2008.00304.x

O'Neil, C. (2016). *Weapons of math destruction: How big data increases inequality and threatens democracy*. Crown Publishing.

OECD. (2023). *Skills outlook 2023: Enabling lifelong learning for all*. OECD Publishing. DOI: 10.1787/14d2c4b9-

Oh, S., & Moon, J. Y. (2016). Calling for a Shared Understanding of the 'Sharing Economy'. *Proceedings of the 18th Annual International Conference on Electronic Commerce: E-Commerce in Smart Connected World*, 35:1-35:5. DOI: 10.1145/2971603.2971638

Øko-net. (2000). DanmarksDeklarationen – Erklärung über eine dänische Agenda für nachhaltige Entwicklung im 21. Jahrhundert. https://www.oeko-net.dk

Olfert, K., & Steinbuch, P. A. (1999). *Personalwirtschaft* (8th ed.). Kiehl.

Osterwalder, A., & Pigneur, Y. (2010). *Business model generation: A handbook for visionaries, game changers, and challengers*. John Wiley & Sons.

Owyang, J. (2016). *Honeycomb 3.0: The Collaborative Economy Market Expansion | Web Strategy by Jeremiah Owyang | Digital Business*. https://www.web-strategist.com/blog/2016/03/10/honeycomb-3-0-the-collaborative-economy-market-expansion-sxsw/

Ozanne, L. K., & Ballantine, P. W. (2010). Sharing as a form of anti-consumption? An examination of toy library users. *Journal of Consumer Behaviour*, *9*(6), 485–498. DOI: 10.1002/cb.334

Pandey, M., Bhati, M., Shukla, D. M., & Qureshi, I. (2021). Resourcing and value creation: A case of sharing economy model at the base of the pyramid. In *Sharing Economy at the Base of the Pyramid* (pp. 197–218). Springer. DOI: 10.1007/978-981-16-2414-8_9

Pansera, M., & Shanker, D. (2014). Social construction of innovation narratives: Implications for management studies. *IIM Bangalore Research Paper No. 457*. DOI: 10.2139/ssrn.2422759

Parés, M., Ospina, S. M., & Subirats, J. (2017). *Social innovation and democratic leadership: Communities and social change from below*. Edward Elgar Publishing. DOI: 10.4337/9781785367885

Pasricha, P., Singh, B., & Verma, P. (2018). Ethical leadership, organic organizational cultures and corporate social responsibility: An empirical study in social enterprises. *Journal of Business Ethics*, *151*(4), 941–958. DOI: 10.1007/s10551-017-3568-5

Paulus, P. B., & Nijstad, B. A. (2019). *The Oxford handbook of group creativity and innovation*. Oxford Library of Psychology. DOI: 10.1093/oxfordhb/9780190648077.001.0001

Pellicer-Sifres, V., Belda-Miquel, S., López-Fogués, A., & Boni Aristizábal, A. (2017). Grassroots social innovation for human development: An analysis of alternative food networks in the city of Valencia (Spain). *Journal of Human Development and Capabilities*, *18*(2), 258–274. DOI: 10.1080/19452829.2016.1270916

Peltoniemi, M. (2011). Reviewing Industry Life-cycle Theory: Avenues for Future Research. *International Journal of Management Reviews*, *13*(4), 349–375. DOI: 10.1111/j.1468-2370.2010.00295.x

Pérez-Pérez, C., & Benito-Osorio, D. (2025). Sharing is not for the weak: A systematic review of the main drawbacks of the sharing economy. *Journal of Management & Organization*, *31*(5), 2555–2571. DOI: 10.1017/jmo.2025.10020

Persson-Fischer, U., & Liu, S. (2021). The impact of a global crisis on areas and topics of tourism research. *Sustainability (Basel)*, *13*(2), 906. DOI: 10.3390/su13020906

Pesonen, R. (2022). Argumentation, cognition, and the epistemic benefits of cognitive diversity. *Synthese*, *200*(4), 295. DOI: 10.1007/s11229-022-03786-9

Petrini, M., De Freitas, C. S., & Da Silveira, L. M. (2017). A Proposal for a Typology of Sharing Economy. *Revista de Administração Mackenzie, 18*(5), 39–62. https://doi.org/DOI: 10.1590/1678-69712017/administracao.v18n5p39-62

Pfeffer, J., & Salancik, G. R. (2003). *The External Control of Organizations: A Resource Dependence Perspective* (Parental Adviso). Stanford Business Classics.

Pfeiffer, S., & Meyer, V. (2023). Engage with Fungi. Berlin Universities Publishing. DOI: https://berlinup.books.tu-berlin.de/produkt/978-3-98781-008-4/

Phills, J. A., Deiglmeier, K., & Miller, D. T. (2008). Rediscovering social innovation. *Stanford Social Innovation Review*, *6*(4), 34–43.

Piekkari, R., Welch, C., & Paavilainen, E. (2009). The case study as disciplinary convention: Evidence from *International Business Journal. Organizational Research Methods*, *12*(3), 567–589. DOI: 10.1177/1094428108319905

Pieler, D. (2000). *Weiterbildungscontrolling: Eine systemorientierte Perspektive.* DUV. DOI: 10.1007/978-3-322-97808-0

Pippin, R. B. (2010). *Nietzsche, psychology, and first philosophy.* University of Chicago Press.

Plambech, T., & Konijnendijk van den Bosch, C. C. (2015). The impact of nature on creativity – A study among Danish creative professionals. *Urban Forestry & Urban Greening*, *14*(2), 255–263. DOI: 10.1016/j.ufug.2015.02.006

Pless, N. M., Murphy, M., Maak, T., & Sengupta, A. (2021). Societal challenges and business leadership for social innovation. *Society and Business Review*, *16*(4), 535–561. DOI: 10.1108/SBR-10-2020-0129

Plewnia, F., & Guenther, E. (2018). Mapping the sharing economy for sustainability research. *Management Decision*, *56*(3), 570–583. DOI: 10.1108/MD-11-2016-0766

Politis, J. D. (2005). Dispersed leadership predictor of the work environment for creativity and productivity. *European Journal of Innovation Management*, *8*(2), 182–204. DOI: 10.1108/14601060510594693

Polk, M. (2015). Transdisciplinary co-production: Designing and testing a transdisciplinary research framework for societal problem solving. *Futures*, *65*, 110–122. DOI: 10.1016/j.futures.2014.11.001

Porter, P. K., & Scully, G. W. (1995). Institutional technology and economic growth. *Public Choice*, *82*(1), 17–36. DOI: 10.1007/BF01047727

Pouri, M. J., & Hilty, L. M. (2021). The digital sharing economy: A confluence of technical and social sharing. *Environmental Innovation and Societal Transitions*, *38*, 127–139. DOI: 10.1016/j.eist.2020.12.003

Prasetyono, H., Tjitrosumarto, S., Setyohadi, J. S., Hapsari, S., & Ramdayana, I. P. (2024). Analysis of improving innovative work behaviour of vocational high school teachers in terms of servant leadership with knowledge sharing as an intervening variable. *Jurnal Pendidikan Vokasi*, *14*(1), 110–120. DOI: 10.21831/jpv.v14i1.65445

Purwati, A., Budiyanto, B., Suhermin, S., & Hamzah, M. (2021). The effect of innovation capability on business performance: The role of social capital and entrepreneurial leadership on SMEs in Indonesia. *Accounting*, *7*(2), 323–330. DOI: 10.5267/j.ac.2020.11.021

Qalati, S. A., Zafar, Z., Fan, M., Limón, M. L. S., & Khaskheli, M. B. (2022). Employee performance under transformational leadership and organizational citizenship behavior: A mediated model. *Heliyon*, *8*(11), e11374. DOI: 10.1016/j.heliyon.2022.e11374 PMID: 36387554

Qureshi, I., Bhatt, B., & Shukla, D. M. (2021). Overview of Sharing Economy at the Base of the Pyramid. In Qureshi, I., Bhatt, B., & Shukla, D. M. (Eds.), *Sharing Economy at the Base of the Pyramid: Opportunities and Challenges* (pp. 1–23). Springer Nature. DOI: 10.1007/978-981-16-2414-8_1

Qureshi, I., Pan, S. L., & Zheng, Y. (2021). Digital social innovation: An overview and research framework. *Information Systems Journal*, *31*(5), 647–671. DOI: 10.1111/isj.12362

Radel, T. (1997). Die Formatierung horizontaler Netzwerke: Ein Rahmen für Innovationsprozesse? In Heidelhoff, F., & Radel, T. (Eds.), *Organisation von Innovation: Strukturen, Prozesse, Interventionen* (pp. 105–126). Rainer Hampp.

Ragin, C. C. (1997). Turning the tables: How case-oriented research challenges variable-oriented research. *Comparative Social Research*, *16*, 27–42.

Raisch, S., & Birkinshaw, J. (2008). Organizational ambidexterity: Antecedents, outcomes, and moderators. *Journal of Management*, *34*(3), 375–409. DOI: 10.1177/0149206308316058

Rammert, W. (2008). Technik und Innovation. In Maurer, A. (Ed.), *Handbuch der Wirtschaftssoziologie* (pp. 291–319). VS. DOI: 10.1007/978-3-531-90905-9_15

Ranjbari, M., Morales-Alonso, G., & Carrasco-Gallego, R. (2018). Conceptualizing the sharing economy through presenting a comprehensive framework. *Sustainability (Basel), 10*(7), 2336. DOI: 10.3390/su10072336

Rasheed, M. I., Hameed, Z., Kaur, P., & Dhir, A. (2024). Too sleepy to be innovative? Ethical leadership and employee service innovation behavior: A dual-path model moderated by sleep quality. *Human Relations, 77*(6), 739–767. DOI: 10.1177/00187267231163040

Rawls, J. (1971). *A theory of justice*. Harvard University Press. DOI: 10.4159/9780674042605

Raworth, K. (2017). *Doughnut economics: Seven ways to think like a 21st-century economist*. Chelsea Green Publishing.

Reginster, B. (2009). *The affirmation of life: Nietzsche on overcoming nihilism*. Harvard University Press.

Reichert, L. (2021). *Evolution und Innovation*. Duncker & Humblot.

Reischauer, G., & Mair, J. (2018). Platform Organizing in the New Digital Economy: Revisiting Online Communities and Strategic Responses', Toward Permeable Boundaries of Organizations. *Research in the Sociology of Organizations, 57*, 113–135. DOI: 10.1108/S0733-558X20180000057005

Reiser, D. B., & Dean, S. A. (2017). *Social enterprise law: Trust, public benefit, and capital markets*. Oxford University Press. DOI: 10.1093/oso/9780190249786.001.0001

Reiter-Palmon, R. (2018). Are the outcomes of creativity always positive? *Creativity, 5*(2), 177–181. DOI: 10.1515/ctra-2018-0016

Remenyi, D., Money, A., Price, D., & Bannister, F. (2002). The creation of knowledge through case study research. *Irish Journal of Management, 23*(2), 1–17.

Renko, M., El Tarabishy, A., Carsrud, A. L., & Brännback, M. (2015). Understanding and measuring entrepreneurial leadership style. *Journal of Small Business Management, 53*(1), 54–74. DOI: 10.1111/jsbm.12086

Rhodes, R. (1986). *The making of the atomic bomb*. Simon & Schuster.

Richter, C., Kraus, S., Brem, A., Durst, S., & Giselbrecht, C. (2017). Digital entrepreneurship: Innovative business models for the sharing economy. *Creativity and Innovation Management, 26*(3), 300–310. DOI: 10.1111/caim.12227

Ritala, P., Hurmelinna-Laukkanen, P., & Nätti, S. (2012). Coordination in innovation-generating business networks – The case of Finnish mobile TV development. *Journal of Business and Industrial Marketing*, *27*(4), 324–334. DOI: 10.1108/08858621211221698

Ritella, G., & Hakkarainen, K. (2021). Knowledge Practices. *Theoretical Investigations: Philosophical Foundations of Group Cognition*, *18*, 149–167. DOI: 10.1007/978-3-030-49157-4_7

Ritzer, G., Dean, P., & Jurgenson, N. (2012). The Coming of Age of the Prosumer. *The American Behavioral Scientist*, *56*(4), 379–398. DOI: 10.1177/0002764211429368

Rochet, J.-C., & Tirole, J. (2003). Platform competition in two-sided markets. *Journal of the European Economic Association*, *1*(4), 990–1029. DOI: 10.1162/154247603322493212

Rockström, J., Steffen, W., Noone, K., Persson, Å., Chapin, F. S., Lambin, E., & Foley, J. (2017). A safe operating space for humanity. *Nature*, *461*(7263), 472–475. DOI: 10.1038/461472a PMID: 19779433

Rogers, E. M. (2003). *Diffusion of innovations* (5th ed.). Free Press.

Rojak, J. A., Sanaji, S., Witjaksono, A. D., & Kistyanto, A. (2024). The influence of transformational leadership and organizational culture on employee performance. *EDUKASIA: Jurnal Pendidikan Dan Pembelajaran*, *5*(1), 977–990. DOI: 10.62775/edukasia.v5i1.926

Rosso, B. D. (2014). Creativity and constraints: Exploring the role of constraints in the creative processes of research and development teams. *Organization Studies*, *35*(4), 551–585. DOI: 10.1177/0170840613517600

Rowe, H. A. (2024). *Problem solving and intelligence*. Taylor & Francis. DOI: 10.4324/9781032636696

Ruben, B. D., & Gigliotti, R. A. (2016). Leadership as social influence: An expanded view of leadership communication theory and practice. *Journal of Leadership & Organizational Studies*, *23*(4), 467–479. DOI: 10.1177/1548051816641876

Runco, M. A., & Jaeger, G. J. (2012). The Standard Definition of Creativity. *Creativity Research Journal*, *24*(1), 92–96. DOI: 10.1080/10400419.2012.650092

Sachs, J. D. (2015). *The age of sustainable development*. Columbia University Press. DOI: 10.7312/sach17314

Safranski, R. (2002). *Nietzsche: A philosophical biography*. W. W. Norton & Company.

Sanz-Hernández, A., & Covaleda, I. (2021). Sustainability and creativity through mail art: A case study with young artists in universities. *Journal of Cleaner Production, 318*, 128525. DOI: 10.1016/j.jclepro.2021.128525

Sarooghi, H., Libaers, D., & Burkemper, A. (2015). Examining the relationship between creativity and innovation: A meta-analysis of organizational, cultural, and environmental factors. *Journal of Business Venturing, 30*(5), 714–731. DOI: 10.1016/j.jbusvent.2014.12.003

Satena, A. A., Damessa, D. D., Dadiye, T. A., & Kant, S. (2024). Effect of Servant Leadership Style on Organizational Performance Among University Employees In Ethiopia. *International Journal of Social Science. Management and Economics Research, 2*(2), 42–63.

Saunders, M., Lewis, P., & Thornhill, A. (2016). *Research methods for business students* (7th ed.). Pearson.

Saunders, R., & Bown, O. (2015). Computational Social Creativity. *Artificial Life, 21*(3), 366–378. DOI: 10.1162/ARTL_a_00177 PMID: 26280077

Saunders, R., & Gero, J. S. (2001). *Artificial creativity: A synthetic approach to the study of creative behaviour. Computational and Cognitive Models of Creative Design V.* Key Centre of Design Computing and Cognition, University of Sydney.

Sawyer, R. K. (2010). Individual and group creativity. *The Cambridge Handbook of Creativity*, 366–380.

Sawyer, R. K. (2014). *Group creativity: Music, theater, collaboration.* Psychology Press. DOI: 10.4324/9781410609090

Scaraboto, D. (2015). Selling, Sharing, and Everything In Between: The Hybrid Economies of Collaborative Networks. *The Journal of Consumer Research, 42*(1), 152–176. DOI: 10.1093/jcr/ucv004

Schacht, R. (1983). *Nietzsche's critique of morality.* Routledge.

Schmelzer, F. (2014). Innovative Innovationsberatung. In *Mut zu Innovationen: Impulse aus der Forschung, Beratung und Ausbildung* (pp. 131–150). Springer. DOI: 10.1007/978-3-642-40227-2_11

Schmid, G. (1970). Niklas Luhmanns funktional-strukturelle Systemtheorie: Eine wissenschaftliche Revolution. *Politische Vierteljahresschrift, 11*(2–3), 186–218.

Schor, J. (2016). Debating the Sharing Economy. *Journal of Self-Governance and Management Economics, 4*(3), 7–22.

Schor, J., & Attwood-Charles, W. (2017). The "sharing" economy: Labor, inequality, and social connection on for-profit platforms. *Sociology Compass*, *11*(8), e12493. DOI: 10.1111/soc4.12493

Schot, J., & Steinmueller, W. E. (2018). Three frames for innovation policy: R&D, systems of innovation and transformative change. *Research Policy*, *47*(9), 1554–1567. DOI: 10.1016/j.respol.2018.08.011

Schumpeter, J. A. (1931). *Theorie der wirtschaftlichen Entwicklung: Eine Untersuchung über Unternehmergewinn, Kapital, Kredit, Zins und den Konjunkturzyklus*. Duncker & Humblot.

Schwarz, R., & Ewaldt, J. W. (2008). *Innovationsorientiertes Bildungsmanagement: Hochschulentwicklung durch Sicherung der Nachhaltigkeit von eLearning*. VS.

Schwarz, R., & Ewaldt, J. W. (2008). Über den Beitrag systemdynamischer Modellierung zur Abschätzung technologischer Evolution. In Möhrle, M. G., & Isenmann, R. (Eds.), *Technologie-Roadmapping: Zukunftsstrategien für Technologieunternehmen* (pp. 409–425). Springer. DOI: 10.1007/978-3-540-74755-0_20

Scott, J. W. (1988). *Gender and the Politics of History*. Columbia University Press. DOI: 10.7312/scot91266

Sen, A. (1999). *On ethics and economics*. OUP Catalogue.

Şengüllendi, M. F., Bilgetürk, M., & Afacan Fındıklı, M. (2024). Ethical leadership and green innovation: The mediating role of green organizational culture. *Journal of Environmental Planning and Management*, *67*(8), 1702–1723. DOI: 10.1080/09640568.2023.2180347

Shaw, A. (2021, January). Teaching or cheating? Using collaboration and technology to support student learning. In International Journal on E-Learning (pp. 47-58). Association for the Advancement of Computing in Education (AACE). DOI: 10.70725/703731kdsrzb

Shier, M. L., & Handy, F. (2020). Leadership in nonprofits: Social innovations and blurring boundaries. *Voluntas*, *31*(2), 333–344. DOI: 10.1007/s11266-018-00078-0

Shiundu, T. W. (2024). Ethical leadership and its implication on decision-making in organizations: A literature review. *Journal of Human Resource & Leadership*, *8*(1), 59–67.

Silver, J. (2013, August 3). The sharing economy: A whole new way of living. *The Observer*. https://www.theguardian.com/technology/2013/aug/04/internet-technology-fon-taskrabbit-blablacar

Sindakis, S., Kitsios, F., Kamariotou, M., Aggarwal, S., & Cuervo, W. J. M. (2024). The effect of organizational culture and leadership on performance: A case of a subsidiary in Colombia. *Journal of General Management*, *49*(2), 115–132. DOI: 10.1177/03063070221100048

Sinnott-Armstrong, W. (2018). *Think again: How to reason and argue*. Oxford University Press.

Siuskaite, D., Pilinkiene, V., & Zvirdauskas, D. (2019). The Conceptualization of the Sharing Economy as a Business Model. *The Engineering Economist*, *30*(3), 373–381. DOI: 10.5755/j01.ee.30.3.21253

Šmite, D., Moe, N. B., & Gonzalez-Huerta, J. (2021). Overcoming cultural barriers to being agile in distributed teams. *Information and Software Technology*, *138*, 106612. DOI: 10.1016/j.infsof.2021.106612

Solis-Navarrete, J. A., Bucio-Mendoza, S., & Paneque-Gálvez, J. (2021). What is not social innovation. *Technological Forecasting and Social Change*, *173*, 121190. DOI: 10.1016/j.techfore.2021.121190 PMID: 36536954

Souto, J. E. (2022). Organizational creativity and sustainability-oriented innovation as drivers of sustainable development: Overcoming firms' economic, environmental and social sustainability challenges. *Journal of Manufacturing Technology Management*, *33*(4), 805–826. DOI: 10.1108/JMTM-01-2021-0018

Specht, G., Beckmann, C., & Amelingmeyer, J. (2002). *F&E-Management–Kompetenz im Innovationsprozess. 2. Überarb. Und erw*. Auflage. Schäffer-Pöschel.

Srivastava, S., Pathak, D., Soni, S., & Dixit, A. (2024). Does green transformational leadership reinforce green creativity? The mediating roles of green organizational culture and green mindfulness. *Journal of Organizational Change Management*, *37*(3), 619–640. DOI: 10.1108/JOCM-09-2023-0364

Stambovsky, P. (2021). *Myth and the Limits of Reason* (Vol. 39). Brill.

Statens Museum for Kunst (SMK). (2024). Anne Marie Carl-Nielsen Chatbot: Against All Odds – Historical Women and New Algorithms. https://www.smk.dk/en/article/anne-marie-carl-nielsen-chatbot/

Stein, S. M., & Harper, T. L. (2012). Creativity and innovation: Divergence and convergence in pragmatic dialogical planning. *Journal of Planning Education and Research*, *32*(1), 5–17. DOI: 10.1177/0739456X11417829

Stembert, N. (2024). Co-creation. In *Springer Handbook of Internet of Things* (pp. 841–864). Springer International Publishing. DOI: 10.1007/978-3-031-39650-2_35

Stephany, A. (2015). *The business of sharing: Making it in the new sharing economy*. Springer. DOI: 10.1057/9781137376183

Stroh, D. P. (2015). *Systems thinking for social change: A practical guide to solving complex problems, avoiding unintended consequences, and achieving lasting results*. Chelsea Green Publishing.

Suarez, F., & Utterback, J. (1993). Patterns of industrial evolution, dominant designs, and firms' survival. *Research on Technological Innovation. Management and Policy*, *5*, 47–87.

Sugiono, E., & Nurhasan, A. (2025). The Influence of Organizational Culture on Organizational Citizenship Behavior (OCB) With Job Satisfaction as An Intervening Variable at The Indonesian Quarantine Agency. *International Journal of Management Science and Information Technology*, *5*(1), 160–166. DOI: 10.35870/ijmsit.v5i1.3771

Sukhera, J. (2022). Narrative reviews: Flexible, rigorous, and practical. *Journal of Graduate Medical Education*, *14*(4), 414–417. DOI: 10.4300/JGME-D-22-00480.1 PMID: 35991099

Suriyankietkaew, S., Krittayaruangroj, K., & Iamsawan, N. (2022). Sustainable Leadership practices and competencies of SMEs for sustainability and resilience: A community-based social enterprise study. *Sustainability (Basel)*, *14*(10), 5762. DOI: 10.3390/su14105762

Taamneh, M., Aljawarneh, N., Al-Okaily, M., Taamneh, A., & Al-Oqaily, A. (2024). The impact of ethical leadership on organizational citizenship behavior in higher education: The contingent role of organizational justice. *Cogent Business & Management*, *11*(1), 2294834. Advance online publication. DOI: 10.1080/23311975.2023.2294834

Tabares, S. (2020). Insights from corporate social innovation: A research agenda. *Social Enterprise Journal*, *16*(3), 317–338. DOI: 10.1108/SEJ-08-2019-0057

Tajfel, H., Turner, J. C., Austin, W. G., & Worchel, S. (1979). An integrative theory of intergroup conflict. *Organizational Identity. REAd (Porto Alegre)*, *56*(65), 9780203505984–16.

Täuscher, K., & Laudien, S. M. (2018). Understanding platform business models: A mixed methods study of marketplaces. *European Management Journal*, *36*(3), 319–329. DOI: 10.1016/j.emj.2017.06.005

The Danish Government. (2002). A shared future: Balanced development. Denmark's national strategy for sustainable development. https://mst.dk

Thom, N. (1980). *Grundlagen des betrieblichen Innovationsmanagements*. Peter Hanstein Verlag.

Tidd, J., & Bessant, J. R. (2014). *Strategic innovation management*. John Wiley & Sons.

Tufekci, Z. (2018). *Twitter and tear gas: The power and fragility of networked protest*. Yale University Press.

Tushman, M., Smith, W. K., Woody, R. C., & Westerman, G. (2010). Organizational designs and innovation streams. *Industrial and Corporate Change*, *19*(5), 1331–1366. DOI: 10.1093/icc/dtq040

Udin, U. (2024). Leadership styles and sustainable performance. *Multidisciplinary Reviews*, *7*(8), 2024171. DOI: 10.31893/multirev.2024171

Udin, U. (2024). Transformational leadership and organizational citizenship behavior: The role of person-job fit and person-organization fit in social exchange perspective. *Human Systems Management*, *43*(3), 325–339. DOI: 10.3233/HSM-230039

Uhl-Bien, M. (2006). Relational leadership theory: Exploring the social processes of leadership and organizing. *The Leadership Quarterly*, *17*(6), 654–676. DOI: 10.1016/j.leaqua.2006.10.007

Umesi, D. A. (2024). The role of educational management in enhancing effective teaching and learning in 21st century schools. *Brock Journal of Education*, *12*(3), 66–75.

UNESCO. (2022). UNESCO global report 2022: Reshaping policies for creativity – Addressing culture as a global public good. .DOI: 10.18356/9789210015240

UNESCO. (n.d.). Cultural heritage and climate change. Intangible Cultural Heritage. https://ich.unesco.org/en/climate-change

United Nations Department of Economic and Social Affairs. (2025). The Sustainable Development Goals Report 2025. New York. (revision August 2025). https://unstats.un.org/sdgs/report/2025/

United Nations. (2015). *Transforming our World: The 2030 Agenda for Sustainable Development. Sustainable Development Knowledge Platform*. https://sustainabledevelopment.un.org/post2015/transformingourworld/publication

United Nations. (2015). Transforming our world: The 2030 agenda for sustainable development. https://sdgs.un.org/2030agenda

V. meer. (n.d.). MY-CO SPACE. https://www.v-meer.de/my-co-space

Vågen Svensson, L. E., & Smærup Sørensen, I. (2023). *Nordic Green Roadmap for Cultural Institutions (Nord 2023:041)*. Nordic Council of Ministers. DOI: 10.6027/nord2023-041

Vahs, D., & Brem, A. (2013). *Innovationsmanagement: Von der Idee zur erfolgreichen Vermarktung* (4th ed.). Schäffer-Poeschel.

Valaei, N., Rezaei, S., & Ismail, W. K. W. (2017). Examining learning strategies, creativity, and innovation at SMEs using fuzzy set Qualitative Comparative Analysis and PLS path modeling. *Journal of Business Research, 70*, 224–233. DOI: 10.1016/j.jbusres.2016.08.016

van Bezouw, M. J., van Der Toorn, J., & Becker, J. C. (2021). Social creativity: Reviving a social identity approach to social stability. *European Journal of Social Psychology, 51*(2), 409–422. DOI: 10.1002/ejsp.2732

Van de Ven, A. H., Polley, D. E., Garud, R., & Venkataraman, S. (1999). *The innovation journey*. Oxford University Press.

Van Fleet, D. D., & Yukl, G. A. (1986). *Military leadership: An organizational behavior perspective*. No Title.

van Lente, H., & Peters, P. (2022). The future as aesthetic experience: Imagination and engagement in future studies. *European Journal of Futures Research, 10*(1), 16. DOI: 10.1186/s40309-022-00204-8

Van Ooijen, C., Ubaldi, B., & Welby, B. (2019). *A data-driven public sector: Enabling the strategic use of data for productive, inclusive and trustworthy governance*. Academic Press.

Van Tulder, R., & Van Mil, E. (2022). *Principles of sustainable business: Frameworks for corporate action on the SDGs*. Routledge. DOI: 10.4324/9781003098355

Vandermerwe, S., & Rada, J. (1988). Servitization of business: Adding value by adding services. *European Management Journal, 6*(4), 314–324. DOI: 10.1016/0263-2373(88)90033-3

Villari, B. (2018). A Service Design Approach to Analyse, Map and Design Sharing Services. In Bruglieri, M. (Ed.), *Multidisciplinary Design of Sharing Services* (pp. 3–24). Springer International Publishing. DOI: 10.1007/978-3-319-78099-3_1

von Au, D. (2010). *Strategisches Innovationsmanagement: Eine empirische Analyse betrieblicher Innovationssysteme in der spezialchemischen Industrie in Deutschland*. Gabler.

Voorberg, W. H., Bekkers, V. J. J. M., & Tummers, L. G. (2015). A systematic review of co-creation and co-production: Embarking on the social innovation journey. *Public Management Review*, *17*(9), 1333–1357. DOI: 10.1080/14719037.2014.930505

Voytenko Palgan, Y., Zvolska, L., & Mont, O. (2017). Sustainability framings of accommodation sharing. *Environmental Innovation and Societal Transitions*, *23*, 70–83. DOI: 10.1016/j.eist.2016.12.002

Wakjira, G. G., Debela, K. L., & Kant, S. (2024). Effect of Entrepreneurial Orientation on Performance of SMEs in Ethiopia. *Horn of African Journal of Business and Economics*, *7*(1), 155–176.

Waldman, D. A., & Siegel, D. (2008). Defining the socially responsible leader. *The Leadership Quarterly*, *19*(1), 117–131. DOI: 10.1016/j.leaqua.2007.12.008

Wang, J., Hussain, Y., Mao, C., & Jiang, F. (2025). Effective educational management strategies: Enhancing institutional performance and student success. *Journal of Education, Humanities, and Social Research*, *2*(2), 1–12. DOI: 10.71222/yqw52v02

Watson, E. (2007). Who or What Creates? A Conceptual Framework for Social Creativity. *Human Resource Development Review*, *6*(4), 419–441. DOI: 10.1177/1534484307308255

Weber, W. (1985). *Betriebliche Weiterbildung: Empirische Analysen betrieblicher und individueller Entscheidungen über Weiterbildung*. Poeschel.

Weigel, S., & Hadwich, K. (2019). Erfolgsfaktoren von Dienstleistungsnetzwerken im Kontext der Servicetransformation – Eine qualitative Analyse. *Schmalenbachs Zeitschrift fur Betriebswirtschaftliche Forschung = Schmalenbach Journal of Business Research*, *71*(1), 1–43. DOI: 10.1007/s41471-019-00062-4

Weisberg, R. W. (2016). *Creativity: Understanding innovation in problem solving, science, invention, and the arts*. John Wiley & Sons.

Weisz, J. D., Muller, M., Houde, S., Richards, J., Ross, S. I., Martinez, F., & Talamadupula, K. (2021, April). Perfection not required? Human-AI partnerships in code translation. In *Proceedings of the 26th International Conference on Intelligent User Interfaces* (pp. 402-412). DOI: 10.1145/3397481.3450656

Wengenroth, U. (2010). Innovationsprozesse in Wirtschaft und Gesellschaft – Vorbemerkung. In Hof, H., & Wengenroth, U. (Eds.), *Innovationsforschung* (pp. 1–5). LIT.

Wessels, K. R. (2022). *Pedagogy of entanglement: A response to the complex societal challenges that permeate our lives*. Springer Nature. DOI: 10.1007/978-3-031-15787-5

Westley, F. R., Tjornbo, O., Schultz, L., Olsson, P., Folke, C., Crona, B., & Bodin, Ö. (2013). A theory of transformative agency in linked social-ecological systems. *Ecology and Society*, *18*(3), art27. DOI: 10.5751/ES-05072-180327

Westley, F., & Antadze, N. (2010). Making a difference: Strategies for scaling social innovation for greater impact. *The Innovation Journal*, *15*(2).

West, M. A., & Farr, J. L. (1990). *Innovation at work*. John Wiley & Sons.

West, M. A., & Richter, A. W. (2024). Climates and cultures for innovation and creativity at work. In *Handbook of organizational creativity* (pp. 211–236). Psychology Press. DOI: 10.4324/9781003573326-11

West, S. M., Whittaker, M., & Crawford, K. (2019). *Discriminating systems: Gender, race, and power in AI*. AI Now Institute.

Westwood, R., & Low, D. R. (2003). The multicultural muse: Culture, creativity and innovation. *International Journal of Cross Cultural Management*, *3*(2), 235–259. DOI: 10.1177/14705958030032006

Wigger, L. (2013). Argumentationsanalyse als erziehungswissenschaftliche Forschungsmethode. In Friebertshäuser, B., Langer, A., & Prengel, A. (Eds.), *Handbuch Qualitative Forschungsmethoden in der Erziehungswissenschaft* (4th ed., pp. 351–364). Beltz.

Wilkinson, R. G., & Pickett, K. E. (2009). Income inequality and social dysfunction. *Annual Review of Sociology*, *35*(1), 493–511. DOI: 10.1146/annurev-soc-070308-115926

Worku, M. A., & Debela, K. L. (2024). A systematic literature review on organizational citizenship behavior : Conceptualization, antecedents, and future research directions. *Cogent Business & Management*, *11*(1), 2350804. Advance online publication. DOI: 10.1080/23311975.2024.2350804

World Economic Forum. (2023). *Future of jobs report 2023*. Geneva: WEF.

Wruk, D., Oberg, A., & Friedrich-Schieback, M. (2019). Quantifying the sharing economy: An approach for measuring the ecological, social, and economic effects. *Gaia (Heidelberg)*, *28*(1), 184–189. DOI: 10.14512/gaia.28.S1.3

Wruk, D., Oberg, A., Klutt, J., & Maurer, I. (2019). The Presentation of Self as Good and Right: How Value Propositions and Business Model Features are Linked in the Sharing Economy. *Journal of Business Ethics*, *159*(4), 997–1021. DOI: 10.1007/s10551-019-04209-5

Yin, R. K. (2003). *Case study research – Design and methods* (2nd ed.). Sage.

Yin, R. K. (2013). *Case study research: Design and methods* (5th ed.). Sage.

Yoo, Y., Henfridsson, O., & Lyytinen, K. (2010). Research commentary—The new organizing logic of digital innovation: An agenda for information systems research. *Information Systems Research, 21*(4), 724–735. DOI: 10.1287/isre.1100.0322

Yukl, G. (2009). Leading organizational learning: Reflections on theory and research. *The Leadership Quarterly, 20*(1), 49–53. DOI: 10.1016/j.leaqua.2008.11.006

Zabich, C., & Breßler, J. (2016). Anforderung und Vermittlung von Innovationskompetenzen in der Automobilindustrie. *Working Papers of the Chair for Innovation Research and Technology Management, TU Chemnitz,* 06-01.

Zahn, E., & Weidler, A. (1995). Integriertes Innovationsmanagement. *Handbuch Technologiemanagement, Stuttgart, 1995*, 351.

Zehrer, A., & Muskat, B. (2016). Der Treiber Innovation in touristischen Unternehmen. In Siller, H., & Zehrer, A. (Eds.), *Entrepreneurship und Tourismus: Unternehmerisches Denken und Erfolgskonzepte aus der Praxis* (2nd ed., pp. 29–46). Linde International.

Zeng, L., Proctor, R. W., & Salvendy, G. (2011). Can traditional divergent thinking tests be trusted in measuring and predicting real-world creativity? *Creativity Research Journal, 23*(1), 24–37. DOI: 10.1080/10400419.2011.545713

Zhang, Z., Sangsawang, T., Vipahasna, K., & Pigultong, M. (2024). A mixed-methods data approach integrating importance-performance analysis (IPA) and Kaiser-Meyer-Olkin (KMO) in applied talent cultivation. *Journal of Applied Data Sciences, 5*(1), 256–267. DOI: 10.47738/jads.v5i1.170

Zhao, J., Li, Y., & Liu, Y. (2016). Organizational learning, managerial ties and radical innovation: Evidence from an emerging economy. *IEEE Transactions on Engineering Management, 63*(4), 489–499. DOI: 10.1109/TEM.2016.2597290

Zheng, Y., Epitropaki, O., Graham, L., & Caveney, N. (2022). Ethical leadership and ethical voice: The mediating mechanisms of value internalization and integrity identity. *Journal of Management, 48*(4), 973–1002. DOI: 10.1177/01492063211002611

Zhou, J., & Hoever, I. J. (2014). Research on Workplace Creativity: A Review and Redirection. *Annual Review of Organizational Psychology and Organizational Behavior, 1*(1), 333–359. DOI: 10.1146/annurev-orgpsych-031413-091226

Ziegler, R. (2017). Social innovation as a collaborative concept. *Innovation (Abingdon), 30*(4), 388–405. DOI: 10.1080/13511610.2017.1348935

Zimmermann, O. (2018). Sustainability culture: Fresh thinking is what the country needs! On the cultural dimension of the sustainability debate. In: German Almanac of Sustainability 2018: Ideas and actions. *Transformation (Durban)*, 50–57. https://www.nachhaltigkeitsrat.de/wp-content/uploads/2019/02/Almanac_2018_Zimmermann_190213EN.pdf

Zuboff, S. (2019). *The age of surveillance capitalism: The fight for a human future at the new frontier of power*. PublicAffairs.

About the Contributors

Ziska Fields is an Associate Professor in the Department of Business Management, College of Business and Economics, at the University of Johannesburg (UJ). She is also a certified FourSight and Neethling Brain Instruments (NBI) Practitioner, specialising in developing creative thinking skills in educational and organisational contexts. She holds a BA in Communication Sciences, a Diploma in Management Studies, an MBA (Cum Laude), and a PhD in Business Administration. With 16 years of higher education experience and over a decade in the financial industry, Professor Fields teaches and supervises management and entrepreneurship at undergraduate and postgraduate levels. Her research focuses on theoretical and applied creativity across disciplines, with a particular interest in youth and higher education. She has developed two models to measure creativity in South Africa and serves as an Advisory Board member and Ambassador of World Creativity & Innovation (WCI) in South Africa. Professor Fields has edited nine scholarly books and authored 23 book chapters on creativity, sustainability, the Fourth Industrial Revolution, global collective intelligence, wicked problems, and creativity in higher education. She is committed to empowering people to reach their full potential and believes creativity and entrepreneurial action are key to building a sustainable, inclusive future.

* * *

Julia Breßler is in her role as Innovations architect at TeleskopEffekt GmbH. She holds a PhD in Management of Innovation and a diploma in business education from Chemnitz University of Technology in Germany. She is interested in Management of Innovation and Education.

Aditya Kumar Gupta is an Associate Professor in the Department of Philosophy, University of Delhi. He earned his Ph.D. from the University of

Allahabad in 2011 and specializes in Indian philosophy, particularly the Upani ads, ethics, social and political thought, meditation, yoga studies, and philosophy of religion. With over a decade of teaching and research experience, Dr. Gupta has published extensively, including two books and numerous research papers. He has supervised doctoral and M.Phil scholars, delivered lectures internationally, and led research projects on meditation, ethics, and Indian philosophical traditions.

Anja Herrmann Fankhänel (M.Sc.) works at the Chair for Innovation Research and Technology Management at the Technische Universität Chemnitz, Germany as a teaching and research assistant. She holds Master and Bachelor Degrees in Management and a PhD in Management of Innovation. She is interested in social innovation and creativity.

Stefan Hüsig is holder of the chair for Innovation Research and Technology Management at the Technische Universitat Chemnitz, Germany. Before he had several positions in academia such as Interim Professor at the Chair of Innovation Research and Sustainable Resource Management at the TU Chemnitz, as an Associate Professor at the Department of Innovation and Technology Management at the University of Regensburg, Germany or as Deputy Director and founder of a new Institute for Innovation and Technology Management at the University of Economics in Prague (Czech Republic). Moreover, he had visiting positions at the Leeds School of Business at the University of Colorado (USA), Aston Business School, Aston University in Birmingham (UK) and the Fudan University in Shanghai (China). In addition to his academic activities Prof. Dr. Hüsig was active in research and consulting projects in collaboration with Mannesmann, Vodafone, Continental or the Fraunhofer Institute. He holds a Habilitation in Business Administration, a PhD in Innovation Management and a Diploma in Business Administration from University of Regensburg.

Mustafa Kayyali is an ardent advocate for excellence in higher education, driven by a relentless pursuit of quality, recognition, and innovation. Their journey in academia started with a Master's in Quality Management and Evaluation in Higher Education from Universitat Oberta de Catalunya, followed by a Ph.D. in Quality Management from Azteca University. These academic pursuits have laid a strong foundation for their expertise in Accreditation, Quality Assurance, and Higher Education Rankings. As an entrepreneur, researcher, translator, and publisher, they are deeply involved in various facets of the academic world. Their diverse interests encompass Management, Translation, Interpretation, and Academic consulting, contributing to a well-rounded understanding of the industry. Throughout their career, they have made significant contributions to academic literature, with more than 40 published papers and 30 book chapters to my name. Additionally, they take pride in having translated 6 books, bridging language gaps, and promoting knowledge exchange on a global scale. They are committed to fostering positive change in higher education and contributing to its continuous improvement.

Sooraj Kumar Maurya currently holds the position of Assistant Professor of Philosophy and serves as the Teacher-in-Charge at the Department of Philosophy within Zakir Husain Delhi College (Evening), affiliated with the University of Delhi. He boasts an illustrious academic background, having earned his B.A., M.A., and D. Phil degrees from the esteemed Department of Philosophy at the University of Allahabad. Dr. Maurya exhibits an unwavering commitment to scholarly pursuits and has significantly enriched the field of philosophy. His scholarly achievements include over 35 published research papers featured in esteemed international and national journals and conferences. Dr. Maurya's research interests span a broad spectrum of philosophical themes, with a particular focus on social philosophy, political philosophy, and moral philosophy.

Vikash Ranjan Singh is a faculty member in the Department of History at Zakir Husain Delhi College (Evening), University of Delhi. His academic interests include the study of historical narratives and their intersection with contemporary issues. Dr. Singh is dedicated to enriching the learning experience of his students, emphasizing critical thinking and historical analysis. He is actively involved in research and contributes to the academic community with his insights and publications. Dr. Singh can be reached at vikashatdelhi@gmail.com for further academic inquiries.

Sapna Tiwari is an Assistant Professor with a strong academic and literary background. She has contributed to the Kavya Desh Project and published several research articles in UGC-listed journals. Her work shows her involvement with literature and critical studies. Her literary insights appeared as a book review in Pustak Sanskriti, the magazine of the National Book Trust. Besides her academic work, she regularly participates in Akashwani (All India Radio) programs. There, she takes part in discussions about literature and culture. She has also been involved in many national workshops and seminars, enhancing her academic and professional experience.

Anca Unertl is owner of the cultural management agency ArtisLogistics and Head of Press and Public Relations at the Mannheim State University of Music and Performing Arts.

Yohannes Mekonnen Yesuf (Ph.D.) is an Assistant Professor of Management at Woldia University and a Postdoctoral Research Fellow at the University of

Johannesburg (UJ). He holds a Ph.D. in Management and specializes in research areas including creativity, innovation, entrepreneurship, leadership, and strategy. His academic work focuses on exploring the intersection of these fields to drive business resilience, organizational development, and strategic decision-making. Through his research, Yohannes aims to contribute to both theoretical advancements and practical applications that foster innovation and leadership in various business and academic settings.

Laura Zebisch is sustainability manager at Goethe-Institut with a particular focus on strategic sustainability management.

Index

A

C

D

E

H

I

K

L

M

N

O

P

S

T

U

W

www.ingramcontent.com/pod-product-compliance
Lightning Source LLC
LaVergne TN
LVHW080905300926
849162LV00003B/564